Conventional literary history has virtually ignored the role of newspaper syndicates in publishing some of the most famous nineteenth-century writers. Stephen Crane, Henry James, Rudyard Kipling, Robert Louis Stevenson, and Mark Twain were among those who offered their fiction to "syndicates," firms which subsequently sold the work to newspapers across America for simultaneous, first-time publication. This decentralized process profoundly affected not only the economics of publishing, but also the relationship between authors, texts, and readers. In this, the first full-length study of this publishing phenomenon, Charles Johanningsmeier evaluates the unique site of interaction syndicates occupied between readers and texts. He shows how the economic practicalities of the syndicate system influenced the consumption and interpretation of various literary texts, and through a wealth of historical detail helps revise our understanding of what the term "literary history" can legitimately encompass. He explores the vital role the syndicates played in the professionalization of the literary sphere; they constitute, he argues, a transitional moment between the highly centralized literary publishers of the early nineteenth century, and the emergence of mass-market magazines which accompanied the growth of industrial capitalism. Johanningsmeier's study provides a literary and historical context for understanding the ordinary reader's response to crucial developments in nineteenth-century writing.

FICTION AND THE AMERICAN LITERARY MARKETPLACE

CAMBRIDGE STUDIES IN
PUBLISHING AND PRINTING HISTORY

GENERAL EDITOR

David McKitterick

TITLES PUBLISHED

*The Provincial Book Trade in
Eighteenth-Century England*
by John Feather

Lewis Carroll and the House of Macmillan
edited by Morton N. Cohen & Anita Gandolfo

The Correspondence of Robert Dodsley 1733–1764
edited by James E. Tierney

Book Production and Publication in Britain 1375–1475
edited by Jeremy Griffiths and Derek Pearsall

*Before Copyright: The French Book-Privilege
System 1486–1526*
by Elizabeth Armstrong

The Making of Johnson's Dictionary, 1746–1773
by Allen Reddick

*Cheap Bibles: Nineteenth-century Publishing and
the British and Foreign Bible Society*
by Leslie Howsam

*Print Culture in Renaissance Italy
The Editor and the Vernacular Text, 1470–1600*
by Brian Richardson

*American Literary Publishing in the Mid-Nineteenth Century
The Business of Ticknor and Fields*
by Michael Winship

FICTION AND THE AMERICAN LITERARY MARKETPLACE

The role of newspaper syndicates, 1860–1900

CHARLES JOHANNINGSMEIER
State University of New York at Cortland

CAMBRIDGE
UNIVERSITY PRESS

Published by the Press Syndicate of the University of Cambridge
The Pitt Building, Trumpington Street, Cambridge CB2 1RP
40 West 20th Street, New York, NY 10011-4211, USA
10 Stamford Road, Oakleigh, Melbourne 3166, Australia

© Cambridge University Press 1997

First published 1997

Printed in Great Britain at the University Press, Cambridge

A catalogue record for this book is available from the British Library

Library of Congress cataloguing in publication data

Johanningsmeier, Charles
Fiction and the American literary marketplace.
The role of newspaper syndicates, 1860–1900 / Charles Johanningsmeier
p. cm. – (Cambridge studies in publishing and printing history)
Includes bibliographical references and index.
ISBN 0 521 49710 8 (hardback)
1. American newspapers – History – 19th century.
2. Serialized fiction – History and criticism.
I. Title. II. Series.
PN4864.J64 1997
071′.3–dc20   95-52430 CIP

ISBN 0 521 49710 8 hardback

CE

Contents

List of illustrations	page	viii
Acknowledgements		ix
List of abbreviations		xii
Introduction. Newspaper syndicates of the late nineteenth century: overlooked forces in the American literary marketplace		1
1 Preparing the way for the syndicates: a revolution in American fiction production, distribution, and readership, 1860–1900		11
2 The pioneers: readyprint, plate service, and early galley-proof syndicates		34
3 The heyday of American fiction syndication: Irving Bacheller, S. S. McClure, and other independent syndicators		64
4 What literary syndicates represented to authors: saviours, dictators, or something in-between?		99
5 What price must authors pay? The negotiations between galley-proof syndicates and authors		126
6 Pleasing the customers: the balance of power between syndicates and newspaper editors		151
7 Readers' experiences with syndicated fiction		183
8 The decline of the literary syndicates		206
Notes		228
Bibliography		266
Index		281

Illustrations

1 Portrait of William Frederic Tillotson. Courtesy of the *Bolton Evening News*, Bolton, England. *page* 49
2 The *Bolton Evening News* and *Weekly Journal* building. Courtesy of the *Bolton Evening News*, Bolton, England. 51
3 Offices of the *Evening News* and *Weekly Journal*. Courtesy of the *Bolton Evening News*, Bolton, England. 52
4 Portrait of S. S. McClure. Courtesy of The Lilly Library, Indiana University. 68
5 S. S. McClure and John S. Phillips. Courtesy of The Lilly Library, Indiana University. 69
6 Portrait of Irving Bacheller. From *Best Things from American Literature*, ed. Irving Bacheller (New York: The Christian Herald, 1899) 70

Acknowledgements

This book, like all research projects, has been from the start a collaborative effort. I could neither have conducted my research nor written my book without the assistance of many individuals in both the United States and Great Britain.

First, I would like to thank the librarians, curators, and archivists who helped me locate and photocopy materials that often had not been looked at in many years. Their prompt responses to my inquiries certainly made it easier for me to collect the disparate pieces of the syndicate puzzle. Chief among these persons are Saundra Taylor, Curator of Manuscripts, the Lilly Library, Indiana University, and Lynn Ekfelt, University Archivist, Owen D. Young Library, St. Lawrence University. I am very grateful for permission to use materials not only from these libraries but also from the Newberry Library; the Clifton Waller Barrett Collection, Alderman Library, University of Virginia; the Amherst College Archives; the Rare Book and Manuscript Library, Columbia University; the Houghton Library, Harvard University; the Manuscript Division, Library of Congress; the Special Collections Library, Duke University; the Department of Rare Books and Special Collections, Princeton University Libraries; the Beinecke Rare Books and Manuscript Library, Yale University; the Chicago Historical Society; Bowdoin College Library; the Huntington Library; Knox College Archives; the Harold B. Lee Library, Brigham Young University; the Robert W. Woodruff Library, Emory University; the Rare Books and Manuscripts Division, New York Public Library; The Curators of the Bodleian Library, Oxford, England; the Miller Library, Colby College; Special Collections and Archives, Utah State University; and the Winterthur Library. Andrew C. Smith, Editor in Chief, and John Waters, Managing Director, of the *Bolton Evening News* in Lancashire, England, have also been very forthcoming with answers to my queries and with permission to use materials in the possession of the company.

Also deserving thanks are those librarians who made my research in England during the summer of 1994 so productive and enjoyable. Michael Turner, Head of Conservation at the Bodleian Library, graciously shared with me all the materials he used in writing his B.Litt. (1968) thesis about the Tillotson's Newspaper Fiction Bureau. In Bolton, various members of the Bolton Metro Library provided invaluable assistance. In the Archives and Local Studies Searchroom there, Kevin Campbell, Barry Mills, Sharon Harrison, and Julie Lamara were always willing to help in whatever way they could and made me feel extremely welcome.

Second, I greatly appreciate the financial assistance provided me by the Kaltenborn Foundation, the College of Arts and Sciences, Indiana University – Bloomington, the Bibliographical Society of America, and the Bibliographical Society (England). Research and travel grants from these organizations were indispensable to the completion of this project.

Third, I am grateful to have had the opportunity to talk or meet with Mr. Peter Lyon and Mr. Marcus Tillotson. The former, a grandson of syndicate pioneer S. S. McClure, not only wrote an important biography of McClure but also provided me with a number of important pieces of information. Mr. Tillotson, grandson of syndicator William Frederic Tillotson, warmly received me at his home, shared his memories of Tillotson family history, and made available to me a number of significant documents relating to the Tillotson syndicate. I am grateful to both men, too, for granting me permission to use materials related to the two syndicates.

Fourth, I would like to thank Professors Christoph Lohmann, Terence Martin, David Nord, and David J. Nordloh of Indiana University for their contributions to the intellectual content of this book. They, along with Michael Winship of the University of Texas at Austin, suggested many ways to improve this text and encouraged me by always believing in the project's worth. I am especially grateful to David J. Nordloh for his many challenging questions and rigorous editorial suggestions, which constantly forced me to reexamine my ideas and write more clearly and concisely.

Fifth, I was fortunate to have enjoyed the support of many family members. Mary A. Mastin and Ed Johanningsmeier often asked about the project, took the time to listen to the answers, and helped remind me how important history is. In addition, my parents transmitted to me their love of books, newspapers, and learning; for these gifts I am very thankful.

Finally, this book is dedicated to my wife, Gina, whose intellectual, financial, and emotional support has never wavered. Simply put, this book would never have existed without her. In the tradition of Anna Bacheller and Hattie McClure, wives of syndicators Irving Bacheller and S. S. McClure, she gave me a reason to push on and patiently waited while encouraging me to pursue the syndication Idea.

Grateful acknowledgement is made to the following for permission to reprint or adapt from previously published material: *Publishing history*: for "Newspaper Syndicates of the Late Nineteenth Century: Overlooked Forces in the American Literary Marketplace," 37 (1995). copyright © 1995. Reproduced by permission of Chadwyck-Healey, Ltd. *American periodicals*: for "Redefining the Scope of 'Periodical History' for Literary Studies: Irving Bacheller's Newspaper Syndicate," 5 (1995). Copyright © 1995. Reproduced by permission of the University of North Texas Press.

Abbreviations

APA-LC	American Press Association Papers, Library of Congress, Washington, DC.
BL-Turner	Tillotson's Newspaper Fiction Bureau materials in the possession of Michael Turner, Bodleian Library, Oxford, England; these are available by application to Mr. Turner.
B-StL	Irving Bacheller Papers, Special Collections, Owen D. Young Library, St. Lawrence University, Canton, NY.
CWB-Alderman	The Clifton Waller Barrett Collection, Manuscripts Division, Special Collections Department, Alderman Library, University of Virginia, Charlottesville, VA.
ECSP-Columbia	Edmund Clarence Stedman Papers, Special Collections, Rare Books and Manuscripts, Butler Library, Columbia University, New York, NY.
KAHB	*Kellogg's Auxiliary Handbook: Containing a History of the Origin of Auxiliary Printing; With Opinions of Publishers; and Day-Book and Journal Combined: Being a Model System of Keeping Advertising Accounts; Together with Various Useful Articles, Tables, and Calendars.* Chicago: A. N. Kellogg, 1878.
MP-Lilly	S. S. McClure Papers, The Lilly Library, Indiana University, Bloomington, IN.
VLP-Newberry	Victor Lawson Papers, the Newberry Library, Chicago, IL.
ZBEN	The Bolton Evening News Archive, Archives and Local Studies, Bolton Metro Library, Bolton, England.

INTRODUCTION

Newspaper syndicates of the late nineteenth century: overlooked forces in the American literary marketplace

> For the most part the newspaper syndicate is the sewer of the author.
> Edward W. Bok, "The Modern Literary King," *Forum*, 1895

> The newspaper has not only monopolized the news – its proper field – but it has drawn to itself the best of literature. Both magazines and publishers of books complain that the newspapers are more attractive to writers and pay more than they can afford, while their cheapness appeals to the readers. To the future historian the point is not without interest.
> Worthington C. Ford, Report to the American Antiquarian Society Council, 1918[1]

The Ansel Nash Kellogg Company; the American Press Association; the Western Newspaper Union; S. S. McClure's Associated Literary Press; the syndicates of Irving Bacheller; Tillotson's Newspaper Fiction Bureau; the Authors' Alliance; the Authors' Syndicate; the Editors' Literary Syndicate; the United Press; the International Literary and News Syndicate. American newspaper readers of the late nineteenth century in rural areas, small towns, and large cities throughout the country were very familiar with either the names or the work of these syndicates, which supplied printed material in various forms to the rapidly increasing number of country weeklies and metropolitan dailies. Through their operations, a single written work would appear simultaneously in from twenty to perhaps 1,000 newspapers across the United States. Most important for this study, these syndicates distributed thousands of short stories and novels in serial form. Every major American and British fiction author of this period had at least one work first published through the syndicates, and from 1861 to 1900 these organizations probably exposed a greater number of American readers to more works of fiction than did books and magazines of all kinds. Today, however, few students of American literature even recognize the names. No systematic study of their operations and role in the literary marketplace has been done, and thus the available information about them consists mainly of scattered scraps tucked away inconspicuously in biographies, bibliographies, or surveys of the rise of the American newspaper. Given the size and influence of the syndicates, the paucity of information about them is striking.

I

There are many reasons why newspaper syndicates can no longer be overlooked by literary scholars, chief among them that they afford entry into an almost completely neglected fiction publishing venue: the newspaper. The increases in production and readership of American newspapers between 1860 and 1900 were phenomenal; newspapers became a part of the lives of almost every American. There were 4,051 different newspapers published in the United States in 1860, with 387 of these being dailies and 3,173 being weeklies. By 1899, there were 18,793 newspapers published in the United States; 2,226 were dailies and 12,979 were weeklies.[2] Given that the vast majority of daily and weekly newspapers included syndicated fiction, the readership for these materials was quite large. One syndicate alone, McClure's Associated Literary Press, distributed 155 short stories and one serial novel in 1885 and 119 short stories and 16 serial novels in 1899, each of them to an average of 20 newspapers, from Boston to San Francisco, with circulation per newspaper ranging from 10,000 to 120,000 copies. If one accepts the usual estimate of three readers per copy, this one syndicate thus made fiction available to at least as many readers in a year as did any of the supposedly pioneering national mass-market magazines founded in the late 1880s and early 1890s.

Syndicates are also important because they reached different readers than those previously believed by scholars to have been the main audience during this period for what middle-class cultural arbiters of the time deemed "quality" fiction. (While in the last twenty years literary scholars have largely deconstructed the terms of "quality," "serious," "popular," and "artistic" fiction and literature, for the purposes of this study it is useful to acknowledge the distinctions made at the time by critics and others between "quality" fiction that was supposedly more "serious" and "artistic" and written not primarily for financial ends, and "popular" fiction that was allegedly written solely for commercial purposes and intended only to amuse readers.)[3] The readers of syndicated fiction were of both genders and came not only from a wide geographical expanse outside of the Northeastern United States but also from a broad socioeconomic spectrum. This was made possible by their unique distribution system. Syndicates were often based in New York or other East Coast cities, but the points of actual publication were decentralized in cities across the country. Unlike magazine, book, and story paper publishers, syndicates (except for readyprint syndicates) did not produce already laid-out, complete print products in New York, Boston, or Philadelphia and then ship these bulky works throughout the country to subscribers and jobbers. Instead, most syndicates sent stereotype plates, flong mats, or galley proofs via the mail or rail express services to newspaper editors in Toledo, Minneapolis, New Orleans, and Los Angeles, among other places, and allowed them to incorporate these fictions into their newspapers however they chose. These newspapers were subsequently widely circulated throughout the regional market area in general stores and by periodical kiosk vendors, newsboys, and the postal system. In addition, because newspapers sold for an average price during this period of either 2 or 3 cents daily and 5 cents on Sunday or weekly, they and their fictions were easily available to a broad socioeconomic group that previously had been shut out from first publication reading of "quality" fiction by the 25 or 35 cent price of a literary magazine or $1.25 or $1.50 for a cloth-covered book. However, although syndicated fiction ended up inadvertently benefiting lower-class readers with little money to spend on reading materials, newspaper editors aimed their choice of syndicated fiction primarily at the middle-class female reader, who was presumed to have the buying power to purchase the goods advertised in the newspaper. In general, editors hoped that syndicated fiction would appeal to female readers as well as the traditional male newspaper reader, thus creating a higher readership in general and thereby boosting advertising revenues. Overall, then, the syndicates reached the new, more diverse national audience slightly before mass-market magazines did in the 1890s.

Furthermore, the syndicates helped create unique sites of interaction between readers and fiction texts. The contexts in which syndicated fictions were presented to and read by readers differed radically from those that obtained in the case of books and, to a lesser extent, magazines. Newspaper editors during this time created intertextual printed salad bowls where non-fiction stories and advertisements mixed on the pages with syndicated fiction, and these visual and ideological melanges undoubtedly helped influence readers in their attitudes towards such fictional works. In addition, readers clearly read newspapers in different environments and approached reading with a different attitude than they did books and magazines. Only in the past few years have some scholars begun to appreciate the difference between reading short stories and novels in magazines rather than in books; no one, however, has yet taken newspapers into account.[4] Scholars interested in understanding how millions of nineteenth-century American readers interacted with fiction texts and in general how the contexts of the reading experience influence interpretation should be very interested in the newspaper as a venue.

Another reason to investigate the syndicates is that they played a vital role in the professionalization of the fiction author. Their operations demanded that they procure many times the number of fictional works that magazines could publish in a year; as a result they supported a large number of authors of all levels of popularity and critical reputation. Syndicates purchased works from a very heterogeneous group that included authors whose names are unrecognized today, those who were once popular but are now known only to a few, and many authors who have been and are the object of extensive scholarly research, such as Henry James, William Dean Howells, Mark Twain, Mary E. Wilkins (Freeman), Sarah Orne Jewett, Charles Chesnutt, Robert Louis Stevenson, Arthur Conan Doyle, Rudyard Kipling, Stephen Crane, H. G. Wells, and Jack London. The syndicates were important outlets for the work of all of these authors. What most attracted them was that some syndicates were often able to offer higher sums for their works than individual magazines could and also a great deal of publicity. The competition between syndicates and magazines for authors' works had a far-reaching impact on the profession of authorship.

Possibly most important, syndicates represent an important but overlooked stage in the evolution of the American literary publishing industry. Most literary historians narrate the development of the relationship between the author and the publishing industry in the late nineteenth century as proceeding directly from the stable era of "Gentlemanly Publishing" (to use Susan Coultrap-McQuin's term), when literature was produced and published by a relatively small group of persons with "serious" artistic tastes and intentions, to the more plebeian, competitive environment dominated by the impersonal organizational structures of the mass-market magazines founded in the 1890s. These were supposedly headed by commercial-minded, autocratic editors who regarded literature as a commodity like any other and who hegemonically controlled and manipulated their authors and readers.[5] However, the organizational structure and operational methods of most syndicates bore little resemblance to those of magazines. To a great extent, the syndicates represent a transitional stage between the more personalized "old-fashioned" literary publishing industry (although one must be careful not to over-romanticize it) and the highly-capitalized and complexly organized one of the mass-market magazines and modern book publishing houses.

II

The role of these syndicates may be almost forgotten today, but in the late nineteenth century syndicates were given their due as major factors in the literary marketplace. They were mentioned in numerous periodical articles, and there were frequent debates about their impact on authors, publishers, and readers. The editor of the *Journalist* magazine introduced an 1888 article on the subject of syndicates: "They are here and are growing rich and powerful. The very fact that they provoke much discussion, criticism and praise, is proof positive that they are a very live factor in newspaper work." Detailed knowledge of the syndicates is assumed in almost all contributions to the debate. One commentator in *Writer* (New York) magazine could in 1888 "presume that everybody knows by this time what is the province of the syndicates."[6]

Unfortunately, for the most part only one side of the debate about the syndicates has been passed down over the years. The view that has held most stubbornly is that expressed in a stinging diatribe written in 1895 by Edward W. Bok, editor of the *Ladies' Home Journal*. In a *Forum* magazine article entitled "The Modern Literary King," Bok surveyed the American literary scene and could see nothing but decay. Bok argued that authors no longer wrote to share their divinely inspired artistic visions with others but now were solely influenced by money, the "modern literary king." In this mad, competitive rush for money, the old, stable bonds between publishers and authors had been broken. Bok placed the blame for this state of affairs almost entirely on the newspaper syndicates, which supposedly had come between authors and respectable publishers and turned the author "into a veritable machine" who wrote works "to order." "The syndicate is in business for money: for literature it cares very little," he alleged, adding that because syndicates lacked standards and taste, they took the second-class work of famous and not-so-famous authors and paid high rates for it, thereby enervating literature as a whole.[7]

What has gone unnoticed, however, is that Bok – like many of those who criticized the syndicates – was not a disinterested party in the matter. Founder of a short-lived syndicate himself in 1886 and editor of the *Ladies' Home Journal* from 1889 to 1919, he competed directly against the syndicates for the work of many authors. In 1891, for instance, S. S. McClure had outmaneuvered and outbid him for serial rights to Mark Twain's novel *The American Claimant* (1892). Bok's assessment of the syndicates was thus not objective; furthermore, it was not universally shared. Opposing voices who defended the syndicates at the time and pointed out their positive contributions problematize Bok's judgment. For example, one of his contemporaries countered many of the popular arguments against the syndicates when he wrote, "The [syndicate] system enables newspapers to obtain first-class articles at a moderate cost – while the middleman is able to pay authors high prices, and to introduce them to a larger circle of readers than they could obtain through any magazine, or book." Another concluded, "the syndicate system is doubtless a benefit to the writer, the publisher and the public," because with it, "the well-known author can command a higher price for his work . . . than any individual publication is willing to pay him," and receive wide publicity; he added that "the public is also a gainer, in being afforded an early reading of fiction of the first quality."[8]

For many reasons, researching the true history of the syndicates in order to offer a more sober assessment of the role they played in American literary history is a difficult task. One reason is that the subject is immense and largely uncharted; there is very little previous scholarship to consult and build on. There are also practical obstacles to overcome, such as the relative inaccessibility of important relevant materials. Quite often the newspapers in which syndicated fiction appeared were not saved before the acidic content of the paper itself reduced them to yellow dust. In addition, even when such newspapers are available, the inquiring scholar must be extremely patient to scroll through roll after roll of microfilm and try to decipher the small print of these papers. The lack of adequate indexing in all but a few instances also greatly deters exploration of this print medium. Despite all of these obstacles, however, it was possible to find a great deal of material about these syndicates and their operations. This book gathers the numerous scraps of contemporary accounts, information gleaned from numerous hours of looking at microfilm of old newspapers, the smaller amount of published secondary information on the syndicates, and a great deal of unpublished archival material, and consolidates it all to provide the first detailed histories of these syndicates.

In fact, in order to make this study more manageable for both the writer and the reader, some limitations have been imposed. To some extent the availability of materials helped define the scope of the present work: archival materials and information on some of the syndicates – those of S. S. McClure, Irving Bacheller, Tillotson and Son's, Ansel Nash Kellogg, and the American Press Association – is more available than on others. In addition, it begins in 1861, the year when Ansel Nash Kellogg first printed "patent inside" newspapers in Baraboo, Wisconsin; it continues to 1900. The choice of 1900 as an ending point is in some ways arbitrary and in other ways not. Syndicates did not stop distributing fiction to newspapers in 1900; in fact, they continued to operate for many years after this. After about 1900, however, an increasing percentage of syndicated fictions were not original publications but rather reprints, having first appeared in book and magazine form. The year 1900 is also a convenient stopping place because the second largest American galley-proof syndicate of this time, Irving Bacheller's, folded in 1898, and the attempt of William Dean Howells to gather well-known authors into a syndicate failed in 1899. Worthington Ford in 1918 might still write that the newspaper "has drawn to itself the best of literature," but in general the comments of Hamlin Garland in 1902 that "There are, I believe, fewer stories printed serially in the newspapers now than ten years ago," and the "The story syndicates are passing rather than coming on" were accurate assessments.[9]

This book also confines itself to prose fiction printed in American daily and weekly newspapers, printed sheets whose primary content is news, not fiction. Except for a brief description of them in chapter 1, family story papers such as the New York *Ledger* and Gleason's *Pictorial Weekly* are excluded, because they included little news, and syndicates marketed few materials to them. Furthermore, only syndication in United States newspapers is included in any depth. While the American operations of the British syndicate of Tillotson's Newspaper Fiction Bureau are examined, the operations of Tillotson's and various American syndicates in the United Kingdom, Continental Europe, Australia, India, and other British colonies are not. Finally, because of the limited space available, the relations between the syndicates and only a relatively small number of fiction authors are detailed, although every effort has been made to ensure that they constitute a representative sample.

III

Within these parameters, this book will provide what anthropologist Clifford Geertz would call a "thick description" of these syndicates and how they procured, processed, and disseminated fiction. To comprehend how the syndicates generated their cultural product, however, requires more than just a descriptive history. Elizabeth Fox-Genovese's advice is heeded here; she argues that "History, at least good history, in contrast to antiquarianism, is inescapably structural ... by structural, I mean that history must disclose and reconstruct the conditions of consciousness and action."[10] What little history has been written of the syndicates has implied that the personalities of individual syndicate managers were the sole governing factors in each syndicate's operations. This work, however, attempts to offer a description of certain types of organizations rather than a biography of their managers. It recognizes that syndicates did not have a single *mentalité* of operation, since each functioned differently according to the persons involved, the programs of the firms, and the operating capital available to them. At the same time, since all syndicates of each type (readyprint, plate, and galley-proof) shared a roughly common organizational structure with other syndicates in the same category, one can justify grouping them together and making some generalizations based on evidence gleaned from only a few of them.

Moreover, in this work the history and operations of these

syndicates in relation to other print media and their representatives will be documented, but this information will not function as mere background to fiction texts. Too often an amorphous agent called capitalist "power" or "the 'inevitable' forces of urbanization, commercialization, and industrialization" are invoked as responsible for historical change or cultural production.[11] This work instead uses the information available to examine how not only the personalities of the syndicators themselves but also specific historical and cultural conditions of the period – technological advances, economic concerns, cultural prejudices, and copyright laws – influenced the organizational modus operandi of the syndicates and the cultural products they produced.

Even more specifically, in chapters 4, 5, 6, and 7, this work asks and attempts to answer a number of vital questions about the hegemonic power of the syndicates in the marketplace. First, how did the newspaper syndicate outlet influence what fiction authors produced and how they did it? Did it force them to become mere "wordsmiths under contract," as is commonly charged, or did it empower authors and afford them relative artistic freedom? Were authors forced or prompted to produce more short stories and works with less characterization and more action to suit the supposed itinerant newspaper reader? Did they choose certain subjects over others in an attempt to appeal to the newspaper audience? Second, were the syndicates the forerunners of the kind of centralized editorial control later exerted by editors and publishers of national magazines in the 1890s? Third, what degree of freedom – of both choice and interpretation – did the syndicates offer readers? Overall, do the newspaper syndicates support or refute the claims of many scholars that, as in other industries, the production and consumption of American literature during this time became more urban-oriented and centrally controlled, usually from New York City? Intertwined with all of these questions is the issue of the stringency of the operating limitations: who or what generated them, and how were they made known or "enforced"?

Related questions will also be investigated. For instance, how and why did newspaper syndication of fiction threaten the arbiters of "high" culture of the period? Were the managers of these syndicates actually uneducated materialists who cared only for the financial bottom line and believed literature could be manufactured like iron stoves, as they have sometimes been portrayed? What factors were primarily responsible for the gradual disappearance of first publication syndicated fiction from the newspaper? Finally, what were the implications of the end of this era for the average reader and American print culture as a whole?

Up to this point the voices that have spoken for the entire text of syndicate history have been almost exclusively negative ones. Allegations as to the low quality of literary work distributed through the syndicates and the heavy-handed treatment of authors by syndicators have been made on the slightest of evidence. Many of these charges are colored by cultural biases and rely on incomplete evidence; they come closer to rumor and myth than to historical accuracy. Too often, for example, literary scholars have unquestioningly sided with authors who claimed they were "wronged" by the syndicates because businessmen such as syndicators are often seen as enemies to art. These negative views of the syndicates, however, should not be accepted as the last word without more extensive investigation. Here the numerous more positive voices – those of authors, critics, agents, and readers – that have not been heard will join the negative ones. This is not, though, a simple defense of the syndicates. Rather, it is an attempt to test the commonly held assumptions about the syndicates and to adjudicate the debate over their role and significance.

CHAPTER I

Preparing the way for the syndicates: a revolution in American fiction production, distribution, and readership, 1860–1900

> It is a universal and much-expressed regret that the literary output has of late years become almost a flood ... Men and women are perplexed to know where they shall begin their reading and where end it.
>
> Francis Whiting Halsey, *Our Literary Deluge*, 1902
>
> Is it not better to welcome and rejoice over this recent "literary deluge" than to decry it?
>
> Frank Norris, 1903[1]

Syndicates that distributed fiction to newspapers did not spring fully formed from nowhere, and as they developed they did not operate in a vacuum. This chapter situates the syndicates in the print ecology of the period 1860–1900 by detailing the production, distribution, and readership conditions of the larger American publishing industry within which they emerged, operated, and competed. Syndicates were only one part of an unprecedented explosion of print during these years. The extent of this explosion – particularly of print forms capable of carrying fiction – and how certain technological, legal, social, educational, and economic boundaries directed the particular forms which it took – are described here, along with the modi operandi of the various publishers involved in this proliferation. The special conditions affecting newspaper publishing receive special attention, since it was in newspapers that fiction distributed by syndicates was published. The broad understanding obtained here of how fiction was produced, procured, and distributed for and by book, story paper, and magazine publishers provides a valuable benchmark against which the operations of the syndicates can be compared. Most important, such information allows one to more fully comprehend why the newspaper syndication of fiction flourished at this particular moment in American literary history rather than before 1860 or after 1900.

I

In the period between 1860 and 1900, the American publishing industry grew immensely, producing an ever-increasing amount of print. Population more than doubled, from 31 million in 1860 to 76 million in 1900, but the number and variety of print forms – especially those containing fiction – available to American readers grew exponentially. Cloth-covered books, paperback books, story papers, magazines, and above all newspapers, seemed omnipresent. Many American readers began to feel inundated with print. In 1881 the noted psychologist George Beard went so far as to posit that the greatly increased number of periodicals that the average American was expected to read contributed heavily to the condition he diagnosed as "American Nervousness."[2]

Some of this deluge was made up of print designated as nonfiction, but a large majority of it was made up of print labelled as fiction. For hardcover book publishers, the dramatic rise in the numbers of volumes of fiction published and sold had begun in the 1850s. Whereas in the 1830s a volume that sold 6,500 copies was considered a bestseller, by the 1850s a book was a "decided hit" only if it sold in the tens of thousands. According to one report in 1858, only eight works of fiction had sold more than 25,000 copies, with *Uncle Tom's Cabin* leading the way at 310,000 and Maria Susanna Cummins's *The Lamplighter* far behind in second place at 90,000 copies sold. Not only were more copies of each work being sold, but more separate volumes were being published: in 1855 American publishers reportedly issued about 2,000 separate titles, and some 400 of these were works of fiction. After the Civil War, however, these numbers would seem small by comparison. Measuring exactly how much of the increased output was made up of hardcover fiction is difficult to determine, because no comprehensive or reliable production figures for the entire industry exist before 1880, and the *Publishers' Weekly* annual survey that began in that year relied solely on publishers' reports and did not break down book production into clothbound or paperback, new volume or new edition categories. Yet we do know that in 1881, American book publishers reported having published 587 works of fiction; in 1890, 1,118; and in 1900, 616 new volumes and 662 new editions of fiction. Selling at the comparatively high average price during this period of $1.25, most hardcover volumes of fiction failed to break even, but those that did often sold in hitherto unimagined numbers. By the end of the century a bestseller was measured in the hundreds of thousands, and there were a few of these each year.[3] Most of the real growth in fiction book sales, however, came not from hardcover volumes published by old guard publishers such as Harper's, Scribner's, Lippincott's, Putnam's, or Appleton, but rather from nickel and dime paperback editions by publishers who wanted to reach the market constituted by the new, mass reading public. The year 1860 marks the publication of the first so-called dime novel (even though it sold for 15 cents), a reprint of Ann S. Stephens's *Malaeska–The Indian Wife of the White Hunter* (1839). Such novels, usually published weekly in a series, made up a large percentage of the books published and sold. Their low price was possible because most were reprinted works whose already proven popularity decreased publishers' risks and the advertising budget needed to sell them, pirated works by foreign authors that until 1891 were unprotected by American copyright law, or highly formulaic works produced by American writers willing to write for low wages. The pocket-size (usually 4" x 6"), 100-page volumes were enormously popular among Civil War soldiers, and their low price appealed to a mass civilian audience as well. Sales of each dime novel usually ranged from 35,000 to 80,000 copies, but because of the great number of titles produced, they appeared omnipresent.[4]

In the 1870s these series of cheap fictions were often consolidated under the aegis of "libraries" such as Donnelly, Lloyd and Company's *Lakeside Library* (founded in 1875) and Munro's *Seaside Library* (1877); by 1877 there were at least 14 such programs, ranging in price from a nickel for volumes of *Beadle's Half Dime Library* (1877) to 10–30 cents for copies in *Lovell's Library* (1882). In their peak year of 1886, 26 cheap libraries printed 1,351 volumes.[5] As competition reduced profit margins in the late 1880s, however, many firms went out of business. The death-knell for these "libraries" came in March 1891, when Congress passed the Chace Act, bringing the United States into accord with the 1886 Berne Convention regulations concerning international copyright. This Act, the most important legislation affecting authors during this period, for the first time provided copyright protection under American law for works by foreign authors – provided that the typesetting for the work was done in the United States. Because of this, American cheap book publishers could no longer reprint the works of foreign authors for free or next to nothing, as they had previously. Despite John Lovell's attempt in the early 1890s to make cheap paperback publishing profitable again by merging many of these reprint libraries into one firm, the American Book Company, it and other cheap reprint houses soon went bankrupt.

To compete with these extremely cheap paperbacks, mainstream American book publishers in the 1870s came out with their own libraries of cheap paperback fiction. These series reprinted many popular British works but also often published American copyrighted works; while non-copyrighted material sold for 25 cents, copyrighted works sold for the slightly higher price of 50 cents. Less popular than their cheaper and usually more sensational competitors, their average sales were a respectable 10,000 copies each.[6] Houghton-Mifflin's *Riverside Library* (begun in 1877) and Harper's *Franklin Square Library* (founded in 1878 and specializing in British fiction) were joined in the 1880s by Scribner's *Yellow Covers*, Ticknor's *Paper Series*, Houghton-Mifflin's *Riverside Paper Series*, and Appleton's *Town and Country Library*. These series remained in business even after the Chace Act of 1891, but declined in the 1890s as their publishers realized the negative effect they had on sales of the more expensive and profitable editions that they also published.

Another very important source of fiction for American readers was the literary weekly, often referred to as the story paper, which was the precursor to and contemporary of the nickel and dime novels. In their early days in the 1830s, story papers generally sold for 3 cents and were physically huge (deemed "blanket sheets"), four-page weekly miscellanies consisting mainly of pieces clipped from other newspapers or magazines but also including some news stories. By their heyday in the 1850s and 1860s, they usually sold for 5 or 6 cents and contained more original material, including "anywhere from five to eight serialized stories, as well as correspondence, brief sermons, humor, fashion advice, and bits of arcane knowledge." The pioneers in the field were the *Philadelphia Saturday Courier* (begun in 1831), Park Benjamin's *Brother Jonathan* (1839) (which Benjamin left a few months after founding it) and *New World* (1839), and the *Saturday Evening Post*, which began its life as a story paper in 1821. Later entrants include *Frank Leslie's Illustrated Newspaper* (1855), Street and Smith's *New York Weekly Dispatch* (revitalized in 1855), Robert Bonner's New York *Ledger* (1856), James Elverson's *Saturday Night* (1865), Beadle and Adams' *Saturday Journal* (1870), and Norman Munro's *Family Story Paper* (1873). As indicated by the last title, these story papers strove to present morally upright material that would offend no one in the family. Sold nationwide at newsstands and by subscription through the mails, they reached a substantial readership. The *New York Weekly* claimed that its circulation climbed from 80,000 per week in 1859 to 150,000 in 1863 and 300,000 in 1870, while the New York *Ledger* claimed to have a circulation of 400,000 per week in 1860. By the late 1870s, however, a glut of these weeklies on the market and the appearance of other cheap forms of printed fiction led to their lessened importance.[7]

Many magazines also contained fiction. In general, until 1885 the literary magazine field was dominated by a few genteel publications that were usually affiliated with a book publishing firm; after 1885 the advent of nonaffiliated, illustrated, mass-market magazines significantly altered the character and sales of magazines. The increasing number of both genteel and mass-market magazines were part of an overall boom that continued unabated throughout the period. While there had been only 700 American magazines of all kinds published in 1865, there were 1,200 in 1870, 2,400 in 1880, 3,300 in 1885; 4,400 in 1890, and 5,500 in 1900. Thus, while the population of the United States increased 113 per cent from 1865 to 1900, the number of magazines published from 1865 to 1900 increased 686 per cent. In addition, the overall production and circulation of magazines skyrocketed. It should be noted that for a variety of reasons, completely reliable circulation figures for magazines and newspapers during this period are almost impossible to obtain. Yet even taken in round terms, Richard Altick's statement about the circulation increases of late nineteenth-century magazines is striking: "in 1885 the only four magazines with circulations of over 100,000 had sold an aggregate of 600,000 a month; by 1905 there were five times as many [selling over 100,000 per month], and their total sale was more than 5,500,000 copies."[8]

From 1860 to the mid-1880s, the monthly magazines that printed fiction were few in number and catered primarily to a culturally select audience, most of whom lived in the urban Northeast, and whose members could pay the relatively high price of 25–35 cents per copy or $4.00 a year. The model magazines of this type were *Harper's New Monthly Magazine*, founded in 1850, and the *Atlantic Monthly*, founded in 1857 and affiliated throughout its career with a number of different Boston book publishing firms. Other magazines of the type included *Godey's Lady's Book* (1840–1898), *Graham's* (1840–1858), *Peter-*

son's (1848–1892), *Galaxy* (1866–1878), *Harper's Bazar* (1867–1929), *Lippincott's* (1868–1915), *Appleton's* (1869–1881), *Scribner's Monthly* (founded in 1870, it was sold to the Century Company in 1881 and returned from 1887 to 1939 as *Scribner's Magazine*), and *Century* (1881–1929). In 1860, the average individual circulation of all monthly magazines stood at 12,000, and most of the aforementioned periodicals continued to have relatively small circulations throughout the period 1860–1900. For example, the *Atlantic Monthly*, considered by many as the most prestigious venue for quality fiction, had only 12,000 subscribers in 1881 and 14,000 in 1898. More successful at reaching a large audience later in the century were *Harper's Monthly*, *Harper's Bazar*, *Harper's Weekly* (a slightly less genteel magazine published between 1857 and 1916), and *Century*. *Harper's Monthly* circulated 200,000 copies per issue in 1885, while *Harper's Bazar*'s circulation stood at 150,000 copies per issue in 1880; *Century* averaged approximately 200,000 copies per issue through the 1880s. Yet, by 1900 the circulation of *Harper's Monthly* and *Century* was down to about 100,000 each.[9]

Why did these magazines experience a decline in sales just as total magazine production and consumption was increasing so dramatically? Much of the reason lies in the appearance in the late 1880s of a new type of magazine: relatively cheap (5 to 15 cents per copy), copiously illustrated, and full of timely articles and fiction by the most famous authors of the day. This group included *Ladies' Home Journal* (begun in 1883), *Cosmopolitan* (1886), *Golden Argosy* (1887), *Collier's* (1888), *Munsey's Magazine* (1889), *McClure's Magazine* (1893) and the *Saturday Evening Post*, reorganized in 1897 under the control of Cyrus Curtis. According to Richard Brodhead, these magazines "began to encroach on American high culture's established literary domain" by luring quality authors to write for the masses, more precisely the middle-class masses. As one literary historian notes, in the late 1880s, "the country's non-magazine-buying millions were ripe for anyone who could interest them in reading. As yet there was no popular literature for them, no middle ground of periodicals between the Augusta dreadfuls [story papers] and the ponderous reviews dealing in subject matter the average man cared nothing about at a price he couldn't afford to pay."[10] A whole new reading public, not previously attracted to magazines, responded vigorously to these cheaper versions and, as noted previously, bought them in record numbers.

One might expect that all of these books, story papers, and magazines would have satisfied the appetite of the American public for fiction, but they did not. Possibly the most prolific purveyor of fiction – yet so seldom thought of as such that it has rarely been discussed in literary histories – was the newspaper. Although the primary mission of newspapers throughout the period between 1860 and 1900 remained the dissemination of supposedly non-fictional information, the majority also contained a good deal of fiction, much of it supplied by syndicates. As the century progressed, newspaper production and readership figures far outdistanced those of books, story papers, and magazines. E. L. Godkin, editor of the *Nation*, was led to observe in 1890 that while "the number of books, serious as well as light, undoubtedly increases rapidly, and so does the number of those who read them ... they do not increase in anything like the same ratio as the number of newspaper readers."[11]

The phenomenal growth from 1860 to 1899 in the total number of American newspapers supports Godkin's assessment; the most reliable figures indicate an increase of 363 per cent. The number of newspapers rose fairly slowly in the first decade and a half after the Civil War but grew much more rapidly during the 1880s and 1890s. In 1860 there were 387 daily newspapers in the United States and 3,173 weekly papers, by 1880 there were 971 daily newspapers, by 1890 there were 1,731 daily newspapers, and by 1899 there were 2,226 dailies and 12,979 weeklies. Major cities were swamped with newspapers: in 1870 New York City had 29 daily newspapers, Philadelphia 24, and San Francisco 21; in 1879 Chicago had 18 dailies and 138 weeklies. While urban areas had a surfeit of newspapers (on average, by 1880 each of the 389 cities or towns in which daily newspapers were printed had 2.5 newspapers), other areas were also widely covered: of the 2,605 counties in the United States in 1880, newspapers – either daily or weekly – were published in 2,073 of them.[12]

Not only did the number of different newspapers grow by leaps and bounds, but so did their circulations. As with magazines, though, newspaper circulation figures are quite inexact and must be taken as such; publishers clearly benefited from reporting inflated circulation figures. Furthermore, even if publishers accurately reported the numbers of copies printed, those numbers do not imply that all were sold or read. Even given a substantial discrepancy between reported circulation and the actual readership of the newspaper, however, one must acknowledge that newspaper reading became an established part of daily life for most Americans during this period. To cite the figures from just one year, 1870, the 574 daily newspapers issued a total of 806,479,579 copies, and the 4,295 weeklies issued 550,921,436 copies – this in a year when all other periodicals combined printed a total of only 150 million copies.[13]

The circulation of metropolitan dailies was especially large. In 1860 the *New York Herald* was deemed the world's largest daily newspaper with 77,000 copies sold. By the 1880s, though, the larger New York City papers commonly circulated 100,000 copies each, and such papers as Joseph Pulitzer's New York *World* and William Randolph Hearst's New York *Journal* claimed to circulate 600,000 and 430,000 copies respectively in 1896. Outside of New York City, circulation figures were usually much lower but still considerable. The *Boston Globe* in 1884 reported an average circulation of 121,480; in 1889, 139,971; and in 1898, 230,515; the *Detroit Free Press* recorded a daily average of 17,209 in July 1885; the Philadelphia *Evening Item* circulated 182,497 copies on average in 1892; the *Indianapolis News* reported an average daily circulation in 1891 of 26,000; the *Los Angeles Times* circulated 18,179 copies on average in 1896; and the St. Paul *Pioneer-Press* claimed an average circulation of 32,320 in 1890.[14]

Paralleling and then surpassing the increased circulation of daily newspapers was that of the Sunday newspapers. The number of Sunday editions affiliated with daily newspapers rose dramatically, from 113 in 1880 to 257 in 1890 and 567 in 1900. Filled with a smorgasbord of international and national news, features, fashion advice, children's pages, and fiction, these Sunday newspapers were, as the *Boston Globe* proclaimed itself in 1891, "THE PEOPLE'S FAVORITE MAGAZINE."[15] Until the mid-1880s, most metropolitan Sunday editions sold for 3 cents; from the mid-1880s to the end of the century, despite the increase in typical size from eight pages to forty-eight pages, the price remained 5 cents a copy or 2 dollars a year.

The pattern of Sunday circulation exemplified by the *Boston Globe* was repeated throughout the country. In 1891, the *Globe* reported a Sunday circulation in July of 153,668, which was just barely above the average daily circulation in May of 150,548. By 1899, though, the reported average of 253,182 for the Sunday edition was far beyond the daily's average 190,743 circulation.[16] By virtue of its being the newspaper touted as being read by the entire family, the Sunday newspaper can safely be assumed as having had at least two readers for each copy, which means that the approximate readership of each Sunday edition of the *Boston Globe* in 1899 was 506,364. Much as was the case with magazines with heterogeneous contents, it is impossible to determine what percentage of newspaper readers – whether on Sunday or any other day of the week – read any one particular item contained within it, such as fiction. Yet it can safely be asserted that simply on the basis of the sheer number of copies sold, Sunday and daily newspapers that contained fiction constituted a significant force in mass readership. By extension, syndicated material such as fiction that was printed and sold for simultaneous publication in 20 or more of these metropolitan newspapers at a time can be said to have reached a large mass audience.

II

Why did the production of these various types of printed materials skyrocket in the late nineteenth century? Numerous technological innovations introduced in the publishing industry during this time certainly contributed to the rise. These advances are generally well-known yet worthy of brief mention. Further development of the electrotype and stereotype plate processes, the discovery of the soda-alkali process (1860s) and then the sulfite process (1880s) of making paper from wood pulp (instead of from scarce and expensive rags), the wider use of continuous-roll paper dryers and of rotary and web perfecting presses after the Civil War, along with the introduction in the 1880s of Ottmar Mergenthaler's linotype machines that greatly speeded typesetting, made larger production runs of books, magazines, and newspapers possible. Most important, by reducing the cost of materials and the amount of labor involved, they decreased the costs of production and subsequently lowered the price of most printed materials for the purchasing public.

Studying the changing means of production, however, affords only a partial understanding of how and why Americans were flooded with printed materials after the Civil War. The expansion of the markets for such materials, for instance, was a crucial catalyst for increased production, and these markets could not have expanded without an improved distribution system. Clearly, without improvements in the capabilities of this system, it would have been impossible to reach the growing number of potential readers, and countless numbers of books, story papers, magazines, and newspapers would have rotted in warehouses where they were printed instead of making their way into readers' hands.

Some of the greatest difficulties in distributing printed materials to readers throughout the country had diminished by 1860. The march of transportation advances in the 1830s, 1840s, and 1850s – steamboats, canals, and railroads (especially the extension of the railroad network in the 1850s beyond the Alleghenies and the completion of the transcontinental railroad in 1869) – had gone a long way toward regularizing a distribution system that previously had suffered vagaries of weather like frozen waterways or roads made impassable by spring rains. The most important advance in distribution during the period under discussion was the enormous growth in total railroad miles in operation from 30,626 in 1860 to 166,703 in 1890, a more than five-fold increase, which greatly benefited both publishers and readers.[17]

One important result of the improved and extended rail system was the ability of the book, story paper, and magazine publishing industry to concentrate in Boston, Philadelphia, and New York, and to send its products cheaply and in a timely manner to other areas of the country. One scholar has concluded that by 1875, "A few eastern centers – New York, in particular – were supplying books for the whole country, and the age of regional [book] publishing was at an end." The majority of magazines that deemed themselves national in purview, too, were printed in these cities; in 1880 one quarter of the country's monthlies were published in New York City, and most of the rest were published in Boston or Philadelphia.[18]

Such centralization was also made possible in part by new, large organizations that almost completely dominated magazine, newspaper, and to a lesser extent, book distribution by the end of the century: wholesale distributors such as the International News Company, the American News Company (ANC), and the United States Post Office Department. By the mid-1880s the American News Company (founded in 1864) had a virtual monopoly on magazine distribution, and reportedly, "this giant distributed practically all the magazines sold in America." In the 1890s the International News Company, which distributed foreign periodicals in the United States, teamed up with the ANC.[19] The importance of such wholesale distributors has been largely overlooked, yet such firms played a vital role in efficiently moving large numbers of magazines, newspapers, and books from their publishers to readers throughout the country.

Providing an even more direct distribution route from publisher to consumers/readers was the United States Post Office Department. The number of operating post offices increased from 28,498 in 1860 to 76,688 in 1900.[20] Furthermore, improved railroads and roads, along with societal imperatives for the free, democratic diffusion of print information among the American citizenry, led to lower postage rates for magazines and newspapers during this period. Story papers, too, were widely distributed by mail.

Books, on the other hand, remained during this period the object of comparative postal rate discrimination. One writer commented in 1900 that "To-day's extended market for books" is "practically coextensive with the mails."[21] Yet while the possibility of receiving books through the mail existed, the relatively higher postal rates on them discouraged purchases by this means. Only books such as those in cheap series or "libraries" that by virtue of their regular weekly or monthly publication masqueraded as periodicals could pass cheaply through the mails at the magazine rate. The rates on other kinds of books declined, but not nearly as rapidly as the rates for magazines and newspapers. As just one example, the 1885 Postal Act that equalized the rate on all periodicals (including many paperback books disguised as periodicals) at 1 cent per pound decreed that clothbound books would cost 8 cents per pound to mail.

Other actions taken by the postal service from 1860 to 1900 also served to extend print access to more readers throughout the country. In 1863, City Free Delivery was established in every city with a population of over 50,000, and in 1873 this service was extended to every city with a population over 30,000. By 1890, 19 million of the nation's 76 million people had mail delivered free to their door, mainly in urban areas. Service to rural areas also improved somewhat during this period, but truly equal access to story papers, magazines, books, and newspapers through the mail for rural residents came only after the turn of the century with the extension of the Rural Free Delivery (RFD) system.[22]

Due to all of these developments, the US Post Office became a major print distributor. A flood of materials, especially magazines and newspapers, almost inundated the post offices of America. In 1868 the US Postal Service delivered 16,910,715 newspapers, and in 1871 it delivered 32,610,353. By 1880, this number had skyrocketed: 812,032,000 newspapers passed through the mail, along with 40,148,792 magazines and other periodicals.[23] Unfortunately, accurate figures for second-class mail are not available after this date, but one can assume that the Post Office continued to be swamped with this class of material, especially considering the generous periodical rates stipulated in the 1885 Postal Act.

Despite the expanded rail network and all the improvements introduced by the ANC and the Post Office, however, it must be remembered that throughout the period of this study, equal access for Americans in all geographic areas to print products containing fiction – especially to books, magazines, and story papers – remained far from a reality. Certain areas of the country, such as the South and West, were not covered as extensively by the all-important rail networks. Rural readers, even in inland areas of the East Coast, were relatively isolated from print compared to their city cousins, mainly because the Post Office, like the book, story paper, and magazine publishers located in the major cities, found it too expensive per capita to try and reach them. Distribution systems had improved, but it was still cheaper and easier for book and magazine publishers to reach population concentrations in metropolitan areas and along rail lines rather than reach the more dispersed population of rural areas. Magazine and book publishers thus especially envisioned themselves as serving an urban, chiefly Northeastern, market. Cyrus Curtis, publisher of the *Ladies' Home Journal*, believed that in 1891, 75 per cent of the magazine's circulation was in towns with populations of over 10,000, many of them Eastern suburbs. There is some evidence that such magazines, along with some story papers and books, were being read outside the Northeast and in some relatively rural areas. Yet at present, one must conclude that because of the limits of the distribution network, during most of the period from 1860 to 1900 the majority of the readers of print products produced in East Coast cities appear to have lived in Eastern and North Central cities and towns along or near rail lines. Monthly magazines did eventually reach beyond these areas – by 1900, for example, half of the *Atlantic Monthly*'s circulation was west of the Mississippi – but in general, publishers were slow to react to the fact that increasingly higher percentages of Americans were living in Western areas, and that a great number of potential readers lived in rural districts.[24]

The only print form that carried fiction which does not conform to the centralized publication and distribution configuration of book, magazine, and story paper publishing during this period – and thus the only one that did not experience all their difficulties – is the newspaper. Unlike magazines and books, newspapers were primarily published at numerous outlying points and distributed and read locally and regionally. The distribution pattern of most weekly and daily papers published in rural areas was quite simple: they were usually both produced and read within the same county, and often distributed by the US Post Office, which carried them for free within their county of origin.

The large metropolitan daily newspapers, though, succeeded at blanketing not only their cities of publication but also their entire geographic regions. In cities, newspapers were sold (along with magazines in lesser numbers) at numerous newsstands, and newsboys hawked the papers on the street and in trolley cars. These newspapers also achieved extensive distribution within regional areas by having copies travel short distances by horsedrawn wagons or streetcars and longer distances through the mails or by express trains. The greatly improved and expanded rail service of the 1870s allowed even more rapid same-day service to ever larger circulation areas. New York City papers, for example, were well-known for their efficient distribution system that utilized "special trains" engaged solely for carrying newspapers. One observer reported in 1885 that "The special train business has become quite a feature in the metropolitan newspaper world," and by 1900 one writer noted that not only were nine special trains out of New York engaged to distribute the Sunday editions of daily papers, "in addition there are wagon services from diverging [rail] points, so that the country within a radius taking in Boston, Washington, Pittsburg, and Buffalo is gridironed, and the papers are delivered by noon." One report in 1890 noted that "The quiet streets of Washington [DC] ring with the cries of negro newsboys, who arrive with the New York papers in time to intercept people just as they are returning from morning service at church."[25]

Hoping to increase their circulations and their profits, large metropolitan newspapers throughout the country strove to become regional papers with ever-widening territories. The *Atlanta Constitution* is an excellent example of one such paper. As early as 1884, an editorial could boast: "Early and swift trains now carry the Daily Constitution out on every road that reaches out from Atlanta. It reaches almost every point in Georgia, and penetrates into every adjoining state on the day of publication." Another example is the *Detroit Free Press*. In 1885 it provided a detailed list of newsdealers' badge numbers and addresses to show it was not just a Detroit paper but a Michigan paper as well (significantly, many of these dealers were from small towns). Furthermore, as one newspaper historian writes, "The Weekly *Free Press* was read from New York to San Francisco. When nationwide circulation had reached 120,700 in 1891, only 37,720 copies were being sold in Michigan." The *Boston Globe*, too, was read by many outside the metropolitan area; an 1891 contest to guess the murderer in a mystery serial drew responses from rural areas of Massachusetts and small towns in every New England state. In addition, Edgar Watson Howe observed in 1891 that "Even in the west the big St. Louis dailies are delivered three hundred miles away by ten o'clock on the morning of publication," and the "Chicago dailies are delivered on the Mississippi River by breakfast time." Finally, there are indications that papers in the far West were also circulated to a wide area: in 1894 *The Colorado Weekly Sun* listed sales of over 1,000 copies in each of eight states, from Texas to Washington.[26]

What other factors contributed to the increasing flood of printed matter in the United States from 1860 to 1900? All of the production and distribution developments that made print products cheaper and more available, it can be said, would have been useless if there had not been an increased number of readers literate enough to be able to read them. In fact, the period 1860–1900 witnessed a remarkable extension of at least minimal literacy to a great number of people from various socioeconomic classes. No figures measuring literacy exist for this period, but the United States census does mark the decline of illiteracy from 20 per cent in 1870 to 10.7 per cent in 1900. The chief reason for this declining illiteracy rate was the public school movement. In 1870 there were 6,872,000 public school students, representing 17 per cent of the total population, and by 1900 this number had grown to 15,503,000, or 20 per cent of the total population. To get an even more accurate figure of the overall increase in school enrollment, one would also have to add to this latter figure the many millions of adult immigrants and their children enrolled in religious schools. The level of literacy such public and religious schooling produced in students (despite nostalgic assertions to the contrary) was probably quite low but still significant. As Harvey J. Graff reports in his study of literacy in some Ontario cities of the nineteenth century, "Common schooling experiences were not in most cases likely to produce more than imperfectly skilled individuals." Even this low level of literacy, however, had a large impact on the American publishing industry. Richard Altick underscores this point when he writes that the low level of American literacy in 1900, especially among recent immigrants, "did not encourage the average working-class reader to aspire beyond the magazines and newspapers that were carefully designed for his limited comprehension."[27] The influence of this new reading public is evident in the contrast between the stagnant circulations of periodicals such as the *Atlantic Monthly*, *Century*, and New York *Commercial-Advertiser*, all of which required a high literacy level, and the exploding circulations of magazines and newspapers such as *Cosmopolitan*, *Munsey's Magazine*, the New York *World*, and the *Boston Globe*, all of which used more illustrations and less sophisticated vocabularies.

As seen in the above descriptions, a large number of technological, distributional, and educational developments converged in the United States in the late nineteenth century to provide more print products to more readers than ever before. What is rarely noticed, however, is that while some mass-market magazines after 1885 captured an audience among readers of both genders from a broader socioeconomic spectrum, both before and after this time the print form that most cut across various demographic lines was the newspaper. Newspapers reached readers in rural areas, small towns, and large cities alike. Furthermore, although in some cities there were enough newspapers to allow individual ones to target certain audience sectors, in most places large daily newspapers could no longer afford to orient themselves toward only one group such as a political party or specific ethnic group; this type of targeting was done by smaller, usually weekly, newspapers. Cheap, easily available, containing information valuable to all classes and groups, and requiring little literacy or time to read, the metropolitan daily newspaper was read by men and women from almost all walks of life. Typical of this type of newspaper was the *Chicago Daily News*, which one knowledgeable writer noted in 1893, "goes everywhere in Chicago. It is read by rich and poor alike, for the carrier service reaches every street and every square in the city. It is a matter of record that as many copies are sold per 1,000 people in the silk stocking wards as in the district where the workingmen live."[28] Furthermore, in an attempt to reach beyond the traditional male readership of newspapers and reach women readers, newspapers began including Women's Pages and other features of interest to them. Such broad readership among so many demographic groups was multiplied many times in numerous local and regional markets. Given the aggregate presence of these newspapers in the daily life of most Americans during this period, the fiction that syndicates made available to readers in this print form clearly deserves closer scrutiny.

III

The American publishing industry, as outlined above, thus underwent a transformation of monumental proportions from 1860 to 1900. Along with this transformation came major changes in the way various publishing companies were run. In 1860 most of the large book and magazine publishing houses were fairly small scale family-owned businesses or were closely associated with the individuals at their heads: Scribner, Harper, Appleton, Putnam, Lippincott, and others. While their altruistic love of literature can easily be overstated, these publishers – if only symbolically – "liked to believe they were members of a profession requiring special scholarly training and a sense of dedication which rose above material gains."[29] The great newspaper editors of the day – Greeley, Bennett, and Bryant, to name a few – supposedly shared this disinterested love of truth over financial gain. As 1900 approached, however, these sanctums of high ideals were allegedly invaded by outsiders with crass, materialistic aims who pandered to the tastes of an altered reading public rather than seeking to elevate it, and who consequently were blamed for ruining literary and newspaper publishing by turning it into a centralized big business like that producing any other commodity.

The methods that book, magazine, and newspaper editors used to procure, edit, and sell printed materials certainly did change drastically during this period. For example, because they had deadlines to meet and more money at stake in these businesses, which required larger amounts of capital than before to establish and operate, publishers and editors were increasingly unwilling to wait for unsolicited submissions that might or might not meet their needs. Instead, they tried to insure a steady flow of written material on the topics they wanted by constructing salaried staffs of in-house writers. Fiction authors were rarely kept on salary by magazines, but their editors did actively pursue these authors for contributions. Representative is *Atlantic Monthly* editor Horace Scudder, who, when he searched for fiction, reportedly "did not wait for volunteer contributions any more than he did in conducting the other departments." This general change in procedure resulted in a decline in the number of unsolicited manuscripts published, especially in the magazines. "Magazines," one self-proclaimed "literary hack" wrote in 1895, "are planned by the editors for months in advance of publication. They are not thrown together from what material happens to be on hand." Donald Sheehan states that the same situation obtained in book publishing.[30]

In addition, following the societal trend towards greater "scientific management," empowered editors not only more frequently suggested topics for articles, but they also financed their research, and exercised more editorial control over authors' and reporters' work. Daniel Borus posits that "publishers and editors ... placed orders for specific treatments, and demanded significant and drastic revisions as a condition of publication." Borus and others quote Frank Norris's essay "Salt and Sincerity" (1903) to support their contention. Norris writes therein, "The publisher again and again picks out the man ... suggests the theme, and exercises, in a sense, all the functions of an instructor during the period of composition."[31]

Many scholars have further charged that even when editors were not directly coaching the fiction writer, they exerted a great deal of control over what was written and how by specifying the guidelines to which authors had to adhere in order to be published and paid. William Charvat states that "by 1870 almost all recognized novelists were selling their work first to magazines and were making the necessary compromises in matter of chapter division, construction, arrangement of incident, style, and moral and social prejudice."[32] Most mass-market magazine and story paper publishers required that serial installments be of a certain length, wanted each one to end with an exciting incident or cliffhanger, and followed the dictum that material printed must be such that it could be read in the "family circle," which included many "impressionable" daughters. Sex, unpunished or rewarded villains, and, in general terms, lack of adherence to social norms were all frowned upon. These requirements were made known to authors in letters from publishers and sometimes in formalized "style sheets."

What has most concerned literary scholars about the transformation of the publishing industry during this period has been how the technological developments, innovations in distribution, recognition of the new reading public, altered editorial conduct, greater attention to the financial aspects of literary publishing, and new organizational structures of these publishing enterprises might have institutionalized a greater control or hegemony over fiction authors and readers. According to one view, fiction authors and readers, like steel workers, shoe assemblers, and department store consumers, were caught up in the inexorable modernization process that left little room for genuine personal artistic autonomy. While fiction authors might have been better able to obtain higher fees and make a respectable living, so this argument goes, they had to sell their artistic freedom for it. For example, despite Henry James's oft-expressed desire for a stable contract, one scholar laments that in 1883 "James signed the first of a series of agreements with [Boston publisher James] Osgood and thereby 'mortgaged' his literary freedom." Further, Susan Coultrap-McQuin concludes, "What had previously been a relatively autonomous career [authorship] was now [at the end of the century] more closely directed by editors and publishers who increasingly commissioned the articles they wanted written." Michael Anesko concurs when he writes, "the conditions by which such phenomenal growth [in publishing] was achieved carried with them new threats to the writer's integrity and to the very habits of mind that made possible the creation of a lasting and significant literature." In Britain, too, N. N. Feltes charges, "The writer's work [in the late nineteenth century] was produced in a journal within relations of production analagous to those prevailing in a textile mill."[33]

Readers – especially mass-market magazine readers – were also allegedly transformed by all these developments. According to some scholars, they were turned into manipulated "consumers" of mass-produced print products by cultural managers in Northeastern cities who made their reading choices for them and directed their reading practices. Christopher Wilson argues that in the United States, the low-priced mass magazines of the late 1880s represented "a world of illusory power and participation that masked delimited options and prefabricated responses" from readers.[34] In this view readers did not benefit from the wider choice of print vehicles. Instead, libraries, schools, bookstores, and newsstands in this view were thus sites of false "choice" where readers' desires were acted upon by the hegemonic intentions of librarians, teachers, editors, and other cultural managers.

Some of these charges accurately depict the evolution of literary publishing in the United States during this time. However, the description is problematic for a number of reasons. First, such a paradigm overstates the freedom for authors that existed before this type of mass publishing appeared on the scene in the late 1880s and understates the advantages of the new conditions for them. Second, it implies that readers were much more passive than they actually were, and that they were incapable of making empowered choices from among the proliferating print products. Most important for the subject at hand, though, is that while many of these conditions might have obtained in book, magazine, and story paper publishing, these were not the only print mediums available to fiction authors and readers. Almost completely overlooked in this cultural paradigm is the newspaper as a fiction medium and the syndicates that supplied them with this fiction.

When one closely examines the comfortable image of the pre-1880 relationship between authors and publishers as full of mutual respect and authorial freedom, with a minimum of commercial influence, one begins to see that it was not all it seemed. To characterize this era before modern, mass publishing as pre-commercial and offering great autonomy to authors and readers is extremely deceptive, since publishers of all types had always had at least one eye fixed on the financial bottom line and were trying to exert their control over production and consumption to maximize profits, as will be described in greater detail in chapter 4.

Fortunately for American authors, the conditions affecting their profession began to change in the late 1880s. The American public's greater demand for fiction, the establishment of numerous new fiction outlets – including syndicates and mass-market magazines – the rise of the literary agent, and then the 1891 Chace Act concerning copyright helped promote for authors greater remuneration and advances as well as more contracts that provided authors with security. Authors also now had many more rights to sell in a single work. One could first sell or lease serial rights to a single magazine or newspaper publisher or syndicate operator, then to a book publisher, who might also pay for cheap clothbound or paperback rights, then (if American) to a magazine or book publisher in Britain or (if British) the United States, and finally to the German publishing firm of Tauchnitz for a European edition.

Some of the responsibility for helping authors secure and retain their higher rates and authorial rights must be given to personal literary agents. These agents were made much more of a necessity by the proliferation of outlets, the greater complexity of publishing contracts, and the need to coordinate British and American publication of literary works (the latter was essential after the 1891 Chace Act, which required adherence to a strict timetable in order to secure American copyright and not lose British copyright). Bitterly resented by publishers, agents were engaged by almost every professional writer by the 1890s. In Britain, the pioneers were A. P. Watt, who opened for business in the late 1870s, the agency sponsored by the Society of Authors and run by William Morris Colles beginning in the early 1890s, and James Pinker in 1896; the first professional agent in the United States was Paul Revere Reynolds, who began in the early 1890s. For a usual fee of 10 per cent of the sale price of a work, these agents relieved authors of distracting business arrangements such as placing the work with a publisher and negotiating a price. Henry James in 1888 heartily endorsed his new agent A. P. Watt in a letter to his brother William: "'the relief & comfort of having him take all the mercenary & selling side off one's mind is well worth the cost.'" These agents also helped authors take advantage of the increased competition and secured for them advances, higher royalty rates, and more frequent payment on acceptance by magazine publishers. Furthermore, agents helped authors play magazine publishers against one another and thus procure competitive bids from them. The overall financial benefit of an agent is indicated by Bret Harte, a very satisfied client, who wrote to A. P. Watt in 1885, "I am quite convinced that the commission I pay you has been fully returned by the appreciation of the market value of my work through your efforts."[35]

For many, fiction writing thus changed in the late 1880s from a calling that required divine inspiration and a vow of poverty to a fairly easily entered and practiced profession where one could possibly earn a respectable middle-class income or even a fabulously lavish income if one were successful. The newly-won apparent advantages of the literary life in turn inspired more people to try their hand at fiction writing and increase the amount of fiction available for printing and distribution. In 1895 a confessed "literary hack" wrote, "There is scarcely a village in the land without two or more aspirants for literary fame, and bids come even from the farm-houses; while in the cities no one, young or old, appears to be free from the scribbler's mania."[36] Certainly, American fiction authors were not completely happy with the editorial restrictions and conditions placed upon them and their work in the late 1880s and 1890s. Yet most, unlike modern scholars, in general welcomed the new marketplace conditions, for they wanted greater remuneration and financial security and understood that these high fees – especially those paid by mass-market magazines – were not possible unless they gave up some artistic control over their work.

What is also overlooked in the conventional portrayal of the American literary marketplace during this time is that a great number of readers also benefited in ways from the new conditions. To some, the literary deluge might have been daunting, but surely the proliferation of fiction in story paper, book, and magazine form was greeted by many others as a positive, democratic movement that more than ever before made a greater choice of low-priced print forms more available to readers from a wider socioeconomic and geographic spectrum. Surely, too, not all readers – even those with little formal education – were easily manipulated by urban Northeastern editors and publishers into making certain choices and reading in certain ways. As Janice Radway and others have so persuasively shown, readers whom academics believe are usually passive in making "supposed choices" in fact often resist the machinations of cultural managers and exert great control over their reading choices and behavior.[37]

Finally, the most significant difficulty with the common depiction of the evolution of the American literary marketplace during the latter decades of the nineteenth century as increasingly centralized, standardized, and regulated, is that it has traditionally focused almost exclusively on publishers of books, genteel and mass-market magazines, and story papers, and has assumed that their modes of operation – including their interaction with authors – represented modern publishing as a whole. This scholarship has thus overlooked the production and consumption patterns of the newspaper as a fiction medium, along with the operations of its most important fiction suppliers: patent inside, plate service, and galley-proof syndicates. Like magazines, newspapers employed staffs of reporters and writers and directed their subject matter and method of treatment, but they did not employ staff fiction writers to produce short stories and novels to order, as dime novel houses did. Instead, newspaper editors relayed their needs and desires to the syndicates, who negotiated with the authors or their agents. In addition, as noted previously, newspapers were not published in one or two centralized Northeastern locations but rather were published throughout the country in small towns and large cities alike. As a result, they were able to penetrate many socioeconomic and geographic spaces not reached until after the turn of the century by most books, story papers, or magazines. Furthermore, unlike these other print forms, newspapers cannot be considered manifestations of national mass culture – with all the usual connotation of reader control this term suggests – because they were not repeated performances of the exact same thing on a national scale. Syndicated patent inside, plate service, and galley-proof fiction might have been distributed throughout the country, but the overall makeup of each individual newspaper, including the choice and presentation of syndicated materials, differed widely according to the preferences and strategies of its editor.

Within the cultural stockpile of print expectations in the late nineteenth century, newspaper syndicates emerged and helped fill a niche in the print ecology previously unrecognized by publishers. Newspapers in the United States during this era needed more material to fill their pages and satisfy their readers and advertisers, and the syndicates emerged to procure these materials for editors for a relatively low price. In this way they represent a further manifestation of the increasing specialization of roles within the publishing industry. The syndicates examined in this book, one should note, did not deal only with fiction. The major ones such as Tillotson and Son's, McClure's Associated Literary Press, Irving Bacheller's variously-named syndicates, the American Press Association, and the A. N. Kellogg Company all bought and sold non-fictional pieces such as Women's Page and Children's Page materials, humor columns, interviews with famous people, and features about foreign countries, exotic travels, and new inventions. S. S. McClure wrote in 1891, "I publish not only the best fiction but [also] articles by leading writers of history, biography, science, travel, and practical papers in all fields of work and enterprise," and he was not alone in doing so.[38] Frederick Douglass contributed European Letters, Rudyard Kipling American Letters, and Hamlin Garland reports about life in the West to the McClure syndicate; Stephen Crane wrote Western sketches and John Muir authored numerous articles for Bacheller.

To maintain its focus, however, this study will follow the lead of the syndicators themselves in their reminiscences and preserved records, and concentrate on their practices of syndicating fiction. Possibly because they believed their future reputations depended chiefly on their contact with famous fiction authors, when syndicators and their colleagues recorded their memories of early syndication, they rarely mentioned the non-fictional materials; the available archival records also provide much less information on the latter subject than on fiction. One result of this bias is that it is very difficult to determine whether fiction or non-fiction syndicated materials were more profitable. What is most important to this study is that such syndicates began purchasing and distributing fiction, and that they did so with methods hitherto untried and to a print vehicle – the newspaper – not previously expected to contain fiction. By doing this, the syndicates were among the most potent catalysts for the many positive changes that came in the literary marketplace in the 1890s for both authors and readers. To more fully appreciate the significance of these syndicates, first their histories must be reconstructed, and second their operating methods need to be analyzed. Only then can scholars begin to understand what they meant to the hundreds of authors, thousands of editors, and millions of readers whose lives they touched.

CHAPTER 2

The pioneers: readyprint, plate service, and early galley-proof syndicates

> Please inform me in regard to the motive and methods of your organization.
> Clementine Cole, prospective author, to the American Press Association, 1892[1]

Properly situating newspaper syndicates in the American literary marketplace of the late nineteenth century has proved difficult in the past, primarily because detailed information about their histories, organizational structures, and operating methods was not readily available. As a result of this dearth of information, what little research done on syndicates has misunderstood or overlooked the important differences between the syndicates and publishers of magazines, story papers, and books. These differences are important, for they help define the important niche in the print ecology that the syndicates occupied. Readyprint companies acted much like publishers, but plate service and galley-proof syndicates functioned more as middlemen, procuring materials that newspaper publishers would later put into print. What unites these varied types of syndicates is that they all distributed fiction and other materials for eventual publication in newspapers. To assess the impact of all of these syndicates on authors and readers, one must first document their histories and understand how they operated.

The term "syndicate" is itself the source of some confusion, and thus a definition of this term is helpful before proceeding. I include under this term readyprint newspaper publishers who printed material on one side of sheets of newsprint and sold these to newspapers; plate service providers who sold actual stereotype plates to newspapers; and companies that distributed texts to newspapers primarily in galley proof or copy form. None of these firms at first described themselves as a syndicate, a word more commonly used in the late nineteenth century to describe large business combinations in copper, cattle, and other commodities. Most readyprint companies instead used "union" in their company titles: the New York Newspaper Union, the American Newspaper Union, the Chicago Newspaper Union, and the Western Newspaper Union were some of the most prominent of these firms. "Union" did not signify corporate ownership of a chain of newspapers but rather a company that supplied a group of newspapers with materials their editors had requested. Each union usually served a number of different "lists" of papers, named for the city in the area where a branch office of the company was located. An individual newspaper could withdraw from its union or list at the end of the contracted-for period without any penalty. These readyprint companies saw themselves as helpful partners with the local papers, as is indicated by the latter often calling themselves "co-operative" papers. "Association," the term used by one of the largest plate service providers discussed in this study – the American Press Association – denoted much the same thing as union. Furthermore, none of the firms that distributed material in copy form at first included the term syndicate in their titles. When William Frederic Tillotson of Bolton, England, began syndicating material in 1873, this part of his business was known as Tillotson's Newspaper Fiction Bureau. The most important American syndicators of this type, Irving Bacheller and S. S. McClure, in 1884 first operated under the respective company titles of "Bacheller and Co." and the "Associated Literary Press."

Among newspaper people in the 1880s, "syndicate" most commonly referred to a group of newspapers provisionally formed to purchase and publish only one work. In November 1884 for example, Charles A. Dana, editor of the New York *Sun*, solicited other newspapers to join him "in a new syndicate," referring to a group of newspapers formed for the one occasion of simultaneously printing Bret Harte's "Sarah Walker." S. S. McClure's first publicity circular (4 October 1884), echoed Dana when it stated that McClure would furnish materials "for simultaneous publication in syndicates of leading newspapers." In 1887, McClure still wrote of multiple syndicates within his own "syndicate service."[2] The members of the syndicate would change according to whether newspaper editors liked the work offered to them, whether they had the funds available to buy fiction, and whether or not they had space for it.

Only after 1887 did "syndicate" begin to take on its more modern meaning of a certain type of business concern that supplied newspapers with various materials. In general, readyprint publishers and plate service providers did not incorporate the word into their company names and were rarely referred to as syndicates. Some companies that distributed materials in copy form, however, did add the word syndicate to their titles, possibly to appear wealthier and more powerful than they actually were. Bacheller and Co. became the Bacheller Newspaper Syndicate in 1887, operated under this aegis until 1894, and from its incorporation in 1896 until its demise in 1898 was known simply as the Bacheller Syndicate; the Associated Literary Press became the McClure Newspaper Syndicate in May 1900. In the 1890s, these companies were joined in the marketplace by the Authors' Syndicate, the Albert Bigelow Paine Syndicate, and many other companies similarly named. It was not until after the turn of the century that groups of newspapers owned by a single individual or company came to be referred to as syndicates.

I

The beginnings of the syndication of materials in the United States can be traced to as early as 1768, when Boston area patriots sent printed copies of the "Journal of Occurrences" to many East Coast newspapers for reprinting. Over seventy years later, in 1841 the New York *Sun* printed President Tyler's message to Congress on half-sheets and sold them to a number of New York State and New England newspapers for insertion between the locally printed sheets. The first syndication in what became known as "readyprint" form occurred in 1847, when Andrew Jackson Aikens, editor of the Woodstock, Vermont, newspaper *Spirit of the Age*, arranged to have a Boston newspaper print President Polk's address to Congress on one side of folio sheets and send these to him; Aikens then printed local matter on the other side. After 1851, the New York *Sun* regularly printed one side of folio sheets and supplied them to the publishers of the *Staten Islander*, who printed their own typeset material on the other side. Yet despite the growing use in Britain in the late 1850s of what were there called "partly printed sheets," little use was made of this revolutionary idea in the United States until 1861.[3]

In July 1861, Ansel Nash Kellogg, the twenty-nine-year-old publisher of the *Baraboo [Wisconsin] Republic*, found himself short of printing labor because his printer had enlisted for service in the Civil

War. In order to continue printing a four-page paper, Kellogg asked David Atwood and Horace E. Rublee, the publishers of the Madison *Wisconsin State Journal*, to print war news on both sides of half-sheets and ship these to him so that he could insert them in his other home-printed sheets. The following week, Kellogg asked Atwood and Rublee to print war news on one side (the inside pages, two and three) of folio sheets; in Baraboo, he would typeset and print local material on the other side (the outside pages, one and four). On 10 July, 1861, Kellogg printed his first four-page newspaper with the aid of these sheets, later called "patent insides" because of the patent medicine advertisements so prevalent in the material published in this way. Kellogg continued to print his newspaper with patent insides, while Atwood and Rublee in Madison slowly expanded their service, by 1865 furnishing insides to thirty country papers.[4]

Recognizing the business opportunities afforded by such an idea, Kellogg soon became a publisher of patent insides himself rather than of a single newspaper that used them. In 1862 he sold the *Republic*, and in 1865 he established a Chicago office and a printing plant. His first customers were five Illinois papers, two from Wisconsin, and one from Minnesota. By the end of 1865, Kellogg was supplying 53 weekly papers in four states with his patent insides, and by 1871 he was serving approximately 300 weekly papers. Despite the loss of his plant in the Chicago Fire of 1871, Kellogg continued to expand his business, primarily by acquiring other newspaper unions that had been established around the country and by signing up more newspapers as subscribers. Incorporated as the A. N. Kellogg Newspaper Company in 1881, the firm continued to expand even after Kellogg's death in 1886. The number of newspapers it served rose from 701 in 1877, to 1,588 in 1886, and to 1,957 in 1900. Most of these newspapers had individual circulations of less than 1,000, but by using "the usual estimate of five readers to a [country] paper" – not unlikely, given the scarcity at this time of printed materials in rural areas – one biographer of Kellogg calculated that Kellogg's patent insides and outsides were read by a total of 1.7 million weekly newspaper readers in 1875.[5] Using this basis and taking into account the number of newspapers served, this would mean that by 1900 approximately 4.7 million people read newspapers that included materials distributed by Kellogg alone.

Others soon joined Kellogg and Atwood and Rublee in the readyprint business (also known as cooperative or auxiliary printing) to serve the large numbers of papers that wanted to avail themselves of this service. In 1878, Kellogg reported that his own firm plus nineteen others were supplying 2,500 papers with readyprint, and in 1880 it was reported that 3,238 weekly newspapers – two-fifths of all weekly newspapers in the country – took readyprint from twenty-one different companies operating from coast to coast. Due to the consolidation of some firms, by 1886 there were fourteen companies distributing materials to 5,811 American newspapers.[6]

Kellogg's first major competitor was the firm of Cramer, Aikens, and Cramer, publishers of the Milwaukee *Evening Wisconsin*. Andrew Jackson Aikens, who had used patent insides once many years before in Vermont, had by the mid-1860s moved to Wisconsin and urged his partners to begin printing patent insides. In 1869 the firm provided material to 117 newspapers in eleven states, and in 1871 it moved to Chicago and assumed the name of the Chicago Newspaper Union. In this same year, Aikens combined with George Rowell and Samuel French to form the New York Newspaper Union, and this organization, along with other Cramer, Aikens and Cramer firms such as the Southern Newspaper Union and the Aikens Newspaper Union of Cincinnati, operated under the aegis of the American Newspaper Union, which in 1877 supplied a total of 1,150 newspapers with readyprint; later this firm was again known simply as the Chicago Newspaper Union. In 1877, James H. Beals of Boston bought the New York Newspaper Union from Cramer, Aikens, and Cramer. He expanded the business rapidly by establishing the New England Newspaper Union in 1880, buying the Publishers' Union of Atlanta in 1883, founding the Charlotte Newspaper Union in 1884, and forming the Birmingham Newspaper Union in 1886; this conglomerate was known as the Atlantic Coast Lists by 1895.[7]

Further adding to the competition was the Western Newspaper Union, established by George A. Joslyn and three partners in Des Moines, Iowa, in 1880. Like the firms of Kellogg, Beals, and Cramer, Aikens, and Cramer, the Western Newspaper Union expanded by acquisition and establishment of branch offices. Joslyn, who became president of the company in 1890, moved its base of operations to Omaha, but by 1890 its coverage extended east to New York City and west to Denver, with other offices in St. Paul, Detroit, Dallas, St. Louis, Lincoln, Nebraska, and Chicago, and by 1895 it led all other unions in the number of newspapers on its lists. In the 1890s, these four main firms and others vigorously competed against one another for the patronage of rural weekly newspapers; *N. W. Ayer and Son's American Newspaper Annual* for 1891 listed sixteen newspaper unions serving approximately 7,337 newspapers, and in 1895 one advertising agency listed eleven unions providing material to 7,871 newspapers.[8]

Because the economic and qualitative advantages of readyprint were so clear, marketing patent insides to the editors of the growing number of small weekly newspapers was not very difficult. By contracting – usually for a period of one year – to have the readyprint house collect, edit, typeset, and print two pages of the paper, local editors and publishers not only had more time to cover local issues but also saved a great deal of labor and thus money. As one editor noted, "The saving in composition is a very important item; but of not less importance is the saving of labor in editing the Kellogg side of my paper. To edit so well would require the employment of another man and a large increase of my exchange list." In addition, because the advertising carried in these sheets defrayed the readyprint publisher's expenses, the printed sheets cost an editor little more than the blank paper would have. Finally, many editors appreciated the quality presswork, which was commonly regarded as superior to that of the local product.[9]

Details of the methods these readyprint firms used to procure, process, and distribute their materials – including fiction – are relatively unknown, and numerous gaps remain in our understanding of them. However, enough information exists to sketch an outline of their operations. In general, the main office of each readyprint firm – whether in Milwaukee, Chicago, or New York – functioned as a large systematizer of the "exchange" system that already existed. For decades it had been common practice for newspaper editors to clip news articles, features, fiction, and so forth from other "exchanged" newspapers and magazines and reprint these items. In the absence of strict copyright enforcement and with a prevalent laissez-faire attitude among editors about reprinting material, few persons were prosecuted for this practice, so long as the reprinting editor gave proper recognition (and hence publicity) to its source with one line such as "St. James Gazette" or "Harper's Weekly."

Readyprint publishers obtained most of the various materials they reprinted through this exchange system. Fiction was included in readyprint editions possibly as early as 1865, but most certainly by 1870, when Kellogg began printing serial installments of novels. In 1876, almost one full page of each readyprint edition supplied by

Kellogg was regularly made up of fiction and poetry. In what might be assumed to be an average week, the first week of July 1876, Kellogg offered fifteen different fictional works for various editions; other firms probably circulated slightly lower numbers. Before the mid-1880s, editors in Kellogg's employ clipped all of these short stories and serials from British and American magazines and newspapers for reprinting. The fiction came from a wide variety of American and British magazines, plus many American newspapers, most of them from New York City. As the company claimed in an 1878 publication, "we select, as far as possible, our literary and miscellaneous matter from the original publications, so as to duplicate nothing that has ever before appeared." As for other readyprint companies, one commentator noted in 1890, "In most of the establishments the reading matter used in auxiliary sheets is prepared with great care by a well-trained corps of editors. An exchange list, consisting of the best metropolitan dailies and the leading American and foreign magazines, is scrutinized every day, and the choicest matter selected." In general, the practice of paying readyprint company editors to do the work formerly carried out by local editors – but on a larger scale – represents one more example of the increasing specialization of roles within the publishing industry and American culture as a whole during this era.[10]

After the mid-1880s the methods readyprint publishers used to procure fiction changed somewhat. Competition with plate service companies, an 1879 Post Office regulation against mailing materials that violated copyright, and the Chace Act of 1891, enabling foreign authors to secure American copyright, seem to have spurred readyprint firms into more frequently paying authors or their agents for first or second serial rights to the fiction they used. One 1887 report noted, "a recent move [by the Kellogg Company] has been the furnishing of a certain amount of original matter ... to their sheet customers," but most fiction appears to have continued to be reprinted from elsewhere. Readyprint firms usually contracted with intermediaries to pay for reprint rights to these works. In 1889, for example, the syndicate of Irving Bacheller began to supply the Kellogg Company with material for reprinting after it had first been published by Bacheller's daily newspaper clients. How much fiction was supplied under this agreement, however, is unclear. Of the writers named in an 1889 advertisement of the Kellogg-Bacheller combination, thirteen have been traced, and all were at the time non-fiction writers or humorists. Wright Patterson, an editor at Kellogg's Chicago headquarters from 1890 to 1898, has asserted that Stephen Crane's *The Red Badge of Courage* – first distributed by the Bacheller, Johnson, and Bacheller syndicate in 1894 to at least nine metropolitan daily newspapers – subsequently appeared in a great number of small daily and weekly newspapers served by Kellogg. Although no such printings of this novel have yet been found, given the agreement between Kellogg and Bacheller, it is not unlikely that Kellogg reprinted (either in readyprint or stereotype plate form) not only Crane's work but also a number of other Bacheller-syndicated works by Joel Chandler Harris, Rudyard Kipling, and Mary E. Wilkins, among others, and that by this means many readers first encountered the works of such prominent authors in small country weekly newspapers.[11]

After editors had clipped and edited materials from different publications, all of which had varying typography, these were set in type and illustrations made. Once the proofs were corrected, the type, advertising copy, and illustrations were set up together and stereotyped. Fiction, either a short story or a serial installment, usually began in the upper-left hand corner, after a reprinted poem by the likes of Joaquin Miller, William Cullen Bryant, Margaret Sangster, or Oliver Wendell Holmes. Possibly fiction was located here – the first part of the page to be typeset – because its length was unpredictable and the printers wanted to make sure that they would not run out of space. Yet it is also possible that fiction was printed in this prominent position because of its popularity. In 1876, most serials and short stories appeared anonymously and only a few were illustrated, none of them copiously. None had copyright notices attached to them, but almost all were accompanied by a line acknowledging their source.

After the two pages were typeset, they were usually printed either as insides or outsides and then sent enough ahead of time through the mail or via an express service to subscribing newspapers so that they would arrive shortly before the scheduled day of publication. There is some evidence, though, that the larger companies sent matrix molds made from the set-up material to its branch offices, where plates were made and the papers were printed and sent to customers in that region. In both the receiving post office or express office, if the editor had not paid in advance, he paid for the sheets on delivery; under no circumstances were they to be released on account.[12] In the local newspaper office, the printer sprinkled the sheets with water to moisten them for the new impressions and with homeset type printed the rest of the paper.

II

Many rural weekly papers with slightly larger circulations than those which took readyprint, along with weeklies and dailies from smaller cities, did not want to commit themselves to two or four full pages a week of matter printed elsewhere. These papers were thus attracted to stereotype plate service, a form of syndication which Kellogg and George Rowell of the American Printers' Warehouse introduced on a broad scale in the United States in 1875. However, the idea of selling multiple copies of stereotype plates had originated much earlier and, as with readyprint, its roots were British. In 1858, Isaac Heyes of Sheffield, England, syndicated material in plate form, and the Central Press Agency of London began sending stereotyped news stories to provincial papers in 1863. Between 1871 and 1880 a number of technical developments in the United States spurred more widespread plate service there. One was the invention by B. B. Blackwell of New York in 1871 of a thin, lightweight stereotype plate that could be made type high at the printing shop by affixing it to wooden or metal blocks; this was much cheaper to ship through the mail than an entire block of type-high plate. In 1875 Ansel Nash Kellogg and James J. Schock developed an easier, more efficient way of fastening the thin stereotype plates to the wooden backing blocks to make them type high; a year or two later they introduced a way to cut stereotype plates after they were already attached to these blocks and a butterfly spring on the back of plates that allowed them to be easily fitted into metal frames. In the late 1870s Kellogg pioneered the celluloid plate, which lowered shipping and handling costs even further.[13]

Some of the largest plate service providers were the same companies that had published readyprint; Kellogg and the Western Newspaper Union were two of these. A number of new firms founded in the 1880s and 1890s, though, dealt exclusively in plate service and had such names as the Central Press, International Press Association, Continental Press, Union Associated Press, and the Mail Plate Company. Readyprint publishers found it a relatively simple matter to make extra plates of the material they had already typeset for readyprint and to ship these to subscribers instead. In fact, the company that would become the nation's largest plate service provider, the American Press Association, began as a readyprint publisher but discontinued this line of business after only a year or two. This firm, founded in Chicago in August 1882 by Orlando Jay Smith, R. W. Nelson, and G. W. Cummings, played a very important role in the development of plate service and the evolution of syndication. (It was supposedly at the American Press Association office in Chicago, in fact, that the term "boilerplate" was coined to describe plate matter; it came, supposedly, from a printers' joke about the Association's shop being in the same building as an iron foundry.) The Association expanded rapidly, and between 1883 and 1890 it established offices in Cincinnati, New York, Boston, Buffalo, Omaha, Atlanta, St. Paul, Dallas, Philadelphia, Pittsburgh, and San Francisco. By 1892, the American Press Association's main bureau was in New York City and was supported by twelve other bureaus; in 1896 this number had risen to fourteen. The Association also provided some of its material in galley-proof form beginning in 1884 (this was sometimes known as "slip-service"), but most of its customers continued to purchase stereotype plate. In 1886, the Association reportedly provided 600 daily and 1,200 weekly customers in twenty-eight states with plate service, and by 1890 the Association advertised that it was supplying over 6,000 daily and weekly papers with material. One report in 1892 stated that nine-tenths of the daily newspapers in the country took plate service from the Association, and that many daily papers from large cities were now subscribers.[14]

All plate service providers had the same basic principles of operation. After matter had been chosen – either from other printed sources or from manuscripts, depending on the company – and edited, it was typeset in a central office, where subsequently matrix molds were made. In the Association's case, molds were sent to the branch offices, where stereotype plates were cast from them and sent to area subscribers; in this way the high cost of shipping plates long distances was avoided. Local newspaper editors chose beforehand from a large menu of materials including Humor Columns, Women's Pages, Agricultural News, Horticultural features, and so forth, and as with readyprint indicated if they preferred these materials to have a certain regional or political viewpoint; unlike with readyprint, they could choose between illustrated and non-illustrated versions of the same works. Plates containing the specified matter (in one-column-wide lengths) were then sent to local newspaper editors, who could saw them however they wished to fit the makeup of their papers. All plates for syndication were probably flat rather than circular, for use with flatbed cylinder presses employed by smaller newspapers at the time. It is possible that some large daily papers could have used a combination of flat plate and home-typeset material to make up formes, then created a flexible flong mould of this page, and used this mould to cast a curved plate for use on a rotary press, but unfortunately, no information is available on whether anyone followed such a practice. After about 1886, the Association was also able to provide "electrotype shell plates with copper face and steel bases." Like readyprint, plate service was usually either paid for in advance or sent COD and sent by express service or regular mail. The cost of the matter depended on how much advertising – sold by the plate service company to advertisers who wished to relieve themselves of the burden of contacting hundreds of newspapers individually – the local newspaper was willing to print; accepting more advertising meant a lower price for the other material. Through this system, newspapers saved a great deal on editing and typesetting costs. As newspaper editor Edgar Watson Howe noted in 1891, plate service made "it possible to run a very good evening paper with two printers, a foreman to set the advertisements, and a boy..."[15]

In addition to providing various news and feature items, some plate service companies such as Kellogg, the American Press Association, and the Western Newspaper Union sold fiction to subscribing newspapers. The methods Kellogg and the Western Newspaper Union used to obtain, edit, and distribute fiction were much the same as those they used for readyprint, although Kellogg appears to have reserved more original material for plate service.[16] The American Press Association, though, operated differently than these other firms, and its methods represent an important evolutionary step toward those later employed by syndicators of materials in galley-proof form.

Possibly to differentiate itself from the readyprint publishers providing chiefly reprinted fiction for their customers, the Association mixed a large amount of fiction for first printing with its reprinted fiction. "Unlike other [plate matter] concerns," one writer noted in 1886, the Association "adopted the plan of furnishing original matter." An Association prospectus of 1891 confirms this observation, stating that "A large number of the serials which we are now offering are copyrighted productions of leading American writers." Other plate companies followed suit. In 1889 one report stated that among such companies, "There is a tendency toward the use of copyrighted stories by American authors in place of pirated productions from abroad. The best plate houses appear to think that success lies in that direction."[17] Given the increased number of American literary aspirants during this period, one might assume that it was a relatively simple task for the Association and other plate companies to obtain original American fiction of a level of quality acceptable to its customers. However, this was not the case: the Association had to expend a great deal of effort to obtain the fiction it needed.

Much of the fiction used by the American Press Association came from authors who submitted unsolicited manuscripts. Short stories and serials from unknown amateurs and better-known professionals poured into the New York headquarters of the Association. Beginners sometimes eventually became regular suppliers, while the firm also accepted numerous manuscripts from mid-rank professionals such as Mary Kyle Dallas, John Milton Edwards, Alfred H. Calhoun, and Maurice Thompson. The then unknown Stephen Crane in August 1892 wrote the Association to ask if it would finance a trip of his to the American West to gather material that he would write up for the firm, and in late 1895 he inquired if the editors would be interested in a serial novel of his. A struggling young writer named Jack London reportedly also sold some stories – most likely unsolicited – to the Association, and Charlotte Perkins Stetson (later Gilman) submitted a poem for approval in July 1890. The Association was clearly known among writers throughout the country: unsolicited submissions came not only from large cities but also from such far-flung places as Bendena, Kansas; Dexter, Maine; Seattle, Washington; Portland Mills, Indiana; Fayetteville, Tennessee; Santa Ana, California; and Double Springs, Alabama.[18]

How did all of these authors find out about the American Press Association? Many of the letters of submission written to the Association indicate that the author was referred personally by someone connected to a local newspaper who understood how the newspaper secured its material. For example, Stetson wrote, "I have your address from Miss Lilian Whiting of The Boston Budget, who has published some of my work; and venture to submit to you a poem."

In addition, newspaper staff members frequently recommended a local author's work to the Association editors. Authors also were probably responding to notices about the Association printed in the *Journalist* magazine, possibly placed at the company's behest. One such notice in 1887 stated that the Association was "buying original short stories for use in their syndicate and plate matter," and asked "Aspirants for literary success ... [to] please send their MSS. to the American Press Association."[19]

The Association and other plate service companies also obtained fiction from literary agents, book publishers, other syndicates, and occasionally from newspapers themselves. Only rarely was an author directly solicited by the Association. One such case occurred in 1887, when the Association approached W. D. Howells about syndicating *The Rise of Silas Lapham* (1885) (a deal was never made); another came in 1896, when the Association asked for and obtained Kate Chopin's permission to reprint the stories "In and Out of Old Natchitoches" and "In Sabine" from *Bayou Folk*. In addition, the humor writer Opie Read was commissioned to write a Decoration Day story in 1893. Agents were also in regular contact with the Association to offer the work of their clients, either for first or second serial use, and book publishers such as Cassell's, J. B. Lippincott, and G. P. Putnam's Sons frequently made special arrangements with the Association to print newspaper serials of recently published books in order to promote sales. Another major source of plate service fiction was other syndicates. In Kellogg's case, fiction might have come from Bacheller as part of a regular contract. The Association, on the other hand, had no such contractual arrangement but regularly received offers of fiction from McClure's Associated Literary Press, Tillotson's Newspaper Literature Bureau, the Authors' Syndicate of London, the United Press, and the Wilson Press Syndicate, and sometimes bought stories from them.[20]

The details of how the Association marketed its service – including fiction – remain uncertain, but what is known is that occasional advertisements in such trade journals as the *Journalist* were supplemented by circulars sent directly to editors. The many advantages of plate service probably made it easy to sell. Local editors were attracted to plate service primarily because of its flexibility compared to readyprint and the financial savings realized through not having to obtain, edit, typeset, and stereotype this material. In addition, fiction from plate service companies was probably sold to editors with the pitch that it would attract both readers and consequently advertisers; editors certainly used it as a drawing card. The inroads of national magazines in the late 1890s into rural areas and smaller towns and cities served by newspapers taking plate service, however, eventually made its fiction less desirable. Jason Rogers, author of a series of articles in 1897 addressed to editors on the topic of how to increase circulation, advised them, "Don't use those old chestnuts [of fiction] sold in plate form. Such literature has probably been read by your readers years ago. Plate stories may be better than nothing, but don't count as compared to original and first-published matter."[21]

Readyprint publishers who also provided plate service probably edited fiction the same way they did fiction for circulation as readyprint. The editing practices of the American Press Association were somewhat different. Like readyprint publishers, the Association had its editorial staff in one central location, in this case its main office in New York City. There, short stories and serials were examined and judged. Acting more like book and magazine editors and unlike readyprint editors, however, editors at the Association wrote readers' reports on the fiction manuscripts submitted to them and dealt personally with their authors (famous authors whose works were obtained through agents or for second use did not receive this type of treatment). Manuscripts were subject to a good deal of editorial criticism and suggestion. If the manuscript was accepted, these suggestions, along with the manuscript, were returned to authors, who were expected to make necessary revisions. When the revised manuscript was returned to the Association office, it was typeset and printed in proof form. One copy would be sent to the author for final correction, and one to the illustrators. The Association very early on understood the importance of illustrations as a selling point, and its in-house illustrators on average provided one head illustration and two text illustrations (most unsigned) per short story or serial installment. In 1886 one report noted, "The work of illustration is in charge of Mr. S. H. Horgan, and some of the cleverest artists of the country furnish sketches," including "Cusachs, Miranda, Parker, Taylor, and Meeker"; by 1892 the list also included "Fitzgerald, Gribayedoff, Hencke, Kendrick, Kerr, Knickerbocker ... McDougall, Trowbridge, Verbeck, [and] Zenope." These illustrations appear to have been photoengraved line drawings from which zinc plates were made. As a writer described the operation in 1892, "The photographing [of drawings] is done by electric light, and the original of every picture made is kept and filed away in the American Press Association archives; so is every pen-and-ink drawing, and every photograph from which a drawing is made." Once the author's corrections were returned and final copy was set, the Association would use galley slips to register the copyright in either the author's or the firm's name.[22] The molds were then sent out to Association bureaus, where plates were cast from them and sent to newspaper editors to use however they chose, except for the requirement that it be published simultaneously or nearly simultaneously with other newspapers receiving the same materials.

III

Readyprint and plate service publishers supplied a great number of newspapers with fiction, but one important and fast-growing market segment remained underserved: the large metropolitan daily newspapers. Some of these papers did use a small amount of plate matter, but because they frequently had sizeable – and after the introduction of the linotype machine in the 1880s, mechanized – typesetting operations, they would not have saved significant labor costs by using plate service. Thus, they preferred to receive syndicated material in galley-proof form and typeset it themselves. The American Press Association furnished a few large dailies with feature material in proof form rather than in plates, but in general until about the early 1880s the larger dailies got almost all of their fiction from the exchange or from individual authors who sold their manuscripts for single publication. Few famous fiction authors were published in this way, however, because the cost to a single newspaper of buying such a manuscript was prohibitively high and would probably not have provided a profitable return on the investment.

In the early 1880s, however, an idea that had been born in France in 1836 and introduced and developed in Britain in the 1870s began to revolutionize fiction publication in American newspapers: if more than one newspaper could share the costs of purchasing the first serial rights to an author's work, and if all simultaneously printed the same serial installment or short story, the group of newspapers could purchase higher-priced and supposedly higher quality fiction from famous authors for first publication and make it appear to local readers as if the fiction were exclusive to the local paper alone. In France, the "feuilleton" – a space reserved for serial fiction in daily

1. William Frederic Tillotson, founder of Tillotson's Newspaper Fiction Bureau, circa 1888

and weekly papers sent to or printed in the provinces – had been a popular feature since its introduction in 1836.[23] Ironically, the first syndicate to sell galley proofs of fiction in the United States was British.

This syndicate was neither based in London nor well-connected in the British literary publishing world. Instead, its founder was William Frederic Tillotson, a newspaper publisher from the Lancashire mill city of Bolton. Tillotson, the owner of the *Bolton Evening News* (founded 1867) had in November 1871 established the *Bolton Weekly Journal*. In 1873 he created the Lancashire Journal Series, which consisted of the *Bolton Weekly Journal* and five other weekly Lancashire papers, and began to purchase serial novels from leading writers of the day for first, simultaneous publication in these papers (which were all typeset and printed in Bolton). The first novel Tillotson purchased and published in this way was Miss Mary Elizabeth Braddon's (Mrs. John Maxwell) *Taken at the Flood*, which was published in the *Bolton Weekly Journal* between August 1873 and April 1874. The French antecedents of such a scheme were clear; one report noted in 1881, "Messrs. Tillotson & Son, of Bolton, appear to be carrying out energetically the plan of publishing Novels as 'feuilletons' in Newspapers." Tillotson's had the field almost completely to itself, having only one chief competitor for the British provincial newspaper market in the late 1870s and afterwards: W. C. Leng, proprietor of the *Sheffield Telegraph*, who sold stereotype plates and galley proofs of fiction to British newspapers and, at least in 1888–89, to American newspapers (after approximately 1900 another competitor, the Northern Newspaper Syndicate, vied for the British newspaper market).[24]

Realizing that he could make money by selling the first serial rights in the works he was publishing to other newspapers besides those in the Lancashire Journal Series, Tillotson soon founded Tillotson's Newspaper Fiction Bureau (later sometimes known as Tillotson's Newspaper Literature Syndicate) to regularize this part of his newspaper business, and he began selling stereotype plates of the fictions to subscribing newspapers. Encouraged shortly thereafter by his success at selling serial novels and stories to British newspapers in plate, matrix, and galley-proof form, Tillotson expanded the sales territory to include all of the United Kingdom, the European Continent, various British colonies, and the United States. The first serial whose American serial rights Tillotson's purchased was Florence Marryat's *Fighting the Air*, which was published in the *Bolton Weekly Journal* between November 1874 and May 1875; it is still unclear, however, whether this was ever published in an American newspaper or magazine, as no appearances have been located. Most probably, in the later 1870s Tillotson's sold American rights in works

2. Architect's drawing, including inset aerial view, of the new *Bolton Evening News* and *Weekly Journal* building, which opened in 1890. From these premises Tillotson's Newspaper Fiction Bureau distributed short stories and novels for serial publication in newspapers throughout the English-speaking world

3. Inside the front door of the *Bolton Evening News* and *Weekly Journal* building, circa 1908

only to magazines such as *Harper's Monthly* and *Harper's Weekly*; significantly, for example, Braddon's *Taken at the Flood* was serialized in *Harper's Weekly* between November 1873 and May 1874. By the early 1880s, the Fiction Bureau appears to have been somewhat successful in penetrating the American newspaper market, selling fiction to the *Cincinnati News*, the Louisville *Commercial*, the *Fort Worth Gazette*, Springfield (MA) *Republican*, Philadelphia *Press*, and St. Louis *Republican*. Thus, in the mid-1880s the Fiction Bureau, with only about eight to ten full-time employees in Bolton and small branch offices in London and Berlin, was reaching millions of readers on almost every continent.[25]

The Tillotson Newspaper Fiction Bureau expanded its American business after the head of the firm, William Frederic Tillotson, visited the United States in 1884. Shortly after this visit, Tillotson arranged with the American syndicator S. S. McClure to market British novels whose serial rights Tillotson had purchased. As McClure wrote in one circular of May 1886, "Messrs. Tillotson & Son have authorized me to negotiate the sale of these Serials to the American Newspaper Press." It is probable that McClure did not actually buy or even lease these rights but rather worked on commission. In March 1887, McClure visited Tillotson in Bolton and worked out a new arrangement whereby, as he put it, "I pay him 3/5 of all I get in America for English authors, & he pays me 3/5 for all he gets in the rest of the world for Am.[erican] authors." Relations with McClure did not remain warm for long, however, and after Tillotson felt McClure had dealt unfairly with him, the agreement was discontinued around the summer of 1888.[26]

Possibly because of the end of his arrangement with McClure or because he anticipated the need to bring American syndication more under the British firm's control and cut out an extra middleman, Tillotson visited the United States again in the autumn of 1888, at which time he established a branch office in New York City. Michael Turner has argued that the American Chace Act of 1891 precipitated "the collapse of the American market for Tillotsons [at least for its British fiction]," but this does not appear to be true, for the New York office even after 1891 continued to do a good job of syndicating British and American fiction to American newspapers. It was reported that in 1892 Tillotson's distributed 22 serial novels, 10 novelettes, and 60 short tales for publication in the United States. Significantly, of the 29 authors whose works Tillotson's reportedly were to publish in the United States in 1893, the majority were British. As late as 1899, however, Tillotson's was still marketing a mixture of American and British fiction to American newspapers. Furthermore, the firm continued to maintain a New York office under the direction of Mr. Frank Graves and operate in the United States at least until 1900. Clearly, the copyright law did not make it impossible to syndicate British fiction in the United States.[27]

Unlike readyprint publishers and plate service providers in the United States, Tillotson's initially sought to obtain the first serial rights to works by authors who already stood near the top of their profession and whose names would be instantly recognized by newspaper readers, although of course it also ended up publishing many works by lesser-known authors. In the 1870s Tillotson's syndicated the works of the popular Wilkie Collins, Miss Braddon, and Charles Reade, and after 1881 Thomas Hardy sold a number of stories and serials to the firm. Obtaining such a grade of fiction required active solicitation of work from authors. Such direct solicitation and commissioning of fiction was relatively unknown in the 1870s, when magazine and book publishers tended still to rely on authors to come to them with their manuscripts. By the 1890s, however, the methods first established by Tillotson were routinely used not only by those syndicates that followed their lead but also by book and magazine publishers. In the early years of the syndicate, William Frederic Tillotson himself appears to have negotiated for works either personally with authors or by mail. Such negotiation by Tillotson, however, was ended by his premature death from pneumonia in March 1889. Various representatives of the firm subsequently had to take over the task of soliciting fiction. Robert Sheppard was one such representative from about 1890 to 1919. He would often go to authors rather than expect them to come to him; he later recalled how he once went to meet a young author at a train station who "had written a novel ... which he wanted to sell. He was to be identified by the red tie he was wearing and his name, of course, was Arnold Bennett."[28]

Even before 1890, Tillotson's had also begun obtaining work from famous British authors and some American authors living in Britain through the literary agent A. P. Watt. Later, Tillotson's would secure the works of authors such as H. Rider Haggard, H. G. Wells, Rudyard Kipling, and Arthur Conan Doyle either through Watt, James Pinker, or other agents. In 1899 Stephen Crane (living in England at the time) sold material to Tillotson's through his British agent, James B. Pinker, and in at least one case it is clear that Tillotson's initiated this contact.[29]

Materials from authors not as famous as Hardy, Doyle, and Crane were obtained by Tillotson's in a variety of other ways. A number of works as early as 1878 appeared in the *Bolton Weekly Journal* as "Prize Stories," indicating that the Fiction Bureau ran prize contests that would have brought many authors and works to them for consideration, not only for the contest but also for later publication. Some British fiction was for second printing, and this was supplied by "other newspaper proprietors, publishers and syndicates"; a number of fictions, for example, came from W. C. Leng of the *Sheffield Telegraph*.[30] The arrangement Tillotson's had with S. S. McClure supposedly provided the company from 1887 to 1888 with a supply of American fiction for near-simultaneous publication, but it is unclear whether Tillotson's used any of this material. The New York office of Tillotson's in 1889 also helped the firm obtain American material directly, although the amount of this material was quite limited.

Tillotson's also received a great many unsolicited manuscripts. In June 1894, Mudie's, Smith's, and other smaller circulating libraries issued new requirements for the books they would purchase that effectively ended the reign of the lengthy three-decker novel. One repercussion was that there were fewer book publishers willing to assume the financial risks of publishing marginal novels, because there was no longer a guaranteed market for them. According to Nigel Cross, this led many writers to turn to Tillotson's in order to supplement their income. Even before this date, many authors had sent unsolicited works to Tillotson's, whose reputation became increasingly widespread due to favorable notices about it in British and American magazines and newspapers. In 1886, for instance, the *Critic* magazine reported that Tillotson's actively protected authors' copyright. In the United States, submissions might have resulted from advertisements such as those that frequently appeared in the *Journalist* magazine and from articles that mentioned Tillotson's as a purchaser of short stories. One syndicated newspaper column, "Literary Leaves," promoted Tillotson's as a positive factor in helping authors to gain a living wage. An author who was possibly inspired to submit material to Tillotson's as a result of such notices was the young Jack London, who in 1899 sent work to Tillotson's American bureau.[31]

Selling fictions by these authors was initially very difficult; most newspaper editors were unwilling to pay high prices for first printing rights. Yet Tillotson's did eventually succeed in selling hundreds of works to American editors, and the marketing practices that it developed created a set of precedents that other syndicates would later build on and refine.

As stated earlier, it is possible that previous to 1882 Tillotson's did not even attempt to sell to American newspapers the "American serial rights" it had purchased from British authors. Instead, it appears that the firm was trying to sell these rights chiefly to American magazines. There is some evidence of Tillotson's selling works to a few American newspapers in early 1882, but it was only in late 1882 that William Frederic Tillotson began soliciting advice from British publisher John Maxwell about the American newspaper market. One of Maxwell's first recommendations was to "send out circulars largely [widely]: don't spare postage."[32] Tillotson clearly took this advice; the firm began marketing fiction more aggressively to newspapers after this date.

The greatest difficulties Tillotson's encountered in marketing fiction in the United States before Tillotson's established its American office in 1889 were caused primarily by the amount of time necessary for business communications to pass back and forth between England and the United States. The Fiction Bureau editor in Bolton typically wrote to American newspaper editors to offer upcoming works of fiction for publication in their papers. In Britain, editors each September were sent a Programme of serials available in the coming year. These commonly included the reasons why the newspaper editor should purchase the fiction, which would certainly have been presented to American editors as well. One 1894 Programme said that such fiction would "raise the rank of a paper" and "increase the circulation," which would supposedly attract advertisers. Similar promotional materials were sent to American newspaper editors as early as 1885. One dated in this year listed "WORKS OF FICTION for SERIAL PUBLICATION in NEWSPAPERS" and gave the dates when they were scheduled to begin; the earliest was to start in July 1885 and the latest in September 1887. Such general, inclusive announcements, though, were clearly insufficient to sell the works to American editors. In the United States, although short stories were often sold in blocks, serial novels were marketed individually. In the general absence of firm, long-term contracts with newspapers, the Fiction Bureau editor regularly had to send circulars that provided the title, the author's name, a synopsis, the price, and fairly accurate estimations of length of both stories and serials. These circulars were sent to multiple newspapers within the same circulation area; only one newspaper could purchase the rights in that area, so whoever replied first secured the rights. Editors were encouraged to respond quickly; as one Tillotson circular stated in December 1882, "we hold ourselves at liberty to decline any acceptance of these terms if in receipt of an earlier order from the same State, or if unable to concede the exclusive area requested." These circulars had to be sent from Bolton at least six weeks in advance of the planned publication date; John Maxwell told Tillotson that "Letters [offering fictions to American editors] take 13 or 14 days [each way] out and back. Allow 3 days for thought and reply. The earliest answer can only reach you 29 to 30 days after day of sending out." After an order was received in Bolton, proofs then had to be sent to editors, and this took another two weeks. It is little wonder that by 1884 American newspaper editors were encouraged to cable their orders to speed up the process. After Tillotson's New York office opened in 1889 and these marketing tasks were assumed by its managers, the lead time would have been significantly reduced.[33]

To reach American newspaper editors after 1889, Tillotson's New York representative at that time, W. Philip Robinson, continued to send syndicate circulars to editors, but apparently he became discouraged at the lack of response to this tactic. As a result, he began to regularly place advertisements directed towards editors in the *Journalist* magazine of New York City. The advertisements throughout late 1891 and most of 1892 were relatively subdued, reading, "Dear Mr. Editor / When you want a Serial Story, When you want a Short Tale, When you want a London Letter, When you want a Woman's Letter, When you want a Children's Letter, send to the undersigned [Tillotson and Son in New York City], who will reply by return mail, furnishing lists and all particulars." By late 1892, however, the firm's advertisements indicate an even greater willingness to accommodate the individual needs of newspaper editors. One in October 1892 asked "SUNDAY EDITORS (AND OTHER EDITORS)" to "Send for Lists, and state **what** you want, **when** you want it, and about **how much** you are prepared to pay for a Service." Another advertisement a few months later more boldly stated, "ORIGINAL COPYRIGHT NEWSPAPER FICTION IN ALL SHAPES: SERIALS or SHORT TALES IN VARIOUS LENGTHS."[34]

Another obstacle Tillotson's had to surmount in selling its offerings in the United States was its high price relative to what newspaper editors had previously paid more obscure authors or reprinted free. Newspaper editors were accustomed to paying aspiring fiction authors – if they did at all – $3–$10 for short stories and often less than $100 for a full-length serial. In contrast, in 1883 and 1884 Tillotson's offered a 26–week, 6,000–words-per-installment serial novel by Mary Elizabeth Braddon for £25 (approximately $125), and in 1884 the *Chicago Daily News* paid $550 for Wilkie Collins's *The Evil Genius*, a 27–part serial. In 1896, it was reported that an "international syndicate" (probably Tillotson's) was offering 50 stories of 2,000–2,500 words each over the course of a year to American newspapers for $2,000, or $40 each. These prices seem very low compared to what a magazine with the same circulation would have paid for some of these magazine-grade serials. Yet for newspaper editors such as Victor Lawson of the *Chicago Daily News* they appeared high, as indicated by his frequent complaints. Probably like many other editors, too, Lawson was not always happy with Tillotson's payment requirements. One 1882 circular spelled these out: "Draft on London for half the subscription must be remitted on receipt of opening chapters, and for the balance when the concluding copy has come to hand." Finally, somewhat surprising – and possibly irritating to some editors – was that fictions were offered at the same price to all newspapers, no matter how large or small each paper's circulation. The only variables in determining price were the fame of the author and the form in which fiction was received (stereotype plates, which were available only to British newspapers, cost on average 50 per cent more than galley-proof sheets).[35]

The methods that Tillotson's used to edit and illustrate the fiction were quite similar to those used in major magazine offices of the time. In Bolton, there was an editor in charge of the Fiction Bureau and all its operations. William Brimelow, the partner of William Frederic Tillotson from 1874 to 1912 (and editor of *Bolton Evening News* from 1871 to 1913), appears to have edited some syndicate materials until March 1889, when Tillotson died and Brimelow was forced to assume many of his duties. John Nayler served as Bureau manager in the late 1880s and early 1890s, and in 1893 he was succeeded by William Frederic Tillotson's second son, James Lever

Tillotson. As "Lever" Tillotson became more involved with other of the company's activities, though, a replacement was needed. Sir Philip Gibbs then managed the Fiction Bureau from 1900 to 1902, Isaac Edwards filled the position from 1902 to about 1912, and Robert Sheppard was in charge of the Bureau during the First World War. These men were probably responsible for the editing of manuscripts (often submitted as handwritten but usually converted to typescript by the firm for editing purposes). It is unknown whether these editors sent their recommendations to authors and required extensive revisions. After the text had been agreed upon by the editor, the works were subsequently typeset and proofs pulled. These were sent to their authors for correction and returned to the Bolton office. In the case of American authors' works obtained by the New York office, these were probably edited in that office by W. Philip Robinson and later, Frank Graves; there is no indication of contact between these authors and the Bolton office. In England, not only authors were checking the proofs. As John Nayler recalled many years later, "Proofs for reading were deposited on one of the tables and were read and corrected by whoever happened to be in the office at the time. There was no regular reader – we all helped."[36]

As all of this work was being done on the text, illustrations were being made. The first illustrations accompanying Tillotson's fiction were published in late 1886 in the *Bolton Weekly Journal* and were fairly simple; they were most likely photoengraved line drawings, executed at the Bolton plant. Illustrations were clearly used to lure the readers to new serial novels; in the late 1880s and early 1890s the first few installments of serial novels in the *Weekly Journal* were usually accompanied by two or three illustrations but subsequent installments were non-illustrated. Some materials syndicated by Tillotson's in the United States in 1894 followed this pattern, but by 1899 they were not usually illustrated.[37]

Because of the technical exigencies of newspaper syndication, the methods Tillotson's used to distribute fiction were quite different from those used by book and magazine publishers. In Britain, much of Tillotson's early business in the 1870s and 1880s involved casting stereotype plates at the Bolton plant and sending them in columns 21 inches long to other provincial newspapers. The firm continued to make plates available to those British papers that wanted them all the way until the syndicate's sale in 1935. However, the demand for these plates decreased because of their high price compared to galley-proof copy and because most larger papers moved away from presses that used flat stereotype plates. Most British newspapers buying Tillotson's fiction, then, received it in the form of advance sheets or galley-proof slips (often called "reprint"), which were first made available to customers in 1875. In fact, many of the works listed in a Tillotson notebook circa 1885 were available "in Reprint only." The American market, on the other hand, was always served with advance sheets and galley-proof slips, mainly due to the high shipping costs involved in sending stereotype plates across the ocean. Before 1891, these sheets and proofs were either printed at the British book publisher's plant or in Bolton. Because of the provision in the Chace Act of 1891 requiring American typesetting of foreign works to secure American copyright, however, after this date the American branch office probably arranged for the typesetting and printing of proofs in the United States.[38]

Tillotson's distribution of fiction in proof form in the United States presented many problems in respect to copyright registration, especially before 1891. Before this date, the United States was not a signatory of the Berne Convention regulations concerning copyright, and thus works first published there could be legally pirated by publishers elsewhere in the world. One result was that if a British author's work appeared in the United States even only a few days before its publication in Britain, British copyright would be vitiated and it could be legally printed by any British publishers who so desired. Since the printing of the galley proofs themselves did not constitute "publication" for copyright purposes in Britain, and because one could not register the copyright before a work was published, Tillotson's outlined strict rules for American newspaper editors to follow. Tillotson's circulars sent to American newspapers in the early 1880s stressed that a work could only be published in the United States "within a day or so of [after] its appearance in British and Colonial newspapers," never before. This same circular also stipulated that editors must make sure "that each weekly instalment is published as divided in the printed copy, and that none of the Novel is published in anticipation of the issue in England," and continued, "The practical monopoly of earliest issue is so obtained in America without injury to the British Copyright, which must be protected under all circumstances." To insure that the British copyright was protected, Tillotson's, acting on the advice again of John

Maxwell, provided American newspapers with proofs of only one installment at a time, and sent these only fourteen – or later, ten – days before the date of publication. In this way, it was impossible or at least very unlikely that the installment would be published first in the United States. As Maxwell succinctly told William Frederic Tillotson in 1883, "10 days advance to New York: 15 days to San Francisco = co[pyright] safe: longer time *unsafe*."[39]

IV

Quite possibly it was William Frederic Tillotson's early efforts and his personal visit to the United States in the spring of 1884 that inspired a number of Americans to begin to syndicate, in galley-proof form, fiction by famous authors for first, simultaneous publication. Two of the first syndicators were Charles Taylor, the editor and publisher of the *Boston Globe*, and Charles A. Dana, editor of the New York *Sun*. In June 1884 the *Boston Globe* published the serial "The King's Men" by John Boyle O'Reilly, Robert Grant, John T. Wheelwright, and J. S. of Dale (F. J. Stimson) and reportedly syndicated it to four other papers for simultaneous publication. A *Boston Globe* advertisement in November 1884 for Wilkie Collins's "Royal Love" (not syndicated by Tillotson's) and Taylor's sale of at least one story to a Chicago newspaper in 1888 also indicate that Taylor was an early experimenter with syndication.[40]

As for Dana, the claim of one of his former subordinates that he "originated the now familiar idea of syndicated newspaper fiction" in 1877 or 1878 is incorrect. Dana first syndicated works – by Henry James and Bret Harte – to a select few newspapers across the country in the summer of 1884. Textual variants among the separate publications of these stories indicate that they were not printed from stereotype plates sent by Dana but rather were typeset at individual newspaper facilities from galley proofs, which were probably printed at the *Sun* plant. Dana most likely contacted these authors directly to obtain permission to syndicate their work. In June and July 1884 he syndicated Henry James's "Pandora" and "Georgina's Reasons," plus Bret Harte's "A Blue Grass Penelope"; a work by Howells was promised to editors but never delivered. These works were heralded in one Syracuse newspaper as "SOME NEW AMERICAN STORIES / Produced by a Combination of Newspapers and Published Serially, in Parts, Every Sunday." They were hardly eye-catching features;

they were not illustrated and did not have subheadings.[41] Newspapers besides the *Sun* included in Dana's syndicates from June 1884 to February 1885 were the Cincinnati *Enquirer,* Philadelphia *Times,* New Orleans *Times-Democrat,* St. Louis *Globe-Democrat,* Springfield (MA) *Republican, Syracuse Daily Standard,* Savannah *Morning News, Boston Herald, San Francisco Chronicle, Boston Globe,* and *Atlanta Constitution.* Not all of these papers took each fiction Dana offered; rather, combinations among these papers were formed for each work.

Very little is known about Dana's methods of syndication. One piece of evidence that sheds some light on this matter is an announcement in the *Sun* on 1 January 1885 for Bret Harte's "A Ship of '49" (slated to begin in the *Sun* on 22 February 1885). Unlike earlier announcements of fiction syndicated by Dana, it does not name the other subscribing newspapers. Instead, it states, "We shall be glad to hear from those of our contemporaries in other places who may wish to join THE SUN in a syndicate for the contemporaneous publication of this attractive story." Clearly Dana had already bought the rights to this story before he began marketing it, and thus he had incurred the full expense without guarantee of recovering any portion of it. Further, those who would share the costs obviously had no say in the choice of the work. This notice also demonstrates fairly passive marketing, much like Tillotson's. Dana apparently assumed that he could sell materials through advertising in the pages of his own newspaper, without writing to other newspaper editors or leaving New York to make personal calls on them. This lack of initiative, combined with Dana's inability to attract a larger number of more popular authors to his venture, was most responsible for the discontinuation in early 1885 of his attempts at syndication. One contemporary concluded that the plan "was dropped, from lack of support from the newspapers." But part of the problem might also have been that readers were not properly prepared for fiction in the newspaper. After publishing one of Dana's syndicated stories and failing to receive a positive response from readers, for example, the business manager of the *Chicago Herald* reportedly commented, " 'I soon made up my mind that the scheme was a fizzle.' "[42]

Readyprint publishers, plate service providers, and the first syndicators of fiction in galley-proof form thus all operated very differently not only from book, magazine, and story paper publishers, but also from one another; no one type of syndicate could satisfy the widely varied demands of all newspapers. Of the three types of syndicates, those which distributed fiction in galley-proof form to larger daily newspapers would eventually prove to be the most successful in bringing the fiction of famous and critically respected authors to the greatest number of American newspaper readers. Yet in the fall of 1884, this type of syndication was still at an early, critical stage of development in the United States. Tillotson's had not yet successfully negotiated the American newspaper marketplace, Charles Taylor's syndication efforts were only occasional and haphazard, and Dana's syndicate scheme was a soon-to-be-aborted experiment. In late 1884, however, two individuals with little capital were beginning their own syndicates; with a combination of personal zeal and modified operating strategies, they would significantly affect the literary and newspaper worlds through the end of the nineteenth century and beyond. Their stories are the subject of the following chapter.

CHAPTER 3

The heyday of American fiction syndication: Irving Bacheller, S. S. McClure, and other independent syndicators

[Syndication] is an attempt to give to the great mass of people through the newspapers reading equal to that which appears in the best magazines.

S. S. McClure, 1891

I had a hard struggle in about the most difficult kind of business that any man ever attempted. I was a pioneer in the newspaper syndicate business.

Irving Bacheller, 1938[1]

Despite the different methods they used to distribute their materials, the syndicates operated by readyprint companies, plate service providers, Tillotson's, Dana of the New York *Sun*, and Taylor of the *Boston Globe* had two things in common that distinguished them from later syndicates: all owned their own printing plants and did not rely solely on syndicating fiction for their revenues. In 1884 two young Americans, Addison Irving Bacheller and Samuel S. McClure, building on and inspired by the example of these earlier syndicators, pioneered their own innovative type of syndicates that did not have the advantage of a great amount of operating capital, a large staff of editors and illustrators, or a printing plant. Yet these two syndicators and their numerous imitators became sources of abundant and inexpensive newspaper material, primarily original fiction. A great number of newspaper editors and publishers, including Dana and Taylor, welcomed the opportunity to shift the responsibility for obtaining, marketing, processing, and distributing fiction – and assuming all the financial risks inherent in this type of operation – to these firms.

The syndicate forms described in the previous chapter evolved within the tradition of newspaper publishing. The type of syndicate Bacheller and McClure introduced, however, had different antecedents. Although Bacheller may have described his company in 1886 as "Publishers and Correspondents," and McClure's first letterhead in 1884 listed "S. S. McClure, Publisher," these statements were not literally true. Unlike book, magazine, and newspaper publishers who usually either owned printing plants or had standing arrangements with printers to print what they had purchased from authors, neither Bacheller nor McClure owned a printing establishment until the mid-1890s. Furthermore, while McClure might have believed he was emulating the Associated Press when he named his syndicate the Associated Literary Press, seeking to provide the most current fiction instead of the freshest news, he did not act as a newspaper publisher combining and contracting with other newspaper publishers: he was merely a salesman to them. The more important and immediate predecessors and early contemporaries of these two syndicators were not newspaper, book, or magazine publishers but rather the literary bureaus and manuscript brokers that in the late 1870s and 1880s offered business – and sometimes editorial – advice for a fee to aspiring authors. These companies, with names such as the Athenaeum Bureau of Literature, the New York Bureau of Literary Revision, the Literary Interchange, the Writers' Literary Bureau, the Managers' National Literary and News Bureau, the Literary Exchange, and the Western Literary Bureau promised to help both the aspiring author and book and magazine publishers. Since the literary bureau managers and manuscript brokers made it their business to understand the needs of various publications, they claimed that they were more likely to know where an author's manuscript stood the best chance of being accepted and thus would relieve authors of the expensive and time-consuming task of mailing and remailing their submissions, in the process increasing their acceptance rate and income.[2]

Like the managers of these bureaus and exchanges, Bacheller and McClure – as Tillotson had before them – acted as middlemen who helped authors make arrangements with multiple newspapers. There was, however, an extremely important difference between literary bureaus and syndicates. Whereas literary bureaus guaranteed themselves a return on their labor and greater financial stability by charging a flat fee for their services in addition to a percentage commission on the fiction's selling price, an independent syndicator usually bought the manuscript outright or contracted to purchase it, only making money if he was successful in selling it to enough newspapers to cover his initial outlay.

At first glance, the role played by independent syndicators also seems closely akin to that beginning to be played in the 1880s and 1890s by literary agents; indeed, syndicators often thought of themselves as agents and were described as such by others. The British author Ouida (Louise de la Ramée), for example, conflated the terms "syndicator" and "agent" in a letter to the London *Times* in 1891, and in 1890 S. S. McClure did the same and implied a comparison to the most famous literary agent of the era when he wrote to Robert Louis Stevenson, "There will be no more A. P. Watt nor Tillotson & Son. There is just room for one person in *this business of mine*" (emphasis added).[3] Like later personal agents, independent syndicators helped authors market their fiction and had a positive effect on their remuneration. However, agents and syndicators usually operated quite differently. Agents like A. P. Watt charged a standard fee of 10 per cent of the work's selling price for their services but did not have to risk any capital of their own; furthermore, agents usually arranged to have publishers pay any author's fees or royalties directly to them and took their 10 per cent before giving the remainder to the author. Syndicators, on the other hand, risked their own capital to buy publishing rights from authors and had no certainty of return; independent syndicators commonly paid the author on delivery of the manuscript, or part upon delivery and part later, without knowing whether newspaper editors would buy it. In those cases when an author was not paid upon delivery, syndicators still were under contract to turn over any sales revenues to the author first, before taking any profit for themselves. Thus, there was great potential for a syndicator to actually lose money on a transaction.

Outlined on paper, the organizational plans and tasks of Bacheller, McClure, and their later imitators seemed simple enough. As McClure naively believed, he would buy a short story for $150, a higher price than that paid by most magazines of the time, sell it to one hundred newspapers for 5 dollars each, and thus make a substantial profit for himself. As he later recalled, "News was syndicated in this way, and I did not see why fiction should not be."[4] In the United States, because of the rapidly growing number of metropolitan daily newspapers, the market appeared virtually unlimited, and regularly forming syndicates of one hundred newspapers each seemed simple. To make their ventures successful, Bacheller and McClure, while introducing some innovative methods of their own, continued to operate along many of the lines established by

Tillotson and Dana: buy work from currently popular authors, arrange to sell it to a large number of newspapers whose circulation areas do not overlap, guarantee them exclusive use in their territory, send them galley-proof copy in advance so they can typeset it in their own plants, require them to print a copyright notice identifying the author or syndicate, and make sure they all publish a work simultaneously. The outline of this type of business seems straightforward, sensible, and profitable; success appears easy to achieve. The details of the history of these syndicates and their operating methods, however, reveal a complex business proposition that was very difficult to manage.

I

Bacheller and McClure, although not widely known by scholars today, were ubiquitous in the Anglo-American literary publishing world of the 1880s and 1890s. Authors and publishers of all types frequently referred to them in their correspondence, reminiscences, and even literary works. According to most accounts Bacheller, a poor boy of Yankee stock from northern New York State, was the more favored of the two. His friend Hamlin Garland described him as "large of frame and ruddy of face, with smiling blue eyes and blond hair .... [whose] voice is gentle, and his glance absent-minded yet humorous." Arthur Waugh, who eventually became an editor at Chapman and Hall, met Bacheller in the late 1880s and recalled that he "was a man whom everyone liked instinctively; there was a continual sense of contrast between the bustling business out of which he was making a livelihood and his own naturally quiet, dreamy temperament."[5]

In contrast, McClure, a self-made Irish immigrant who grew up in Indiana, is always remembered as fiercely determined and full of frenetic energy. The key aspects of his personality are captured in Ida Tarbell's description of her first meeting with McClure, in Paris in the early 1890s: "A slender figure, ... a shock of tumbled sandy hair, blue eyes which glowed and sparkled. He was close to my own age, a vibrant, eager, indomitable personality that electrified even the experienced and the cynical. His utter simplicity, outrightness, his enthusiasm and confidence captivated me." And, as she noted, McClure "was as eager as a dog on the hunt – never satisfied, never quiet." Lloyd Osbourne, Robert Louis Stevenson's stepson and

4. S. S. McClure, founder of the Associated Literary Press syndicate, February 1887

5. S. S. McClure (left) and Managing Editor John S. Phillips (right) in the New York City office of the Associated Literary Press syndicate and of *McClure's Magazine*

6. Syndicator Irving Bacheller, circa 1899

occasional collaborator, seconded Tarbell's opinion, writing that in the 1880s McClure was "vibrating with energy, endowed with an ability, initiative, and originality that at times almost approached genius." Finally, Ray Stannard Baker described his boss as "all intuition and impulse, bursting with nervous energy, one of the most unorganizable, impatient, and disorderly men I ever knew." These qualities, admirable in some ways, often made it difficult for "the General," as he was called by *McClure's Magazine* staffers in later years, to get along with those less energetic and enthusiastic than he. His reputation eventually spread; Joseph Conrad wrote in 1899, "S. S. McClure is a sort of Holy Terror – I hear [,] but *why* he is terrible I'm damned if I know. Sort of Silas Lapham I understand. [However,] I dare say he is no more beastly than any other animal of that sort." William Dean Howells, the author himself of *The Rise of Silas Lapham* (1885) and a man who knew McClure fairly well, is often credited with having used McClure as the model for the character of Fulkerson the syndicate manager in *A Hazard of New Fortunes* (1889); he later said, however, that this character was inspired by someone else. McClure was, though, the model for a number of fictional characters, from Reuben Tracy in Harold Frederic's *The Lawton Girl* (1890) to Jim Pinkerton in Robert Louis Stevenson and Lloyd Osbourne's *The Wrecker* (1891).[6] Yet, despite the contact these two very different syndicators had with so many of the era's leading literary figures, Bacheller's and McClure's complete stories have never been documented.

Accurately tracing the syndicate operations of Irving Bacheller is a rather arduous task, given the paucity of available manuscript and secondary materials. Most scholars have had to rely primarily on Bacheller's two autobiographies, *Coming Up the Road: Memories of a North Country Boyhood* (1928) and *From Stores of Memory* (1938). Unfortunately, Bacheller's memory of events that took place at least thirty years earlier is faulty at times, and he rarely provides specific dates in his meanderings through his syndicate experiences. The many inaccuracies and uncertainties in these autobiographies have in turn produced incorrect scholarly and popular accounts. To corroborate and correct Bacheller's memories, the present study draws not only on the autobiographies but also numerous other sources.

Accounts of when and how Bacheller began to syndicate materials differ widely. Bacheller himself later claimed that his "was the first newspaper syndicate in America," and that "There was no such [syndicate] preparation by the [New York] *Sun* or the *Boston Globe* [in 1884]"; a colleague wrote in 1888 that "What credit there is in the invention and the development of a new and important system belongs exclusively to Mr. A. I. Bacheller, and no one else."[7] So far, however, scholars have been unable to agree on when exactly Bacheller began syndicating fiction. The year 1883 is most often given as the date when he founded the American Bureau of Fiction or the New York Press Syndicate, although 1884, 1887, and even 1894 have also been offered. This last date, however, is as inaccurate as one scholar's statement that Bacheller – who was from upstate New York and lived most of his adult life in New York City and Connecticut – was a famous "Indiana author."[8]

In fact, Bacheller made his first attempt at syndicating fiction – under what title is uncertain – in the fall of 1883, but it was unsuccessful. An 1882 graduate of St. Lawrence University, he was working as a drama reporter for the *Brooklyn Daily Times* when he met the English novelist Joseph Hatton in October or November 1883. Hatton, who was accompanying the British actor Henry Irving on his first American tour in order to ghostwrite Irving's account of it, suggested to Bacheller that he try to syndicate a novel of Hatton's, a practice he told Bacheller was by then commonly used by Tillotson's in Britain. Bacheller then "wrote a circular offering the novel to a large list of newspapers," but was rebuffed. Instead he sold "The Mystery of Margaret Willoughby" to the *New York Ledger* for $3,500, taking a $500 share for himself for acting as an agent; the novel was published serially between 3 January 1885 and 16 May 1885.[9]

Hatton, learning of Bacheller's failure with the novel, subsequently proposed to write a potentially more marketable London Letter that would include a number of interviews with leading British writers and personalities; he would send them to Bacheller, who would syndicate them to American newspapers. This arrangement between Hatton and Bacheller probably was not made earlier than 1 April 1884, when Hatton returned to New York after touring the country with Irving and before his return to England. It was most likely after this meeting with Hatton that Bacheller travelled to Boston, Chicago, Kansas City, Washington, D. C., and points between, contracting with enough newspapers to insure a steady income supplementing his salary at the *Brooklyn Daily Times*. The first-known Joseph Hatton "London Letter" is dated 15 May 1884, and appeared in the *Boston Herald* on 25 May 1884; the last was published in the

Washington Post on 8 February 1885 (both were presumably published in other newspapers as well). A letter of payment for the Hatton letters dated 25 January 1885 and addressed to Bacheller at the *Daily Times* is further evidence that they were published in the second half of 1884 and early 1885; the address also suggests that Bacheller did not quit his reporting job to become a full time syndicator until the spring of 1885, much later than he claimed.[10]

It is very possible that Bacheller began to successfully syndicate fiction only after S. S. McClure syndicated his first work for publication on 15 November 1884. The first fiction I have located that appears to have been syndicated by Bacheller was Opie Read's "Old Amazin' Grace," which was published on 29 November 1884. Certainly by the spring of 1885 Bacheller was syndicating fiction in earnest. A Rochester, New York, newspaper editor wrote to S. S. McClure on 23 May 1885: "They tell me in Brooklyn Bacheller has gone up in literary supply business, [sic] and gone west himself," as if this were a relatively recent development.[11]

Tracing Bacheller's history as a syndicator after these beginnings is also difficult, in part because from 1884 until the end of his syndicating operations in the spring of 1898, Bacheller frequently changed the name of his company (these name changes were always precipitated by a change of partners or investors). From 1884 to 1887 it was known as Bacheller and Co.; from 1887 to the spring of 1891 it was named the Bacheller Newspaper Syndicate; from this date to November 1894 it was called the Bacheller and Johnson Newspaper Syndicate, and from 1894 to May 1896, with the addition of his brother Wilbur, the Bacheller, Johnson, and Bacheller syndicate. At this point, the firm was incorporated and renamed the Bacheller Syndicate, the title it held when it was sold in March 1898 to John Brisben Walker of *Cosmopolitan* magazine. Walker kept Bacheller on as the manager of the renamed International Literary and News Service, but Bacheller left the firm in the late spring of 1898, and the syndicate folded in November of that year. Over the years, Bacheller's syndicate expanded geographically, with offices in Washington, DC, London, and Sydney, and though its service also broadened to include other types of printed materials, it apparently syndicated fiction throughout its fourteen years of operation.

The genesis of Samuel S. McClure's Associated Literary Press is also obscured by autobiographical discrepancies and repeated inaccuracies. In *My Autobiography* (1913), for example, McClure boasted,

"I was launching a business that had never been tried before," and those who do not credit Bacheller as the first syndicator usually – as a result of McClure's constant repetition of his story – name him as the first. Yet many years earlier McClure had acknowledged the debt to his predecessors, writing in an 1887 letter to the *Critic* magazine that in the summer of 1884, when he formulated his own plan, "I [had] noticed the success of Mr. Dana's plan, and of Mr. Tillotson's." In his first syndicate circular of 4 October 1884, too, McClure indicated that he already knew of British and French syndication ventures that preceded his.[12] Clearly, McClure's autobiographical memories also need to be corroborated and clarified.

When he began his syndicate in 1884, McClure, a recent graduate of Knox College in Illinois, had completed only two years of print industry experience (gained in Boston and New York). He later claimed that during a short leave from his duties as an editorial assistant at *Century* magazine in July 1884, "One evening ... I sat down and in a few hours invented the newspaper syndicate service which I afterward put through. I saw it, in all its ramifications, as completely as I ever did afterward, and I don't think I ever added anything to my first conception." Despite such a sweeping statement, however, in other places McClure made clear that he did not "invent" the syndicate in just one evening. In 1934, he recalled that the germ of the idea had come in 1870 when, as a country boy in Valparaiso, Indiana, he had wished that he could receive good fiction that was being distributed only in and near big cities. This inspiration, combined with his familiarity with the patent insides that were common in the Midwest during his youth and the syndicate examples of Dana and Tillotson, resulted in the plan he took to Frank Scott of the *Century* in late July 1884 and subsequently to Roswell Smith, its editor. That plan was to syndicate stories from *St. Nicholas* magazine, also published by *Century*, to small country newspapers throughout the country for second publication, so as "to supply good reading matter for the country boys and girls."[13] Smith rejected the proposal and probably pointed out to McClure the basic problem with his plan: there already existed stiff competition from the readyprint and plate service companies who syndicated this type of material, and newspaper editors who were used to clipping the best pieces from *St. Nicholas*, *Youth's Companion*, and *Century* and reprinting them without fee were very unlikely to pay for such a service. Smith also suggested that McClure find other employment.

It has not been previously noticed, though, that the plan McClure began putting into motion in August 1884 bore little resemblance to the idea he proposed to editors at the *Century* in July. In late July or early August McClure seems to have suggested to his friend and Knox College classmate John S. Phillips an entirely different concept. Instead of distributing children's fiction to daily and weekly country newspapers for reprinting, he would form syndicates of larger metropolitan dailies to buy fiction from the leading American authors for first printing. McClure only once mentioned the difference between these plans, noting in a 1939 interview, "First, I thought of sending such a story to the county [sic: country] newspapers throughout the country. Then it developed into sending other stories to all the great newspapers."[14]

Also like Bacheller, McClure began with little financial backing; his biographer notes that McClure "had less than twenty-five dollars in the bank [and] no capital to buy the stories he proposed to sell." Nonetheless, full of hope, McClure in September 1884 visited the homes of many fiction authors in New England to ask them if they would sell him some of their works and allow him to syndicate them. By October, he and his wife Hattie had moved from East Orange, New Jersey, to a New York City apartment at 114 East 53rd St., which doubled as their office. As he noted in his autobiography, "If I were going to launch a new venture, I had, of course, to have a New York address." McClure later recalled that he and his wife ran a cottage industry: "we had it there in the flat with us; we ate in the office; the syndicate was a member of the household."[15] In December, McClure's fortunes had improved enough to allow him to move to a separate office.

In September 1885 McClure expanded his fiction offerings by establishing a Youth's Department, which over the years contained children's fiction by Joel Chandler Harris, Mary E. Wilkins, Sarah Orne Jewett, Frank Stockton, and others. McClure expanded geographically as well, eventually syndicating works around the world. As noted in chapter 2, in March 1887 he made an arrangement with Tillotson's whereby McClure would supply Tillotson's with American fiction for distribution in Britain and its colonies and in return Tillotson's would supply McClure with British fiction for distribution in the United States. Upon conclusion of the negotiations McClure wrote to John Phillips, "we engaged in a treaty offensive, & defensive to monopolize the syndicate serial service of the world." Thus in 1888 McClure could accurately report that fiction he procured was being syndicated to newspapers not only throughout the United States but also in Canada, Great Britain, Ireland, Australia, New Zealand, India, and the West Indies. After McClure's arrangement with Tillotson was abrogated in late 1888, McClure sought to expand the geographic reach of his own syndicate's distribution capabilities. In the summer of 1889, he established a permanent London office of the Associated Literary Press to obtain British fiction and market fiction to British newspapers. Yet, after he encountered substantial difficulty in more extensively entering the British market in 1889, he wrote in a more humble tone, "I will confine my operations more exclusively to America." By 1890 McClure had reversed course and made new plans to expand the syndicate onto the European continent, with offices in Paris and Leipzig. Such plans were spoiled, however, when McClure took a hard financial loss on Stevenson's *South Seas Letters* (1891); the idea of offices in Paris and Leipzig was permanently shelved. Yet English-language syndication of McClure materials throughout the world continued unabated. McClure told Seth Low in August 1891 that his Youth's Department was being "published in leading newspapers in most of the large cities of the United States, Great Britain, Australia, and New Zealand." This extensive reach is partially corroborated by Rudyard Kipling's comment in January 1890 that he knew of McClure's "association [syndicate] while in charge of a weekly in India," and the publication of some McClure-syndicated works – most notably Twain's *The American Claimant* – in Australia in 1892.[16]

In 1893 McClure turned his energies in a different direction, taking up a long-held dream of becoming a magazine editor and publisher. The first issue of *McClure's Magazine* was dated June 1893. After the founding of the *Magazine*, McClure was not so directly involved in the syndicate's operation and left most of the day-to-day work to his brothers Robert, Tom, and John, along with Robert J. Finley, whom S. S. McClure knew from Knox College. Under their direction the syndicate offered a somewhat reduced amount of fiction but continued to do fairly well. As the firm turned the corner into the new century, the McClure Syndicate continued to distribute fiction to newspapers not only in the United States, Canada, India, and Australia, but also in South Africa.[17]

II

The brief organizational histories of the Bacheller and McClure syndicates tell only part of their stories. Even more revealing are the details of the innovative methods they used to obtain, market, process (edit, print, illustrate, and copyright), and distribute fiction.

To obtain the necessary amount and quality of fiction from authors that would be saleable to newspaper editors for first printing, Bacheller and McClure used strategies much more complex and aggressive than those used by patent inside companies, plate service providers, and early galley-proof syndicators. They visited and wrote to famous authors, solicited recommendations of local authors from newspaper editors, conducted prize contests, worked with literary agents (after 1887), appointed their own representatives to seek out fiction, and occasionally combined with various publishers to purchase works. All of these methods were rather innovative in 1884, when most American publishers tended still to rely on authors to submit unsolicited manuscripts. Because their businesses required them to recruit well-known authors who were more or less bound to specific book and magazine publishers by the informal practices of trade courtesy, neither Bacheller nor McClure could play by the traditional rules for obtaining fiction that gentleman publishers generally followed. Their disregard for these rules helped make Bacheller and McClure two of the key figures involved in breaking open the literary marketplace in the late 1880s.

To successfully operate their businesses, Bacheller and McClure each needed to procure many more fictions than any single magazine did. As early as July 1885, Bacheller was reportedly syndicating short stories of various lengths for publication on six days of the week.[18] Given his later pattern of supplying many stories that ran for two, three, four, and even five and six days, it is probable that the number of separate fictions he syndicated in each of his first few years of operation was about 100. He needed fewer fictions between late 1888 and late 1894, because during this period Bacheller marketed illustrated fictions only sporadically. In November 1894 he returned to providing short stories and novelette installments six days a week, mostly by well-known authors, and advertised a "Six Day Serial Service," offering short stories and short serial novels (novelettes) for publication on Mondays through Saturdays and that could be published in no more than six installments.

In the first few months of his operation in late 1884 and early 1885, McClure syndicated only about 5,000 words a week, either a complete short story or one part of a longer short story of two or three installments. Beginning in April 1885, he offered three to six different stories per week (a total of about 9,000 words), three of them translations of foreign works. For the entire year of 1885, 158 short stories are known to have been syndicated by McClure, with 36 of them foreign translations. In September 1885 McClure wrote to editors that he would use 300 stories in his daily and weekly service in the coming year, and that he planned to increase the number of American stories to five per week.[19] McClure expanded his service by syndicating his first book-length serial, "Mrs. Peixada" by Sidney Luska (Henry Harland) in December 1885. Because he offered larger serials, McClure syndicated a total of 82 fictions in 1891; of these, 22 were serials, and 12 of those were book-length. In 1899 this trend away from short stories was reversed, and McClure syndicated 120 short stories and fourteen serials.

To obtain the works of well-known authors, Bacheller and McClure relied heavily in the early years of their operations on personal visits and letters. Bacheller wrote that one of the first things he did after becoming an independent syndicator was to visit John Greenleaf Whittier, Oliver Wendell Holmes, and Mark Twain at their homes to solicit material from them. Unfortunately, he recounted, "None of these great men would do business with me." As early as 1888, Bacheller was delegating much of the responsibility for author visits and correspondence to his partner, James W. Johnson, who "was able to give me good help in the traveling and soliciting and on the task of finding the copy we required." After about 1890, Bacheller also entrusted some of the work of fiction solicitation to his office manager, Arthur Stedman. In his capacity as Bacheller's representative, the well-connected Stedman (son of the famous poet Edmund Clarence Stedman) visited and wrote to authors to ask for material. Edmund Clarence Stedman himself, in his informal position as a part-time editor for Bacheller, also steered a number of authors toward Bacheller. One of the more interesting methods Bacheller used to solicit works by mail was to enclose a check with the letter to the author, as he did once with Brander Matthews.[20]

McClure also relied at first on personal visits to authors and written solicitations to obtain materials. He made his first trip in search of authors' work in September 1884, going to New England to visit the homes of Sarah Orne Jewett, Elizabeth Stuart Phelps, Harriet Prescott Spofford, and Helen Hunt Jackson. McClure, whom Phelps described as "the indefatigable editor of a New York literary syndicate, to whom distance is a myth," would in the late 1880s track down Phelps on her South Carolina farm and in the early 1890s find Henry James in London, securing works from both. In addition, as early as the fall of 1884, McClure was writing to Mary Noailles Murfree and Frank Stockton to ask for contributions; in such letters McClure usually enclosed circulars describing his service. His most successful strategy was to get an author to merely promise his or her next work, which was much easier to get than an actual manuscript. One instance of this strategy occurred when McClure visited Robert Louis Stevenson late in the winter of 1887 at his cottage in Saranac Lake, New York. McClure on this visit obtained Stevenson's promise of the sequel to *Kidnapped* (1886) whenever he might write it – which turned out to be five years later. Significantly, there are in the McClure papers no copies of formal written contracts with authors during these early years that would have made such promises legally binding; after about 1890, however, formal agreements are more common, due primarily to the influence of literary agents. McClure continued to write to more famous authors until 1891 and to visit them until 1894, but after these dates he delegated more of these responsibilities to others.[21]

Bacheller and McClure also developed other methods for obtaining the fiction they needed. As noted previously, in 1885 almost one quarter of the material McClure syndicated was foreign work unprotected by American copyright. His wife Hattie found much of this and directed its translation; in September 1885 she wrote to her mother: "You know I am working all the time for Sam, translating, reading to find good stories at the libraries and bookstores [,] looking for things he can use ... ," and to make the search easier, one month later McClure began subscribing to *Le Petit Journal*, a French newspaper known for its feuilleton fiction. In addition, in 1885 McClure asked newspaper editors with whom he had contact to forward to him the names and addresses of promising local writers. McClure and his managing editor, John Phillips, also kept a close personal eye out for promising young authors. McClure sent Ambrose Bierce a syndicate circular in 1892 and asked him for a contribution, writing,

"I have often noticed your stories in the [San Francisco] Examiner"; furthermore, it was probably Phillips who spotted Frank Norris's work in the *Wave* magazine of San Francisco and advised McClure to offer him a syndicate job in New York and to ask Norris if the Associated Literary Press could syndicate his work.[22]

Both syndicators also obtained fiction by sponsoring prize contests, whose benefits for them included publicity and hundreds of manuscripts to consider. After the winner and second place finisher had been paid extraordinarily large sums, Bacheller and McClure could contact some of the non-winning authors and offer them much smaller fees. McClure preceded Bacheller in sponsoring prize contests and appears to have run them more regularly. He began his first contest in May 1885 and conducted others in 1886, 1888, 1890, 1893, and 1894, respectively. Entries were usually solicited with small advertisements in newspapers with which McClure did business, and these directed interested authors to contact McClure for further information. One example of what respondents received in return in 1886 was a printed sheet with detailed "INSTRUCTIONS to Young Writers intending to write for prizes or for publication in the McClure Syndicate of Newspapers," which advertised four first prizes of $75 each and four second prizes of $50 each in the categories of "Stories of the late War," "Stories of Adventure," "Dialect Stories," and "Stories not of these kinds." Manuscripts for the 1885 contest flowed in at the rate of twenty stories a day, and in 1894 the prize story reportedly was chosen from about 1,000 entries. Not all contestants could win the big money, of course, but as one advertisement for the 1885 contest reassured authors, "Other stories submitted for the prize, if of sufficient merit, will be purchased at the regular rates." An advertisement of $2,250 in prizes offered by McClure's Youth's Department in 1890 undoubtedly also attracted the attention of many authors.[23]

Bacheller, too, conducted similar prize contests but quite possibly rigged their outcome. In one contest for the best 3,000-word story, which ran from July 1886 to August 1887, the winner of the $300 prize was F. R. Burton, for his story "Smith's Bell." As it turns out, however, Burton was an employee of Bacheller's, raising the suspicion that Bacheller reaped great publicity from the contest but never actually had to pay the prize. Bacheller sponsored another contest beginning in late 1894 for the best detective story; first prize was an exorbitant $2,000 and second prize was $500. Three thousand entries were received, and in June 1895 it was announced that "The Long Arm," a story co-written by Mary E. Wilkins and J. Edgar Chamberlin, editor of the *Youth's Companion*, had won the contest. Of course it was not mentioned publicly that Bacheller and Arthur Stedman had for a few months actively solicited an entry from Wilkins and probably arranged her victory.[24]

Also important as sources of material for both Bacheller and McClure were the literary agents who represented an increasing number of authors during this period. Both Bacheller and McClure dealt with all the major agents of the period on both sides of the Atlantic: A. P. Watt, Wolcott Balestier, James Pinker, Paul Revere Reynolds, William Morris Colles (acting as an agent of the Authors' Syndicate), and John Chartres.

In addition to relying on literary agents to bring material to them, though, both Bacheller and McClure engaged their own agents in Britain and established permanent offices there. Over the years Bacheller made a number of trips to Europe in search of material, but in general he relied on his personal representative in London, Arthur Waugh, whom he appointed in 1887. Waugh wrote that during Bacheller's initial visit he "got me to take him round town among the editors and the literary agents." Bacheller later remembered that Waugh, from the London office – which was maintained from 1887 until 1898 – "sent us the first tales of W. W. Jacobs, Stanley Weyman and Anthony Hope and some by James Payn and George Gissing."[25]

As previously described, McClure procured some British works between 1886 and 1888 by simply acting as Tillotson's agent in the United States. But McClure, like Bacheller, also travelled to Britain to meet with authors and publishers. McClure recalled that in February 1887, he "heard that Bacheller was going to Europe," and this helped spur his decision to make a trip himself. Fearing that Bacheller would notice his name on a passenger list and somehow beat him across the Atlantic, McClure sailed on 26 February under the name of "S. Sidney." On this trip he engaged Harold Frederic as his London representative. More important for his supply of British fiction, however, was McClure's journey to Bolton, England, on 8 March to meet with William Frederic Tillotson. The resulting agreement (noted previously) whereby, as McClure wrote to John Phillips on 9 March, Tillotson "will secure all possible serials from all the names worth having in Europe [and] I will secure all worth having in America," must have seemed a dream come true for McClure, who badly needed the prestigious and popular works by British authors. He wrote to Phillips, "Success, absolute, and cloudless is ours," and told his wife, "Bacheller is utterly routed and badly beaten." Soon, however, this agreement would not be enough for McClure, who realized that he could make more money by bypassing Tillotson's and negotiating directly with British authors and their agents for American rights. The end of his arrangement with Tillotson was precipitated when McClure in June 1888 insisted on syndicating Stevenson's "The Outlaws of Tunstall Forest" to British newspapers, a step Tillotson's regarded as a violation of the spirit of their contract (it was implied that Tillotson's would not try to market materials directly in the United States if McClure did not try to market materials in Great Britain and British colonies). In late 1888, McClure placed his younger brother Robert in charge of a London office. Described by Joseph Conrad as a "perfectly harmless man who knows nothing of literature," Robert McClure served in this position from 1888 until after the turn of the century. Others, too, were enlisted to recruit authors: as one report noted in 1890, S. S. McClure's "agents in every large city of the world are constantly on the lookout for novelties in the world of letters."[26]

Another way Bacheller and McClure occasionally obtained fiction – usually when a large amount of money was involved – was to act as agent for someone else who had more capital; in return they would secure distribution rights for themselves. Bacheller, for example, acted on behalf of the New York *World* to persuade Arthur Conan Doyle to break his standing agreement with Sir George Newnes of the *Strand* magazine. And in the case of Stevenson's *South Seas Letters* (1891), McClure served as an agent for the New York *Sun* and the British magazine *Black and White*. He was to contact Stevenson and bring him the financial offer tendered by Charles Dana of the *Sun*; in return, McClure expected to receive special publishing rights in the work. However, when Stevenson sent McClure material unacceptable to the *Sun*, McClure was forced to become the chief financial backer of the deal, and he suffered a large loss. McClure also acted as an agent for William Dean Howells's *The Quality of Mercy* (1891). Again, Dana used McClure to tender an offer to Howells for serial rights to this novel; in return, it appears that McClure was allowed to buy or lease the right to distribute this work through his syndicate. Finally, McClure obtained six European letters from Mark Twain in

1891–92 not on his own but as an agent for William Laffan, managing editor of the New York *Sun*.[27]

Finally, all of these more regular sources of material were supplemented by unsolicited manuscripts. These two syndicators became increasingly well-known to aspiring fiction authors across the country not only because of advertisements for prize contests but also because articles about them in such magazines as the *Journalist*, *Critic*, and *Writer* often included their addresses. A *Journalist* report in 1890 that "S. S. McClure is still yearning for stories, poems, and articles, and his check-book is still open for payment for them" was also an open invitation to such writers. Probably as a result of such notices, after about 1890, Bacheller later recounted, a "great mass of manuscript was now arriving every day from all sides of the continent for our consideration."[28]

III

Armed with promises from authors and sometimes some form of written agreement with them, Bacheller and McClure next had to market their wares to newspaper editors across the country. Their sales techniques differentiated them from early syndicators and the mainstream book and magazine publishers of the mid-1880s even more strikingly than did their solicitation practices. Neither Dana nor Tillotson's undertook the laborious task of calling on or writing to every potential American newspaper customer, and no book or magazine editor would have entertained the idea; this, though, is precisely what Bacheller and McClure had to do in order to sell these fictions. Making sales especially difficult was the common practice of newspaper editors – at least in the early years – of reserving the right to read the material offered before deciding whether or not to pay for its use. Certainly no magazine publisher could survive if all potential purchasers were allowed to read the magazine's contents before deciding whether or not to buy it. Bacheller and McClure responded to these unusual conditions with marketing strategies quite different than those used by salesmen of other print forms. Understanding these processes is crucial to determining the control this type of syndicate exercised over the market, and to understanding why the mass-market magazines succeeded financially and syndicates did not.

There has arisen a general presumption that in 1885 the market was extremely congenial to the syndication business, and one scholar has written that when McClure "came to their offices, editors welcomed him because of the yawning empty columns they had to fill daily and on Sunday." In fact, however, in 1884 and 1885 the more characteristic replies McClure received from newspaper editors were: "We are now overloaded with interesting local matter"; "Advertisers have pre-empted every available inch of space"; and "I regret that I have no space in the Appeal for stories." Many years later, McClure recalled that "There was no definite demand on the part of the newspapers for this sort of stuff [fiction]." One editor, Milton McCrae, later remembered the many times when Bacheller "came to sell me something which I could not often buy," and he was probably not alone.[29] Resistance to this new type of product was quite strong.

Bacheller and McClure had to face other difficulties as well in selling their wares. One commentator noted that in the United States, "where the magazines play Lord Bountiful and throw open their treasure-houses to every editor who comes along, it is not easy even for so pushing a canvasser as the agent of a 'Syndicate' to persuade the proprietors of newspapers to pay for similar things to those which hitherto they have been able to get for nothing." Making sales even more difficult was the mediocre reputation of the patent-inside and plate-matter fiction that had previously been supplied to newspapers. Bacheller later recounted that because of these obstacles, "There was a steep grade in the way of the syndicate man those days."[30] Tillotson's had already encountered such resistance, but it was Bacheller and McClure who best adapted to editors' stated concerns and modified the basic principles of syndication in order to do well in the United States. To sell their services, Bacheller and McClure – acting as competitors with each other – had to create a demand for what they were offering, make a variety of attractive promises, aggressively market a better product than the other exchange and syndicate fiction available, and offer it at a lower cost than newspapers had been paying.

Two of the most important promises Bacheller and McClure made to editors, and what they hoped to create a demand for, were the closely allied concepts of "originality" and "exclusivity" in fiction. In a world increasingly filled with mass-manufactured and standardized goods, many products labelled "original" were gaining a certain added value. Bacheller, McClure, and many newspaper editors believed that if they handled syndicated fiction correctly, they could – without lying outright – succeed in giving readers the impression that it was original and exclusive, and thus of great value. To sell their services and aid editors in this mild deception, Bacheller and McClure guaranteed that the fiction they distributed – unlike exchange fiction clipped from other publications or reprinted patent inside and plate service fiction – would be purchased directly from the authors and be printed in subscribing newspapers for the first time anywhere; thus, this mass-reproduced fiction could, by stretching the definition, fairly honestly be promoted as "original." Bacheller certainly did not mind that many editors printed fiction that he syndicated under headlines such as "The Observer's Original Stories" and "The Journal's Original Stories"; in fact, he very likely suggested they do so.

The promise of exclusivity was equally important to editors, since it helped further promote the illusion of originality and because it led readers to believe that the work of famous authors was appearing in the local paper by virtue of the efforts of the local editor. Newspaper editors at this time operated within an extremely competitive culture that highly valued and publicized the "scoop" and exclusive coverage of certain news events. In buying originality, exclusivity, and simultaneity in fiction, an editor bought the right to crow about beating out the competitors and being the preeminent local paper, just as he would if he were to "scoop" another paper on a news story. Like Tillotson's, neither Bacheller nor McClure represented to individual editors that they would be the only ones in the entire country to receive printing rights to a certain work; what each promised editors was exclusive use in their circulation area. This exclusivity made it highly unlikely that any but the more widely-travelled and better-read readers who saw the same work in another city's newspaper would discover the truth that the fiction was neither original nor solely printed in the local paper. Not only did Bacheller and McClure have to guarantee exclusive use within a certain territory, but they also had to promise that all newspapers would print the same works simultaneously, so that each editor could somewhat truthfully claim that he was the first to print it; when simultaneity was not achieved, editors complained.

When editors believed that syndicators' promises were violated and that they had been deceived into buying a work previously printed or misrepresented, sparks flew. In October 1885, for example, the angry editor of *The San Franciscan* enclosed in a letter to S. S. McClure a newspaper clipping that read, "A newspaper syndicate in this country is now publishing a story by Julian Hawthorne, called 'Uncle Bloodstone's Will.' It has been running in the *San Franciscan*, among other journals, as a new story, with the line at head 'Copyright 1885.' The same story was published in the Springfield *Republican* for 25 May and 1 June 1879. Somebody has been deceived." In his letter, the editor demanded of McClure, "Am I deceived – or you? or both of us?" (it is unknown if or how McClure replied). Bacheller was in fact once deceived by an author and as a result inadvertently misrepresented some fictions to editors as original. In 1887 author Lew Vanderpoole sold stories to Bacheller and others (including McClure and *Cosmopolitan* magazine) that he claimed were original manuscripts by George Sand, left to him in her will to sell posthumously for the estate. Bacheller appears not to have been among the publishing industry insiders (McClure was among them) who as early as March were aware of Vanderpoole's activities. Although Vanderpoole was not arrested for forgery until September (at the behest of editor Frank B. Smith of *Cosmopolitan*), news of his deception probably spread fairly quickly in newspaper circles. Unfortunately, Bacheller had already sold some of these fraudulent works to a number of newspapers, including the *Syracuse Herald*. The *Herald*, which had regularly taken materials from Bacheller in early 1887, discontinued its association with him in June, quite possibly because of his inadvertent misrepresentation of Vanderpoole's stories.[31]

Bacheller and McClure conveyed their promises and made their services known to editors in a number of ways. Two prevalent methods were to mail circulars directly to newspaper and magazine editors and to place advertisements in the *Journalist* magazine. Most often, however, McClure simply sent duplicate copies of typed letters to editors detailing his offerings. In the mid-1880s, Bacheller at one point saved money by having a sample of his Christmas page offering printed on the back of his letterhead stationery; by 1894 the circular appears to have been a separate sheet, but it was much more crudely printed than McClure's. These syndicators, however, found the efficacy of such printed sheets alone rather minimal; as one *Journalist* article reported, typically "The editor receives the syndicate man's circular and promptly dumps it into the waste basket, and forgets all about it until he wants to buy syndicate matter." To complement such appeals, Bacheller, McClure, and other syndicators thus also often tried to reach editors by placing advertisements in trade magazines.[32]

Recognizing the minimal response to these sales strategies, Bacheller and McClure adopted a direct sales approach and travelled extensively to sell their wares in person to editors, making contacts that could later be maintained with circulars and letters. Tillotson's had used this strategy in Britain but not in the great expanse of the United States. Bacheller wrote that twice a year he travelled to meet with editors, taking "many journeys up and down the continent. For making th[ese] I slept on Pullman cars; I climbed innumerable flights of stairs, late at night, to ratty editorial rooms in all the big cities. After fifteen years of it I estimated that I had traveled seven hundred miles up stairs and down in quest of managing editors." Bacheller was convinced that personal visits to editors were more effective than letters and circulars. While working for the syndicate of John Brisben Walker in 1898 he wrote to his boss: "We have written and are writing many letters [to editors], and, of course, they are doing some good but personal solicitation is the thing needed – argument and persuasion." Just as Bacheller hired others to help him procure fiction, so too he enlisted the help of his partner James W. Johnson in travelling to meet with editors, and by 1892 he was employing a staff of agents working on commission to relieve him of some of the burden of these sales trips.[33] Until 1894, McClure also travelled a great deal to make sales calls on various newspaper editors. Reading McClure's itineraries during these early years is tiring even to those more accustomed to jet travel; it was not uncommon for him to cover the entire western United States in three weeks, stopping in one or two cities per day to visit with editors and, like Bacheller, sleeping on the train on his way to the next city.

To sell their wares, Bacheller and McClure also promised editors a wide variety of choices as to authors, genres, and lengths. The majority of works they offered were by lesser-known authors, but they also knew that they frequently had to offer works by famous authors in order to sell their services; after all, the promise of works by these authors constituted one of the most significant differences between their services and those of readyprint and plate service companies. In addition, while McClure's personal taste ran to adventure stories and Bacheller tended to prefer local color fiction, they did not limit themselves to these genres. As one literary historian has correctly noted of McClure, he catered to the varied market with "a potpourri of styles ... [that included] both realist and romantic texts"; the same can be said of Bacheller.[34] Finally, both syndicators appealed to editors (whose availability of space varied) by promising a diversity of lengths.

Bacheller and McClure further enticed editors with prices for original fiction by well-known authors that were lower than those offered by Tillotson's and which in some cases were much lower than or equal to the $3–$10 usually paid by newspapers for original stories by unknown writers. In July 1885, for example, Bacheller offered his service to the *Pittsburgh Chronicle* for 50 cents per column (approximately 1,500 words) or $3 per week, and in 1890 the *Chicago Daily News* paid only $15 per week for the serial story service. Somewhat surprising is that in 1894, those few customers who took their fiction from Bacheller in plate form still paid only 50 cents per column, about $3.35 per 5,000-word story.[35] Because the extant documents include only one Bacheller contract form for plate service, it is unknown if he acted as McClure did, varying the price for each fiction in galley-proof form according to the length of the piece, the author's fame, and the size of each city's potential readership.

McClure's contract with the tiny *Hoosac Valley News* of North Adams, Massachusetts in November 1884 set a price of 50 cents per thousand words of fiction, slightly higher than Bacheller's price. However, McClure soon realized that he could not sell fiction at this price to every paper. If he bought a 6,000 word story for $150, at fifty cents per thousand words he would have to sell it to 50 newspapers just to break even, many more than the forty or so papers to which he was usually able to sell a single work. A more common price for a 7,000-word short story or two-part serial in November 1884 was $8 to $15. Unlike Tillotson's, McClure did not offer fictions at one set price; instead, he varied the sale price according to the city's population, regardless of whether one paper's circulation was greater than another's. In 1892, newspapers such as the Omaha *Bee* and the Kansas City *Times* could purchase short stories by Rudyard Kipling, Bret Harte, and Arthur Conan Doyle (the second series of Sherlock Holmes stories) for $2 to $3 each, while the much larger Chicago *Journal* would be offered the Doyle stories for $25 each. Much more expensive was Mark Twain's *The American Claimant* (1892), a twelve-part serial novel. It was offered to the Philadelphia *Times* for $1,250, but the selling price in Detroit was $500, and Atlanta and Richmond newspapers could purchase the entire serial for $150. Even more appealing to editors than Bacheller's and McClure's promise of low prices was their promise of easy payment plans whereby one could pay for the work after rather than before publication if one chose – unlike the readyprint and plate service companies, which usually required payment in advance, and Tillotson's, which wanted half payment on receipt of the first chapters and the other half upon delivery of the final ones.[36]

The process of determining which newspaper in each city would receive the rights to print a short story or novel was quite complicated. McClure typically sent out – far in advance of the projected publication date – 125 to 160 circulars with the names of authors, the titles of the works offered, and the price of the offerings to the specific newspaper. If one newspaper had a standing contract with McClure, no circulars were sent to the other papers in that city. Usually, though, circulars were usually sent to all of the newspapers in each city, and the first one to respond won the right to print the work. In such a way, he would supposedly never lose an entire metropolitan market. Such an uncertain situation, however, made Bacheller and McClure very anxious. Whenever possible they preferred to lock in a steady cash flow with long-term contracts to supply individual newspapers with fiction; few editors, though, desired such a commitment.

In response to the uncertainties of the marketplace and the low profit margins they earned, Bacheller and McClure sought out alternative markets for their fiction. Under Bacheller's 1889 agreement with Kellogg, for example, he sold second serial rights to the numerous smaller country weeklies that Kellogg served; McClure, too, sold some second rights to both Kellogg and the American Press Association. Additionally, after about 1890 both Bacheller and McClure began regularly selling selected syndicate materials to magazines rather than newspapers. The reason for shifting to this new market in America is apparent in an 1891 letter from McClure to the editor of the magazine *Christian at Work* regarding a serial story: "I should like to sell the story at once as I need the money just now and do not like to wait for a chance to use it serially in my newspapers. This would prevent me from realizing [a return] on my investment for many months." Bacheller apparently sold second serial rights in some materials to *Ev'ry Month* magazine, edited by Theodore Dreiser, and in Britain, Bacheller and McClure sold most of their syndicate material to magazines such as *The Idler*, *Black and*

White, and the *English Illustrated Magazine*, primarily because the British newspaper market was difficult to penetrate. As McClure and then Bacheller became involved with their own magazines (*McClure's Magazine* and *Pocket Magazine*) in the mid-1890s, they also in a sense sold syndicate materials to these magazines, for they profited from using each work two times. For example, half of the 49 stories that appeared in the first eighteen monthly issues of *McClure's Magazine* had either first been printed through the syndicate or were in the syndicate files, and almost every story Bacheller published in the *Pocket Magazine* had previously been published through the syndicate.[37]

IV

After expending energy to obtain and market fiction, Bacheller and McClure – like book and magazine publishers – still had to process these materials. Their methods of editing and illustrating were much like those used by other publishers, but those for printing and transmitting texts and illustrations to newspapers and magazines were quite different.

Bacheller and McClure at first personally edited the fiction they syndicated, probably because they lacked the financial resources to hire trained help. The first editor Bacheller hired appears to be B. B. Vallentine, one of the founding editors of *Puck* magazine, who served with Bacheller from March 1887 until at least December 1891. Wright Patterson, an editor for the Kellogg firm in Chicago, in 1947 claimed that under the terms of the Bacheller–Kellogg agreement of 1889, Kellogg employee John E. Barman in Chicago and later Patterson himself would read copy and do the headline writing for Bacheller. He wrote, "Bacheller bought the stories in New York, and sent the copy to Chicago. Few of the MS were type written." Yet their responsibilities probably did not include editing; manuscripts were almost certainly edited by Bacheller or an employee in New York. Bacheller clearly tried to retain editorial control over the copy sent to the metropolitan dailies, as indicated by his attempt in 1890 to hire Edmund Clarence Stedman as his full-time literary editor in New York. Stedman preferred to maintain his distance and offer limited editorial advice on a part-time basis, but even so, if Bacheller needed or was pleased with the job being done by Kellogg's editors in Chicago, he would probably not have tried to hire Stedman.

Apparently, Bacheller's editorial staff had more work than it could handle; sometime between 1891 and 1894 Bacheller acknowledged, "Not half the things we publish – in all about 60,000 words a week – are ever seen by me [before they go out]." To help deal with this mass of manuscript, about 1894 Bacheller hired Charles Kelsey Gaines, a friend and St. Lawrence professor, as an editorial assistant, and Gaines had an assistant named Edward B. Lent.[38]

Like Bacheller, McClure began by editing all manuscripts himself but then hired others to help him with the work. In December 1885 McClure reported that he had "a good corp [sic] of clerks" (including his office manager A. H. Chadbourne) to help in the office, but he probably continued to edit all materials himself. Also in this month, McClure tried to entice his friend and Knox College professor Melville B. Anderson to come East to act as "managing editor of the United States," but with no success. Only in September 1886 did McClure find someone he could trust to provide the editorial help he needed: his college friend John Phillips, fresh from graduate study at Harvard and Leipzig, returned to the United States in August and shortly thereafter joined McClure as his right-hand man. Besides balancing McClure's impetuous nature and providing him with prudent financial advice, Phillips served as managing editor of the Associated Literary Press from this point until shortly after *McClure's Magazine* began in June 1893. In addition to all of his other duties, Phillips read manuscripts and appears to have had a great deal of authority as to which works were accepted or rejected. Ray Stannard Baker described Phillips as an editor with "so much of the creative touch, a kind of understanding which surprises the writer himself with unexpected possibilities in his own subjects."[39] Phillips, deflected from a life of scholarship into publishing, probably helped shape the syndicate's offerings as much as McClure did.

In later years McClure hired a number of qualified editors in addition to Phillips. In 1889 he named novelist Frances Hodgson Burnett as editor of the Youth's Department, although her day-to-day involvement is uncertain. Also in 1889, McClure engaged Edmund Gosse as European editor to recommend manuscripts to Robert McClure at the London office. In 1891, McClure scored a coup by engaging Eliza Anna Farman Pratt, the editor of the children's magazine *Wide Awake*, as the new editor of his Youth's Department. McClure proudly announced, "This is the first time that a skilled and trained editor has been connected with syndicate work." Besides helping choose and edit manuscripts, Pratt used her friendship with authors such as Mary E. Wilkins to help the syndicate obtain submissions from prominent authors. In 1894 Mrs. Pratt moved on to another editorial post on a magazine, and Mary Bisland assumed her editorial duties. Frank Norris worked for the syndicate in an unclearly defined role in 1898 and 1899, Edward Marshall (formerly an editor at the New York *Press*) helped with editing in 1899, Shurmer Sibthorp helped Robert McClure with manuscripts in London in the late 1890s, and Samuel Hopkins Adams was editor of the syndicate service in 1900–1901.[40] In addition, all McClure family members, Tom, Harry, Robert, and John, had some editorial input in syndicate matters, at least after 1893.

Bacheller, McClure, and their editorial assistants worked both on holograph manuscript, typewritten manuscript, and sometimes on advance sheets prepared for book publication. For example, Bacheller once wrote to Edmund Clarence Stedman, "I will hand you the ms. [of a Mary E. Wilkins story] when you call – am having it typewritten." And in the cases of Howells's *The Quality of Mercy* (1891), Crane's *The Third Violet* (1896), and Kipling's works printed by John Lovell, the copy submitted to McClure was either already typewritten (*The Third Violet*) or already typeset.[41]

Once the initial editing of the manuscript copy was completed, McClure usually returned it with his editorial suggestions to the author for revision. When the author's revised copy was returned to McClure – at least in 1884 and occasionally in 1885 – he set his wife Hattie or a stenographer to work writing out multiple copies of the fiction in longhand to send to newspapers. By October 1885, the firm had hired its first stenographer, an Irish immigrant named Flynn, but Hattie and this stenographer no longer wrote out every copy sent to the newspapers; an editorial note in the *Detroit Free Press* of December 1885 indicates a new method employed for textual transmission. This editor opined that some recently received Julian Hawthorne stories were "written evidently with a stylograph pen with a sort of aniline (purple) ink." This is only partially correct. Instead of using a stylograph pen (a mechanical device linking multiple pens to an original) to produce a number of near-holograph copies, McClure probably used a hectograph process whereby one copy, handwritten with aniline ink, would be pressed onto a prepared thin gelatin surface; from this, multiple copies could be made by pressing clean sheets of paper onto it.[42]

No samples of the copy Bacheller provided to newspapers in the early years are available, but it is quite possible that he was the first to employ an alternative method of producing multiple copies that McClure began using in 1885 and other syndicates did in later years. Instead of having someone write out multiple longhand copies of authors' texts or reproducing handwritten or typewritten copies with the gelatin hectograph process, Bacheller probably – and McClure most definitely, beginning in 1885 – would contract with a newspaper to typeset the author's revised manuscript and print a few galley proofs. One copy would usually be returned to the more famous authors for proof corrections (less-famous authors probably did not have this privilege), and one copy was given to illustrators. Once the author's proof corrections were received at the syndicate office, the text would be corrected, and enough galley proof copies printed to send to all subscribing newspapers and to the Librarian of Congress for copyright registration. In return for performing this valuable service, the one newspaper would receive printing rights to this one fiction gratis.[43]

Until he left the *Brooklyn Daily Times* in early 1885, Bacheller might have had proofs printed there, and between the fall of 1887 and 17 June 1888, Bacheller probably used his own small, short-lived newspaper, the *New Yorker*, to print galley proofs. After this point, Bacheller probably relied on the Kellogg firm or the New York *Press* to print proofs. The problem of printing proofs was apparently solved in late 1894 or early 1895 when, as Bacheller recalled, "We enlarged our suite of rooms [in the Tribune Building] and had a capable office force, our own illustrators and photoengraving plant," and presumably printing facilities. Given such a plant, it is unlikely that Bacheller continued to farm out galley-proof printing in 1895 to the *Nebraska State Journal*, as one scholar has claimed.[44]

McClure's Associated Literary Press in 1885 also began to contract with certain newspapers to provide typesetting and galley-proof printing in exchange for free syndicate material. In 1885 alone McClure had type set for various fictions at seven different papers, from Portland, Maine, to Philadelphia. By 1891 the New York *Sun* had begun to handle most of this printing and seems to have continued to do so until the mid-1890s. Here again, however, McClure was frustrated at not being in control of the entire production process. He later remembered, "Often the paper that supplied these proofs would be late; sometimes, after I had spent an anxious day or two waiting for them, they would come just in time for me to rush them off on the first mail"; occasionally they arrived too late and McClure lost customers and money as a result. One would expect that after McClure became the owner of his own printing plant in 1896 (for *McClure's Magazine*), galley proofs would be pulled there, but this was not the case; in the last few years of the century the syndicate had the *Boston Globe* do its printing.[45]

While the author was revising proofs and his or her corrections were being set in type, the illustrators were hard at work. Both Bacheller and McClure very early recognized the value of illustrations in selling their fiction to newspaper editors, very few of whom until the 1890s could afford to employ their own illustrators. The first illustrated stories distributed by Bacheller that I have located were Julian Hawthorne's "The Devil's Christmas" and Rose Terry Cooke's "A Gift of God," both published in December 1885. Most illustrations up to 1890 appear to have been line drawings; Bacheller employee John Young Taylor indicated in 1892 that he was selling electrotype "cuts" for another branch of Bacheller's business, but whether Bacheller sent electrotypes, stereotype plates, or zinc plate photoengravings for fiction illustrations is still unknown. In fact, the only extant copy observed of the galley proofs Bacheller sent to editors indicates that subscribing newspapers might not have received plates of illustrations at all. In this instance, the illustrations were printed on the same sheet as the text, suggesting that individual newspapers were expected to make their own photoengravings of the illustrations from these proofs. At least in the early years, Bacheller's illustrators were almost certainly free-lancers rather than regular employees. Between Bacheller's agreement with Kellogg in 1889 and 1894, it is possible that Kellogg's illustrators in Chicago were executing illustrations (Kellogg's had an office in the same building with Bacheller in New York, but it is unknown whether illustrators were employed there). After the establishment of its own photoengraving plant in 1894 or 1895, however, the Bacheller firm had its own staff of illustrators in an art department under the direction of G. Y. Kauffman. From 1894 to late 1896, each installment of a short story or novelette was usually accompanied by one head illustration and two in the text; in fact, subscribers were guaranteed "that the matter furnished in any one week (six days) shall be accompanied by not less than twelve or more than fifteen illustrations." To keep up with the increasing size of illustrations in the rest of the newspaper, in late 1896 these illustrations went from one column in width to two, and in 1897 they occasionally spread across three columns.[46]

As yet the form in which McClure provided illustrations to customers is also undetermined. McClure in his autobiography stated that the first story he had illustrated for syndication – in whatever form – was Robert Louis Stevenson's "The Outlaws of Tunstall Forest," in the spring of 1888. McClure's memory in this area, however, was faulty; he was offering illustrations at an additional cost as early as December 1884. In 1891 McClure established his own art department, headed by Charles Stuart Pratt, the former art manager of *Wide Awake* and the husband of Eliza Farman Pratt. Pratt did illustrations himself but also oversaw the work of illustrators W. P. Bodfish for the Youth's Department and V. W. Newman for the Woman's Page. In 1891, McClure usually provided two or three small one-column wide illustrations for each short story or installment; by 1899 the adult fiction texts were regularly accompanied by only one large two- or three-column wide illustration.[47] By July 1900 McClure was offering to send halftone engravings, which could either be printed directly or used for making a stereotype.

For book and magazine publishers, the actual forms in which readers would encounter the texts and illustrations were fixed after the revised proofs and illustrations were printed in book or magazine form. This was not the case with syndicated fiction (Bacheller provided only a few small newspapers with stereotype plates that contained a text that was difficult to alter). More commonly, Bacheller and McClure still had to coordinate sending galley slips of the text and illustrations in whatever form to a large number of subscribing newspapers. In 1885 McClure promised most domestic newspaper editors that proofs would be mailed to them one week in advance of publication, although copy for West Coast newspapers had to be mailed ten days in advance; Bacheller most likely followed this timetable as well.[48] In the early days when only one story was sent per week, one story was enclosed in each mailing; those who took all six stories offered per week in late 1885 probably received all of them at once. It is unlikely, however, that more than one week's material was ever sent at one time, since this would increase the risk of non-simultaneous publication and endanger the copyright. Distributing these texts was quite troublesome, chiefly because the United States mail was not always reliable; copy was often caught in Rocky Mountain snowstorms or otherwise delayed and could not be printed on time. When these materials finally did arrive at the newspaper office, they were frequently edited further, and the illustrations were occasionally modified. After these alterations were made, the text was typeset, stereotype plates made of this and the illustrations, and the newspaper printed. As one can well imagine, such a system inevitably created a great number of textual variants.

v

Despite the many difficulties of syndicating fiction in galley-proof form, numerous individuals and businesses, the majority of them very small and underfunded operations, followed Tillotson's, Bacheller, and McClure, and vied with them for the patronage of American newspaper editors. Most were based in New York City and lasted only a few years, and they tended to syndicate short stories by unknown writers, offered for extremely low prices. Firms of this type include the American Short Story Company, the American Press Company, Frank Carpenter's Newspaper Syndicate, the International Syndicate of Baltimore, the Albert Bigelow Paine Syndicate, the Editors' Literary Syndicate, the Pacific Press Syndicate, the Syndicate Exchange, the Lorraine Literary Press Association, the Authors' Co-Operative Company, and the Wilson Press Syndicate.

Some other independent syndicates with more substantial financial backing succeeded in offering original fiction by better-known authors to American newspapers. One about which virtually nothing is known is the Authors' Alliance, a British firm which in 1891 and 1892 supplied works by Rudyard Kipling, Walter Besant, Jules Verne, Frank Stockton, Bret Harte, and others to newspapers such as the New Orleans *Daily Picayune*, the *Boston Globe*, the *Syracuse Daily Standard*, the *Syracuse Journal*, and the *San Francisco Chronicle*. Another is the United Press, which was founded in 1882 and devoted primarily to distributing news and features. Under the direction of manager Edward S. Van Zile, a novelist himself, the Literary Department of the United Press syndicated serial fiction and short stories for Sunday publication from 1890 until the company's bankruptcy in 1897.[49]

The Authors' Syndicate, founded by the British Society of Authors in 1890 to serve its members, was the most significant of these other syndicates. William Morris Colles, a barrister, was appointed as its first head, and he remained in this position until his death in 1926, long after the syndicate had broken its ties with the Society in 1898. In the United States during the 1890s, literary agent John Chartres in New York helped the syndicate obtain and market fiction. The Syndicate received a 25 per cent commission in return for editing manuscripts and marketing them to newspaper, magazine, and book publishers for one-time use. Some authors welcomed such help, especially the legal expertise regarding international copyright that Colles provided. In general, though, Colles appears to have been fairly incompetent; one biographer of Arnold Bennett writes that "Colles failed to acknowledge receipt of stories, failed to sell them, [and] had to be advised by Bennett where to sell them." Unlike the syndicates run by Bacheller and McClure, the Authors' Syndicate did not want to purchase works by the unknown authors who needed it most. An 1891 advertisement proclaimed, "Authors are warned that no syndicating is possible for them until they have already attained a certain amount of popularity." Stephen Crane, George Meredith, H. G. Wells, Arnold Bennett, and George Gissing, among others, availed themselves of Colles's services. As one scholar has noted, however, once these authors attained more than the requisite modicum of fame, they usually deserted the syndicate and engaged their own agents.[50]

By procuring, editing, and distributing thousands of works of fiction from 1883 to 1900, galley-proof syndicates – especially those operated by Tillotson's, Bacheller, and McClure – played an important role in the Anglo-American literary marketplace. Virtually every major or minor author of the period had at least one work first published through these syndicates, and millions of American newspaper readers read syndicated materials. McClure kept ahead of Bacheller and Tillotson in the strident competition for the American market in the 1880s and early 1890s, but as McClure became more involved with *McClure's Magazine* after 1893, Bacheller was able to gain the lead. Making success more difficult for these three syndicates in the 1890s, however, was the growing number of competing syndicates and the cheap mass-market magazines, which lowered their prices from 15 to 10 and then even to 5 cents a copy.

Achieving a significant presence in the marketplace required a great deal of hard work. All of these syndicators found it much more difficult and less profitable than they had imagined to actively solicit fiction from authors, market this fiction to newspaper editors across the country, process it, and coordinate its shipment to and simultaneous publication in multiple newspapers. Bacheller made no understatement when he later described syndication as "about the most difficult kind of business that any man had ever attempted." John Phillips, S. S. McClure's partner and able assistant, had foreseen the main difficulties of this type of syndication as early as August 1884; in reply to McClure's proposal Phillips wrote, "On the whole it seems to me impracticable because of the extensiveness of the plan – and the consequent difficulty of bringing the many incongruous elements into harmony. Am afraid of trouble in both directions – getting literary men to make contracts for writing, and papers for publishing." Forty-nine years later, McClure acknowledged to Phillips, "you predicted [in 1884] much that had happened [would happen], which I realized after I had started the plan."[51] Between the former and the latter statements, however, came desperate attempts not only by McClure but by other syndicators as well to succeed in managing these "incongruous elements" – authors and editors – of the literary and newspaper marketplaces.

CHAPTER 4

What literary syndicates represented to authors: saviours, dictators, or something in-between?

A great many stories are published in the papers and sent out by these syndicates, but the competition of writers is so exceedingly great in this matter that the rates are not worth working for.
      William H. Hills, editor of *The Writer*, 1888

The Sunday newspaper magazine, supplied with fiction by the syndicates, "has lifted the man of letters out of the slough of despond and given him a chance in the struggle for existence. It has eliminated Grub street [sic], and has enabled genius to market its literary wares at a figure somewhat commensurate with their value. The author of merit no longer burns the midnight oil in a garret; oftener than otherwise he revels in the blaze of electricity and lives in marble halls, because he is able to reach a world of readers through the Sunday magazine. That he can do so is due in large part to the development of the 'syndicates.'"
      John Young, 1915[1]

In Britain and the United States during the final few decades of the nineteenth century, fiction-writing evolved from a primarily non-remunerative activity to a profession in which more authors than ever before could make a modest living and enjoy relative job security. One of the most important reasons for this change was the newly-developed ability to reach many more readers with fiction than before. British authors benefited from the advent of numerous British periodicals printing fiction and, at least until the mid-1890s, from the steady market of the circulating libraries. For American fiction authors, the mass-market magazines founded in the late 1880s and early 1890s are usually identified as the main catalysts of this evolution, supposedly having been the first print forms to reach a large, national American audience and thus the first to be able to offer authors greater sums for their work. What is usually overlooked in discussions of this transformation of the literary marketplace, however, is the role that newspaper syndicates played in distributing the works of both British and American authors to this American audience. In reaching such an audience before the mass-market magazines did, syndicates helped encourage American fiction authors and provided British authors greater recompense from American publication. Both readyprint publishers and plate service companies distributed fiction to newspapers across the country, yet in general they had a relatively minor impact on authors. On the other hand, the new galley-proof syndicates of the 1870s and 1880s substantially altered the working conditions for hundreds of authors in the Anglo-American literary marketplace. What advantages did these syndicates offer? Were their overall effects on authors more positive or negative? Most important, did the syndicates – in return for any advantages – allow authors substantial artistic autonomy, or did they act as forerunners of the prohibitive editorial practices used by 1890s magazine editors to regularize literary production?

Because the term "syndicate" encompassed a great many different types of print enterprises and because the syndicates dealt with an extremely wide variety of authors, it is difficult to make broad statements about the relationship of all authors to all syndicates. In general, however, within each category – readyprint publisher, plate service provider, and galley-proof syndicate – each individual company shared the same difficulties and objectives with the other companies in its category, and these in turn dictated common methods of dealing with authors. Thus, despite some individual differences, it is possible to discuss each category of syndicate as a group. The discussion of how authors felt about syndicates and dealt with them, though, must be more nuanced. The syndicate manager's personality, for instance, affected authors' views on syndication. Furthermore, an author's nationality, business savvy, and popularity influenced his or her views of the advantages and disadvantages of syndicate publication and to a large degree determined how much relative power he or she held in negotiating issues of remuneration, subject, treatment, length, editing, and publication. What was true for the literary hack who ground out formulaic pieces to assure him or herself a minimal income, for example, rarely obtained in the case of authors with more serious artistic intentions or those with more than a modicum of fame to trade on. The letters and published impressions of better-known and canonized authors are much more accessible than those of the countless unknown authors who dealt with the syndicates, and this imbalance threatens to give only one view of the syndicates. To correct this imbalance, I have whenever possible represented or deduced from other information the experiences of many lesser-known and relatively forgotten authors. After all, as archaeologists will attest, much of the best knowledge about past cultures comes from examining the artifacts left behind in dumps by "common" people rather than those specially chosen items preserved in the burial vaults of esteemed leaders. The result, I believe, is the most complete picture possible of the working relationship between syndicates and authors.

I

Almost all of the fiction used by readyprint firms was taken without payment from other printed sources or was purchased for a small sum from intermediaries for reprinting; as a result, editors of readyprint firms had little direct contact with authors to negotiate compensation or discuss editorial suggestions. Readyprint editors do appear to have had fairly rigid requirements as to what subjects and treatments in fiction they deemed acceptable for publication; the fiction they printed was uniformly moral, avoided sectarian disputes and partisan politics, and usually ended happily.[2] Yet because readyprint companies were rarely the primary market for any author, it is highly unlikely that authors composed their fictions with these guidelines in mind; rather, editors chose for reprinting materials that already met their conditions.

Undoubtedly, few authors celebrated when their work was chosen by a readyprint firm for publication, since these companies had little regard for their artistic and property rights. Editors presumably did not want to contact authors whose property they were usually using without permission, and thus they would not have consulted the authors if they edited the texts or adjusted their length with a pair of scissors; most certainly, authors would not have been allowed to correct proofs or have a say in how and when the published text would appear. What hurt authors most was the way readyprint piracy damaged their financial interests. Readyprint firms did not commonly pay authors for reprint rights and they did not usually attach copyright notices to the fictions they printed. Consequently, the texts were unprotected from further widespread pirated reprintings, for which their authors received no compensation. The humorous story writer Bill Nye summed up his complaint against these firms by writing in 1885, "I am convinced that the value of my 'stuff' is depreciated by the convenience with which it has been gobbled up by every crossroads paper and 'patent inside' in the country."[3] For authors, the only positive effect of being published by a readyprint firm might have been the wide publicity it afforded, which would possibly help sell future works to magazine and book publishers. Surely, though, authors would have preferred direct payment for their artistic labor and protection of their property and creative rights in the texts. Many encomiums about readyprint publishers were written by newspaper editors and readers, but since the benefits these two groups derived from readyprint – cheap copy and comparatively good fiction – came at the expense of authors, it is understandable that no written endorsements by authors have been found.

II

Many plate service providers also distributed reprinted fiction, and thus they dealt with authors in much the same way that readyprint publishers did. The American Press Association (and a few other small concerns), however, operated differently, not only paying for reprint rights but also dealing directly with many authors for first publication rights. Yet because one of the most important selling points of the Association's fiction was its low price – lower even than that of fiction syndicated in galley-proof form – it could only purchase works from beginners or low-level professionals who were desperate to get in print, had few other publishing options, and thus were more willing to accept low wages. Only occasionally did the editors of the Association have to negotiate with famous (and thus more powerful) authors, and in these cases the Association usually bought reprint rights rather than primary rights. These authors, who often submitted advance sheets from their book publishers to the Association, clearly did not regard the Association as their primary market or compose their works with the Association's guidelines in mind. With the more numerous lesser-known authors, however, the Association was able to exert greater control over their work.

For most authors the advantages of syndication by the American Press Association were publicity and income. For those who submitted unsolicited manuscripts from America's hinterlands, syndicated publication represented an opportunity to reach a national audience. The Association understood the dreams of these authors and thus told them in one handbook, "To the author the simultaneous publication of his work in scores of prominent papers in different sections of the country offers the advantage of wide-spread and immediate circulation." Many authors wrote to the Association that they had published their work previously in a local paper but now, in the words of one hopeful, wished to "seek a wider circle of readers." Beginning authors hoped that when their work was published nationally through the Association, it would catch the eye of someone in a book or magazine publishing house in the Northeast and lead to a profitable career in fiction writing. More experienced professional authors believed the publicity might help them to achieve further success with the better-paying magazines or boost sales of their books. In 1891 one commentator concluded that authors were justified in such hopes, writing, "It is worth something to an author to have his name in papers all through the country. If he is a writer for a [plate service] syndicate he gets an advertisement in this way which nothing else could procure for him." In at least one instance the publicity worked; a reader from rural Hoosick Falls, New York, wrote the Association to ask if one syndicated work had been published as a book, because he or she wished to buy a copy.[4]

The plate service companies also offered financial benefits to many authors. A small number of British authors whose works were not in demand by American magazines found they could supplement their incomes with payment from the Association for American serial rights. Most important, though, in a market dominated by British fiction that could be had by newspaper and magazine editors for little or no payment to authors, the Association offered American authors a new and at least reasonably remunerative market for their work. The Association paid much less for fiction than did the large magazines, but it represented a step up from the usual $3–$10 that most unknown authors received from local papers for their short stories. One author's explanation of why he was submitting material to the Association is typical; he wrote, "I have been a regular contributor to the Chicago Daily News for more than a year," but then added that he wished to secure "a foothold with some syndicate that could pay for work more liberally than any one newspaper could." Many aspirants were probably also attracted by the reports that unlike with many magazines, at the Association, "Payment is always made upon acceptance, and manuscripts are passed upon with startling rapidity."[5]

The rates paid by the Association and sought by legions of hopeful contributors were in fact quite modest. In 1887 the Association paid $20 per short story of between 1,500 and 2,500 words, and in the early 1890s it appears to have paid $10 per thousand words for short stories and about $120 total for serials, or roughly what it had been paying in 1887. In the late 1880s these wages had bettered those of most individual urban dailies and equalled those of some of the smaller magazines, but by the mid-1890s, while the Association's rates remained higher than those paid by many individual metropolitan dailies, most magazines paid much more liberally. As the humor writer Opie Read informed the Association in 1893, "lest you think that you are paying to [sic] much, let me say that the *Cosmopolitan* magazine has just paid me three times as much for a story of about the same length."[6]

Beginning writers were not the only ones willing to work for these wages. In the overcrowded literary market of the 1880s, low- to middle-rank professional authors also found the Association a welcome additional source of income. William Wallace Cook (John Milton Edwards) referred to the Association as "Another market for the Edward's [sic] product." In 1895 the Association paid Kate Chopin $5 per thousand words for reprint rights to two of her stories (for a total of $42), which she termed "fair enough compensation," and in 1898 it paid her $70 – the second highest payment she ever received for a short story – for first publication rights to her story "A Family Affair."[7]

In return for these modest publicity and pecuniary advantages, authors had to write fictions that conformed to guidelines established by the Association. Only two fiction authors have been identified who worked under a long-term contract with the Association that bound them to produce a certain number of works meeting specifications dictated by the Association editors. In the majority of cases there was no prior agreement, yet the Association made it clear to authors which subjects and treatments were most acceptable. In their initial contact with the Association, many authors inquired as to the company's guidelines. Most were subsequently sent the Association's style sheet entitled "Styles of Composition." No copies of these guidelines have been found, but the sheet's contents can be inferred from how authors promoted their fictions in their cover letters. In 1891, for instance, one author declared, "There is no crime in it and nothing which could offend any person or class, the prime requisites, as I understand it, in a story for general circulation. I have also of course avoided any tincture of questionable morals, religious, sectional or political intimations." Another noted, "I have complied with the conditions you require, so far as I know them, in the matter of tone and character; i.e. there is no suggestion of a political, religious or sectional nature, no incident of a revolting or unpleasant sort." Besides avoiding displeasing topics and treatments, authors were also expected to make their work exciting. Probably hoping to mirror the treatment suggested by the style sheet, author Will Lisenbee pitched his serial to the Association editors by assuring them it was "full of strange incidents and dramatic situations," and he added that he believed "a newspaper serial should be rapid in movement, and the interest never allowed to flag." If an author failed to adequately follow these guidelines during composition, Association editors appear to have suggested how authors could change their work to make it more acceptable. In response to an editor's remarks regarding his manuscript, for example, one author resubmitted his story and noted, "I suppose I had better kill the villain & send Arizony back to Virginia."[8]

The Association also had fairly rigid guidelines as to the acceptable lengths of short stories and serials. The maximum length for storiettes was 1,200 words, while the desired length for short stories varied somewhat over the years. In 1887 short stories were supposed to be from one to one and one half columns in length (1,500–2,250 words), but by the early 1890s the minimum was 5,000 words and the maximum 6,000 words. In addition, the Association appears to have preferred fairly short serials, anywhere from 30,000 to 60,000 words long.[9]

Some minimal resistance to the length limitations is evident in authors' correspondence with the Association, but most authors seem to have internalized these requirements and either wrote to meet them or passively accepted the editing they knew was necessary to make their works conform. One author spoke in 1896 of his willingness to "saw out chunks [of his story] to the extent of 5,000 words to suit the A.P.A.," and another freely gave her permission to editors to make her work the desired length, writing that she knew her storiette was longer than the 1,200 word limit but adding, "your editor is at liberty to cut it." An examination of many short stories syndicated by the Association indicates that these limits were generally adhered to. Authors also believed they understood the desired length of longer serials and their installments. As one author noted, "I am writing it in installments suitable for your use and should like to submit you the story when it is completed. It will contain 30,000 words, perhaps, for I shall condense it as much as possible." Despite the implication in this letter that the Association required authors to write with specific installment lengths in mind, however, the wide range of actual installment lengths of works the firm distributed, from 1.5 columns (approximately 2,250 words, given the standard length of one newspaper column = 1,500 words) to 5.3 columns (7,950 words), refutes such a hypothesis.[10]

In enforcing the guidelines regarding subject, treatment, and length, editors at the Association do not appear to have drawn the ire of authors. Many beginning authors in fact asked for and welcomed advice from Association editors because they believed it would help them improve as writers and increase the marketability of their fiction. Editors I. D. Marshall and A. A. Hill often took the time to give advice to authors whose manuscripts were accepted or rejected. There are numerous letters from authors thanking these men for their attention; typical is one author who wrote, "It is a great thing for me to have this help, and if the future brings me any great success, I shall know where much of the credit belongs." It is of course difficult to distinguish between genuine gratitude and an obsequious tone adopted to please the editors. Yet in support of the argument that these words were genuine is the significant fact that of all the letters examined, only one contains a complaint from an author about the editing of the Association. Author A. S. Cody explained, "It goes so terribly against my grain to write without the artistic descriptions you so much object to, that I prefer to write them in in the first place and then cut them out with a ruthless sweep of the pencil." In general, though, most authors seem to have enjoyed warm relations with these editors; one wrote to editor Hill, "I appreciate deeply your encouragement," and he was not alone. Further, the common practice of the Association editors in returning galley proofs to the authors for correction indicates at least a passing recognition of the rights of authors to control their texts.[11]

After proofs had been corrected and the work set in type and stereotyped, however, the plate service system allowed the author little control over where, when, and how the fiction text would be used. The Association firmly maintained the right to determine which papers received these texts and approximately when they would be printed. In addition, neither authors nor the Association had any control over how the texts would appear in individual newspapers: editors were free to cut the plates to fit the space available and to place it in the paper wherever they chose. Finally, while the Association copyrighted the fiction it distributed, to what degree it protected their property rights by prosecuting any publishers who pirated this material is unknown.

Compared to readyprint publishers and other plate service companies that obtained almost all of their fiction with a pair of scissors, the Association (and other plate service companies purchasing chiefly original fiction) represented greater opportunity to authors, primarily those on the lower rungs of the literary ladder. The Association offered publicity, a subsistence wage, and some editorial assistance. In exchange for these advantages, however, the Association required authors to adhere to fairly strict guidelines during composition; furthermore, the Association exhibited a general disregard for textual integrity. Judging from the hundreds of aspirants who sent unsolicited manuscripts and the many who were disappointed when their work was rejected, however, it appears that to authors who had little power to negotiate better conditions, the advantages of plate service syndication outweighed the disadvantages.

III

The syndicates that most significantly affected British and American fiction authors in the late nineteenth century were Tillotson's Newspaper Fiction Bureau, McClure's Associated Literary Press, and Irving Bacheller's variously-named companies, all of which distributed original fiction in galley-proof form. These syndicates and others like them dealt with a greater number of famous authors than readyprint and plate service companies and in almost all cases bought original manuscripts directly either from authors or their agents. This closer contact put such syndicates in a position where they had more opportunity to influence the construction of fiction texts, and thus more authors, contemporary commentators, and literary scholars were and have been moved to record their opinions of them.

The received opinion on how these syndicates treated authors is quite negative. Some fiction authors at the time complained that they interfered too much in the composition process, telling them what to write about, how to write it, and what length it should be. Jack London believed he had ascertained what at least one syndicate (probably Tillotson's) demanded of its authors. His fictional character Martin Eden, a struggling literary aspirant much as London had been, studied the works published by one syndicate and concluded: "the newspaper storyette should never be tragic, should never end unhappily, and should never contain beauty of language, subtlety of thought, nor real delicacy of sentiment." Accordingly, to compose a work that would be acceptable, "Martin consulted 'The Duchess' for tone, and proceeded to mix according to formula. The formula consisted of three parts: (1) A pair of lovers are jarred apart; (2) by some deed or event they are reunited; (3) marriage bells. The third part was an unvarying quantity, but the first and second parts could be varied an infinite number of times." He further noted that "In quantity, the formula prescribed twelve hundred words minimum dose, fifteen hundred words maximum dose." British novelist Ouida (Louise de la Ramée) was equally sure of the pernicious effects of syndicates on authors and their texts. In a letter to the London *Times* in 1891, she charged that syndicates transformed authors' selves into products standardized to meet syndicate specifications. She described a syndicate as "an 'immense organization' which treats authors precisely as the Chicago killing and salting establishments treat the pig: the author, like the pig, is purchased, shot through a tube, and delivered in the shape of a wet sheet (as the pig is in the shape of a ham), north, south, east, and west, wherever there is a demand for him."[12] When even these homogenized texts failed to meet approval, some authors complained, the syndicates proceeded to butcher their texts in editing or in printing.

Partially as a result of such statements from authors, many contemporary commentators were equally unkind in their portrayal of the syndicates and their managers. One described S. S. McClure as "the newspaper syndicate man, who buys and sells literature as a market commodity." And, as noted previously, in 1895 Edward Bok, longtime editor of the *Ladies' Home Journal*, condemned the syndicates for transforming the author "into a veritable machine" who "sinks art into trade" in exchange for high wages.[13]

Literary historians have combined these opinions with statements made by the syndicators themselves and concluded that an author who contributed work to the syndicates was no more than an assembly-line worker in a factory where in the name of efficiency the managers (syndicators) did the planning and dictated to workers (authors) how to manufacture (compose) the homogeneous and standardized product (fiction). N. N. Feltes, for example, refers to Tillotson's and the *Bolton Weekly Journal* and concludes, "fiction writers entered their pages as hand-loom weavers entered a factory." S. S. McClure has drawn the most criticism, since he provided numerous statements in his autobiography and elsewhere to sufficiently condemn him as a materialistic boor who treated authors' artistic talents as incidental to literary production. McClure's attitude toward literary artistry and the ancillary role of the author is apparently summed up in his making such remarks as: "To a man of large creative powers the idea is the thing; the decoration of phrase is a very secondary matter"; "Often I was able to suggest to writers a subject profitable to them and to me"; and that "When an author's manuscript becomes sacred, then either the author or the editor is decadent." McClure also boasted of how much he could control production; he frequently referred to "my" authors who wrote "for" him, and on one occasion he told newspaper editors, "I can secure anything I want from almost any writer." Given these statements, it is not surprising that his biographer argues McClure had "the notion that good fiction could be ordered by the pound, like mackerel," and that other scholars have concluded McClure commissioned many fictions for his syndicate. These commissions, curiously enough, are almost invariably portrayed as instruments of authorial oppression. In one case, Stephen Crane made a long-term commitment in 1896 to supply McClure with a series of war stories in return for a secure income, and one commentator has written that while Crane initially "sensed in a generous and naive way that the agreement might be too good," his "naiveté was one day to wither in the discovery that he was in virtual peonage."[14]

Bacheller, too, is sometimes portrayed negatively. One piece of evidence often used to condemn him is his heavy-handed editing of Crane's *The Red Badge of Courage*; Bacheller caused the manuscript to be cut by two-thirds to make it a more plot-driven work (to satisfy newspaper readers) and to fit the length requirements spelled out in his contracts with newspaper editors. Yet, because of his later largesse with Crane, Bacheller has largely avoided the sharper criticism aimed at McClure.[15]

Finally, in cases where no evidence has been found that syndicates enforced strict guidelines, it has been charged that newspaper publication itself forced authors to use inartistic subjects and treatments. Three different commentators on Henry James's story "Georgina's Reasons," for example, have asserted that James's perception of what newspaper readers wanted forced him to write one of his weakest and most sensational stories for publication through Charles Dana's syndicate.[16]

Many of these charges against the galley-proof syndicates, however, have either been taken out of context (in the case of authors' statements) or have been based on little empirical evidence. McClure's braggadocio of self-representation and authors' complaints, for instance, have been allowed to stand as fact without close examination of whether they reflected the true situation of his syndicate. Closer investigation reveals not only that a great number of authors of all levels saw numerous advantages in galley-proof syndicate publication, but also that the weak marketplace position of these syndicates relative to book and magazine publishers made it very difficult for the syndicates to regularize the production of fiction as they may have wanted to; they simply could not afford to be as restrictive with authors as the commonly cited evidence suggests.

IV

Most literary historians have accepted the verdict handed down in *The Cambridge History of American Literature* (1917) that "The [mass-market] magazines were indeed a saving influence in the life of the hard-pressed American author."[17] Authors certainly welcomed these magazines as new and remunerative outlets for their work. Yet the galley-proof syndicates also supported many American authors after the mid-1880s (and British authors beginning in 1873) by providing expanded opportunities for publication and by increasing the overall prices paid for short stories and serials. At a time when the supply of fiction was growing astronomically but many American authors were crowded out of the American magazine and book market by low-cost or free British fiction, these syndicates appeared and began to purchase (at competitive prices) a seemingly endless number of works of American fiction.

The chief reason why American authors had few publishing opportunities in the 1880s was that before the United States entered into an international copyright agreement in 1891, British authors' works were unprotected by American copyright law, and thus American publishers could reprint works from British magazines and books for either very little or no fee. In addition, although the works of American authors were protected in the United States by American copyright law, this tended to hurt their financial position rather than to help it. American book and magazine editors, given the choice between cheap or free British fiction and American fiction for which they would have to pay the author half profits, royalties, or serial right fees, generally chose the British. As just one example of how American authors were effectively shut out of the American market by the cheapness of foreign materials, one can cite Brander Matthews's report that in 1886 only one of the 54 volumes (46 of which were fiction) published in Harper's *Franklin Square Library* was authored by an American. Moreover, before 1891 American authors living in the United States were unprotected by British copyright law, and thus often did not realize the full profits on their works sold there. In 1888 the situation led American author John Boyle O'Reilly to lament "the wretched conditions in which our professional *littérateurs* are left through the cheap reprints and translations of European books"; he added that because of the current state of copyright law, "the literary man, the most defenseless and surely one of the most precious possessions of the country, is literally robbed and disregarded."[18]

The practice common in the literary publishing industry until the late 1880s that also depressed the incomes of many American authors developed out of a policy known as "trade courtesy," first used by American book publishers in the 1820s to minimize the harmful competition among themselves for advance sheets of foreign authors' wares. Under trade courtesy, it was understood that publishers would not try to lure a foreign author away from his or her present publisher with promises of higher fees. Somewhat the same situation obtained with American authors. Donald Sheehan succinctly describes this as "a code of ethics which attempted to place limits on the overtures which a publisher could make to an author already identified with another house"; authors were generally discouraged from shopping for a better wage and switching publishers. While this informal, non-legally-binding understanding was occasionally broken in the scramble for a particularly lucrative author or when an author was very dissatisfied with his or her current publisher, it continued until the 1880s for American authors. One might add that since most of the genteel monthly magazines were affiliated with a book publisher and an author was expected to publish in the magazine connected with his book publisher, authors were under pressure not to submit work to other magazines. Some authors liked trade courtesy because its "rules" informally obligated book publishers to accept works not up to an author's usual standard in order to keep that author in the publisher's fold, and because it relieved the author of the often difficult and time-consuming task of submitting the manuscript to multiple publishers and negotiating the best deal he or she could. Other writers felt inhibited by this loose system. While acknowledging the benefits of trade courtesy for some authors, Susan Coultrap-McQuin concludes that this system "and the aim of noncompetition between publishers over authors actually disadvantaged authors from seeking competitive bids in the marketplace."[19]

With only minimal demand and competition for their short stories and novels, most American fiction authors worked in a very financially insecure environment. Not only did they have problems finding a publisher, but also, since authors could move from one firm to another only with difficulty, there was little reason for publishers to offer authors either advances or contracts for future work. Without such a contract or cash advance, even successful authors usually had to shoulder the burden of living expenses while writing, with the possibility that the publisher might reject a year's worth of work and pay nothing. In addition, authors also frequently had to harrass their book and magazine publishers for payment. Book publishers usually paid only twice a year, at mid-summer and year's end; also, except for the various Harper magazines, magazines usually paid on publication, not on acceptance. Magazine editors frequently accepted a work yet did not publish it for many months, not only delaying payment to authors for the serial publication but also precluding book publication and sales, for books could not be published until after the serial had concluded.

Another principal cause of insecurity for the American author of "serious" fiction until the mid-1880s was the severely limited number of magazine outlets. American fiction authors who desired to steer clear of the undignified story papers and dime novel factories knew there were only a handful of American magazines interested in this type of fiction: *Harper's Monthly*, *Century*, *Scribner's*, and *Atlantic Monthly*. As a result, they were flooded with submissions. One report stated that *Harper's Monthly* received 12,024 manuscripts, half of them poems, between January 1886 and January 1887, and used a total of only 200 of these items. It was also reported that in 1890 the *Ladies' Home Journal* received 15,205 manuscripts of all genres and accepted 497; of these, 300 were solicited in advance. As monthlies, these magazines could publish only a very small number of works of fiction each year; at best they could buy one or two serial novels and a dozen or so short stories. In 1874 Henry James wrote to William Dean Howells, then editor of the *Atlantic Monthly*, "The *Atlantic* can't publish as many stories as I ought and expect to be writing." In 1885 the *Century* simultaneously serialized James's *The Bostonians* and Howells's *The Rise of Silas Lapham*, indicating that Americans were beginning to break into the American magazine market, but this does not mean the market had greatly expanded. For these two authors such publication was a prestigious coup; however, as one scholar has noted, it constituted "a cheerless prospect for those American authors who saw the *Century* closed to their work until the eminent serialists had unwound their plots many months ahead." By 1895, one self-professed "literary hack" argued – probably correctly – that "not one voluntary contribution in fifty had any chance of acceptance in a first-class magazine." Furthermore, even for those whose work was accepted, the financial rewards were not all that large; because of their limited circulation these magazines generally paid high in prestige and low in money.[20]

American authors were not the only ones working in an insecure environment. Readers and editors in the United States previous to the Chace Act of 1891 might have enjoyed reading and publishing works by British authors for a low price, but British authors did not benefit from this. The United States at this time represented a potentially large and lucrative market, but British authors were frustrated by their inability to reap their just rewards from it. The low fees that American publishers were willing to pay for advance sheets of works by the type of authors Tillotson's was marketing before 1891 are indicated in a number of letters from Tillotson and Son to Henry Holt and Co. during this period. Significantly, these letters indicate that the syndicate was forced to adopt a markedly subservient and plaintive tone. In 1885, for example, Tillotson's wrote regarding one series of short stories, "if you had felt £10 to be too large a sum we should have been willing to accept such a sum as you felt justified in offering." Further, one 1889 letter refers to an "honorarium" for one novel and concludes, "We are hoping that your sales of the book will enable you to forward us a handsome remittance." John Maxwell, husband and agent of author Mary Elizabeth Braddon, expressed in an 1885 letter to William Frederic Tillotson sentiments quite common among these authors. Disgusted at the low offer of £20 from *Harper's Magazine* for American serial rights to the Braddon novel *Wyllard's Weird*, he commented satirically, "I am sick – very sick – of such Princely encouragement of literature!"[21]

With the galley-proof syndicates, on the other hand, the chances of the British and American amateur, the professional hack, and the writer with serious artistic intentions were much greater. They were the sole hope for those whose works were not solicited by magazines or stood little chance of being accepted there, and functioned as vital secondary outlets for authors whose works were often published in magazines. For British authors, who faced a crowded domestic magazine market and had been hurt by the American copyright situation before 1891, Tillotson's, and then later, American syndicates, offered new and lucrative outlets, purchasing British, Colonial, and American serial rights to numerous works by British authors. The insecure working conditions for American authors made syndicates especially attractive to them. As Julian Hawthorne concluded in 1888, "if our native authors are not to find an outlet in syndicates, the prospect for them is dark. The magazines are all overstocked, and no author can live on the royalties of his books."[22]

Not only did syndicates need to buy many more manuscripts than the magazines did, but because they were the first to reach a true mass audience by combining a great number of relatively small local newspaper markets, they could usually – until the 1890s – offer higher rates for serial rights to authors than individual newspapers and magazines did. To authors who previously had published only in local metropolitan newspapers or with plate service providers such as the American Press Association, the pay scale of these syndicates represented a marked step up. In the 1880s and early 1890s many commentators acknowledged the potential gold mine the syndicates represented to authors. Probably remarking on the high prices Charles Dana paid Henry James for stories contributed to Dana's syndicate, one report in 1884 stated that "daily papers combine, but magazines cannot, and it is beyond question that ten wealthy, powerful dailies can outbid one magazine, however wealthy, in buying a supply of original fiction." In 1889 one observer concluded, "The result of this [syndication] must be that every author will become a rich man," and publisher Charles Scribner later remembered that in the 1880s, "the authors all expected to become rich on the newspaper syndicates." A few disgruntled authors did complain that the syndicates robbed them of their local newspaper markets; in 1896 one wrote to the American Press Association that "the Bacheller Syndicate has run me out of two places [newspapers] with cheaper and better work."[23] Yet the almost universal response to such complaints was that if a piece of fiction was any good at all, it could find a place in the syndicate and the author could get paid more for it in this way.

Establishing a benchmark for the average amount paid to fiction authors for American magazine work is extremely difficult, since this amount varied widely. In 1884 one report stated that authors were still receiving only about $10 per thousand words of fiction, the same as thirty years earlier, and this is seconded by a scholar who notes that in the 1880s "only quality magazines offered over one cent a word [$10 per thousand words] and standard payment was usually three-fourths of a cent a word [$7.50 per thousand words]." In the 1890s prominent magazines appear to have paid unknown authors only about $5 per thousand words of fiction and well-known authors on average about $7.50 per thousand words.[24] Rates offered British authors – when at all – were probably much less.

In comparison, in the 1880s and early 1890s the syndicates generally appear to have paid much more for fiction. Tillotson's, which usually kept a close watch on what other syndicates and various story papers paid authors, was usually quite liberal with authors' compensation. In 1888 Bret Harte, living in Britain at the time, received £455 (approximately $2,275, computed at the approximate equivalence during this period of £1 = $5) for the American serial rights and all British rights to a 31,000 word story, "The Argonauts of North Liberty." Harte was thus being paid the exorbitant sum of about $73 per thousand words for this short serial, a rate that remained constant for him throughout the 1890s. Not all authors received such princely sums, of course, but it appears that many authors soon saw that Tillotson's was willing to pay high rates for what it wanted. As for Irving Bacheller, Hamlin Garland credited him with being "careful not to overpay his authors," but in 1886 Bacheller, referring to all syndicates – though probably mainly to his own – wrote that syndicates usually paid between $10 and $100 per thousand words for fiction, "depending entirely upon the fame of the author and upon the quantity of matter which he is producing." In December 1884 McClure announced that he would pay authors $20 to $40 per thousand words, and in fact, in November 1884 H. H. Boyesen received approximately $45 per thousand words for the first story McClure syndicated. In 1888 one knowledgeable commentator reported that McClure's syndicate paid only $5 per thousand words to beginning authors, but McClure's office manager John Phillips was probably more accurate when he noted that the syndicate paid average writers between $10 and $20 per thousand words and established authors between $20 and $50 per thousand. For example, in 1889 McClure offered Edward Bellamy $25 per thousand words for Youth's Department short stories. Except in the case of very famous authors, these rates do not appear to have increased over the years; in 1899 McClure paid authors such as Bret Harte and S. R. Crockett £5 (approximately $25) per thousand words for American serial rights. Yet what had seemed generous in the 1880s by this time seemed very low pay. In 1891 McClure could fairly accurately advertise, "I pay the same rates as the regular magazines," but by the late 1890s the rates paid by his syndicate were much lower than those paid by the major magazines.[25] Tillotson's rates, too, failed to remain competitive toward the end of the century.

Authors at the beginning of their careers who were least likely to have their work published in any of the major magazines especially benefited from the opportunity to earn respectable wages from the syndicates. At least one contemporary, though, differed with this assessment, writing in 1887, "Are writers in general benefited by syndicates? I think experienced ones are, but ... the less well-known find market with difficulty." A Tillotson's circular of 1894 also seems to concur: "A story by an unknown writer is of no value; the announcement of a new story by 'Mr. Jones' or 'Mr. Smith' will attract no one." Yet in fact lesser-known authors were welcomed by the syndicates, chiefly because there was a higher profit margin on works by these writers than on works by famous ones. More accurate portrayals of the situation were offered by an editor at the *Journalist* in 1886: "I fancy these syndicates offer a better market for young and aspiring authors than the magazines do," and by William Dean

Howells, who concluded in 1893 that for the lesser-known authors, syndicates "offered perhaps the best market they have had out of book form." It should be noted, for example, that Stephen Crane submitted *The Red Badge of Courage* to Bacheller for syndication as a last resort, only after S. S. McClure had turned it down for use in *McClure's Magazine*. What was written by one contemporary about W. F. Tillotson can be applied to other syndicators as well: "he has not hesitated to take in hand new writers struggling for fame, not a few of whom have reason to be thankful for their association with him."[26]

In many cases, the money these beginning authors earned from syndicates afforded valuable financial support and time necessary to continued artistic development. As the not-so-fictional Martin Eden wrote, probably mirroring the experience of Jack London and numerous other struggling authors, "Then there are the newspaper syndicates, and the newspaper short story syndicates, and the syndicates for the Sunday supplements. I can go ahead and hammer out the stuff they want, and earn the equivalent of a good salary by it ... I don't care to become as they, but I'll earn a good living, and ... Then I'll have my spare time for study and for real work. In between the grind I'll try my hand at masterpieces, and I'll study and prepare myself for the writing of masterpieces." London himself received much encouragement and a stipend from McClure at a critical time in his life to "attempt the novel he felt he couldn't afford to write." Other writers who found that regular employment in one form or another with the syndicates could support them financially at the beginning of their careers were Frank Norris and Stephen Crane. Norris's work for the McClure syndicate from 1898 to late 1899 gave him space and time to work on *McTeague*, and Crane survived the years 1896–1898 in large part because of McClure's and Bacheller's largesse of loans and steady work. Norris wrote to John S. Phillips: "I remember perfectly well that as far as 'getting on' is concerned I practically owe you everything ... I owe my start to you and whatever measure of success I have achieved so far. You have made it so easy for me that I shall always remember my first experiences in New York as some of the pleasantest years of my life – whereas they might have been the hardest." In 1895 Bacheller financed the Western travels of Crane that later yielded many of his best stories, and Crane was able to find time to write *The Third Violet* in late 1895 and early 1896 chiefly because of the income he gained from syndicate work. Further, while Crane would later speak disparagingly of McClure as a "Scotch ass" and write to friends that he felt entrapped by his agreement with McClure, in January 1896 he had a different opinion and wrote to him, "I think the agreement with you [for a series of stories] is a good thing. I am perfectly satisfied with my end of it."[27]

Authors already well-known also reaped great financial benefits from the syndicates, which had to outbid the magazines to obtain their work. For example, Henry James, who in the 1870s was accustomed to receiving approximately $100–$150 from *Scribner's* or *Atlantic* for one of his short stories, was shocked when syndicator Charles Dana in the summer of 1884 offered to pay him $1,100 - $1,200 each for two short stories. James consequently wrote to his friend Thomas Bailey Aldrich in February 1884 that the stories had "been, in a word, secured, *à prix d'or* in – je vous en donne en mille [I give the price to you in thousands] – the New York Sunday *Sun!*" For James, the amount paid by Dana increased his earnings from American serial rights in 1884 to $4,815, the second highest yearly amount in this category he would ever earn, and it helped make 1884 the third most financially lucrative year of his career.[28]

Robert Louis Stevenson was another author shocked by the high prices syndicates – in his case S. S. McClure's Associated Literary Press – could pay for his work. One literary historian has written that despite his success, Stevenson's "income from writing [from 1870 to 1887] was not enough to support him," and another has noted that in 1886 and 1887 Stevenson had made very little money from American publication of his work because pirates had robbed him. McClure's offer in 1887 of $500 for rights to syndicate Stevenson's story "The Black Arrow," which had appeared four years earlier in Britain, thus pleasantly surprised Stevenson and represented much more equitable compensation for his labor. Stevenson, despite his frequent complaints about McClure's haggling over terms, always knew that McClure was invaluable to his economic survival. In 1892 Stevenson chastised his friend Charles Baxter for causing discord with McClure, writing, "he has put a vast deal more money into my hand than ever I had before ... I would advise you if possible to avoid actual hostilities with the little man, whom you may still find useful."[29]

Other famous authors whose pockets the syndicates lined with gold included Wilkie Collins, Mark Twain, Rudyard Kipling, and

Arthur Conan Doyle. Tillotson's payment of £1,300 to Wilkie Collins for *The Evil Genius*, according to one biographer, "was almost certainly the largest figure he ever received for serial rights." In May 1891, after Twain had already accepted an offer of $6,000 for the American serial rights to *The American Claimant* from Bok of the *Ladies' Home Journal*, McClure entered the bidding and secured British and American serial rights from Twain for $12,000. McClure also outbid *Scribner's* for a Kipling serial, offering either $20,000 or $25,000 compared to the $16,000 that Charles Scribner offered. Irving Bacheller bettered magazine rates, too, in one instance obtaining a series of short stories from Arthur Conan Doyle despite his long-term arrangement to offer his work first to Sir George Newnes of the *Strand* magazine. In 1894 Bacheller visited Conan Doyle in England and found him unwilling to sell his work for first publication, but when he offered Doyle £30 ($150) per thousand words instead of the £15 paid by Newnes, Bacheller recalled, "That mortgage [with Newnes] was breaking loose. It [the offer] had begun to act like a lifting cloud."[30]

In addition to offering popular authors more for the works that they could publish in magazines if they chose, syndicates constituted a lucrative secondary market for the work that they did not wish to or could not place with their primary magazine publishers. In general, Edward Bok was correct when he charged that "the higher-class authors do not first offer their best wares to the newspaper syndicates: they employ them either as a last resort or as a 'special channel' for 'a certain class of their work.'" Occasionally, it is true, the syndicates were the last resort for these authors. For example, Mary E. Wilkins wrote to Harper and Brothers regarding the British serialization of her novel *Pembroke*, "If no other disposal of it can be made [to a magazine], I am quite willing it should be published by a syndicate." In addition, Stephen Crane viewed Tillotson's as a ready source of cash for his lesser works. Living in a large manor house in England at the turn of the century, Crane had enormous expenses and was in dire financial straits. To obtain enough money to pay his creditors Crane wrote a great number of fictions, many of which were below his usual level of quality. To market some of these works he turned to Tillotson's and sold various rights in eight stories for a total of £193 1 sh., or approximately $965.[31]

Just as often, however, well-known authors regarded the fictions they submitted to the syndicates highly and chose to publish through them chiefly because they knew their primary publishers could not print everything they wrote. Mary E. Wilkins, for example, in 1891 had pledged all of her adult fiction to Harper and Brothers for both magazine and book publication, but was very happy to have McClure pay a large fee for the right to syndicate her children's stories. As one scholar notes, "for that work she insisted upon and received higher and higher payments," and by 1894 the Bacheller, Johnson, and Bacheller firm was paying her the high rate of $50 per 1,000 words for her secondary fiction (this is the same rate it was paying Sarah Orne Jewett for a similar grade of stories). In addition, when the literary publishing community was clamoring for more Sherlock Holmes stories from the pen of Arthur Conan Doyle, McClure was willing to pay high prices for his other work (which Doyle regarded as artistically superior to the Holmes stories). McClure bought Doyle's *The White Company* for $375, even though few newspaper editors wanted it, paid him £40 ($200) for American serial rights to "The Doings of Raffles Haw," and in 1892 even paid Doyle £15 each ($75) for his short sketches under the title, "In a Physician's Waiting Room." Robert Louis Stevenson also benefited from the high fees McClure paid him for his comparatively lightweight South Seas Letters. It is doubtful that any magazine could have published nearly as many of these letters as McClure was able to, and while McClure took a financial drubbing from this deal, the money Stevenson earned from it helped him buy a yacht, pursue his dream of sailing to the South Pacific, and construct a house in Samoa. As Stevenson wrote in 1890, of all his current work "the letters [are the] most remunerative."[32]

Tillotson's also bought numerous works that authors liked but which for one reason or another they could not place with magazines. Mary Elizabeth Braddon was a popular British author whose works frequently appeared in both British and American magazines. Yet between 1873 and 1893 she chose to sell serial rights in 23 short stories and novels to Tillotson's (primarily for newspaper syndication) for a total of £8,925 or approximately $44,625, quite a large sum. Bret Harte also was a very prolific writer and found Tillotson's an important outlet for some of his work; he sold the firm worldwide English-language serial rights to 14 short stories and short novels for £1,412, or approximately $7,060.[33]

Besides offering higher direct payments to authors for their fiction, syndicates might have indirectly helped raise authors' incomes by increasing the overall demand for their work and promoting competition among magazine editors (and other syndicators) for it. The very presence of syndicates in the marketplace, William Dean Howells asserted, "no doubt advanced the prosperity of the short story by increasing the demand for it."[34]

Finally, a financial advantage some syndicates appeared to promise – but which in general did not regularly materialize – was payment on acceptance. Many authors during this period were unhappy with the common practice among magazine editors of accepting a manuscript and then holding it for months before publication and payment. Some authors unwilling or unable to wait took their manuscripts to the syndicates for a faster return on their work. In the fall of 1884 McClure offered authors a choice of payment plans: they could either receive "a guaranteed price & 90 per cent of receipts when in excess of [the] price" or "a fixed cash price *at once*." Tillotson's contracts with authors usually stipulated partial payment upon delivery of the first one-third or one-half of the manuscript and the remainder upon completion of the work. However, the more common practice of these syndicates was to delay paying authors until the receipts from newspapers had been collected. Bacheller, who one author said paid on acceptance in 1888, offered Arthur Conan Doyle "cash on delivery of the manuscript" in 1894; yet by 1897 he was often behind in payments to authors. McClure wrote that in 1885, "I got along by paying my authors $10 or $20 on account ... my actual working capital was the money I owed authors. I made no secret of this, and the men who wrote for me were usually willing to wait for their money, as they realized that my syndicate was a new source of revenue which might eventually become very profitable to them." As time went on, however, many authors complained about late payment. As early as August 1885, Sarah Orne Jewett wrote to McClure, "if I do any more work for you I must have my regular price and be paid at once ... Oughtn't you to have put a safe and profitable business in good order by this time? ... You see, it [McClure's unbusinesslike behavior] troubles your writers and makes them lose a little confidence." John Maxwell summed up the frustration some authors felt at being kept waiting when he wrote to W. F. Tillotson, "My wife [Mary Elizabeth Braddon] does not like the position involved in having to wait while you gather in your harvest [receipts]. She thinks the position is alike unprofessional and undignified."[35]

V

Besides direct financial reward, authors were attracted to syndicate publication for the great quantity of publicity it afforded. As one contemporary put it, the author benefited from syndication because "his name appears simultaneously in one hundred leading newspapers, thus presumably enhancing his reputation, and certainly giving his work a conspicuous opportunity to be read and admired." Another observer argued that in the United States syndicates could introduce authors "to a larger circle of readers than they could obtain through any magazine, or book." For authors whose works were syndicated by Tillotson's, the audience was especially large. As one 1885 report in the *Saturday Review* stated, these authors' "wares are vended in the remotest parts of the antipodean world ... no longer confined to the centres of civilisation or the limited areas of railway and postal enterprise." Moreover, syndication by Tillotson's was known to expand an author's exposure among persons of lower socioeconomic classes. In 1889 one writer argued that in accepting an offer from Tillotson's the author found that he "lost none of his old readers and gained hosts of new ones; for not only was he read in thousands of homes where his name would never otherwise be heard, but he was talked about and thoroughly well advertised." The authors of all these comments might have had Britain, India, and Australia foremost in their minds, but they could easily have been describing how Tillotson's increased authors' exposure in the United States. McClure, like the others, understood the potential value of such publicity to authors and used it to help him obtain contributions; in September 1885 he enticed authors with the claim that syndication was "a method of publication that gives an author four times the audience afforded by the largest magazines." Author Octave Thanet (Alice French) apparently agreed, telling McClure in 1892 that she would not raise her asking prices to the level of what she received from magazines, explaining, "We will take the extra money out in '*boom*' [publicity]. You are the best of boomers." Finally, an 1895 article about Mary E. Wilkins's story "The Long Arm," syndicated by Bacheller, concluded: "Her latest effort has been more widely commented on than any previous production" that had appeared in magazine or book form.[36]

For beginning authors, the publicity generated by syndication was frequently invaluable in launching or boosting their careers.

McClure can be credited with having given a number of the period's most popular authors their first national American exposure. An 1893 report accurately concluded that McClure "had the discernment in some cases and the good luck in others to establish connections with rising authors at the happy moment when they were about to step across the threshold of fame. He helped them and they helped him." Frank Norris, for example, who is described by one literary historian as "one of the young writers whom McClure 'discovered' during his meteoric career," used the syndicate to reach beyond the regional audience that publication in the *Wave* magazine of San Francisco had given him. McClure was especially successful in discovering young British authors and giving their work its first major publication in the United States; one 1897 report noted that McClure's "powerful syndicate enterprise ... introduced to the larger American public the British novelists – such as Stevenson, Kipling, Barrie, Crockett, Ian Maclaren, Stanley Weyman, and Conan Doyle – who today divide the literary world among themselves."[37]

McClure was not alone in giving unknown authors needed publicity. Bacheller discovered in his first visit to authors' homes that a few well-established authors such as Oliver Wendell Holmes and John Greenleaf Whittier "had no desire for the publicity I offered," but most authors welcomed it. Stephen Crane realized the power of the Bacheller syndicate shortly after it distributed *The Red Badge of Courage* in December 1894: seemingly overnight the previously unknown Crane found himself nationally famous, and he was pleasantly surprised to receive letters from as far away as California in response to this work.[38]

What most authors hoped to gain from this publicity was help in obtaining a hearing with book and magazine publishers, along with a lever to increase their book royalties and magazine serial prices. An independent report of 1889 noted that "There is an [British] authoress now so full of orders from publishers that she cannot work fast enough. She was first made known to them through [syndicated] newspaper success." One commentator also argued in 1887 that publication through Tillotson's meant the author's "fame increased and relying upon that fact he could make better terms for each successive book not only with Messrs. Tillotson and Son, but with the book publishers." Many beginning authors used syndicate publication as an entrée to other publishing firms. Stephen Crane, for one, "regarded [his newspaper success with *The Red Badge of Courage*] as the best ground for putting himself forward" with the book publisher D. Appleton; instead of appearing as an unpublished, unknown author, Crane could show the firm's editors printed clippings of his abbreviated novel and published reports of his reception at the offices of the Philadelphia *Press* as a rising star of American literature.[39] Book publishers were likely more attracted to authors who had achieved such syndicate success because the syndicates saved them risking their capital on these unknowns before finding out if there was an audience for their work.

In addition, already well-known authors used the publicity generated by syndicate publication as a bargaining chip to increase their rates of compensation elsewhere. Robert Louis Stevenson, for example, credited McClure's "offers – [as] the first thing to make me raise my charges [with other publishers]." Frances Hodgson Burnett also tried to use the syndicate option to her advantage. Her biographer writes that Burnett's husband wrote to Frank Doubleday at Scribner's "that he had Frances' consent to offer it [*Giovanni and the Other*] to *Scribner's Magazine* and mentions an offer 'made for it by a syndicate' [McClure's], obviously in an attempt to get Scribner's to improve their terms." Finally, part of Henry James's motivation for selling two stories to Charles Dana in 1884 was to prove to book and magazines publishers that he could write something that would appeal to a mass audience and thus strengthen his argument for higher pay. In February 1884 James wrote to Thomas Bailey Aldrich that the prospect of these two stories being syndicated in June and July made him "expect to be in the enjoyment of a popularity which will require me to ask $500 a number for the successive instalments of *The Princess Casamassima*."[40]

Some authors also believed that syndicate publicity could help increase sales of their books. Whether or not this belief was borne out by fact is uncertain and probably will remain so, but at least in the 1880s some members of the literary community believed it would. In 1886 one commentator wrote, "The sale of a novel, it is commonly said, is not injured by having been issued as a newspaper serial." An editor at the St. Paul *Pioneer-Press* opined in 1885 regarding Henry Harland's syndicated novel *Mrs. Peixada*, "We doubt not that its publication in our paper will tend to increase its sales in book form, rather than otherwise." Such also appears to have been the case in Britain, where one writer stated that syndication "advertises his [the author's] new book in a great many districts, and so promotes its sale." To help sell both the syndicated fiction and the author's other books, syndicates regularly provided editors with short notices listing these books and a few paragraphs of the author's biography; these were often printed in newspapers directly under or next to the author's name. Yet one can also understand how some book publishers might have worried about the prospective sales of a book such as Joel Chandler Harris's *Plantation Pageants* (1899), first syndicated by McClure; one New Orleans newspaper review of it began, "Mr. Harris' new book was so extensively circulated through the south in the guise of a newspaper serial, that it is a work of supererogation to describe or even to praise it. Everybody knows all about it ..." On the other hand, master promoter Mark Twain believed syndicate publication would help boost sales of the cheap paperback version of his *The American Claimant*; he wrote to Fred Hall that in order to maximize sales, this edition "should issue a little before the last instalment appears in newspapers."[41]

Overall, a statement made about William Morris Colles of the Authors' Syndicate can be applied to almost all authors who contributed work to American and British galley-proof syndicates: "Those who stuck with Colles did so usually for various self-serving reasons, such as to raise their prices, to play one publisher against another, or to extend their markets into areas where they had no previous entrée."[42] Clearly, such syndicates offered authors many advantages, and these made it unnecessary to twist their arms in order to force them to contribute work.

CHAPTER 5

What price must authors pay? The negotiations between galley-proof syndicates and authors

> There would be any amount of blood in the pages but the slaughtering should be of a practical kind and a large amount of rough-cast morality could be worked in ... That sort of work might with advantage be syndicated in America. If you think anything of the notion would you kindly give me (a) your most preferred size and (b) your rates. The story could be compressed or pulled out to suit.
> Rudyard Kipling, letter to S. S. McClure, [1890]

> Syndicate managers, like all others who are buying literary material, find that they can not always secure just what they want.
> "Literary Syndicates," *The Editor*, 1896[1]

The question that naturally arises from the discussion of the previous chapter is, how much of their artistic autonomy and property rights did authors have to sacrifice in return for the advantages that galley-proof syndicates offered? Authors who wrote for dime novel firms had to surrender almost complete control of their work, and the high wages paid by both British and American mass-market magazines in the 1890s appear to have come with fairly burdensome editorial strings attached. To what extent, though, did these conditions obtain among galley-proof syndicates? Did syndicates and their editors indirectly or directly dictate strict limits of subject, treatment, and length of the manuscript, forcing authors to turn out a bland, standardized product? Did syndicates control the pace of artistic production by stipulating and enforcing the delivery date of solicited manuscripts? And once these manuscripts were in the hands of syndicate editors, how much control did authors have over how they were edited and when, where, and how they were eventually published? Finally, to what degree were authors' property rights in their texts protected by the syndicates?

I

What should first be recognized is that although galley-proof syndicates often "contracted for" works from certain authors, there is no evidence that they had any authors under long-term contracts for multiple works that unduly restricted their authorial freedom. In fact, one advantage of syndication not mentioned previously was that it allowed authors a broad range of contractual arrangements. For many authors a contract for a single future, unwritten work, or a standing offer for one's work from a syndicate, was welcomed as a guarantee of income. Edgar "Bill" Nye expressed to S. S. McClure his hope that "if all my writing could be done for your syndicate ... both the writer and the papers [would] be protected from the paste pot and scissors fiends" who were stealing and reprinting his work without paying him. Rudyard Kipling recalled, "I liked and admired McClure more than a little ... Nor did I like him less when he made a sporting offer to take all my output for the next few years at what looked like fancy rates" (Kipling did not accept this offer). Other authors wished, though, to steer clear of such commitments. Tillotson's attempted to restrict authors with contractual clauses that required authors to give the firm first refusal of newspaper serial rights to future works for a period of five years. Most authors, however, balked at this, and the clause was usually deleted from contracts. In fact, authors acted more like independent suppliers to Tillotson's, making individual arrangements for each work rather than accepting a single, standardized contractual agreement imposed by Tillotson's. One of the firm's ledgers is strong testimony to this: each fiction is listed separately, and next to the column entitled "Restrictions by Publisher [Tillotson's]" is a column entitled "Powers and Restrictions by Author," to remind the syndicate of what they could and couldn't do with the work.[2]

What guidelines existed for the production and acceptance of fiction within the galley-proof syndicate system? Syndicators clearly understood that most newspaper fiction was published in weekend editions intended for reading by the whole family – including the women readers so important to advertisers; this knowledge influenced both their ideals and their requirements for fiction. S. S. McClure could have been speaking for all syndicators when in 1891 he wrote to editors that "To be of the greatest profit, this fiction should interest the whole family, both older and younger members."[3] The desire to appeal to this national family audience, in conjunction with the individual syndicators' personal religious beliefs, would seem to have prompted syndicate guidelines that excluded fiction which might offend any readers by being lurid, morally or religiously depraved, biased against any one political interest group, or ending unhappily. In most cases fictions met these guidelines, but the negotiations between authors and syndicates reveal that syndicates sometimes bent these guidelines because they wanted to or because authors held more of the power of production.

William Frederic Tillotson, S. S. McClure, and Irving Bacheller, along with key editors in their employ such as William Brimelow and John S. Phillips, were all described as having relatively strong religious beliefs, and these appear to have had some influence on which fictions were accepted. One literary historian has described William Frederic Tillotson – a teetotaler – as "a leading Congregationalist and Sunday School worker ... [who] held strong views as to the tone of all material in his own papers and the family newspapers that were his clients," and his editor William Brimelow served as a minister in the Independent Methodist Church. In one famous instance Tillotson and Brimelow deemed the text of Thomas Hardy's *Too Late Beloved* (later known as *Tess of the d'Urbervilles*) "unfit for publication in a family newspaper" and asked Hardy to alter its text to make it less prurient, irreligious, and hopeless. A short time after this episode, Hardy submitted a précis of a new novel, in which he indicated that now he knew very well what would please Tillotson's: "There is not a word or scene in the tale which can offend the most fastidious taste; & it is equally suited for the reading of young people, and for that of persons of maturer years." As indicated by a 1911 circular, the type of fiction Tillotson's desired remained the same for many years: "we find confirmation of our past policy, and encouragement to rely for success on fiction which shall be domestic without being mawkish, sensational without being vulgar, and in close correspondence with human nature, yet entirely wholesome."[4]

Bacheller, a Universalist who preferred upbeat American literature, also had high moral ideals for the literature he wanted to syndicate. In 1886 he expressed his belief that "if the great public can get hold of the wholesome productions of literary genius, it will thank God for deliverance from the reign of rot." McClure, too, was quite religious and thus in principle did not want to distribute any fiction that was too sensational or immoral. In 1886 he described his syndicate as "a powerful agency in destroying the market for vile literature," and in 1890 he wrote of his syndicate work, "Never before have I so longed to serve God and to put my work in harmony with him." Also in 1886, McClure sent a standardized style sheet that set more specific limits. His "Instructions to Young Writers intending to write for prizes or for publication in the McClure Syndicate of Newspapers" told authors that in acceptable stories "the literary character and moral tone of the stories must be unexceptionable," and that "Stories of a lower standard, and *merely* sensational [would] not be accepted." Like almost every other editor of the period, McClure disliked depressing endings or realism that was too stark or atheistic. When he did publish a novel by a writer like Emile Zola (*The Dream* [1888]), he took pains to tell editors that the novel "shall be of absolute purity," and included a statement from Zola himself that "Le roman est d'une chastité absolue et qui pourra être mis dans les mains de toutes les jeunes filles."[5] Even if authors were not always directly told that fiction suitable for reading in the national family circle had the greatest chance of acceptance, the tone set by these men probably made the point.

These syndicators not only said they wanted authors to write about pure subjects in a morally inoffensive way, but they also often indicated that they wished authors to steer clear of politically divisive subjects and to supply action-packed fictions that captured and kept the hurried newspaper reader's interest. Some sensitivity to explicitly political fiction on Tillotson's part is implied in one letter from author Justin McCarthy, who was also a prominent politician. He told W. F. Tillotson in 1884, "You may safely reassure your client [an editor]. The novel I am writing for you will not contain one single allusion to political affairs." In the United States the major source of concern was whether the fiction would offend Southern newspaper editors, and thus McClure advised authors in 1886: "no stories calculated to excite sectional feeling between the North and South, or to arouse any class prejudices, will be used." McClure also told authors, "stories will be accepted because they are thoroughly interesting, pure, and well-written." His definition of "well-written" usually coincided with what he and the newspaper editors with whom he dealt found "interesting" and can be ascertained from his advertisement of Frank Stockton's *The Cosmic Bean* to editors: "Absorbing incidents, dramatic situations, episodes of love and intrigue, and passages of sparkling dialogue follow in rapid succession, ...

[making it] a story that is in every way adapted for serial publication in newspapers." McClure was certainly not alone in his belief that a successful serial "dashes along at a lively pace ... [with] few descriptions and no extraneous matter that does not bear upon the plot."[6]

Having a vested interest in the production of works that met these standards, all syndicates occasionally suggested to authors that they produce works with the most marketable subjects and treatments. Bacheller or his assistant Arthur Stedman clearly recommended subjects and treatments to authors in their letters of solicitation. Sarah Orne Jewett, for example, wrote to Stedman regarding one solicited story, "I chose this scheme rather than one or two others which I had in hand, bearing in mind Mr. Bacheller's special message about 'action & excitement.'" Bacheller or Stedman at various times also suggested subjects to Mary E. Wilkins, such as a "New England juvenile story," a detective story for a prize contest, or a sequel to her story "Comfort Pease and Her Gold Ring." McClure, too, often suggested to famous authors a topic or general treatment, such as a children's story, a story for young girls, or something in the vein of the author's previous work.[7]

Despite suggesting subjects and treatments to authors, however, there is little evidence that syndicates were able to force authors to accede to their suggestions and write works about subjects and with treatments they didn't like. In the case of Charles Dana and Henry James, for example, James may have chosen the subjects and treatments he did to satisfy what he supposed the newspaper reading audience wanted, but there is no proof that Dana suggested or enforced such guidelines. In fact, judging from James's letters to his friends in February and March 1884, it appears that Dana had already guaranteed James the large fee for two of his stories in advance, no matter what the subject or treatment.

Thomas Hardy, too, tailored one work to fit what he supposed was the British provincial newspaper audience that Tillotson's served, but he did so without any prompting from the firm. He described one fiction, "The tale is of a light discursive nature. Whether my single eye to the Bolton Journal has influenced the writing I cannot tell, but I naturally contemplated a provincial public." As a result of his writing for this envisioned audience – which he believed less sophisticated and more conservative than the London audience – Hardy assured there would be "No cutting required. every [sic] won

[sic] can be circulated freely in schools & families – nay, in nurseries." Tillotson's did not tell him to write with this audience in mind, however; in fact, the work was circulated in London and other major cities. The minimal involvement of Tillotson's in directing the subject matter of works is also indicated both by the fact that *Too Late Beloved* was turned down only *after* type had already been set for it, and by employee John Nayler's recollection that in contracts with authors, "No reference was made as to the nature of the story."[8]

Bacheller also lacked the power to force famous writers in this way. Mary E. Wilkins was at first reluctant to write a detective story for Bacheller's prize contest in 1895, but she eventually wrote it willingly as an experiment. When Wilkins wished, she could successfully rebuff Bacheller's or Stedman's suggestions; for instance, in December 1895 she wrote to Stedman, "No, I cannot write the other chapter of Comfort Pease ["Comfort Pease and Her Gold Ring"], this Jan. I am sorry, but you don't know how busy I am, and such wretched weather it is, to work in, too." Further, despite the assertion of Richard Cary that with her tale "A Dark Night" Sarah Orne Jewett "yielded to the importunities of the Bacheller Syndicate, turning out this conformable tale" that included "a systematic plot, dauntless and dastardly characters, titillating contingencies, unfamiliar terrain, and mandatory romantic denouement," the subject of this story was not forced on her. David Green argues that in this story – which included many elements of her later novel *The Tory Lover* – "Miss Jewett was trying her hand, on a small scale, at the kind of historical romance or adventure story she had long wished to attempt."[9] Although Jewett was not writing in her usual local color vein, as Bacheller and the market might have expected her to, Bacheller accepted her experiment in historical romance and distributed it. Bacheller also supported other authors who wanted to experiment with subjects and treatments that the public was not used to receiving from them; in 1894 and 1895, for instance, he accepted Hamlin Garland's Western local color stories and Crane's Western sketches.

McClure, too, was generally unsuccessful in ordering fiction on specific subjects and with certain treatments for the syndicate. When well-known authors felt uncomfortable with a suggested subject, they were able to refuse to write a fiction about it and still continue to work for McClure. McClure in fact usually played the weaker role in negotiations with famous authors regarding subject choice. A typical instance illustrating this point occurred when in 1890 McClure solicited Frank Stockton to write a children's story "for" him, to which Stockton replied, "I have nearly given up writing for children." One might interpret this to mean that Stockton no longer wished to write this type of story and had moved on to other subjects. Yet Stockton qualified his statement by adding, "but I expect *occasionally* to do something of the kind, and if you have five hundred dollars to devote to that purpose, I will write you for it, one of my old style fairy tales." Furthermore, just one year later, in response to another request from McClure for a children's story, Stockton wrote, "I have no story, for young people, but if I should have one, I will let you know."[10] In both cases, Stockton remained firmly in control of his subject matter.

In addition, although syndicates occasionally suggested subjects and treatments to authors, such suggestions often could be so broadly interpreted that they only very slightly impinged on authors' freedom in this area. Bacheller's and McClure's suggestions as to subject and treatment were often quite vague. Bacheller's requests that Mary E. Wilkins write "a New England juvenile story" or a detective story, or McClure's requests of Frank Stockton for a "humorous" story and Mark Twain for a "boy's story" do not appear overly restrictive, since the specific subjects and treatments were left to the authors. The less famous authors who had few publishing options and were more desperate to have their work accepted probably closely followed the specific guidelines of style sheets and crafted texts that conformed to their limitations. However, for those authors whose work the syndicates greatly desired and who stood a good chance of having their fiction published in magazines, the guidelines suggested by the syndicates were much more flexible. An idea of how McClure made his suggestions to these authors is glimpsed in numerous letters of solicitation he wrote to them. Typical is the one he sent to Joel Chandler Harris in September 1885, in which he asked, "Now you had an immense story in the last 'Youth's Companion'. Can't you do me one like that?"; he then added, "You couldn't give me a short story (5000) Christmas story, could you? I need 300 stories, and I could use every story you are a mind to write."[11] Rather than sounding like editorial edicts, McClure's requests sound like pleas for help. Quite frequently, too, McClure simply asked famous authors to give him their "next" stories or novels, with no preconditions attached. Finally, authors who submitted advance sheets of their novels to syndicates clearly did not regard them as their primary markets or write with their needs in mind.

Contrary to what one might expect, some authors in fact welcomed the suggestions made by syndicators or their editors, especially early in their careers when they were learning what types of fiction were most in demand by various publications. To many beginning writers, McClure's style sheet might have represented valuable advice rather than a dictatorial document which overly restricted their artistic choices. One author probably spoke for many others when he wrote in 1888 that he appreciated how hard the syndicator (in this case Bacheller) worked to learn the newspaper market, which made him the source of "suggestions which otherwise would never have occurred to the author" and capable of sparing the author "the loss of producing what may be valueless." Stephen Crane, for example, may have later complained about what he saw as an agreement with McClure that confined him to writing war stories, but when he was just starting out and in need of a steady income he wrote to McClure, "I think it will be of great advantage to me to have you invent subjects for me." In the one case I have discovered where McClure directly commissioned a work, the author was certainly happy enough to oblige. Elizabeth Stuart Phelps remembered that she and her husband, Herbert Ward, "were engaged [by McClure] to write these [biblical] novels for a special purpose, and with a special cast and coloring." Yet rather than rail against the subject and treatment guidelines, Phelps reminds her readers, "The one thing which serial publication does *not* require is less art," and she appears proud of the work.[12]

Finally, the most conclusive evidence that syndicates did not overly control the production of fiction and enforce homogeneous in-house styles is the great diversity in subject and treatment of the fictions they distributed. Contrary to the character Martin Eden's assessment of all syndicated fiction as formulaic romances, for example, Tillotson's distributed many adventure stories, and the two Jack London stories syndicated by Tillotson's and which have been located violate every element of the formula Eden had deduced the syndicate wanted. These stories – "The Unmasking of the Cad" and "The Grilling of Loren Ellery" – are biting, thought-provoking satires of the stereotypical love story and criticize the way men falsify themselves in courtship; both end with a decided movement away from wedding bells and conventional happiness. In addition, despite Tillotson's religious background and Ouida's reputation as an author of morally suspect fiction, the firm syndicated many of her works. One can point to Tillotson's refusal of Hardy's *Tess of the d'Urbervilles* and see him as a strict moralist, but one can also note the firm's publication of Zola's *The Dream* (1888), which was sufficiently risqué to elicit a bishop's libel suit.[13]

Many works syndicated by Tillotson's were also overtly political, usually in support of the type of Liberal causes William Frederic Tillotson advocated both in the community and in his own plant. Lord Wingfield's *The Haven of Unrest* (1881) was advertised as a novel which "will deal with a National Institution urgently requiring improved administration – Lunatic Asylums. It will, therefore, be in the best sense a Novel with a purpose and a mission, viz. to inform and arouse public opinion on Lunacy Reform." An advertisement for Compton Reade's *Under Which King* (1884) said it would address "the Question of the Hour, the Enfranchisement of the Agricultural Labourer, a leading purpose of the Author being to promote Hodge's political and social welfare." Tillotson's in general promoted the political novel – and there were many about Lancashire mill workers – because it had "vitality and strength which lift it above the merely sensational competitors."[14] Whether these fictions reached the United States, and if they did, whether they had any meaning for American readers, is unknown. Overall, though, one can see that Tillotson's – at least before 1889 and William Frederic Tillotson's death – did not make all authors conform to dictated subject and treatment requirements.

Bacheller, too, provided works from a wide variety of genres: he syndicated foreign adventure stories, love stories, war stories, local color stories, stories of the fantastic, detective stories, historical romances, and even some works of mild urban realism. Most had happy endings, but many lacked the fast-paced action and sensationalism that most editors believed the average newspaper reader wanted. All of the stories by Sarah Orne Jewett that Bacheller syndicated ended happily, for example, but most were slow-paced and lacking in any material that could be labeled sensational. In addition, an examination of just twenty stories Bacheller circulated in 1895 shows that only roughly half had exciting incidents at the end of each installment or concluded happily. In 1886 Bacheller syndicated "The Scab's Fate," about poor workers, and "Old Sandy" (subtitled "A Chapter in the Life of the Poor"), both of which ended unhappily. And in 1897 the firm syndicated a story by Ruth McEnery Stuart that reminded readers at its beginning, "It is sad to be little and poor and black, and to have no relations. It is sad at any time, but on Christmas it seems even worse." It would thus be inaccurate to accuse Bacheller of being a literary broker who always played it safe.[15]

McClure also had strong opinions about what type of fiction was most marketable, but he did not accept and distribute only those stories that conformed to these beliefs. He learned quickly that no single type of fiction was likely to satisfy all editors, and as a result he offered stories on a wide variety of subjects and with various treatments. His list over the years included stories such as "Edy Adkins, Story of a Slave," works of urban realism by Amélie Rives ("A Story of the Life of Child Workers") and Emile Zola, numerous detective stories, foreign adventures, historical romances, and works of the fantastic.

Furthermore, McClure does not appear to have condescended or catered solely to the mass readers and offered only lowbrow, sensational fiction with happy endings that might have better guaranteed sales. Instead, he occasionally went against what he perceived as market tastes and purchased works that offered subjects and treatments unlikely to meet with popular approval, yet which he felt were important. For example, he syndicated a number of works by George Meredith despite having been told that his "novels were ... quite unattainable to the man of average intelligence." As seen earlier, too, McClure accepted the non-Sherlock Holmes stories of Conan Doyle at a time when he knew readers wanted more of Holmes. McClure also purchased W. D. Howells's *The Quality of Mercy* (1891), even though he believed it would probably not be a popular choice. Shortly after it was published, McClure was clearly relieved that his syndication of such a highbrow author's work hadn't hurt him financially, writing to Howells, "Your novel is taking splendidly. This is somewhat of a surprise to me, inasmuch as I had supposed that your work would not attract the million audience." It is also doubtful that if McClure could have dictated the treatment, he would have asked Sarah Orne Jewett to write "Stolen Pleasures" (1885); its lengthy descriptions and lack of action are contrary to what anyone would expect the newspaper-reading audience to desire. Finally, any reader expecting a happy ending would have been disappointed by Hjalmar H. Boyesen's story "A Case of Heart-Break," which concludes, "Heart-broken, benumbed by the shock, she seated herself at the roadside. She did not know whether she was awake or she slept. But she dreamed that God was dead."[16]

In 1895 Arlo Bates of *The Book Buyer* magazine charged that the better authors of the day were "indirectly urged to lower their standards by appeals on the part of the [syndicate] editor to make their work 'of a popular character,' 'of intense interest,' and so on, for the other euphemisms, which really mean, 'Cater to the popular taste, and get a big price for it.' "[17] Without a doubt, syndicates preferred to purchase fictions that would satisfy the tastes of newspaper editors and readers and thus make them money. Less famous authors probably more frequently succumbed to their requests for such works and traded artistic control over subject and treatment for ready cash. Yet syndicates were often unable to make famous authors write about the subjects and with the treatments they believed were most likely to meet with popular approval. More information about Tillotson's practices in this area is needed. But because Bacheller greatly desired works by Jewett, Freeman, Garland, and Crane, and McClure needed every story he could get from Stockton, Stevenson, James, Howells, and Conan Doyle merely for the luster these names lent to their syndicates, these authors were given almost complete freedom to experiment with subjects and treatments and still be paid well for it.

II

Another parameter by which one can judge the control authors had over their manuscripts is length. In the nineteenth century, authors, editors, and publishers increasingly linked the prices paid for works of fiction to the number of words they contained, and syndicates did the same. Some have argued that this practice commercialized language and encouraged padding, in the process corrupting the artistic integrity of countless works of fiction by inducing authors to write longer fictions and to pay little regard to the effect of this practice on quality. Others have taken the opposite view and hypothesized that because these editors wanted shorter fictions that would fit easily in the spaces between advertisements, they constrained fiction authors from writing works of the longer lengths the authors deemed essential to the artistic integrity of their work. It has further been posited that the length limitations inherent in periodical publication encouraged or even forced authors to produce short stories. Magazine editors are usually portrayed as the principal culprits in forcing authors to write works of certain lengths, but the syndicates are occasionally included in these accusations. Joseph Katz argues that from 1865 to 1905, "writers realized that the steady income they needed as professionals must come from newspaper and magazine work," and he adds, "that is why short stories and sketches dominated the output of the realists: periodicals would be more able to use their short things than their novels." In 1893 William Dean Howells wrote that he believed the syndicates, by increasing the demand and recompense for short stories, encouraged production of this length of fiction.[18] Close examination of the questions of whether syndicates controlled the lengths of the works they distributed and stimulated the production of short stories, however, reveals that syndicates had less power in these areas than it might at first appear.

Syndicates did regularly state some type of length guidelines. Tillotson's regularly included the desired length of works in contracts with authors, such as that installments of novels should be about 6,000 words each, or that a short story should be of a certain length. Bacheller publicized that all stories entered in his 1895 prize contest should be between 2,000 and 6,000 words long, and Sarah Orne Jewett indicated in 1895 that her contract with Bacheller stipulated that her story be 8,000 words long. In addition, she wrote that Bacheller had told her, " 'the story would be printed in instalments of about 2000 words,' " a length he communicated to another author the same year. Bacheller also set out overall length guidelines in the prospectus he sent to editors in late 1894, telling them that stories would be "from four to fifteen thousand words in length." Finally, in 1897 Bacheller asked one author if he could "write a story to divide 2000 wordparts [sic] the whole to contain six to eight thousand words." In 1885 McClure appears to have specified a limit of 5,000 words per story, but by 1886 these limits were looser, and McClure informed authors, "Stories should be about 1,500 words long," and that "the stories must not exceed 2,000 words in length, unless intensely interesting; in that case a few stories of 3,000 words can be used, also an occasional story of 5,000 words." By 1887 these limits had been altered further, and McClure advertised to editors that Sunday stories would be about three columns long (approximately

4,500 words), Saturday stories two columns long (3,000 words), on Monday and Tuesday there would be a two-part story about one column long each day (a total of 3,000 words), and on the other days of the week, complete short stories of about one column each (1,500 words total). In 1896 McClure's syndicate reportedly wanted short stories anywhere between 3,000 and 6,000 words long.[19] The question is, how strictly were these guidelines followed, both by authors during composition and by syndicate editors when deciding which works to accept?

The extraordinarily wide range of work lengths these syndicates accepted and syndicated certainly refutes the idea that syndicates forced authors to produce fictions of standardized lengths. One mid-1880s Tillotson's ledger of current and back-listed works contains the titles of approximately 130 works, and they range from three columns (4,500 words) to 110 columns (165,000 words) long. Michael Turner's examination of numerous contracts between Tillotson's and authors indicates that various types of short stories were from 2,000 to 12,000 words long, novelettes ranged from 15,000 words to 24,000 words long, and serial novels were anywhere from 40,000 to 160,000 words long. To American editors Tillotson's offered "storiettes" (2,000–2,500 words), short stories (4,000–5,000 words), novelettes, and of course serial novels. An idea of the percentage of works in each length range is indicated by the report that in the United States in 1892, the firm distributed 60 short tales, 10 novelettes, and 22 serial novels.[20]

In 1886 and 1887, Bacheller syndicated mainly stories of a length that could be printed entire in one issue (only one story has been found that was long enough to print in two parts), but the length of these stories was far from uniform. In 1886 Bacheller-syndicated stories in the *Syracuse Evening Herald* averaged approximately 2.6 columns long (3,900 words), with a range of 1.3 columns (1,950 words) to 4.1 columns (6,150 words), and in 1887 in this same paper the average was 2.18 columns (3,270 words), with a range of 1.2 (1,800 words) to 3.6 columns (5,400 words).[21] And although Bacheller's promise to editors in late 1894 that all forthcoming fictions would be from 4,000 to 15,000 words long might have discouraged authors from submitting novels to his syndicate, it should be noted that these lower and upper limits gave authors a great deal of latitude with their short stories and novelettes. Of the 92 stories Bacheller syndicated in 1895, 10.9 per cent were published in one part (approximately 2,000 words long); 30.4 per cent in two parts (4,000 words); 22.8 per cent in three parts (6,000 words); 10.9 per cent in four parts (8,000 words); 15.2 per cent in five parts (10,000 words); and 9.8 per cent in six parts (12,000 words). Instead of forcing authors to write short fiction of only one length, Bacheller accommodated the different lengths of fiction by simply expanding or decreasing the number of installments.

Like Bacheller, McClure also offered fiction in a wide range of lengths instead of enforcing strict requirements on authors. One circular for late 1884 and early 1885 advertised works from 5,000 words to 18,000 words long. And despite another circular in early 1885 which promised editors that stories would be between 1,500 and 3,500 words long, providing about 1,500 words or one column per day, many stories exceeded these limits. An examination of the adult fiction distributed by the Associated Literary Press and printed in the *Detroit Free Press* in 1885 reveals that the average length was 4.21 columns per story (6,315 words), and that these ranged from 1.3 (1,950 words) to 9 columns (13,500 words) in length. As late as 1899, there was no uniformity of length among stories distributed for Sunday publication, with stories anywhere from 2,200 words to 5,000 words long. In addition, after December 1886 McClure's syndicate usually published eight to ten serial novels each year, ranging in length from 50,000 to over 100,000 words. In the serial novel service – separate from the daily or weekly story service – editors were told that installments would usually be about 5,000 words long, but even this was frequently not adhered to. To accommodate his lack of control over short story lengths, McClure told editors that they could print longer stories either all at once or in installments, depending on the space they had available. With serials, McClure or his editors either divided novels at exciting moments themselves, no matter whether it was at 5,000 words or 7,000 words, or they simply divided them into more installments of 5,000 words each.[22]

This does not mean, however, that authors were completely free to write works of whatever length they wanted. Works were in fact occasionally rejected because of their length. McClure, for example, wrote author O. O. Howard that although he liked a submitted story, "I am obliged to return it on account of its length." A work by Sarah Orne Jewett, too, was apparently not accepted because of its length, prompting Jewett to write McClure, "I was sorry that the Jaquenot Rose story was too long – I was afraid it would be [,] and it is not fit for a serial." And in 1902 McClure's informed Jack London that his "An Adventure In the Upper Sea" was "too long for our short story service and too short for our long story, and we are, therefore, obliged to return it." Bacheller rejected at least one story on account of its length, and one can safely assume Tillotson's did so occasionally as well.[23]

Numerous instances, though, reveal that syndicates often could not enforce rigid length guidelines that would make fictions fit their categories because they desperately needed as many good manuscripts – especially from famous authors – as they could get. Sarah Orne Jewett, for example, after noting Bacheller's length requirement for her story "A Dark Night," informed him that "Two, or three, of these four chapters will go two or three hundred words beyond" the 2,000 word limit per installment. Probably responding to the same suggestion from Bacheller that her work be 2,000 words long for publication in one installment, Mary E. Wilkins warned Arthur Stedman, "It is understood, is it not, that I may exceed two thousand words? It is only that I fear I cannot write such a story which will be satisfactory to you or myself, within such narrow limits. I will make it as short as I can, but I never write a two thousand word story." When she finally sent Stedman the story shortly thereafter, Wilkins wrote, "I over ran your usual limits, a little, but I made it as short as I could. My children's stories are generally much longer. I find it difficult to keep within less than four or five thousand words." Significantly, too, Wilkins's prize story "The Long Arm," which was supposed to be between 2,000 and 6,000 words long, was in fact approximately 13,500 words long. In contrast, when a less famous author wrote a work whose first installment was 4,500 words long and not easily divisible into 2,000 word installments, Bacheller rejected it, at least for the daily series. Yet Bacheller was not above bending his limits, even for an unknown author, when the work was exceptional. *The Red Badge of Courage*, for example, far exceeded Bacheller's length guidelines, but he accepted the work anyway and then cut it down considerably to make it fit the newspaper serial format.[24]

In McClure's letters of solicitation to famous authors, he usually suggested only very general lengths that gave authors a good deal of creative leeway. The elasticity of McClure's suggested length limits – at least for more famous writers – is exemplified in a letter McClure wrote to Joel Chandler Harris in 1885. McClure wrote, in a very solicitous tone, that he "should like the new story 'A Boston Girl' to be about 30,000 words long," and he asked that another "should be about 10,000 words long"; yet, at no time did McClure state in this letter that a story not of the requisite length would be rejected. Another example of broad guidelines and McClure's tone occurs in a letter to Robert Louis Stevenson in 1890: "I should like from you a short story of ten or fifteen thousand words for my Youth's Department," he wrote, but then added, "I am sure that you will do your utmost to let me have a short story from four to ten thousand words long..." McClure also wrote to William Dean Howells that "A story of about thirty thousand words, divided into ten instalments or chapters, would most nearly meet my requirements," but in a subservient tone then stated, "I feel rather bold in making these requests and suggestions to you."[25]

Authors frequently served notice to McClure that they, not he, were in charge of length. In 1885 H. H. Boyesen wrote of his short story of 3,000 words, "I regret to say I cannot make it shorter." As noted previously, Jewett, too, apologized to McClure for the length of one work, but she sent it anyway, despite knowing beforehand that it did not fit his guidelines. In another case, Frank Stockton indicated that he knew McClure's general requirements for the optimal newspaper serial, but he disregarded them and informed McClure, "I find that the story of which I spoke to you is longer than I thought. It contains about 36,800 words and will conveniently divide into *five* parts of suitable length for newspaper use ... The story is ready for use"; judging from this last sentence, the length was not open for negotiation. Elizabeth Stuart Phelps, too, kept control of the length of her fiction, writing to McClure in one case that she knew she had run at least 300 words per chapter over his suggested limits but telling him, "You must manage as you can" with it. Authors soon understood that if they ran over any length limit, McClure preferred to ask editors to print more installments rather than force the author to cut his or her work drastically.[26]

Authors frequently resisted Tillotson's length requirements as well. George Augustus Sala wrote in 1889 that he was willing to write short stories but added the proviso, "I could not tell the shortest of stories *in my manner*, in fewer than *seven thousand* words." Hall Caine bluntly notified the firm, "By our agreement, I undertook to write a story of 'about 14,500 words in 3 instalments.' I have, however, written about 23,500 words in 4 instalments. The additional matter was not asked for by you, but was written by me in obedience to the artistic compulsion of my subject..." How successful these authors were with their resistance in the cases above is unknown, but Tillotson's clearly did not hold such nonconformity against the authors, for the firm afterwards continued to buy works from them.[27]

In general, then, syndicates were not always in a position to force authors to write fictions of standardized lengths. Instead, they accepted works of a wide range of lengths and did the best they could to sell them to editors. One might conclude, in fact, that the many different programs that McClure's and the other syndicates provided – storiette, daily short story, weekly short story, serial service – should not be understood as restrictive limits that guided production but rather as an attempt to accommodate the various lengths of fictions submitted to them.

III

It has been implied that in addition to controlling the composition of literary works, syndicates controlled the pace of their production. What evidence is available, however, indicates that although syndicates in general were successful in their attempts to control the pace of production by securing delivery of solicited manuscripts by certain dates, they also recognized that their control was at best tenuous, gained only with the cooperation of authors.

All syndicates worked under tight schedules and promised newspaper editors that certain works would be available for publication on specific dates, in order that editors could advertise works in advance and reserve space for them. To maintain the smooth and timely flow of manuscript to publication, syndicates regularly stipulated in contracts with authors the dates – usually mutually agreed upon – by which they wanted authors to deliver the manuscript to them. Most commonly, however, syndicates were forced to adopt solicitous tones, at least with more famous authors. A letter Bacheller wrote to Edmund Clarence Stedman is typical. He commented, "By the way, I hope very much that you will write that war adventure for us immediately, so that it may go out in our service for July 8th," and then he added, "I wish to keep as closely to the schedule as possible... and I fear that most of our customers are counting upon it. Please try to do it."[28] Whether Stedman delivered on time remains undetermined.

Many authors resisted the planned production schedules of McClure, Bacheller, and Tillotson's and made them wait for manuscript delivery. For example, despite McClure's desire to have one manuscript as soon as possible, Elizabeth Stuart Phelps wrote to him that she would "send it to you as soon as possible. It may be two weeks, or thereabouts, before I shall be able to complete it; but shall do the best I can." Sarah Orne Jewett informed McClure on one occasion, "I shall try to have another story before very long, but I must finish some other work first." And Mary E. Wilkins told Eliza Farman Pratt of McClure's Youth Department, "I will most certainly write some stories for you. I will not *promise* a half dozen at once for my own peace of mind, for I am *so* busy, but I will promise two before long."[29]

Some authors struck a similar tone in letters to Bacheller or his representative, Arthur Stedman. For example, in 1894 Wilkins wrote to Stedman, regarding her new story, "[I] will let you have it some time in March. I cannot say the exact date, but will write it as soon as I can. I have some other work which must be finished, first." Jewett also told the firm in late 1894, "I do not see my way clear, just now, toward writing a longer story for your syndicate. I find myself very busy as autumn comes on ... But I shall certainly keep your and Mr. Stedman's own kind proposition in mind." Bacheller's lack of control is also indicated in the escape clause he printed in his contracts with editors: "Bacheller, Johnson & Bacheller reserve the right to omit any [author's] name from the above list and allow credit for one week's service on account of said omission."[30]

Tillotson's, too, often had to deal with authors who did not have their manuscripts ready on time. Usually the contracts were made one year ahead of planned delivery, which would appear to have given authors a great deal of leeway as to when they would write the entire work – or in the case of serial novels, the first third of the novel, later chapters to be delivered after publication had begun. Despite this, numerous authors wrote to Tillotson's asking for extensions and apologizing for the delay in delivery. Tillotson's appears to have been quite understanding in these instances and not to have punished authors in any way. Marie Corelli on one such occasion wrote to Tillotson's, "thank you for the courtesy and patience you have shown with respect to the short story I promised you some time ago," and Hall Caine thanked Tillotson's for extending the delivery date six months after the one on his contract, writing, "I am very sensible of your courtesy and kindness, & trust you may never find reason to regret it." Authors appear to have realized that they did not have to strictly adhere to Tillotson's production schedule; for example, W. W. Jacobs wrote, "I am unable at present to fix a date for the delivery of the stories, but as soon as I can do so I will instruct [Mr. Pinker] to let you know."[31]

Authors – at least famous ones – were thus relatively unconstrained by stipulated delivery dates for manuscripts. Their control of the production schedule in fact caused numerous problems for the syndicates. McClure occasionally found himself explaining to editors that the delay in delivering certain contracted-for works was caused by the manuscript not having yet been delivered to him. In one case, McClure wrote to editors regarding Rudyard Kipling's story "The Son of His Father," advertised for publication on 9 April 1893, "I have not yet received copy of the story ... I will tell you definitely about it just as soon as the story is actually in my hands"; as of November 1893, however, the manuscript was still undelivered. Tillotson's, too, occasionally had to apologize to editors and readers for the delay in delivering a certain fiction. For example, Tillotson's informed those who had anticipated reading Bret Harte's "Found at Blazing Star" on 24 December 1880 that Harte "undertook to deliver the MSS of his story on or before the 30th November, but in consequence of a serious accident ... he claimed fifteen days' indulgence," yet he still hadn't delivered it.[32] The frustration syndicators must have experienced when they could not deliver these fictions on time to their customers can only be imagined.

In general, what syndicates all came to realize was that the production of fiction could not be controlled as easily as the production of most other material goods, for those in control of production, the authors, often had to wait for the muse's inspiration or free time to write, and unlike factory workers or dime novel authors they were not interchangeable.

IV

Once the manuscript had been written and was in the possession of the syndicates, to what degree were authors' artistic rights in the text respected during the editing and publishing processes? So little is known of how Bacheller and how his employees edited that it is almost impossible to determine how much consideration they gave to authors' rights. One author expressed his pleasure that the Bacheller "syndicate gives much time to the editing and illustrating," but it is uncertain how representative his case was. Bacheller's broad acceptance range of 4,000 to 15,000 words per fiction, however, would seem to have allowed him to let authors' works stand much as they were submitted, except for those over the upper limit such as *The Red Badge of Courage*. One indication that authors had some control over their texts is that Bacheller allowed at least a few authors to correct their texts before the final galley proofs were printed and sent to newspapers. But in at least one case – and there were probably more – an author blamed Bacheller's "copyist" for misreading his manuscript and thus making numerous typesetting errors in the galley proofs sent to newspaper editors.[33]

In general, McClure and his editors appear to have been the least respectful of authors' artistic rights in their texts; in this area McClure lived up to the reputation he made for himself with his boasts. Some authors accepted the editing without a great deal of comment. However, in a number of instances, McClure himself edited a manuscript beyond recognition and shipped this version to newspaper editors without the author having a chance to correct proofs. McClure once cut out the first five chapters of a story by Julian Hawthorne, only to find "that these first fave [sic] chapters which I had cut out were the basis of the novel, the part that explained things," and that because a number of characters had been introduced in them, many readers were very confused. Recognizing from experience McClure's propensity to over-edit, Robert Louis Stevenson took measures to minimize textual disfigurement by demanding that all proofs be sent to him at his home in Samoa, even though this often caused McClure unprofitable delays. What is uncertain is how many of the errors appearing in the galley proofs sent to editors were the result of syndicate editing and how many were the result of printers' errors both at the syndicate and the various newspaper plants where proofs for circulation were being printed. McClure apparently tried to minimize printers' errors sent out to newspapers, and in one instance pointed out a number of errors to the editor of the *Portland [Maine] Transcript*, who was printing galley proofs for him. In response the editor noted, "The trouble has been, that in the hurry to get off the proofs to you Thursday, only one reading has been given, & that one the least careful." Apparently as a result of the hasty production process and the resulting errors, many authors requested the same right that Stevenson had to correct proofs, but it is uncertain if McClure honored all these requests.[34]

Authors appear to have had a similar mixture of views about how William Frederic Tillotson and his employees handled their texts. Justin McCarthy recalled in connection with the translation of one of his novels, "I accepted his [W. F.'s] proposed alteration, seeing that it was one entirely in the interest of the author – rectifying a mistake which I had never noticed and which would have told against me. One feels safe in the hands of such a man." Yet Wilkie Collins did not trust the Tillotson's editors as fully; he added to one contract the clause, "no alteration of any sort shall be made in the proofs revised for press by Wilkie Collins without first obtaining his permission." Fortunately for authors, they were usually accorded the right to correct proofs, for the ones printed at the *Bolton Weekly Journal* were, by all accounts, full of printers' errors. Hall Caine wrote, "the proofs [of *The Mahdi*] as you have set them are full of the most alarming errors of every conceivable sort." It is quite possible that such errors were more numerous in works that Tillotson's syndicated in the United States. Proofs had to be sent to American newspapers earlier than to British ones, and as a result there might not have been enough time to receive the corrected proofs from authors and make the required changes before mailing them overseas. In the above instance Hall Caine indicated his concern about this and said on 18 November 1894, "A friend wrote to me that the story was appearing in America. If it is appearing in this condition it will be terrible. Everybody who knows the [Asian] East will think I do not know it." By 3 December Caine's fears were confirmed when he obtained clippings of *The Mahdi* as it had appeared in the *Boston Herald*; he expressed outrage that the text, whether through the fault of Tillotson's or the *Herald*, had been terribly corrupted.[35]

Editing at the syndicates – whether carried out by the heads of the syndicates themselves or by hired editors – was probably neither of the highest quality nor conducted with great sensitivity. None of the syndicators and few of the editors they employed had much literary editorial training, and the time demands of the syndicate operations probably militated against careful, thoughtful editing and proof corrections. Authors who desired such consideration had to demand it, and only famous authors had enough power and influence to succeed in obtaining it.

Not all of the textual errors in authors' texts, however, were the fault of the syndicates. Because of the way syndicates marketed and distributed fiction, once the manuscript had been edited and the proofs corrected, authors had little control over where, when, and in what fashion the work would be published. Syndicates reserved to themselves the right in almost all cases to determine which newspapers and magazines would receive galley-proof copy and when they would print it. Authors occasionally asked syndicates to circulate their works only to certain papers or to delay publication to give them time to obtain copyright or coordinate international and intercontinental publication; many authors' contracts with Tillotson's – especially those with more famous authors – stipulate such limitations. The degree to which other syndicates complied with such requests, though, is uncertain. One case that illustrates how much syndicates controlled the dispensation of manuscripts they had purchased is that of Helen Hunt Jackson and her story "Dandy Steve" (1885). Her biographer claims that after Jackson turned down McClure's request for a story, she sold "Dandy Steve" to Bacheller; a short time later, however, she was reportedly furious upon learning that Bacheller had supposedly sold the story to McClure for syndication. In another case, Bacheller played fast and loose with Mary E. Wilkins's story "The Long Arm" after he had purchased its American serial rights. Wilkins assumed that Bacheller would serialize the story only in newspapers, but Bacheller interpreted his purchase to mean he could also publish it later in his *Pocket Magazine*. Freeman believed this magazine publication violated the terms of their agreement and might hurt book sales; she complained mightily to Bacheller but with no success.[36]

Authors – and syndicates – also lacked control over how fictions would be published in the newspapers. Local newspaper editors could use large, misleading headlines or titles for the fictions, have outrageous illustrations made to accompany them, or place them beside whatever other materials they chose. In addition, newspaper editors could alter the texts as much as they wished, and neither the syndicate nor the author had the right to correct proofs. Further, because type was set at local newspaper shops from the galley-proof copy, numerous variations in the text invariably occurred. Bacheller explained to one author, "I cannot explain why the Herald omitted a part of your article. They certainly had no authority to do so from this office. They were, probably, very much crowded for space."[37]

On occasion, authors complained about this situation. Yet even if syndicates had wished to respond to authors' complaints about violations of textual integrity, they were probably reluctant to retaliate against any newspaper or magazine and drop the offender from their list of customers. After all, syndicates had to work extremely hard to win enough customers to maintain profitability; ceasing relations with a newspaper over a mangled text probably would have seemed an extravagant luxury.

In contrast, syndicates were much more protective of authors' property rights, mainly because their own interests were also involved. To protect copyright, syndicates repeatedly stressed to editors the importance of printing British authors' works only *after* first British publication, and of printing complete and correct copyright notices next to the syndicated fictions. This "copyright *imprimatur*" on syndicated fiction, one commentator noted, "warns off all journals from republishing, which have not subscribed to the special 'syndicate' engaging them." A newspaper's failure to print the proper copyright notice with a work of syndicated fiction allowed other editors to pirate the material; this in turn infuriated editors who had paid for the service and damaged the prospect of future syndicate sales to them. Syndicates also worried that authors who lost income from pirated newspaper, magazine, and book publication would be less likely to contribute stories to them in the future. After all, greater copyright protection was one of the reasons authors were attracted to syndication. As Edgar "Bill" Nye told McClure in 1885, he welcomed the idea of syndicating his work because then it "would not be so freely stolen as it now is."[38]

Syndicates appear to have responded vociferously to any cases of piracy to protect not only their own property rights but also those of authors. Previous to the 1891 Chace Act, Tillotson's could not legally prosecute American newspapers who printed Tillotson's-syndicated British fiction without authorization. Instead, in at least one case the firm took out an ad in the *Journalist* magazine to publicly shame the New York *World* for its piracy. Tillotson's was more protective elsewhere. Responding to a complaint from the editor of the Toronto *Globe* in 1886, Tillotson's successfully prosecuted one Montreal newspaper for its piracy of Justin McCarthy's novel *Camiola, a Girl with a Fortune*; apparently the syndicate pursued other cases in Australia as well. In 1895, shortly after acting less than honorably in the case of "The Long Arm," Bacheller offered to help Mary E.

Wilkins prosecute the Fleming H. Revell Company for its unauthorized book publication of *Comfort Pease and Her Gold Ring*, the serial rights to which Bacheller owned. Only one case has been found where the McClure syndicate threatened pirates with court action, but others probably exist. In 1900 Robert McClure wrote to his brother Tom, "I should proceed against the [Montreal] 'Star' for infringement of those rights, and I would make them pay to the uttermost farthing. If you do not, we will always be bothered in the same way."[39]

v

The syndicates, then, were neither authorial paradises where authors could publish everything they wrote in the form in which they wrote it and receive high prices for it nor absolute tyrants running literary sweatshops. Readyprint syndicates were the least attractive to authors, for they rarely paid authors for their work. Plate service providers offered authors more advantages, but they did so primarily to beginning and unknown authors who were willing to accept the low wages they paid. Galley-proof syndicates, on the other hand, in varying degrees offered hundreds if not thousands of British and American authors in the late nineteenth century wages and working conditions that – when compared to those available through most story paper, dime novel, and magazine publishers – must have seemed quite appealing. These syndicates earned the gratitude of many authors because they were willing to assume the difficult task of making arrangements with multiple newspapers and were among the first to connect authors to a large, national American audience. Furthermore, after the syndicates – not bound by the informal rules of gentlemanly publishing – entered the market, authors had more outlets for their various types of works, and the ensuing competition helped force book and magazine publishers not only to raise their rates but also possibly to treat authors with greater deference.

S. S. McClure's claim that in 1884, "From the authors I got immediate and enthusiastic replies. They would be delighted to be syndicated, would be delighted to write for me" was thus probably quite accurate. Irving Bacheller, too, recalled that although a number of well-known authors turned him down, in 1885 he "was favored ... by the kindly consideration of writers." Upon William Frederic Tillotson's death in 1889, numerous authors remembered him warmly and commented that his syndicate had greatly helped authors (it should be noted that by all accounts, after his death the syndicate continued his policies towards authors). Edward Bok may have decried the situation where "the syndicate manager attracts by the larger sum which his numerous newspaper customers make it possible for him to pay, and the author falls into the temptation," but many authors welcomed the opportunity for higher wages that the syndicates represented.[40]

In return for the advantages that the American Press Association and the major galley-proof syndicates offered, authors had to accept some broad limitations as to their choice of subject, treatment, and length. In addition, after an author sent his or her manuscript or corrected proofs to a syndicate, he or she appears to have no longer retained much control over its final published form, and frequently the author's property rights were not highly respected.

Overall, however, the amount of control implied in the delineation of textual guidelines by syndicates, in the boasts of individual syndicators, and in their proclaimed "commissioning" of works was more fiction than reality. In general, authors who were less famous and who thus had fewer publishing options were more likely to have to accept the limitations spelled out by syndicates without question, often internalizing them and writing formulaic fiction according to their guidelines in order to minimize their risk of rejection, or passively submitting to editorial emendation. At least with the galley-proof syndicates, though, many popular authors often successfully resisted the established limitations, wrote according to their own artistic desires, and continued to have their works accepted by these syndicates.

CHAPTER 6

Pleasing the customers: the balance of power between syndicates and newspaper editors

> By giving me *carte blanche* in the selection of matter of the various classes, you will get the reading fresher than if I send out a proof sheet and await the customer's instructions before filling orders.
> Ansel Nash Kellogg, advertisement directed at newspaper editors, 1875

> From the authors I got immediate and enthusiastic replies. They would be delighted to be syndicated, would be delighted to write for me. But the editors were much more cool in their replies. It was then I learned that the selling end of any business is the difficult end.
> S. S. McClure, 1913

> Mine was a new idea, and in those days energy, hope, faith and persuasion were needed at both ends of the road – the writer being at one end, the editor at the other.
> Irving Bacheller, 1938[1]

More important than the relationships between syndicates and authors in determining what fictions the syndicates purchased and subsequently offered for publication were those between syndicates and their customers, the local newspaper editors. The role of these editors has never been investigated, possibly because it has been assumed that syndicates operated the same way magazines did, distributing texts that were printed in standardized form from coast to coast.

If this were true, the role of local newspaper editors would have been minor indeed; they would have served simply as the passive recipient of the syndicates' wares, persons who subsequently passed them along to readers. In fact, however, syndicate managers and editors in New York and Chicago did not dictate which syndicated fictions the reader eventually encountered at the rural country store, on a crowded horsedrawn trolley car in a large city, or in the drawing room of a middle-class household on a Sunday afternoon. Nor did they dictate its final published form and print context. Instead, the fiction and the context in which it was offered to the reader were determined through negotiations between syndicates and local editors, negotiations in which the local newspaper editor often had more bargaining power. Even in the case of patent insides and outsides, where local editors accepted two or four pages of already-printed matter from the readyprint company, the local editor had some input into what readyprint companies included in those pre-printed pages. Editors who purchased fiction in plate form also influenced the selection of fiction offered them, and they could place this fiction in the newspaper wherever they chose. With galley-proof syndicates, local editors functioned as even stronger gate-keepers, negotiating beforehand with the syndicates what subjects, treatments, and lengths of fiction they were willing to purchase, and thus they influenced in turn syndicates' decisions as to which fictions they would buy from authors. Furthermore, the methods these latter syndicates used to transmit fiction texts allowed local editors to intervene even more substantially between syndicates and readers by editing the texts, writing different titles and subtitles for them, placing them in the newspaper in places most advantageous to the editor, and including or altering illustrations that accompanied the texts. In general, because syndicates of all types had to negotiate with frequently resistant newspaper editors, they exercised less control over the fictions and print contexts offered to the reader than did story paper, dime novel, magazine, and book publishers, who had absolute control over the content and makeup of their print products.

I

The individual newspaper editor in the late nineteenth century was confronted with many choices regarding syndicated fiction. His (almost all editors were men) most important decision was whether to purchase it in any form or to continue relying on exchange fiction or on fiction produced by local authors. After this, he had to decide whether he wanted to receive syndicated material in readyprint, plate (after 1875), or galley-proof (after the early 1880s) form. Which form he chose usually depended on his newspaper's location and circulation. Almost without exception, those who ordered readyprint were editors of small-town, rural weekly papers and couldn't afford the money necessary to gather, edit, and typeset enough material to fill up four or eight pages; plate service and galley-proof copy customers, on the other hand, were usually editors of larger weekly or daily papers who wanted to supplement their local offerings. Having chosen the form in which he would take his syndicated fiction, the editor then had to choose among the many different fictions offered by the syndicates. The consequences of these editorial choices are recorded in the printed copies of the newspapers themselves. What is not so easily discerned from the pages of these newspapers, however, are the behind-the-scenes negotiations that preceded publication.

Almost from the beginning of readyprint, critics charged that by subscribing to such a service the local editor gave up control of his local paper to outside interests and thus was not as worthy as other editors. In 1906 one former readyprint publisher, George Presbury Rowell, recalled, "As these so-called co-operative papers [have] increased in number they have aroused, first and last, all manner of opposition; and the publishers who have used them have been subject to much opprobrium." Later newspaper historians also bemoaned how readyprint decreased the control of local editors over their newspapers and hence their individuality; one has recently argued that with readyprint, "The town press was half slave (to Chicago) and half free. There existed a free press on one side of the sheet, enslaved to a 'foreign' press on the other."[2]

Such concern about outside control was rarely if ever directed specifically at the choice of fiction; articles with more direct political import worried observers more. Yet the process by which fiction was chosen for the readers of these readyprint sheets has political import, for it indicates who had the most power in setting a large part of the fiction reading agenda for newspaper readers in small towns and rural areas across the country.

In many ways, contemporary critics were correct in their criticism that readyprint editors in Chicago and New York controlled what reading matter millions of rural citizens were offered. These editors chose the content of and laid out the pages, which were printed in regional establishments owned and operated by these readyprint companies. These sheets were subsequently shipped to subscribing newspapers, and once they arrived at the local post office or railroad station, the local editor could not alter the texts printed on them.

Furthermore, the requirement of readyprint firms that local editors pay for these sheets in advance, and the fact that most rural papers could not have survived without two pages of non-locally printed material, probably greatly decreased the possibility that any sheets would be rejected after they were delivered. It would appear, then, that readyprint was a blunt hegemonic instrument wielded by urban readyprint editors against editors of small-town papers.

Such a conclusion, however, does not adequately represent the relationship between these two parties. Edgar Watson Howe in 1891 described all country newspapers as looking very similar, yet continued, "of late it does not often occur that any two papers use ready-printed sheets that are exactly alike." This latter statement is seconded by a biographer of Ansel Nash Kellogg, who in 1876 wrote, "The general opinion in regard to the printed sheets is that they are all alike, but in reality there are scarcely two alike." Another observer claimed that even in towns where four or five weekly papers subscribed to the same readyprint house, no one could tell they were supplied by the same company because they were so vastly different from one another.[3] How can one reconcile these seemingly contradictory viewpoints? The answer lies in how the patent inside industry responded to the expressed desires of local newspaper editors for greater choice of column numbers, typography, and content material, including fiction.

In the late 1860s each readyprint company usually provided only one product to all of its customers; there was one typeface, a certain number of columns, and the same content. Yet the Kellogg firm – and probably others – did not remain static, instead soliciting comments and suggestions from local editors. After listening to their concerns, the readyprint managers realized that they could expand their lists of customers by offering editions whose typography and number of columns matched those used by local papers (to make the syndicated material appear home-produced) and whose contents were markedly different for Republican and Democratic papers, papers from different states, and so forth. By 1878, the Kellogg company alone was supplying thirty different editions of readyprint, "embracing almost every conceivable variety of size, politics, and style." In 1886 it was reported that "There are three or four hundred different styles of these sheets published [by Kellogg]." Other readyprint firms also offered a large number of different editions – 100 each week in 1891, according to one report.[4]

It is evident that Kellogg's decision to include fiction was also in response to a perceived need among editors. As one report noted in 1870, "The latest novelty in the business is that introduced by Mr. Kellogg, of supplying country papers with a set of sheets, containing, as a special feature, the successive parts of a serial story, and designed to increase their circulation *a [sic] la [the New York] Ledger.*" Over the years, Kellogg and others would respond to editors' requests for a greater choice of fiction. During the first two weeks of July 1876, for example, Kellogg did not distribute just one fiction to every newspaper that subscribed to his service; instead, for the week of 6 and 7 July he offered editors fifteen different short stories or serial installments, and for the week of 14 and 15 July at least eight different fictions.[5]

One might charge that this choice was more illusion than reality, since the character of this fiction was surprisingly similar; upbeat, morally impeccable tales that avoided political partisanship, sectarianism, and regional biases were the norm. The responsibility for the homogeneous fictions that readyprint firms provided, however, cannot wholly be assigned to the readyprint editors who chose them. They undoubtedly possessed personal preferences of their own in fiction, but the choices they made were also influenced by the desires of local editors. One can infer from the comments of editor Horace James of the *Rensselaer [Indiana] Union*, for example, that some editors wanted readyprint editors to keep their papers free from immorality; he commended Kellogg's service because "There is nothing, so far as I have ever seen, either in the reading matter presented or the advertisements which are admitted, of an immoral suggestion." Most editors who used readyprint addressed rural readers, who were more likely to hold conservative religious beliefs. To insure the success of their newspapers, local newspaper editors had to please these audiences; historian Eugene Harter writes, "Ready-print ... favored its largest circulation market, the dominant Protestant religious majority." Readyprint editors, eager to meet the desires of editors, provided fiction intended to displease no one.[6]

In retrospect it is easy to condemn editors who used readyprint for giving up a great deal of control over the contents of their papers. Yet it must be remembered that without readyprint many local editors would have gone out of business, since they could not afford the labor costs of finding materials through exchange, typesetting it, and printing it. The newspaper that readers encountered was thus the result of a trade-off. In exchange for having only partial control over the layout and content of readyprint pages, editors were able to control and publish in the other half a local forum for news, fiction, and other materials written by local people. Ironically, those who wish the readyprint houses had never come along with their regional advertising, outside fiction, and news to spoil the local nature of newspapers and their individuality did not fully appreciate the economic situation of such editors and would actually have condemned them out of existence.

Given this situation where many editors had little choice but to use readyprint, it is admirable that readyprint publishers catered to their needs as much as they did. Instead of forcing a single product on powerless editors, these firms responded to editors' concerns by providing them with many choices of news, features, and fictions. Editors unhappy with what was offered them did not necessarily submit passively but rather used their limited leverage to influence syndicate policy; one observer wrote, "Everything [in the readyprint pages] must, like the old spinster's bureau drawer, be 'just so,' or one or the other of the thousands of patrons of the [readyprint] house would be sure to file an emphatic protest." Readyprint publishers appear to have responded to their customers' desires; such input, one Kellogg publication noted, "enables us to fully understand and meet the wants of customers." Judging from the numerous endorsements these companies received from local editors and industry observers, this advertisement rings true.[7]

II

Newspaper editors who chose to use plate materials dealt with many of the same issues as did those who chose readyprint. Just as readyprint publishers were portrayed as the enemies of local independent thought, plate service providers were accused of standardizing the content of small town papers from coast to coast. One contemporary spoke in awe of the American Press Association, noting, "no newspaper – no hundred newspapers – ever before wielded such power and influence as this association does to-day," and added that "one is tempted to answer literally the question, 'Who is the true molder of public opinion?' by the response, 'The man who sells stereotype plates to newspapers.'" Such opinions have been echoed by later newspaper historians.[8]

Upon closer examination, however, the argument that plate service companies inflicted a standardized fare – including fiction – on unwilling newspaper editors and readers is not very strong. First, in response to editors' stated desires, the Association expended much effort on providing each editor with materials in typefaces and column widths that matched those in his own paper. Second, editors could choose among a wide variety of materials. The plate service divisions of readyprint firms provided as many choices of fiction and other materials as did the readyprint arms of the firms. Even the American Press Association, though it provided fewer choices of fiction than did large companies like Kellogg's, according to one contemporary offered "stories, poems, novels, and general departmental pages enough ... every week to make a 'home paper' of the most varied and attractive kind." The menu of fictions from which editors could choose was clearly influenced by the reaction from newspaper editors. The Association invited customers to express their opinions; one 1891 Association prospectus stated, "Customers are invited to submit suggestions that may occur to them for the improvement and enlargement of our service." And in 1892 an article in the *Journalist* reported, "The American Press Association owes much of its success to keeping always thoroughly posted as to the needs and demands of its customers, and in responding promptly to every reasonable request from them relating to the service." The Association was not the only plate service that asked for the input of editors. Wright Patterson, who in the 1890s was an editor for Kellogg and later served as editor-in-chief of the Western Newspaper Union, the American Press Association's chief rival, described the local editor as " 'a sort of readers' representative for the people of his community. He knows, or should know ... what his particular folks like to read. It is through what he decides to buy or leave alone that we, in this organization, can feel the pulse of reader interest.' "[9]

The seriousness with which plate service editors took such input calls into question the judgement of one newspaper historian that local editors "exercised little direct control over the selection of the [plate] material."[10] Cumulatively, editors' comments must have influenced which fictions the plate service editors purchased from authors. One can safely assume, for example, that the length limits the Association imposed on fiction authors were not arbitrary but rather were formed in response to the space limitations within which client newspaper editors operated. If such limitations had not existed, Association editors logically would not have risked alienating authors by enforcing them or have expended editorial labor (and thus money) on cutting them to certain lengths.

Responding to local editors' desires was not always easy. It was quite clear to the managers at the American Press Association that they could not satisfy all of their customers with one type of fiction, since the desires of editors varied widely. In 1892 the editor of *The Germantown [Pennsylvania] Telegraph*, for instance, complained to the Association, "There are too many blood and thunder stories on your list. I wish your managers would relent from the multitude of good short foreign stories. It would make a much better matter for readers." In an attempt to please those editors who didn't want such male-oriented action-adventure stories, the Association did provide many romances specifically directed at women readers. The *Hammondsport [New York] Herald* ran one advertisement (probably provided by the Association) that read in part, "Our Lady Readers Will be amused and interested by ... [this] delightful love story ... [which] describes ... the surprising experiences of an eastern woman ON A WYOMING RANCH."[11] At the same time, the firm also provided a steady diet of westerns and adventure stories. The Association may have offered editors a limited number of choices – usually only one short story and one serial each week – but it tried to vary the genres represented in order to please as many editors as possible.

In addition to exercising some control over the types of fiction the Association offered them, editors had a good deal of discretion as to how they would use these fictions. The most important difference for editors between readyprint and plate service was the greater flexibility of layout the latter method of textual transmission allowed. As one contemporary put it, "If a box of these plates is sent to the country editor, he can 'make up' his own paper; can decide in a measure what shall go in and what shall not. That of course he couldn't do with the readyprint sheet, which came to him all printed." If an editor felt he needed the fiction to fit a smaller space, he could cut an inch or two from a story. As one Association publication noted, "To the intelligent editor ... the possession of a saw [for cutting stereotype plate] offers untold possibilities in the way of reconstruction and amendment," although it also advised that the saw be used "judiciously," so as not to "impair the original value of the service."[12] In addition to altering the text itself, editors who took plate service could place the fiction in whichever column or on whichever page of the paper they wanted.

Charges that plate service companies standardized the content and appearance of syndicated fiction in newspapers thus have little validity. One report in 1891 concluded in regard to the entire plate service of the American Press Association and Kellogg, "each concern carries such an immense variety of matter that a man would have to be very cranky, indeed, if he could not be suited by them," and the choice apparently extended to fiction. In addition, because the plates allowed "practically the same freedom in the matter of make-up that the editor has who sets his own paper," even readers of newspapers supplied with the same fiction would have encountered that fiction in widely varying print contexts.[13] Plate service editors did not control the hundreds of newspapers their firms supplied; they merely provided a menu to newspapers, whose managing editors made all the decisions as to which materials they would choose and how they would use them. Granted, this menu was not unlimited, but it certainly offered smaller papers more choice of fiction than they would have had if they had relied on authors' unsolicited submissions. Most important, the plate service editors were well aware that their positions were secure only so long as they pleased the customers, the local newspapers.

III

The financial advantages of obtaining fiction from a readyprint publisher or from a plate matter provider were obvious to newspaper editors. By using materials from these companies the editors greatly reduced the time and money spent on editing, on typesetting, and in the case of readyprint, on printing. The advantages of taking galley-proof fiction, on the other hand, were not so obvious. This original fiction was much more expensive to purchase than readyprint or plate fiction, editorial labor had to be expended to edit it and write titles and subtitles for it, and the text had to be reset in the local newspaper's plant. The only way this type of syndicated fiction could pay for itself, editors soon calculated, would be if its inclusion in the paper increased the number of the right kind of readers sufficiently to attract advertisers and in turn to justify increases in advertising rates. Because of their desire to attract and please readers with this material, editors who purchased syndicated fiction in this form wanted a great deal of say in its selection and use.

In their turn, syndicates of this type had to work harder to please their customers, since so many editors took the fiction on a case by case basis and could, if the fiction offered did not satisfy them, instead easily use works produced by local writers or taken from exchange. To determine what subjects, treatments, lengths, and prices editors wanted, these syndicates assiduously solicited the preferences of their customers. As newspaper publishers themselves, Tillotson's might have been expected to understand newspaper editors' desires. Yet in the early days of his syndicate, William Frederic Tillotson reportedly sent authors' manuscripts to newspaper editors for their opinions on whether to purchase them for syndication. One writer reported that "If the answer were in the negative, Mr. Tillotson would return the manuscript to the author and say he could do nothing with it." In Britain, Tillotson's sales representatives such as Robert Sheppard ascertained editors' wants. One company Programme thus noted, "We make all our purchases [from authors] in the light of experience and of constant contact with editors and with readers."[14] In the United States, though, Tillotson's had fewer staff members and thus a limited ability to ascertain what editors wanted.

Irving Bacheller and S. S. McClure worked very hard at finding out the types of fiction that American editors were most interested in purchasing. Both learned very quickly that it was easier to ask the customer beforehand what he wanted rather than to try to sell him something he neither wanted nor needed. Thus, they frequently visited newspaper editors in their offices. Bacheller reportedly founded his syndicate only "after consulting with a number of leading editors," and his sales trips to editors across the country undoubtedly afforded him ample opportunity to learn what editors wanted. Bacheller continued to ask for input in later years; one editor wrote to Bacheller in 1889, "This is in response to the suggestion of your Mr. Johnson [Bacheller's partner] that you want pointers from your constituents." "Slowly," Bacheller later remembered, "I acquired knowledge of the kind of thing most useful to them [editors]."[15]

McClure also travelled to numerous editors' offices to collect their views, which he then freely relayed to authors. In addition, McClure asked editors to send copies of their newspapers so that he could study them himself and ascertain what might best meet their needs. McClure also constantly wrote to solicit advice from every editor he could induce to offer it. Barely five months after beginning his service, he told editors, "Suggestions, names of possible authors, and criticism generally on the series will be welcomed." Editors responded enthusiastically to this request, sending in the names of many local authors from the Montreal, Philadelphia, New York, San Francisco, and St. Paul areas. Significantly, a number of authors whose names these editors forwarded to McClure eventually had their works published through the syndicate. McClure also inquired as to how editors and readers were reacting to the subjects and treatments of certain fictions. In December 1885, for example, McClure's office manager wrote to editors in one circular, "If you cannot use these stories, please tell me so, with your reason, using the enclosed envelope." By the end of 1885, McClure concluded that the Associated Literary Press had "grown to its present complete form under the tutelage of over thirty editors of successful and first-class newspapers." McClure's interest in editors' opinions did not wane. In 1891 he wrote to editors, "I ... shall make it my special aim to please you. I shall welcome any suggestions from you." In an attempt to satisfy these customers, McClure in at least two instances passed along some editors' comments to authors. In late 1884 he wrote to Mary Noailles Murfree, "I have just returned from an extended tour among newspapermen & have learned the following ..." And in 1893 Octave Thanet (Alice French) wrote to McClure that previously she had not understood what editors wanted, but "That batch of letters from editors that you sent me, once, poured a flood of light on me."[16]

The difficulty for all galley-proof syndicates, however, was that this advice, reflecting the various preferences and needs of individual editors, was often both exacting and conflicting. Not all editors wanted the same authors, the same subjects and treatments, the same lengths, or the same schedule of publication. Many editors worked under the mistaken impression that syndicates controlled a stable of authors who wrote to order, or at least had a stockpile of stories from which they could choose in order to suit the needs of their customers. Clearly, though, syndicates did not exercise the firm control over what authors produced that would have been necessary to fill every order. What the syndicates could do, though, was negotiate a compromise between what editors wanted and what the syndicates could get. The details of these negotiations – which rarely proceeded smoothly or satisfied both parties – are for the most part lost, but some are preserved. The information available on how Irving Bacheller and Tillotson's negotiated with American editors is rather scanty. Thus, the portrayal of such negotiations is here drawn chiefly from the papers of Victor Lawson, editor of the *Chicago Daily News*, and the papers of S. S. McClure. While these sources primarily represent the experiences of only one editor of a major metropolitan newspaper (who, because of his paper's great circulation, probably exercised more power than editors from smaller newspapers) and one syndicate, I believe they accurately represent the negotiations carried out between most other galley-proof syndicates and newspaper editors.

IV

In order to understand the demands that newspaper editors made of these syndicates in the areas of authors, subjects, and treatments, one must first understand that in the 1880s and 1890s the readers that American editors most wanted to attract to their newspapers and thus had to keep foremost in mind were middle-class women who usually directed the household expenditures and toward whom most companies directed their advertising. How to get women to read the newspaper – traditionally a male-oriented print activity – was the subject of much discussion among editors. The best way to reach these women and a greater number of other potential readers, editors concluded, was through the Sunday paper and, to a lesser extent, the evening paper. Editors surmised that Sunday was the one day when women were more likely to have leisure time, and with evening papers, too, editors hoped to reach not only working-class readers who didn't have the time to read morning editions during the day but also more middle-class women whose husbands would bring the paper home after work. According to J. Lincoln Steffens, editor for a time of the New York *Commercial-Advertiser*, "More people have time to read in the evening than in the morning, and, what was still more vital, papers bought on the way home were carried into the family. That insured him [the newspaper editor] advertisers, business."[17]

Editors hoped that by including materials of interest to the whole family, they could induce women to become habitual newspaper readers. Editors frequently implied to women that by reading the Sunday and evening paper together in the safety of the domestic space, the family would become closer and more educated about the world around them. The difficulty was that at the same time, male editors – along with most other members of their gender – wished to keep women and children out of the public sphere, sheltered from the harsh reality represented by the hard news of daily editions. To address these issues editors began to transform the newspaper in general – and the Sunday edition in particular – into a print product that could be brought into the home without offending the supposedly higher moral sensibilities of women and children. In Sunday editions, for example, hard news was downplayed in favor of softer features on music, fashion, and literature, which were often contained in the Woman's Page or Youth's Page.

To procure such materials and create newspapers for the whole family, editors increasingly turned to the syndicates. One of the most sought-after syndicated features used to attract readers was original fiction. Syndicators, though, were sent the clear message that in order to be acceptable, this fiction had to please both women readers and advertisers. As one editor wrote to McClure in 1885, "If our advertisers permit us, we may want to buy your excellent goods ..." McClure for one indicated that he clearly understood what editors wanted, advertising his Woman's Page as a "service of reading matter of special interest to women and to all people who have interest in the expenditure of money for household purposes [i. e. advertisers]." When editors chose among the syndicated fictions offered them and told syndicates what types of fiction to buy, they could not afford to solely indulge their own personal tastes, but also had to keep in mind what women readers and advertisers would want.[18]

v

Most editors told McClure (and presumably other syndicators) that one of the principal selling points of syndicated fiction in galley-proof form (as opposed to plate fiction) was the greater fame of the contributing authors. At a time when companies selling soap, stoves, food, and other products had begun to recognize that promoting name brand recognition positively affected sales, many editors wanted to purchase works by those authors whose names they recognized and which they believed their readers would also recognize and be attracted to. One newspaper trade journal advised in 1896, "Original copyright stories from famous pens affords the publisher an opportunity for advertising and introducing his paper into new homes on a legitimate basis." Another report that year charged that syndicates had "gone into a mad rush for noted names," and in 1900 an observer noted "the eagerness of the syndicates to secure names that already enjoy notoriety." McClure's partner John S. Phillips certainly learned his lesson well, writing that "newspaper novels usually sell according to the value of the author's name as an advertising card that will attract readers to subscribing newspapers."[19] Some newspaper editors, however, did not value name recognition so highly, preferring what they deemed "high quality" works by lesser-known authors. Negotiating whose works the syndicates would offer, and which ones the newspaper editors would purchase, was thus a complicated task.

What editors told McClure to purchase depended primarily on their conception of what authors they believed the local audience wanted. Most editors assumed their middle-class readers wanted fictions from authors whose names were nationally recognized. Thus, they chiefly wanted to purchase syndicated fiction by authors whose works had previously appeared in national magazines; securing such authors as contributors to the local paper represented a coup of sorts for the editor and, he hoped, would elevate that paper's reputation in the minds of local and regional readers. For newspaper editors in smaller cities, the ability to crow about famous fiction authors contributing work to their papers was especially valuable currency in the local marketplace competition. The editor of the *Auburn [NY] Daily Advertiser* told his readers, "That there is no sort of literature too good or too costly for newspapers appears from the growing tendency of writers who have been used to send their work to magazines, to print it now in the daily press," including his own. With a touch of braggadocio he added, "We are little but oh my!" Editors in larger cities also were proud of securing the works of "magazine" writers. In Detroit in 1885, an article entitled "The Free Press Stories / Brilliant Authors Who Are Writing For Our Columns" reported, "A year ago THE FREE PRESS began publishing short stories by the most famous American writers, including the principal contributors to the leading magazines and our most popular local writers. In this time we have furnished our readers as many first-class short stories as the three leading magazines, Harper's, the Century and the Atlantic."[20] Significantly, no mention was made of McClure's role in obtaining these fictions for local printing.

The problem for McClure and other syndicators was that it was very difficult to deliver a continuous supply of quality works by "name brand" authors. McClure's experience in this area is representative. In 1884 and 1885 he could only occasionally provide works by authors with recognizable names such as Stockton, Jewett, and Roe; more frequently he offered works by lesser-known authors. Most editors were displeased by such failure. One wrote to McClure, "We do not like to disappoint our readers. They do not know W. O. Stoddard." A San Francisco editor in January 1885 determined that McClure had failed to live up to his end of the contract to supply works by famous authors, and consequently he was entitled to terminate the contract. "What," this editor asked, "became of the stories by Julian Hawthorne, George Parsons Lathrop, Harriet Prescott Spofford, and others, which were definitely announced? They seem to be indefinitely postponed from week to week, and weaker stories by less known authors take their places." Translations and works by unknown authors could fill time between blockbusters, but the blockbusters had to come. Given the intense competition for works by famous authors, it is no wonder that William Frederic Tillotson – probably speaking for many syndicators – told an interviewer, "'I buy the author, I don't buy the story,'" and "'I would rather give four thousand dollars for a "Braddon" or a "Wilkie Collins" than forty dollars for an intrinsically better story by an author without a name.'"[21]

Yet what made McClure's work – and that of other syndicators – even more difficult was that not all newspaper editors wanted the more expensive works by famous authors or would accept a work solely on the basis of its author's name. Instead, one editor spoke for some of his colleagues when he asked McClure, "Please send me a good short story by some unknown writer. I want one that people who are not 'literary' will appreciate." And the editor of the Pittsburgh *Chronicle* told McClure he wanted high quality work from lesser-known writers because "In most cases the new authors excite more interest than the old stand byes [sic]. You get more originality with the new writers."[22] Finding saleable, "quality" works by lesser-known authors, however, was no easy task for syndicates. As previously described, syndicates used prize contests to attract submissions and also received many unsolicited manuscripts from which they could choose. McClure also tried to locate such works by asking editors for the names of good local writers, and in the process he established an outlet for aspiring authors that bypassed the national magazines. At the outset, though, without a network of editors forwarding quality works by unknowns, McClure had to rely too much on just a few willing middle-rank authors and endure the complaints from editors.

In an effort to satisfy the greatest number of editors (and because he could not obtain a steady supply of works from more famous authors), McClure eventually settled on the strategy of offering a smorgasbord, mixing works by famous authors (Bacheller called these "sky-rockets") with what editors regarded as fairly "high quality" works by lesser-known authors. Tillotson's and Bacheller also adopted this practice; Bacheller, for example, syndicated works by Arthur Conan Doyle and Stephen Crane alongside those of his friend Charles Kelsey Gaines and other unknowns. By 1887 McClure had begun to emphasize in his circulars and advertisements that he would supply not only works by name authors but also "stories from new writers of ability and promise."[23]

Even with this diverse selection, however, McClure could not please everyone. He often found it difficult to sell works by well-known authors because some editors believed their readers were neither patient enough nor intelligent enough to appreciate such fine literature. In addition, editors who wanted works by recognizable name authors were not always pleased with works by lesser knowns, no matter how high their "quality." McClure later recalled that he often tried to sell the works of rising authors to editors "who were mostly ignorant of and didn't know these people," and that when he mentioned a new author named Kipling to editors, "They didn't seem to know him – asked how his name was spelled."[24]

Many years after the demise of the Associated Literary Press, McClure recalled – with patent falsehood – that "In the old days of the Syndicate I selected stories totally irrespective of a man's name, no matter whether he was famous or not." Equally misleading, however, is Edward W. Bok's charge in 1895 that "It is the author's name it [the syndicate] is after, pure and simple. The newspaper editor simply takes the best of what is offered him, and often and again, in his heart, he knows that it is a poor best. But we are all more or less susceptible to the attraction of a famous name, and the average 'supplement' editor of the newspaper is not an exception to the rule."[25] Bok's statement erroneously implies that syndicates offered works only by famous authors, and that newspaper editors played no role in determining whose works the syndicates purchased. In fact, the authors whose works the syndicates offered came from various levels of fame and reputation, and the editors – acting on what they believed readers wanted – were the ones who compelled syndicates to buy works from certain authors.

The name of the author, though, was not the only thing editors looked at when deciding whether to purchase syndicated fiction. Editors also demanded that the subject of the fiction be morally unimpeachable, and that it be full of fast-paced action so as to please readers.

Editors made it clear that one essential attribute of good syndicated fiction was its moral inoffensiveness. Almost all echoed the sentiments expressed by Victor Lawson when rejecting a story offered by McClure in 1890: "We don't want to print fiction that is not suitable for family reading. We aim to keep the columns of our paper clean and unobjectionable on this score. The test we apply to all fiction is, 'Can this story be read aloud in a family circle?' If not, we don't want it." Possibly this desire for morally pure fiction reflected the editors' own primarily middle-class sensibilities. Yet more probably, editors wished to avoid losing advertisers by offending any readers – especially women and children – with immoral fiction. Editor Lincoln Steffens succinctly stated, "The manager of the advertising department of a newspaper opposes any features that are likely to keep the paper out of homes."[26] Editors had to be especially careful with what they printed in their Sunday editions because they did not want to be charged with Sabbath impropriety. After all, numerous clergymen and other devout persons had vigorously opposed Sunday editions in the 1870s, and numerous commentators in the 1880s and 1890s continued to believe that reading newspapers on Sunday violated the Sabbath. It was probably easier, though, for editors and syndicators to follow the Sunday guidelines for fiction when choosing fictions for weekday publication as well.

The moral standards that editors applied to fiction are indicated by their responses when the standards were not met. Instead of welcoming the gritty sensationalism of a story by the popular J. T. Trowbridge, for example, the editor of the Poughkeepsie, New York,

Daily Eagle wrote to McClure, "it belongs to a class of stories which deal only in the horrible, which we prefer not to admit to our columns ... hereafter [we] shall leave out everything of this sensational tragic sort. There is enough that is unpleasant to relate in real life, and we hold that it is inexcusable in fiction." Regarding a Julian Hawthorne story, Talcott Williams of the Philadelphia *Press* told McClure, "The moral was not so bad as it was disjusting [sic]. For a man in fiction to be disappointed at love and the [sic] seek compensation in a house of prostitution is not perhaps impossible but for a hero of a story to do so is abomnible [sic]." McClure was not the only one who had trouble selling certain fictions to editors. Victor Lawson wrote Tillotson's in 1891, "Our criticism [of stories offered] is that all truth is not of necessity, nor in propriety, to be said at all times, in all places, and before all audiences." In addition, Lawson told Tillotson's regarding one Ouida fiction that the *Daily News* published in 1888, "we were obliged to apologise to our readers for publishing [it]," because it was too indecent; he added, "There seems to be a latitude about the publication of a certain sort of fiction in England which does not obtain in this country, we are happy to say, among readers of first-class publications." When Lawson was offered another Ouida story in 1889 he informed Tillotson's, "Whenever Ouida writes anything clean, we want it; when it is unclean, we don't."[27]

Just as some editors preferred works by lesser-known authors, though, a few editors were willing to take a chance on more realistic and depressing fiction, figuring that newspaper readers were more used to the harsh realities of life than genteel magazine readers. While one or more editors complained about stories by Trowbridge, Hawthorne, or Zola, for example, others purchased and printed them. The publication of works by Crane, Norris, London, Chopin, and others by newspapers through the syndicates has even led some literary historians to posit that the newspaper represented a print outlet comparatively lax in morals by comparison to the magazines. Most editors, however, believed that overtly sensational fiction did not pay, either in daily or in weekend editions. More readers might have been attracted to this type of fiction, but they would probably have been the ones editors and advertisers did not want: working class and without much expendable income. Steffens concluded – as did some other editors – that cultivating a small circulation among well-to-do readers, as opposed to a large one among readers with less money, "may be the most remunerative to the advertising trades."[28]

Tillotson's does not seem to have changed course at all in response to these demands from American editors for moral unimpeachability in fiction, possibly because their primary markets were in Britain and commonwealth nations where moral standards were, at least according to Lawson, less puritanical. Bacheller, on the other hand, internalized editors' desires and used them in deciding which fictions to accept. For example, he rejected one story in 1897 and told its author, "I want very much to publish it but alas it *is* so naughty I fear the good old [Boston] Transcript, the [Hartford] Courant and some other papers on our list would lift their voices in a holy outcry." McClure took another approach, accepting a wide range of fictions but emphasizing to editors the moral purity of their subject matter even if he had to bend the truth somewhat to do so. When he did offer a fiction by Zola, for example, he stated that this novel "shall be of absolute purity – [and show] that he can write a story suitable for general popular reading." The McClure syndicate circular for Stephen Crane's *The Third Violet* (1896) certainly shows that the syndicate expected opposition and was moving to defuse it beforehand; it read, "while true to the real conditions of life, the story is in no sense gloomy or morbid. It is, on the contrary, spirited."[29]

Editors not only told syndicates that they wanted morally upright fiction but also that these fictions had to be written in a certain style that would appeal to their readers. Editors believed – probably correctly – that newspaper readers wanted lots of action and suspense and not much extended scene description or character development in their fiction. Victor Lawson distinguished between proper magazine and newspaper treatment when in 1891 he informed McClure that even if he accepted Conan Doyle's *The White Company* he would have to cut it 30–40 per cent because he had "a popular newspaper clientage in mind," advising McClure, "A high-grade magazine constituency would accept long descriptions and disquisitions without objection, but with a popular daily newspaper" this was unacceptable. One Pittsburgh editor concurred, telling McClure, "a reader of a short story in a daily newspaper cares very little about literary polish. He only wants to be interested or amused."[30]

Stories that were not sufficiently action-packed met with a mixed reception among editors and supposedly among readers. Lawson complained to McClure that he could not accept one story because "People are getting a little tired of too much wind and water and so little plot." Edward Phelps of the *New England Homestead* wrote that one Sarah Orne Jewett story "was absolutely plotless and from that standpoint was not worth printing," but added that "it was so truthfully and vividly worked up as to detail that it couldn't help be interesting, and I hear that it was much liked by my readers." On the other hand, Phelps wrote, "Miss [Elizabeth Stuart] Phelps's doctor story seemed to me a remarkably strong piece of introspective literary workmanship, but so far as I have been able to learn it was not generally liked, which is anything but complimentary to my readers." The most damning criticism of a fiction an editor could offer to McClure was that it "seems to me dull and uninteresting."[31] Thus, editors presented McClure with constraining limitations within which he had to operate: on the one hand they wanted fiction by famous authors who had previously published in magazines; on the other, they wanted these same authors to write differently for newspaper publication, providing fast-moving, action-packed works that lacked introspection and lengthy character development.

McClure's advertising rhetoric provides clear evidence that he understood what treatments editors wanted. For example, to sell Julian Hawthorne's *Pauline*, McClure attested that "Hawthorne's stories are good newspaper features, because they always have a good dramatic, original plot; they are plentifully spiced with incident; there are frequent climaxes, and they are invariably written in a clever, interesting style." Another circular letter promised that one story appealed "directly to the tired reader – the class that above all others devotes attention to the Sunday supplement."[32]

McClure and other syndicators did not, however, always provide editors with fast-moving, action-packed fictions. One reason they didn't was that they couldn't; without control over their producers, they were often forced to take what authors supplied, whatever the treatment. In addition, though, the desire of McClure, Bacheller, and probably Tillotson's to elevate the literary tastes of the average newspaper reader and give him or her access to fine literature prompted them to occasionally try and negotiate publication of works that did not meet the editors' requirements in this area. McClure's purchase of James's "The Real Thing" (1892) and Howells's *The Quality of Mercy* (1891) are but two testaments to his willingness to purchase slower-moving works that he believed in advance would not meet with immediate acceptance among editors. McClure and the others knew, however, that if they tried to sell too many works of this type it would spell disaster.

VI

Another subject constantly negotiated by editors and syndicators was the length of fictions. Most newspaper editors had a limited amount of space available and believed their readers had short attention spans; thus they wished to restrict the length of syndicated fictions. Syndicates, on the other hand, had little control over the length authors wrote to and thus sought more flexibility. Resolving these conflicting demands was never easy work.

A great number of editors preferred short stories complete in one issue because, in the words of the editor of the Scranton *Republican*, "our readers include a large class of transient customers, who do not get the Republican every week, and they are better satisfied to have each paper complete." The difficulty for syndicates was that the definition of how many words readers wanted to read in one issue varied from editor to editor. Victor Lawson lectured McClure that short stories should be 1,000 to 2,500 words long and that serials had to divide into installments of 2,000 to 3,000 words, but the editor of the San Francisco *Argonaut* told McClure that he wanted stories complete in one issue that were from 5,000 to 7,000 words long. In December 1884 McClure reported to Mary Noailles Murfree, "They [editors] all want a story of not more than 5000 words complete in one issue," and he later recalled that in 1884 and 1885, "by crowding, we got in a short story of five thousand words, but that is the limit they [editors] would go." As for the optimal overall length of serials, Lawson told Bacheller that he wouldn't accept those shorter than 35,000 words, mainly because he did "not find publication of serials especially resultful except as we spend additional money in advertising them. To advertise a serial effectively it ought to run longer than one of 35,000 words can"; what he actually wanted, he told McClure, were "good serial stories running from 60,000 to 120,000 words."[33]

The syndicates tried whenever possible to satisfy the variety of length requirements stated by editors. A Tillotson's advertisement that appeared in the *Journalist*, for example, promised "Newspaper Fiction in all shapes: Serials or Short Tales in Various Lengths." Yet because syndicates could not strictly control the length of the fictions that authors produced, they frequently found themselves trying to sell works longer than editors wanted. In these cases, editors generally chose between two alternatives: rejecting the fiction outright or somehow accommodating it. Victor Lawson, for instance, turned down the opportunity to print Rudyard Kipling's stories "Black Jack" and the "Strange Ride of Morrowbie Jukes" because at 5,000 words each he deemed them too long for publication in one issue as short stories. The Buffalo *News* also rejected Conan Doyle's serial *The White Company* because of its length.[34]

Other editors used a variety of strategies to accommodate syndicated fiction longer than they wanted. Some squeezed in a long fiction by using a smaller type size for its last few columns; almost every fiction provided by Bacheller to the *New York Times* in 1896 was printed this way. Another simple technique was to continue the story or installment on another page of the paper. In doing so, these editors – probably inadvertently – pioneered the technique of ad-stripping (interspersing subsequent segments of a fiction with advertising) long before Edward Bok supposedly first did so with the *Ladies' Home Journal* in 1896.[35]

When short stories were too long to be accommodated with these strategies, syndicates negotiated their acceptance by suggesting to editors that they publish the first part of a short story on one day and the second on another day, telling editors that this would bring readers back to their newspapers for succeeding installments. In 1891, for example, numerous newspaper editors balked at publishing Conan Doyle's first series of Sherlock Holmes stories, syndicated by McClure, because they felt the stories were too long to publish in one issue. McClure later admitted that "When I began to syndicate the Sherlock Holmes stories, they were not at all popular with editors. The usual syndicate story ran about five thousand words, and these ran up to eight and nine thousand. We got a good many complaints from editors about their length." McClure's biographer claims that eventually McClure "jammed Sherlock Holmes down their throats for six months," but this somewhat misrepresents the actual events. To solve this dilemma McClure merely suggested to editors, "If you find that the story will occupy too much space for one issue, divide it into two parts and publish the second instalment the following week," advice which a number of editors took. After trying this strategy, McClure reported, "the editors of the papers I served began to comment favorably upon the series."[36]

Irving Bacheller, too, had to negotiate this matter of length with editors. Many of the short stories he supplied to newspapers in the years 1885–1893 were longer than most editors preferred for publication in one issue, so they were published in weekly installments. When Bacheller restarted his syndicate fiction service in the fall of 1894, he acknowledged their desires in promising them that the amount of material he supplied each day would be approximately 2,000 to 2,500 words and that he would never have a story of more than six installments (editors with whom he dealt apparently believed readers would not follow longer works). The effects of the editors' requirements are seen in at least one famous case, that of Stephen Crane's *The Red Badge of Courage*. Those who wish to condemn Bacheller for drastically cutting Crane's original manuscript should remember why Bacheller had to do so: the editors who took his service would never have taken a work that ran for as many days (probably about twenty) as the original uncut manuscript would have required. Bacheller gave himself a more heroic part than he deserved when he recalled that after reading the original manuscript, "I sent for Crane and made an arrangement with him to use about fifty thousand of his magic words as a serial. I had no place for a story of that length, but I decided to take the chance of putting it out in instalments far beyond the length of those permitted by my contracts. It was an experiment based on the hope that my judgment would swing my editors into line. They agreed with me."[37] In fact, Bacheller used only about 15,000 words of Crane's novel, and he sent the work out to editors in six installments; neither the length of each installment nor their number exceeded the limits of his contract with editors.

Recognizing that they could not meet editorial needs by strictly controlling the authors producing the fiction, Tillotson's, Bacheller, and McClure formulated quite different strategies in order to satisfy the length requirements of as many editors as possible. Tillotson's offered American newspapers a variety of "services": "Storiettes" (2,000–2,500 words), short stories or tales (4,000–5,000 words), novelettes, and serial novels. After 1894 Bacheller created a service which allowed him to purchase fictions anywhere from 2,000 to 15,000 words long, and in almost all cases he simply doled them out to editors in 2,000 to 2,500 word sections each day for one to six days. McClure, on the other hand, until 1887 offered editors numerous programs of weekday and weekend publication to choose from, each including works of very different lengths. From mid-1887 to 1901, however, McClure changed course and attempted to accommodate authors and editors with one program that offered multiple stories of various lengths for weekend publication only, and he asked each editor to choose which one(s) he wanted.

VII

A much less negotiable topic between editors and syndicates was the specific date of a fiction's first publication. After all, if a single editor published the fiction before another did, it became less valuable a commodity to other editors. For example, if the concluding installment of a serial was prematurely published in the newspaper of one city and copies shortly thereafter reached a second city where the editor was adhering to the syndicate's publication schedule, readers in that city would have no incentive to buy the local paper in order to read this fiction. Furthermore, in the competitive world of late-nineteenth-century newspaper publishing, where exclusives and scoops were highly valued by editors and readers, such premature publication threatened a newspaper's right to claim that its syndicated fiction was an exclusive feature. Tillotson's was especially worried about premature American publication of works by British authors, for this would vitiate British copyright. Even after the American Chace Act of 1891, coordinating the publication date in newspapers in the United States with the publication date in Great Britain remained very important to syndicates, who wished to protect authors' rights and keep them happy. Editors were always free, though, to publish syndicated fiction later than other editors in the syndicate if they desired, and some – possibly because an excess of local material made it difficult to fit in the syndicated fiction – did so.

This is not to say, however, that editors had no control over the schedules that syndicates set. In fact, quite frequently their needs and preferences determined the publication dates. For instance, in order to bolster the readership of their papers during the Christmas advertising season, all editors preferred that fiction by the most famous authors be provided them in November and December. In response, syndicates offered more works by famous authors at this time and even planned it so that popular serials would end in the issues just before or after Christmas day.

Editors also had a great deal of influence over the micro-publishing schedule. The biggest difference among editors was that some believed weekly publication of stories and installments was most effective in keeping their readers coming back, while others believed their readers didn't want to wait between installments and thus preferred daily publication. Victor Lawson, for example, told Tillotson's in 1888, "the only object in using serials is to build up new circulation by them. For this purpose we find that weekly installments are altogether too far apart," and he told McClure in the same year that he wanted three or four installments per week, not just one. Edward Scripps, the head of a fledgling midwestern newspaper chain, also in 1888 offered his opinion "that the greatest circulation for a daily paper can be obtained with ... the publication of stories – especially serial stories daily."[38]

At first, McClure tried to satisfy editors' conflicting desires. By December 1885 he was offering editors "Weekly Stories" for Saturday and Sunday, shorter "Daily Stories" for weekdays, and "Serial Stories" that overlapped the other services. A January 1887 circular offered four different services: "Sunday Stories," "Saturday Stories," "Monday and Tuesday Stories," and "Wednesday, Thursday, and Friday Stories." In mid-1887, though, McClure changed this strategy – possibly due to the desire of most editors with whom he dealt to publish fiction only in weekend editions – and began providing multiple fictions but only for weekend publication. Only in 1901 did the syndicate return to providing stories for weekday publication.[39]

The experience of Irving Bacheller was quite different. From 1884 to about 1893 his syndicate offered fiction only for weekend publication. Possibly in an attempt to capture the market niche deserted by McClure, however, when Bacheller restarted his syndicate in late 1894 he provided fiction to most customers for publication on six days of the week. (In the 1890s Tillotson's, too, provided short stories and serials for daily publication.) Until the demise of Bacheller's syndicate in 1898, most editors purchased fiction from him according to this schedule. Occasionally, though, the editor of a paper liked Bacheller's choice of fiction but disliked this schedule. The *Chicago Tribune*, for example, often printed entire on Sunday a two- or three-part Bacheller-syndicated fiction from the previous week. As far as can be determined, Bacheller did not object to this; in fact, he may have had a small weekly service to serve precisely this type of customer.

Not only did editors have input into the time of year and the days on which fictions would be provided, but they also had a fair amount of control over which chapters of a serial they would publish in each installment. Tillotson's directed editors "that each weekly instalment ... [should be] published as divided in the printed copy," but compliance among editors remains uncertain. With offerings by McClure and Bacheller, it appears that if an editor found himself with a larger or smaller amount of available space on a given day, he would increase or decrease the number of chapters accordingly, so long as he didn't get too far ahead of the other papers publishing the same work. For example, three newspapers (the Boston *Herald*, the Buffalo *Express*, and the Chicago *Inter-Ocean*) began publication of William Dean Howells's *The Quality of Mercy* (syndicated by McClure) on 4 October 1891 and ran this serial for thirteen installments, concluding on 27 December. Yet while the *Herald* and *Express* published chapters 1 through 4 on 4 October, the *Inter-Ocean* published chapters 1 through 5 on this date. As time went on, even the *Herald* and the *Express* publications lacked coordination, with the former on 29 November printing chapters 9 through 12 and the latter printing chapters 11 though 16. The publication dates of materials distributed by the Bacheller syndicate appear to have been more coordinated, yet here, too, there were minor variations. For instance, eight known printings of *The Red Badge of Courage* began on 3 December or 4 December 1894 and continued for six installments; however, the chapter divisions of the Philadelphia *Press* publication are slightly different from those of the other seven. In these seven, the second installment includes chapters 4 through 6, while the *Press* version includes only chapters 4 and 5.[40]

Finally, adding to the difficulties of these syndicates was the constant haggling over price that editors engaged in. Few accepted and paid the prices suggested by the syndicates, which were set according to the population of the newspaper's circulation area (the price for a fiction was higher for a newspaper in a city with a greater population in its circulation area than for one with a smaller population). Most commonly, editors responded to a sales circular by telling McClure that they would buy the story if only the price were x instead of y. In addition, editors often asked for publication rights to a larger area and better fiction for less money.[41]

The process by which a syndicate negotiated the sale of a fiction to editors and arranged the dates for its publication, then, was complex. A syndicate usually could not determine the types of fictions it would offer, when they would be published, or their price without first consulting with editors. Once the galley-proof copy was in the hands of newspaper editors, moreover, negotiations between editors and syndicates came to almost a complete halt, and neither syndicates nor authors from this point on had control over the texts or their presentation.

Newspaper editors reserved the right to edit the fictions sent to them by the syndicates, just as a magazine editor would do with an author's manuscript. One wrote to McClure that "by cutting out two or three paragraphs I greatly bettered the story, as it seems to me." According to one account, "Willa Cather ... heard the Lincoln, Nebraska, *State Journal*'s editor Will Owen grumble as he marked the copy [of *The Red Badge of Courage*] for composing and changed what did not suit him," and Cather herself remembered that "the managing editor ... several times called on me to edit the copy"; such was apparently common practice. If an editor wanted to delete objectionable passages, to shorten it, or to make it faster-moving for his imagined audience of readers, he was free to do so. One editor at the *Boston Globe*, for example, apparently tried to appeal to the hurried reader by editing Jack London's "At the Rainbow's End" so that instead of having to read long paragraphs the reader encountered shorter, more telegraphic ones.[42]

Editors and subeditors also completely controlled the other elements involved in the visual presentation of the text. First, they could alter titles and subtitles to appeal to the perceived audience. For example, one editor clearly believed that the title alone of one Henry James story was not enough to attract the reader's attention and thus used a large type headline that read: 'GEORGINA'S REASONS / The Concluding Portion of Henry James' [sic] Latest Story. / A Woman Who Commits Bigamy and Enforces Silence on Her Husband / Two Other Lives Made Miserable by Her Heartless Action." It is doubtful that James (or a syndicator trying to please James) would have allowed an editor at the *Century* or *Atlantic Monthly* to disfigure the title in this way. Occasionally, too, editors changed the titles to give the story more local appeal. An editor at the *Boston Globe*, for instance, subtitled Frank Stockton's "The Knife that Killed Po' Hancy" as "A Story of a BOSTON MAN," and in the hands of a Utica, New York, editor, Helen Jackson's "Dandy Steve" became "Dandy Steve. A Story of the Adirondacks."[43]

Local editors, too, controlled how the fictions would be illustrated. They could choose whether to use all, some, or none of the illustrations provided by the syndicates and could either use the captions provided or write their own. At least one editor went so far as to commission new illustrations that reworked and elaborated the illustrations provided by Bacheller.[44] Once again, neither syndicators nor authors had the right to review these illustrations before publication, which was common practice with magazine publication.

In addition to controlling the visual presentation of the text itself, editors controlled the print context in which the fiction would appear. Most placed syndicated fiction on prominent pages, either on the last page of an edition or on the first page of a features section. After all, if syndicated fiction was going to pay its way, it needed to be situated in a prominent place where readers could find it easily. Editors could also lay out galley-proof fiction on the individual page for strategic effect. Editors most commonly placed these fictions next to advertisements, probably in an attempt to draw attention to the latter.

VIII

Despite their complaints about authors, subjects, treatments, lengths, prices, and schedules, newspaper editors were generally pleased with galley-proof fiction, probably because they typically got the types of fiction they wanted and had a great deal of latitude as to how to use them. The most important reason editors usually got what they wanted and had so much editorial freedom was the competition among syndicates. From the very beginning of galley-proof fiction syndication in 1884, Bacheller and McClure had competed with one another, but in the 1890s the number of competitors multiplied rapidly.

Such competition helped newspaper editors avoid long-term contractual commitments with any one syndicate. A few signed contracts with McClure for one year, Bacheller for a year (or, in later years, for 26 weeks), or with the United Press for three or six months, but most preferred to remain free from such obligations. As one editor wrote McClure in January 1885, "I do not feel disposed to make any arrangements for a year, but will purchase from time to time as you may offer and we want." The editor of the Scranton *Republican* also reserved "the right to terminate the contract, if at any time the stories should be of less merit or by less eminent writers." McClure was forced in the early years to offer contracts that allowed editors to discontinue the service at any time and without penalty; one 1885 circular noted, "Terms *Weekly*. Contract terminable at pleasure of newspaper by giving notice of one week." Most editors in 1885 took matter on a case by case basis or at least not regularly. Out of the forty-four papers listed in a circular of 10 September 1885, ten published a McClure-syndicated story every day, eighteen printed one story per week (both probably under contract), and the remaining sixteen took material, "but not regularly." By 1891 McClure could write that he could rely on assured income from at least four newspapers in New York, Philadelphia, Chicago and Boston, but during the uncertain economic times of the 1890s most editors probably continued to steer clear of such long-term commitments.[45]

This lack of contractual obligation in turn allowed an editor to pick and choose among the offerings of a number of syndicates instead of being tied to just one, taking those works whose subject, length, and price suited his preferences and needs at the time. Editors purchased syndicated fiction only when they wanted to; quite a few did so only in November and December to increase readership of these financially lucrative, advertisement-packed issues, turning down offers from the syndicates the rest of the year. The end result of all of this competition was that syndicates had to remain flexible as to terms, had to expend a great deal of time and money marketing their wares, and had to provide an extensive product line that would please as many editors as possible.

To a great extent, the balance of power between syndicates and newspaper editors varied according to the methods they used to transmit texts. In the case of readyprint, the local editor had some minimal input into which fictions the readyprint editor clipped from other sources, laid out on the page, and printed for delivery to him. Yet editors who used readyprint often needed it to survive financially, a situation which placed them in a weak bargaining position, and the local editor could not significantly alter the already-printed texts. Editors who chose to use fiction in plate form had slightly more influence over fiction offerings. As long as competition existed between plate companies such as Kellogg's, the American Press

Association, the United Press, and the Western Newspaper Union (as it did until shortly after the turn of the century), the plate companies had to satisfy their customers' preferences in fiction to keep them from defecting to a competitor. Furthermore, companies such as the American Press Association which dealt directly with authors were generally able – because they dealt with less-famous authors who had little power – to procure the types of fiction local newspaper editors wanted simply by enforcing strict guidelines with authors. Finally, because plate fiction came in one-column chunks rather than printed sheets, subscribing editors also had more control over where they placed the texts in their papers.

The galley-proof syndicates afforded local newspaper editors the greatest degree of control. Galley-proof syndicates can best be understood as part-time sub-editors of these papers, doing the hard work of procuring and editing fiction and other features for the newspaper editors in return for uncertain wages. The subservient position these syndicators occupied is indicated by their own self-descriptions as "services," "agents," or "representatives" of newspapers. McClure accurately explained to one author, "You know I am simply agent for the newspapers and must supply them according to their idea of what will suit their papers."[46] Syndicates worked long and hard to satisfy the varied desires of these publishers and editors for fictions by the authors they wanted, about the subjects they wanted, of the lengths they wanted, and at the prices they wanted.

In 1896 one report stated that "The syndicate acts as a middleman, sorting out and rejecting the chaff and bringing to the attention of editors only that which has been declared good [by the syndicate editor]." Such a portrayal would seem to place syndicates in the role of literary gatekeepers with vast power over the fiction offered to editors and thus to millions of newspaper readers. Yet this depiction is inaccurate in that it misrepresents the role of the middleman/syndicator, who to please his customers usually had to satisfy their desire for what they defined as "good" fiction. Upon close examination, what scholars have taken as the preferences of galley-proof syndicators as to subject, treatment, and length of fictions are in fact chiefly the preferences of editors. Primarily middle-class men who wanted to please advertisers and boost readership among women and members of the middle class in general, these editors told syndicators or their agents what they wanted, and syndicators in turn took these desires to authors. McClure later indicated that by the time he founded *McClure's Magazine* in 1893 he had internalized the newspaper editors' requirements, telling an interviewer that " 'There was many a newspaper editor whose brain I had drawn upon unconsciously in the years of going to sell them fiction.' "[47] Only occasionally did syndicates purposely resist what editors wanted, and these cases can usually be ascribed not to syndicators' unwillingness to please editors but rather to their inability to control the fictions written by authors or to their desire to provide challenging rather than purely entertaining fictions.

Furthermore, editors who purchased galley-proof fiction had almost complete control over the venue in which this fiction was published. Unlike magazine, story paper, dime novel, and book editors and publishers in New York City, Boston, and Philadelphia who could control the layout of the final print product distributed to readers across the country, syndicators had almost no control over how a fiction text was used once they sent it to newspaper editors. Because of the individual editor's autonomy, a single syndicated fiction was presented to readers throughout the country in a variety of contexts, not a single one. Charges that "syndicates made for a uniformity and standardization of all newspapers" across the country and ended the era of local, individualistic newspapers thus appear rather poorly supported.[48]

Unfortunately for galley-proof syndicates, they controlled neither their market nor fiction production. Caught in the middle, a syndicator's only recourse was to become an expert negotiator, what cultural theorist Paul DiMaggio has termed a "brokerage administrator" who "serves both management and creators, acting as mediator, double-agent, and advocate for both, with ultimate loyalty to the former." As one contemporary put it, the syndicator "is not, in fact, the judge: he has only to record the judgment of purchasers, and to cater for them." McClure concurred, noting that "The only critic worth listening to is the publisher – the critic who backs his judgment with his money." As a result, instead of offering editors only one choice, McClure – he was no doubt typical of all the syndicators – instead took the position he described to the editor of the Austin (Texas) *Statesman* in 1893: "instead of dividing up the service and making selections myself, I prefer to send you the whole budget and let you make your own selections of material to be actually used."[49]

Local newspaper editors, not syndicators, were the gatekeepers who most controlled the flow of fiction from author to reader in the syndicate system. Only a small portion of the power of determining what fiction would be presented to readers – and how it would be – rested in the hands of syndicates in New York and Chicago; most of it was actually exercised by newspaper editors in Omaha, Poughkeepsie, Austin, Indianapolis, New Orleans, and thousands of other cities and small towns.

CHAPTER 7

Readers' experiences with syndicated fiction

I may find it provoking when seven out of ten of my weekly papers have the same serial, or short story ..., but perhaps the family next door has only one weekly and no daily paper; surely the well-written articles bought by a good syndicate are better for my neighbor's instruction and amusement than would be the trash possibly served to him otherwise.
Adelaide Cilley Waldron, 1887

The creation of a new audience is the most difficult feat known to literature, and the most important. Such work is not often done; when it is done it brings revolution for both writer and reader ... This revolution [caused by S. S. McClure's syndicate], this discovery of a new audience, has multiplied by millions those who read and know the first authors of the day in certain classes of literary work ...
Talcott Williams, editor of the Philadelphia *Press*, [1891]

The Newspaper and enlightenment go together; and the work of the [Tillotson's] Fiction Department has certainly been to the advantage of humanity in all parts of the world. The best literature, perused by intelligent people in various countries, must have an uplifting and an elevating effect on the human minds.
John Nayler of Tillotson and Son's, 1917[1]

As one can readily observe from previous chapters, the processes involved in procuring, editing, marketing, distributing, and printing syndicated fiction were quite complex. All of the parties involved — authors, literary agents, syndicators, and newspaper editors — were forced to negotiate the terms governing the production of this literary product. More difficult to ascertain, however, is the influence that readers had over what was syndicated and how they reacted to and interpreted the fictions presented to them. The chief reason for this difficulty is that historical readers are elusive beings who rarely recorded how they reacted to written materials. There is some evidence that readers had input into which fictions the syndicates distributed and the editors printed. Newspaper editors and syndicators, for example, occasionally noted how readers responded to certain syndicated fictions and said that these responses influenced which fictions the editors bought; this evidence, however, must be viewed with some skepticism. Were the observations made by editors and syndicators based on actual statements or letters they received from readers, or on vague hunches about the preferences of these readers? If the former, the statements might not be very representative, since possibly only those readers literate or empowered enough would take the time to contact editors and the syndicates. Quite possibly, too, editors and syndicators did not listen as intently to the reactions of readers from the lower classes, since they were not the middle-class consumers and readers whom the editors – and thus the syndicators – most wanted to attract and please. At the same time, because these editors were interested in satisfying their readers, their reports of how readers responded cannot be completely dismissed for their bias; they might in fact be quite accurate.

Readers' reactions to syndicated fiction – or any printed material – are guided and prompted by a complex framework surrounding the reading experience. Many elements make up this framework. They include where and when the fiction was read, what expectations the readers brought to reading, the class and gender of the reader, the broad societal attitude towards reading that particular type of printed material, and the print context of the pages on which the fictions appeared. There is certainly much more work to be done in order to fully understand the experiences of the millions of readers of syndicated fiction in the nineteenth century. This chapter, however, seeks to provide as complete documentation as possible of the context of this particular reading experience, so that more informed hypotheses can be made about how actual readers probably interacted with such fiction.

I

One must first ask whether readers even noticed syndicated fiction, since it was usually shoehorned in between advertisements, news stories, and various features. There is some evidence that in larger cities, before readers became accustomed to the concept of fiction in the newspaper, readers sometimes didn't notice it. Talcott Williams of the Philadelphia *Press*, for instance, told S. S. McClure in 1885 that his paper "cut one [serial] in the middle and did not get a single complaint from a single reader." In 1884 a Chicago newspaper editor who printed a Henry James story syndicated by Charles Dana also opined that readers did not respond to it. Having agreed to pay Dana $500 for the right to publish the story, the editor advertised the feature heavily yet "was genuinely surprised to find that nobody seemed at all excited" when it was published. The reporter who recounted this editor's experience concluded that the syndicate idea would never be popular in the United States because the conditions were much unlike those in France, where the *feuilletons* were extremely popular. There, the author wrote, "the principal part of the circulation ... comes from the provinces; from quiet, dull folks who have nothing else to do than to read the papers, and get vastly interested in an exciting story."[2]

Yet despite these initial observations, many readers in urban and rural areas alike eventually noticed syndicated fiction and came to expect it as part of the daily or Sunday newspaper. In 1891, for example, the editor of the Chicago *Inter-Ocean* told S. S. McClure that because of overwhelming demand, he had to print a second edition of the paper containing the first installment of William Dean Howells's *The Quality of Mercy*. Those who took the most cognizance of original syndicated fiction published in metropolitan newspapers appear to have been readers in the countryside, who were hungry for good fiction yet had little access to current magazines and books. McClure paraphrased Charles Taylor, editor of the *Boston Globe*, as telling him that "in a great many families all over New England certain members of the family take the Globe simply for the [syndicated] stories it contains and nothing else." Readers of the *Detroit Free Press* (which was distributed extensively outside the city) clearly noticed at least one serial syndicated by McClure and entitled, "Who Killed Agatha Webb?" In response to a contest in 1899 offering prizes for the correct solution to the mystery, the *Free Press* received guesses from 1,280 readers who were involved enough in the serial to take the time to write.[3]

Not only did readers read syndicated fiction, but they also appear to have appreciated its inclusion in newspapers. Most commendations of readyprint and plate service came from newspaper editors who liked the services because they helped cut down on expenses. Yet many editors also mentioned in their applausive statements that the services had pleased their readers and boosted the circulation of their newspapers. One editor from Aurora, Illinois, for example, wrote the Kellogg Company that he was "thoroughly convinced that they [the patent insides] are very satisfactory to our subscribers." An editor from Henry, Illinois, told Kellogg that his paper's circulation had increased dramatically since he began using patent insides and concluded that this increase "comes simply and solely because they [the readers] approve of the paper, both as to its local and general character," the latter which would have included fiction. Finally, in 1891 a somewhat biased American Press Assocation publication reported "the increased favor with which serial stories are received by newspaper readers."[4]

Readers also reacted positively to fiction syndicated in galley-proof form. Syndicates had promised editors that a prominent author's name attached to a syndicated fiction would serve "as an advertising card that will attract readers to subscribing papers," and a number of objective commentators indicated that syndicated fiction succeeded in delivering on these promises. One trade journal writer told editors in 1896, "The legitimate use of popular literature [in newspapers] has usually been well supported by the public." An 1884 editorial in the *San Francisco Chronicle* noted that the series of stories by Henry James and Bret Harte syndicated by Dana "seems to meet with popular approval." Other editors also appear to have been pleased by the reaction of readers to syndicated fictions. Victor Lawson, who in 1886 wrote that he used syndicated fiction "as a leverage to secure additional readers on Saturday's issue" of the *Chicago Daily News*, in 1888 set out to "find out by actual results whether they [syndicated serials] constitute a drawing feature in our paper or not." Apparently, what he found out was positive: in 1890 he wrote to Tillotson's that syndicated fictions "have become a feature of increasing relative importance in our newspaper publications." In Auburn, New York, one editor commented that a serial by H. H. Boyesen, syndicated by McClure, had "attracted a great deal of attention so far," and he posited just a few months later that McClure-syndicated fiction had boosted the circulation of his paper. Edward Scripps wrote in 1888 that since his chain of newspapers had begun printing original serial stories two years earlier (these were probably provided by syndicates), they had experienced great "success in the way of making rapid increase in circulation." And, as he noted previously, he stated that fourteen years of newspaper experience had taught him "that the greatest circulation for a daily paper can be obtained with the least possible expense of money ... by the publication of stories – especially serial stories daily."[5]

Whether including syndicated fiction attracted the middle-class women readers newspaper editors hoped it would remains uncertain. Newspaper historian Elmer Davis writes that he doubts "any American paper ever accomplished much by printing fiction in its daily issue," yet significantly qualifies this by completing the sentence with, "unless it be that peculiar type of fiction which is written for and found only upon the woman's page of evening newspapers." Editors appear to have succeeded to some extent in making newspaper reading an activity no longer enjoyed solely by men, but this might have been due to the inclusion of other non-fiction features of interest to women or to the loosening of societal restrictions on what women were allowed to read. One observer in 1896 reported his personal experience that "at least on the cars, they [women] read them [newspapers] much more than was formerly the case," and that a newsstand at a summer resort where he was staying "was much patronized by the women of the place." The librarian of the St. Louis Public Library observed that the women who came to the reading room "patronize[d] the daily newspapers fully as much as the others" did. William Dean Howells, on the other hand, offered a somewhat opposing view, reporting in 1893 that "as yet the women, who form the largest, if not the only cultivated class among us, have not taken very cordially to the Sunday edition, except for its social gossip; they certainly do not go to it for their fiction." In 1902 Howells further wrote that "The common notion is that books are the right sort of reading for girls, who are also allowed the modified form of books which we know as magazines, but are not expected to read newspapers." This expectation, he added, was "so prevalent and so penetrant" that he was shocked to see "a pretty and prettily dressed girl in the Elevated train, reading a daily newspaper quite as if she were a man." At the same time, however, one can point out the experience of a Californian named Geraldine Bonner who, while visiting New York City in 1898, read an installment of Frank Norris's syndicated "Moran of the Lady Letty" in the New York *Sun*. This woman wrote that she was drawn to the work by its "brusque and almost defiant sharpness of phrase and the lurid picturesqueness of its setting," and was disappointed when she was unable to obtain and read succeeding installments in the *Sun*.[6] Before mass-market magazines became more easily available throughout the country in the mid-1890s, it is clear, many people relied on newspapers to supply them with syndicated fiction on a daily or weekly basis.

II

To begin to understand how readers reacted to and interpreted syndicated fictions, one must first comprehend the contexts in which they were read. For this discussion I will differentiate between two types of context. One is what I call "non-print context," which includes those factors such as where and when newspapers – and by extension the syndicated fiction printed therein – were read, the reader's class and gender, the various contemporary criticisms of newspaper reading, and the societal expectations of what a newspaper should contain. The second I call "print context," which pertains to the physical newspaper itself: the paper on which the texts were printed and the arrangement and presentation of these texts on the page.

The non-print contexts in which readers encountered syndicated fictions were usually different than those in which they encountered fiction in books and literary magazines. First, according to numerous contemporary reports, newspapers were commonly read in different settings and in a different manner. There is little information on where, when, and how readers specifically read syndicated fiction in the newspaper. However, since it is likely that the contexts in which persons read the newspaper as a whole and the fiction in particular were much the same, I believe that the information available on newspaper reading can reasonably be applied to syndicated fiction reading.

In small towns and rural areas, where newspapers with readyprint and plate service fiction were most likely to be read, newspapers were read more intensively than they were in the cities. This was due in part to the fact that until the late 1880s city newspapers had minimal market penetration into rural areas, and not until the late 1890s would books and magazines become more readily available there. Ansel Nash Kellogg reported in 1878 that papers taking his service "penetrate[d] to districts where no other papers circulate[d]," and this is corroborated by the testimony of one editor who purchased readyprint sheets from Kellogg and noted, "The bulk of my subscribers are those who do not take the daily papers." One newspaperman later recalled that in the 1870s and 1880s, "Not one farmer in three hundred got a daily paper ... Many farmers of the United States were served by a post office to which the mail was brought only once in two weeks." Hamlin Garland, who had first-hand experience of such conditions, described the interior of one Wisconsin house in his story "Up the Coolly" as having "no books, no music, and only a few newspapers in sight." Laura Ingalls Wilder recalled that in her isolated South Dakota home in the 1880s, the chief reading materials were the St. Paul *Pioneer-Press* and Chicago *Inter-Ocean*, both of which included syndicated fiction at about this time. Because of the paucity of fiction in book and magazine form, individual copies of newspapers that included fiction were read intensively by more than one reader. One Kellogg publication posited that "The county paper is frequently shared by two or more families, and passes from one to the other, being read and re-read until it is worn out." Historian Wayne Fuller supports this contention, writing that even in the 1890s, "newspapers and magazines were still scarce enough in country neighborhoods to be saved and passed around." As a result, contemporary observers estimated that five persons read each copy of a country newspaper. In addition, at least before city papers and magazines intruded on the domain of the rural newspaper, families appear to have valued the fiction printed therein in readyprint or plate form. One newspaper historian writes, "Many families regularly clipped the novels, short stories and other entertaining and educational matter from the ready-print and kept it in scrap books for reading and reference"; he adds, "Nineteenth century mothers, north and south, taught their children from scrap-books thick with clippings from the ready-print."[7] One can hypothesize that in rural areas where such practices existed, syndicated fiction was reread frequently and widely discussed.

In the cities, the conditions surrounding newspaper reading appear to have often been quite different. Some of "the vast army of men and women who desire good reading matter on their day of rest" did have the opportunity to read as slowly and as leisurely as their rural counterparts. One writer in the *Boston Herald* in 1885 noted that "At the noon-time respite, or when the day's work is over, the paper is read through [by artisans, mechanics, and laborers]. It is the poor man's theatre, club, and library." A year later another knowledgeable commentator concluded, "The family appetite for the newspaper is at no time so keen as on Sunday morning, when all the household has time to bestow upon its perusal, and when the plans for the coming week both for business and for pleasure are determined by the contents of the newspaper." Such an environment would have been conducive to serious contemplation of syndicated fiction.[8]

More typically, however, city dwellers read their newspapers in very different contexts and manners. Because of the faster pace of life and surfeit of print in late-nineteenth-century cities, readers there probably read newspapers more quickly than in rural areas. One writer posited in 1885 that most papers were "'skimmed over' in the ten minutes which the average city dweller allows himself to read the paper." Many urbanites bought their newspapers from newsstands and read them in transit to and from work and during breaks at work. As one 1895 report put it, "the modern business man never fails to read it [the newspaper] on the train, at least cursorily," and in William Dean Howells's *The Rise of Silas Lapham* (1885), Lapham himself skims through two newspapers in the first twenty minutes or so of a ferry ride. In addition, a contemporary report asserted, "Continuous reading is impossible on a journey which is broken every five minutes by jerks and jolts."[9] It is not unreasonable to believe that even some Sunday papers were read in these settings. Syndicated fictions read under such conditions, one would suppose, were unlikely to be the object of readers' sustained attention.

Socioeconomic class also might have influenced the individual's experiences of newspaper reading. It is quite possible that the less disposable income one had, the more one paid attention to syndicated fiction; those with more money could purchase fiction in book or magazine form and read it in more leisurely settings. And it is very probable that more formally educated readers (or at least those more trained in literary analysis) would have taken syndicated fiction less seriously than the fiction which appeared in monthly literary magazines or in book form and which was deemed "artistic" by cultural arbiters.

Despite these differences, however, there were a number of similarities between newspaper reading practices of different classes. Such reading, for instance, was often a communal activity. At some worksites, especially cigar factories, papers were read to workers as they performed their tasks. As a young man in New York City, future labor leader Samuel Gompers "had a habit of saving any interesting magazine or newspaper articles to read to [his] shopmates," and the narrator of James Weldon Johnson's *The Autobiography of an Ex-Coloured Man* (1912) remarks that "the 'reader' is quite an institution in all cigar factories which employ Spanish-speaking workmen." Communal newspaper reading was also sometimes practiced among members of the middle and upper classes. As one female magazine editor reported in 1895, her brother often "reads aloud to me extracts from these journals [Sunday newspapers] that are entertaining and beneficial." As electric lighting became more available to middle-class homes in the 1890s, however, it is possible that class differences in reading habits were accentuated. For those to whom electricity was neither available nor affordable, communal reading in which one reader sat near the lamp might have continued longer, while among those who had a number of individual electric lights, there might have been less communal reading. As one magazine commentator put it in 1909, the practice of "reading aloud" among families – probably referring to middle-class ones – had greatly declined not only because of electric light but also because of central heating and the availability of cheap books, all of which supposedly caused families to lose their sense of unity and focus.[10]

Gender, too, might have helped shape readers' experiences of newspaper reading and, by extension, of syndicated fiction. In 1885 William Dean Howells drew a sharp distinction between men such as Silas Lapham who remarks, "I get about all the reading I want in the newspapers" and his daughters, who read fiction in volume form. As noted previously, it appears that by 1900 reading newspapers was no longer an experience reserved only for males. Yet one 1896 description of how the Sunday paper was read in homes is quite symbolic: "the father reads it, [and] the wife peruses it over her husband's shoulder." Women clearly did not always read over men's actual shoulders, but this statement indicates that although women were being invited to this male province by newspaper editors, other men were only grudgingly allowing them in. Given such a context, it is not surprising that women's use of their newly-allowed reading materials was watched closely. Would women use the papers to help gain admission to the male public sphere of politics and business? Would their reading make them better-versed on current affairs and thus worthy of greater "respect" from men? This concern was voiced by one female reporter who in 1894 asked a group of women newspaper readers whether they could tell her "the exact status of the Hawaiian question at present, and the latest developments in Brazil and how the Lehigh strike is progressing." The interviewer noted that in response, "There was a perceptible gasp, and each woman looked anxiously at her neighbor," indicating that this was not what they read the newspaper for. However, when these same women answered the reporter's question about whether they read the advertisements, "The five countenances brightened. Then as if they had suddenly decided that it wasn't the proper thing to be 'up' on advertisements, while they gave little heed to the news, the five assumed a careless air." As one can infer from this one exchange, women were under great pressure from some quarters to read the newspaper "properly," i. e. for news rather than for "softer" features and advertising. Did women avoid syndicated fiction because of this pressure? Or did women women resist this pressure, risk societal opprobrium, and read features such as syndicated fiction anyway? If so, it is possible that they might have felt the need to read such fiction instrumentally, as a source of information about history, morality, child-rearing, and so forth, in order to prove to males that this activity was "valuable" and worthy of respect.[11]

Another factor that framed the newspaper reading experience was the general criticism of newspapers towards the end of the century, not only for publishing on Sunday but also for corrupting American morals and language with their sensationalism. As noted previously, many clergymen and religious persons objected to the sale and reading of newspapers on the Sabbath. The attack on modern, "degraded" newspapers and their effect on readers was widespread and often vitriolic. One comment published in *Century* magazine in 1887 is representative. The typical reader, it argued, "lays his newspaper down and rises bewildered by a phantasmagoria of unconnected facts relating to every part of the universe, with his taste vitiated by slang, bad English, loose information, everything which can dissipate his mental energies, and with his heart, it may be, corrupted by grosser evils." Readers in metropolitan public library reading rooms were exposed more directly to this critical attitude. These readers, who either could not or preferred not to pay the two or five cents for a newspaper, usually had to pay the price of listening to a moral lecture from librarians or at least braving their open disdain for newspapers.[12] One can hypothesize that such conditions might have led readers to relieve their feelings of guilt – especially on Sundays – by focusing more on the morally edifying aspects of newspaper fiction than on its other elements.

Possibly the most important non-print context that all readers of syndicated fiction shared was their expectation of what a newspaper should contain. Readers purchased and read newspapers with expectations different than those they would have had of a book or literary magazine. Purchasers would have expected the newspaper to provide useful and timely information that would help them in their roles as social, political, and economic beings, much more so than they would have expected books or monthly literary magazines to do. Indeed, readers were advised to differentiate between these print forms. One columnist wrote in 1893, "If he [the intelligent man] reads the best of what is in the magazines he will read most of the best new fiction before it gets between covers, and will supplement usefully the current information that he gets from the newspapers." This same columnist advised that the best way to read the newspapers was to read quickly, "wresting the news out of them like the meat from a nutshell, and discarding the rest." A series of articles published in 1895 on how a business woman, a variety theatrical manager, a tragedian, and a physician read the newspaper indicates that readers then, as now, were most concerned with information relating to his or her interests and work. In addition, readers would have expected that what they read in the newspaper would provide them with material that they could discuss among their peers. Newspapers, much more than books or magazines, formed a common bond among readers who were also members of the same general community; items in the newspaper would inevitably be discussed at work or at home. In 1885 one writer noted, "One may often hear at the shops, the homes or the customary reports of the working classes in this country a[n] ... intelligent discussion of the news of the day."[13] As a result, readers probably thought of reading the newspaper as an act whereby one gathered information of communal importance – including probably fiction – which one could use in daily conversation. Such was also the case with monthly magazines publishing serials, but one might suppose that serials published in daily or weekly installments in newspapers were even more talked about.

III

What most complicates the task of understanding what meaning readers made of syndicated fiction are the numerous textual and contextual variants in which each fiction appeared. Because of the methods used to transmit them, individual texts in readyprint and plate form were usually almost identical, but texts distributed in galley-proof form rarely were the same in more than one newspaper. Furthermore, these texts were printed in newspapers that had a variety of overall tones; some were sensational, some were serious and dry, and the majority were between these two poles. Finally, because of the great variety of readyprint editions and the fact that local editors controlled placement of the fiction texts in plate and galley-proof forms, they almost never appeared in the same print context. Thus readers across the country did not react to one massproduced and identical text but rather to numerous variations of one text printed in a wide variety of contexts.

Some textual editors and bibliographers have noticed and recorded the variations in fiction texts produced by this system. Such work is undoubtedly valuable for establishing authoritative texts of certain works. However, because our concern here is to understand how readers reacted to texts, I believe we must focus on the actual printed forms – corrupted or not and however far from authorial intention they might be – that were presented to readers. Furthermore, we must recognize that the fiction texts themselves form but single components of larger texts which we must read to understand better how readers made meanings from the fictions. We must broaden our field of focus to include the perceived tone of the periodical as a whole and the other materials appearing on the same page and on other newspaper pages in the same edition. Compared to a newly-discovered newspaper appearance and text of a major work such as *The Red Badge of Courage*, the other printed materials on the newspaper page might seem no more than superfluous, ephemeral banter, unworthy of much attention, but because these too would have influenced how readers responded to a work, they certainly should be taken into account.[14]

Individual newspaper readers undoubtedly made a unique meaning of each text, not only because each reader brought his or her own expectations and life experiences to the textual encounter, but also because the method of textual transmission the syndicates used meant that the print context for each syndicated fiction was different. However, there were some commonalities among readers' experiences, and it is worth examining how the shared experiences of a great number of readers of syndicated fiction texts might have influenced their interpretations. These general suggestions are intended not as definitive answers but as indications of the many directions future research in this field might take.

Readers in the late nineteenth century recognized that each newspaper had a specific bias and tone that made up its "personality"; they chose which newspaper to buy largely because the bias and tone – its general outlook and "message" about what was most important in life – pleased them. Readers' responses to the texts contained in these papers were probably in some ways conditioned by the perceived tone, which as Louis James writes is communicated "through its layout, its selection, arrangement and general presentation, the use or absence of illustrations, the size of columns, paragraphs, [and] the type itself."[15] Because of the subtle yet strong message the newspaper transmitted about how its contents should be read, it is likely that readers – of whatever socioeconomic background – who encountered a syndicated fiction in the "serious" New York *Commercial-Advertiser*, a paper intended for the business community, did not react to it in the same way as did readers of the same work printed in the more sensational *Boston Globe*. The fiction text might be the same, but the tone very probably influenced readers to approach it either as "informative" or "entertaining."

To make meanings of literary texts, all newspaper readers had to negotiate the visual and ideological smorgasbord of intertwined texts that made up the American newspaper in the late nineteenth century. In the 1860s, 1870s, and 1880s, newspapers looked very different from magazines, books, and story papers. Fictions printed in these latter forms generally appeared by themselves on the page. Literary magazines such as the *Atlantic Monthly*, *Harper's Monthly*, and *Century* usually separated fiction from non-fiction texts and relegated advertisements to their back pages, away from the texts. Books, too, contained advertisements only in their end pages, and weekly story papers often did not intersperse advertisements and news items with the fictions. In contrast, readyprint, plate service, and galley-proof fictions rarely appeared by themselves on the printed page. Editors placed the texts, cluttered with their own headlines, sub-headlines, copyright notices, illustrations, and captions, in the midst of a visually stimulating array of illustrated advertisements, news stories with bold headlines, features for women, and so forth. One reader perceptively commented in 1890 that in American newspapers, "The line between what purports to be news and what is fiction is sometimes difficult to draw."[16] There was little differentiation between non-fiction and fiction texts; the word "story" could be applied to texts in both categories, and advertisements frequently were disguised as news stories. Magazines, on the other hand, generally did not follow suit and present fiction, news stories, advertisements, and illustrations together on the same pages until the 1890s.

The lack of differentiation between fiction and non-fiction stories in newspapers, I believe, is quite significant. Only in the 1890s did major metropolitan newspapers begin to be divided into separate sections or departments, which "encouraged selective reading, a habit that appealed to people whose experience of modernity taught them to live life in segments and not as a totality." Before this, the juxtaposition of fiction and non-fiction texts on the page and the general expectation of what was the most important component of newspapers might have led readers to believe fiction provided important information for living life, just as the other articles and advertisements did. This in turn might have led readers to read syndicated fiction more literally than they would have if they had encountered such texts in a literary magazine or book, where the fiction was clearly separated from considerations of real life. Instead of viewing the fiction text as a set of verbal signs whose true meaning could be ascertained only through careful analysis, newspaper readers possibly read fiction texts the same way they did news stories and features: hurriedly and for information. Many newspapers encouraged such a reading strategy by sponsoring prize contests that forced readers to look for clues contained in syndicated fiction serials. Editors thus prompted readers to look only for "valuable" information that would lead them to the prize – just as one looked for "valuable" information in other newspaper items – rather than to pay attention to literary style, characterization, and so forth. One contest in the *Boston Globe* in 1891 to "guess the secret of Austin Craige's strange fate," for example, encouraged readers to disregard the "literary" elements of the preceding serial installments. One advertisement advised readers to "study all the situations and motives that enter into the mystery," and another noted, "The entire novel will be boiled down [in the next day's paper], so that those who failed to read the preceding chapters may get it all in an hour's time next Sunday." The message sent to readers was as clear as that of a plot synopsis intended to help undergraduates avoid reading an entire novel or play: only the plot "matters." One example of this type of reading is provided by author Anzia Yezierska, who would have had ample opportunity to observe how working class readers used newspapers around the turn of the century. Sara Smolinsky, the Jewish, working-class protagonist of Yezierska's novel *Bread Givers* (1925), uses the plot of one newspaper serial as inspirational information. At a turning point in her life she remembers: "The story from the Sunday paper. A girl – slaving away in the shop. Her hair was already turning gray, and nothing had ever happened to her. Then suddenly she began to study in the night school, then college. And worked and studied, on and on, till she became a teacher in the schools." Acting on this newspaper text, Sara promptly sets to work pursuing the goal of becoming a schoolteacher.[17]

Reinforcing the idea that syndicated fictions should be read literally and for information was the fact that they frequently dealt with topics then current. Editors and readers increasingly demanded the latest, freshest news to print in newspapers whose very form emphasized how one had to consume the information of the day quickly before it was made obsolete by the next day's news. Not only did the newsprint on which the fictions were printed begin to decay almost immediately, but the contents were dated and expected to be, in contemporary terminology, "timely." Wire services such as the Associated Press and United Press had been established to satisfy this desire, and the syndicates tried to emulate them by furnishing fictions that dealt with current topics. For example, Frank Norris's "A Salvation Boom in Matabeleland," a short story about the grisly massacre of an American Salvation Army worker by the Zulus, appeared in the *Syracuse Herald* under the regular headline for its syndicated fiction section, "Fiction That Deals With Things That Are Up to Date," at a time when the Boer War was the subject of many news articles. One story syndicated by Bacheller entitled "Manuel: A Cuban Insurgent" was certainly timely, appearing on 21 March 1898, shortly after the *Maine* was blown up in Havana harbor; it was printed in a newspaper containing numerous news stories on the inquiry into the *Maine* explosion and on war preparations.[18]

If readers did read syndicated fictions for information, one must wonder to what degree such texts supported, complemented, or contradicted the supposedly non-fiction texts appearing next to them. When examined closely, the newspaper pages on which syndicated fictions were printed appear as sites where readers were prompted to transfer knowledge between various printed items. For example, how could readers help but transfer what they knew from news reports to their interpretations of "Manuel: A Cuban Insurgent," which was about Manuel Ortega, a young Cuban living in New York who returns with journalists to Cuba, joins the insurgents, and frees his sweetheart from the clutches of the evil Spaniards? Conversely, readers might have used the fiction to help them formulate their views about news stories on the same topic.

Another example of this type of ideological transfer is observed in the frequent juxtaposition of syndicated love stories with articles on how to please a man, how to run a household, and other topics. In one instance, an article entitled, "Fair Bathers. Their Natty Suits and Wonderful Tricks in the Tub. Amusing Wednesday and Saturday Scenes in the Natatorium," with its clearly male and voyeuristic implications, appeared directly to the left of one installment of Henry James's "Georgina's Reasons" in the *Chicago Tribune* (the latter was subtitled by the local editor, "A Woman Who Commits Bigamy and Enforces Silence on Her Husband. Two Other Lives Made Miserable by Her Heartless Action").[19] One might hypothesize that the feature article and subtitle reinforced the idea that women were supposed to be passive objects of men's gaze rather than active agents, and that any deviation from this expectation by a fictional or non-fictional character was to be condemned.

One might also ask how readers transferred information between the syndicated fictions about the interaction of European whites and non-white peoples throughout the world and the news stories and features on this topic that frequently appeared next to them. Dozens of short stories and serials distributed by the syndicates had as their setting British colonies such as India (Rudyard Kipling), and imperialistic hotspots such as South Africa (P. Y. Black, H. Rider Haggard), the Phillipines (Captain Charles King), and Samoa (Robert Louis Stevenson), among others. Many syndicated fictions also had as their subject the relationship between whites in the United States and non-whites such as Native Americans and African Americans. Approximately half of the fictions distributed by readyprint and plate services were westerns, many of which involved the conflict between white settlers and Native Americans. There were many fewer syndicated stories about African Americans, probably because syndicates wished to avoid alienating Southern newspaper editors. Significantly, most of the small number of such stories were written by such whites as Joel Chandler Harris and Richard Malcolm Johnston; only a few were by such African American authors as Charles Chesnutt and Paul Laurence Dunbar. Certainly an investigation of how syndicated fictions reinforced or worked against stereotypes of all of these racial groups would be an interesting topic of future research.

The purposeful juxtaposition of fiction and advertisements by editors could also have had an effect on what meanings readers made of syndicated fictions. One contemporary reader astutely observed that in the New York newspapers, "I experience some difficulty in sifting the reading matter from the advertisements. The two are often adroitly intermingled." Readyprint, plate, and galley-proof fictions were most frequently surrounded by patent medicine and clothing advertisements directed at women, and these advertisements – many of which emphasized timeliness just as news articles did – probably influenced how readers interpreted the fiction texts. The works of Sarah Orne Jewett and Mary E. Wilkins (Freeman), for example, were viewed as very popular drawing cards for women readers, and editors made the most they could of them. When Sarah Orne Jewett's "A Pinch of Salt" was printed in the *Syracuse Daily Journal* in 1897, it was accompanied on the page by a piece entitled, "A Healthy Wife Is a Husband's Inspiration," another on the work of the Syracuse Council of Jewish Women, and one on "Fashion Hints." Advertisements on this page were for Royal Baking Powder, Fairbank's Gold Dust Washing Powder, and Gail Borden Eagle Brand Condensed Milk, touted as having "no equal as an infant food." Wilkins's "Serena Ann. Her First Christmas Keeping," syndicated by Bacheller for publication on 15 December 1894, appeared in the *Utica Daily Observer* and was the only non-advertising text on the page; all the rest of the space was taken up by advertisements for a special Christmas week sale at a local department store, a shoe store that promised "Every purchaser of Women's Shoes or slippers will be given a handsomely bound book," and one for a pants store that suggested, "A Sensible and Very Acceptable CHRISTMAS PRESENT is a Pair of Our $3.00 PANTS!"[20]

In another example from the *Utica Daily Observer*, the first installment of David Wechsler's "When Doctors Disagree," an 1894 serial story syndicated by Bacheller, was almost lost in a sea of advertisements for medicines, many of which were specifically directed at women. (Such was common practice in "patent insides," which got their name from the large number of advertisements for patent medicines.) One for Dr. Greene's Nervura blood and nerve remedy was disguised as an article entitled, "A WOMAN'S SUFFERINGS / Some of the Agonies They Needlessly Endure." Others included one for "Royal Penny Tablets [that] were for LADIES' [sic] ONLY!" and another which, under the headline, "How to Manage A Husband," advised the reader suffering from a husband whose liver ailments were making him cross: "Give him ROUGH ON BILE PILLS."[21]

Such coordination was not only directed at women readers. When the subject of the fiction seemed of more interest to men, the advertisements also sometimes became more male-directed. The appearance in the *Utica Daily Observer* of a story syndicated by Bacheller, Stephen Crane's "A Mystery of Heroism. A Detail of an American Battle," provides one such example. Appearing on the same page as part one of this story was an advertisement for a product called "Magnetic Nervine," which promised in large letters, "VIGOR OF MEN / Easily, Quickly, Permanently Restored"; another one for "Sex-ine Pills" also promised to "RESTORE LOST VIGOR." Part two of this story the next day was accompanied by a large advertisement for "Duke's Mixture" tobacco and an even larger one for "Narcoti-Cure," promised to cure "the tobacco habit in 4 to 10 days or money refunded." In an era when smoking was chiefly a male activity, the intended audience's gender can be easily inferred. And when Crane's "One Dash – Horses," an adventure story set in Mexico, appeared in the *Syracuse Daily Journal* in early 1896, it was accompanied by advertisements for rye whiskey and a new medical book "written for Men Only" and entitled, *Complete Manhood and How to Attain It*.[22]

To what degree, one might ask, did these juxtapositions prompt readers to associate purchasing certain goods and reading certain types of fictions with "femininity" or "masculinity"? Did they encourage readers – especially women – to view the fictions as "healthful," therapeutic entertainment commodities that should be used up and discarded? Could the juxtapositions also have led readers to read the fictions instrumentally, for "information," as one was trained to read the advertisements, rather than as something to interpret and use for personal reflection?

Other visual cues for readers besides advertisements that deserve further attention are the subtitles and illustrations that often accompanied the syndicated fiction texts, all of which functioned as indicators of what readers should look for in the fiction texts. Subtitles in the *Chicago Tribune* for Henry James's "Georgina's Reasons," for example, use terms such as "Heartless," "Whimsical," "Self-Willed," and "Fickle" to describe various characters. Editors were revealing their own attitudes towards these characters, but they were also indirectly indicating to readers the "proper" view of them. Another example of an editor's hint is the subtitle for Norris's "A Salvation Boom in Matabeleland" in the *Syracuse Herald*: "Showing That Although Music Has Power to Calm the Savage Mind, Its Effects Soon Wear Off and the Savage Mind Is Worse Than It Was Before." Readers were thus effectively discouraged from producing alternative interpretations. The reader of the same text in other papers, though, was allowed more freedom of interpretation, for in some there was no subtitle and in others it was simply, "A Tale of Music That Temporarily Charmed in South Africa." In the same way, illustrations might have led some readers to look only for certain scenes in the text, or sent the message that the illustrated scenes, not others, were most important. Not all newspapers, though, purchased the illustrations that the syndicates usually offered, and it is possible that readers of non-illustrated newspapers consequently experienced more interpretive latitude. Furthermore, one must also take into account the captions for these illustrations. Certainly readers could not have missed the message of the caption that the McClure syndicate provided for an illustration of dancing tribesmen that accompanied Frank Norris's "A Salvation Boom in Matabeleland": "They Danced Fiercely About." Without this prompt, one could easily view the dancing tribesmen as happy or celebratory rather than "fierce."[23]

IV

The conditions framing and possibly influencing how syndicated fiction was read were thus quite different from those for books and most literary magazines. It is tempting to posit that readers of syndicated fiction felt manipulated by syndicates and editors and had to passively accept what was offered to them. Most readers did probably feel that they had little input into which fictions were presented to them and how and when they would be. Yet not all readers felt this way. Some readers contacted editors to tell them what they liked and disliked, and these preferences were cited by editors as reasons for choosing certain syndicated fictions over others. Victor Lawson, for one, conveyed his readers' concerns, writing to Tillotson's, "There was considerable complaint about his [Wilkie Collins's] 'Evil Genius' when we published it, one reader even going so far as to charge ... we were palming off a counterfeit." Some readers sent their complaints directly to the syndicates. When McClure edited out crucial portions of a Julian Hawthorne serial, for example, he later recalled, "along came letters from people saying that there were some characters in the story that they did not know anything about."[24] The vast majority of readers, however, probably expressed their approval or disapproval of a particular serial or fiction series by purchasing or not purchasing the newspapers which contained them.

Similarly, readers were also probably less than passive when they interpreted the syndicated fictions. Clearly, readers' interpretations were not tightly controlled by the syndicates, or even by newspaper editors. By strategically placing the fiction texts alongside other texts or advertisements, by including illustrations or leaving them out, and by creating leading subtitles and captions, editors could unintentionally influence interpretation somewhat, but the numerous other factors involved, such as the reader's expectations, life experiences, and when, where, and how the fiction was read, also affected interpretation. As a result, even if syndicated fictions were formulaic or presented in a single identical form, this did not necessarily limit the meanings that readers generated from the texts. This is made especially clear by the letters that readers wrote to the *Boston Globe* in 1891 to explain their numerous and widely divergent "solutions" to a serialized mystery novel; as the *Globe* noted, "Hardly a person mentioned in any part of the story escaped suspicion at the hands of the watchful readers." Until more research is done in this area, one must agree with Janice Radway's conclusion that "In reality we do not know whether mass-produced texts are used up, exhausted, and then discarded by the people who rely upon them to fulfill their need for meaningful stories about their own lives." I believe, however, that the contextualization of syndicated fiction reading provided here establishes a strong foundation for making more accurate hypotheses as to what meanings readers made of such fictions and the possible role they played in readers' lives. Because of the speculative nature of some of the suggestions for further work I have given in this section, the words of David Grimsted fittingly conclude it. He writes, "The richest answers that scholars give are not those that pretend to prove conclusively, but those that suggest realities, connections, and possibilities not fully realized previously."[25]

V

Millions of readers across the country benefited from the syndicates, which took advantage of the multiple local and regional newspaper distribution systems that already existed and placed fiction in affordable and accessible daily and Sunday newspapers. A large and socioeconomically diverse national audience was thus reached by the syndicates before the mass-market magazines did so in the 1890s. Readyprint and plate service fiction appeared in thousands of American newspapers and, from 1884 on, McClure syndicated individual works to anywhere from 20 to 50 newspapers and Bacheller from 20 to 140 newspapers.[26] If each of the papers with whom McClure and Bacheller dealt had an average circulation of 30,000 (a low estimate, given that a large paper such as the *Boston Globe* often sold 100,000 copies and more of each edition), individual fictions had at the very least a potential readership of 600,000; actual readership, however, most certainly numbered in the millions.

Gauging the "quality" level of this fiction is of course a very subjective matter. It was the judgment of contemporary observers that while readyprint and plate service fiction wasn't always by the most talented authors, it was better than what was previously available. One commented that without plate matter local papers would have had to make do with "sentimental poetry and absurd romantic tales by untrained local writers," and another said that Kellogg's readyprint and plate service was, "as a rule, of much higher quality" than locally written material. In many homes, the Sunday paper with its syndicated fiction replaced the more sensational story papers. And although galley-proof syndicates might often have distributed the secondary works of authors such as James, Howells, Jewett, Twain, Stevenson, and so forth, to many observers even these represented a marked improvement over stale exchange fiction. One author opined that Tillotson's "brought to the homes of the poor the works of the greatest modern masters of the art of story writing, and have supplanted sensational rubbish by their superior productions." Regarding syndicates as a whole, one commentator wrote in 1901 that "the public is also a gainer, in being afforded an early reading of fiction of the first quality."[27]

Yet, despite William Charvat's assertion that "it is probable that syndicates helped to spread the reading habit by bringing good if not profound fiction to people who had been reading nothing else of literary quality," it is impossible to determine with any accuracy whether the "higher quality" fiction that the syndicates distributed "improved" (both highly subjective terms) the literary taste of large segments of the American populace. One can hypothesize, however, that the favorable reaction of readers from all socioeconomic levels in America's cities and interior areas alike to syndicated works by Howells, Crane, James, and others encouraged prospective mass-market book and magazine publishers by proving that there was indeed a substantial national audience for works by this type of author. Partially as a result of this reaction, the literary establishment began to include in its envisioned audience the millions of readers across the country who, despite their low levels of literacy, still wanted access to quality fiction. In 1889 one commentator listed the advantages of the daily newspaper and of cheap reprints of "serious" literary works, chief among them their low price, and concluded: "Let the publishers of copyrighted books take a lesson from the daily newspaper and the cheap editions. Let him publish, not for the few at high prices, but for the many at low prices." Awareness of this development is also seen when Basil March, the provincial Northeastern magazine editor in Howells's *A Hazard of New Fortunes* (1889) is lectured on the new national audience by Fulkerson the syndicate manager. Fulkerson tells March, who is worried that their magazine is not receiving much attention from the New York City press, that this is not essential for a magazine's success. "It's the whole country that makes or breaks a thing like this," he advises March; "New York has very little to do with it ... The great mass of readers are outside New York, and the rural districts are what we have got to go for."[28] The syndicates cannot be given credit for discovering these readers, for the same reason Columbus cannot be given credit for discovering America: these readers, like the native peoples of North America, were already there. What the syndicates must be given credit for, however, is helping to make the literary publishing industry, which previously was primarily interested in urban and Northeastern readers, more aware of this audience's existence.

One might contend that readers of syndicated fiction were acted upon and influenced by the syndicates and newspaper editors who made choices for them and who wished to manipulate them in order to make money. The motivations of the managers of readyprint and plate companies are uncertain and probably will remain so. Clearly, though, Tillotson's desire to help the less privileged is clear from William Frederic's commitment to Liberal politics and the philosophy stated by syndicate head John Nayler in the epigraph to this chapter. Irving Bacheller and S. S. McClure, too, wanted more than simply to make large profits. On a number of occasions they stated their desire to provide rich and poor readers throughout the country with access to the best fiction being written. In 1886 Irving Bacheller decried the lack of "an available and adequate medium between the author and the great majority which does not read expensive books and magazines" and opined that "If the great public can get hold of the wholesome productions of literary genius, it will thank God for deliverance from the reign of rot." McClure, too, often voiced his hope that his syndicate would do the American people good. In 1891 he wrote that his syndicate was "an attempt to give to the great masses of people through the newspapers reading equal to that which appears in the best magazines" and further stated, "I cannot but believe that this extensive circulation of good reading among the masses is productive of great good." Some of McClure's statements can be ascribed to self-justification, but his experiences as a poor Irish immigrant farm boy growing up near Valparaiso, Indiana, cut off from mainstream literary culture, appear to have had a profound effect on him. Years later, McClure proudly expressed his belief that his "newspaper syndicate did a good deal to awaken in the country boys everywhere an interest in the new writers of that time, and to create for those writers an appreciative audience, besides all the pleasure such stories gave to minds that would have been emptier without them."[29] After reviewing the activities of all these syndicates, one must conclude that they achieved many of these aims.

CHAPTER 8

The decline of the literary syndicates

> There are, I believe, fewer stories printed serially in the newspapers now than ten years ago. The story syndicates are passing rather than coming on.
> Hamlin Garland, 1902

> We have outlived the superstition that there can be no literature in the true sense of the word except in the form of books ... It will no longer do to sneer at publications [such as newspapers and magazines] which have invaded the literary domain to an extent that enables them to anticipate the triumphs of bookmakers and provide the people with the choicest wares at merely nominal prices.
> St. Louis Globe-Democrat, 1887[1]

Literary syndicates purchased works of fiction from hundreds if not thousands of authors and at one time or another negotiated their publication with almost every newspaper editor in the United States. They did not go out of business *en masse* in 1900. As the century came to a close, though, their influence as purchasers and distributors of fiction waned. The reasons range from the mundane and personal to the more complex and societal. Because the decline of this aspect of the syndicate business had significant consequences for the relationship between fiction authors and the American public and for the evolution of American literary history, these reasons deserve documentation and analysis.

The fate of literary syndicates was that of any organism whose role in nature is made obsolete: gradual decline and then extinction. A number of contemporary commentators noted this decline. One stated in 1896, "The long drawn out serial in the daily paper has had its day," and another concluded in 1900, "At the present time the syndicates proper of this [literary] class have passed away." William Dean Howells, who in 1893 devoted a full page to the syndicates in his article "The Man of Letters as a Man of Business," excised this information from the essay when it was republished in the 1902 collection, *Literature and Life*, which probably indicated his belief that their significance had declined appreciably. Granted, even after the turn of the century, syndicates continued to proliferate: by 1926 there were 100 individual syndicates, and by 1936 there were at least 145. Some of these syndicates hearkened back to 1884 when Charles Dana of the New York *Sun* and Charles Taylor of the *Boston Globe* organized syndicates of papers themselves. The *Chicago Daily News*, New York *Journal*, and New York *World*, for example, in the late 1890s began to sell materials originally appearing in their own pages to other newspapers, thus bypassing independent syndicates. Only a few syndicates, however, continued to distribute fiction; those that did usually bought second serial rights, as was the case in the 1920s with F. Scott Fitzgerald's *This Side of Paradise* and *The Beautiful and Damned*. After 1900, instead of having their works appear first in the newspaper, most well-known and critically respected authors chose to publish first either in the lucrative mass-market magazines or in the "little magazines" that shielded them from marketplace demands.[2]

Readyprint and plate service companies began their decline in the 1890s. After the mid-1890s unknown or lesser-known authors continued to appreciate them as outlets for their original fiction, and better-known authors gladly accepted their checks for second serial rights; Rex Beach, Jack London, Booth Tarkington, and Zane Grey are among those whose works were circulated in readyprint (and probably plate) form. Works by better-known authors, however, rarely appeared first through the agency of such syndicates. The reasons for this might be traced to the constant consolidation and then monopolization of these branches of the syndicate business. In the 1890s the relatively new Western Newspaper Union (WNU), begun in 1880, grew at a rapid pace, outstripping competitors such as the Kellogg Company, the Chicago Newspaper Union, and the American Press Association. In the first decade of the new century the WNU bought out the Kellogg Company (1906) and various other newspaper "unions." In 1917 the American Press Association sold its plate business to the WNU, thereby making the latter the sole provider of readyprint and plate service in the United States until 1952, when it informed its 1,412 remaining readyprint customers that it was discontinuing this service (presumably plate service had been discontinued before this date). The resulting lack of competition for authors among such syndicates probably greatly lowered the rates offered to them and concomitantly the grade of the works they could purchase. News reports about the discontinued service also concluded that readyprint service in general declined "because papers in towns of two or three hundred population have mostly vanished ... [and] the remaining ones are better equipped to prepare their own copy and to set their own type."[3]

Fiction in readyprint and plate fiction form also apparently became less important to newspaper readers. In 1927 Wright Patterson, editor-in-chief of the Western Newspaper Union, argued, " 'Fiction is in very great demand, whether in the form of short stories, novelettes, or serials. It's a little surprising how much fiction the American farmer and his family will read,' " but in fact a number of separate surveys conducted in the early 1920s in New York State and South Dakota showed that of the various types of plate service materials furnished to small town newspapers, the serial and short story were the least read. This decline began in the late 1890s, as improved roads and distribution networks allowed daily and Sunday metropolitan newspapers to start penetrating rural areas in great numbers and replace certain functions of the local paper. Readers who could easily obtain city newspapers with the latest national and international news and syndicated fiction by famous authors had little desire to read days'-old news and warmed-over readyprint and plate service fiction. In addition, the gradual expansion of Rural Free Delivery after 1896 brought low-priced (ranging from 15 cents per copy to 5 cents) national magazines such as *Munsey's*, *Collier's*, *McClure's*, and the *Saturday Evening Post*, all containing original fiction by the most prominent authors, directly to the rural reader's mailbox. By 1899 one commentator could posit, "Very few readers care for, or even read, the ready-print side" of country newspapers.[4]

Some of these factors also contributed to the decline of galley-proof syndicates, but there were many purely personal reasons that contributed as well. In some ways, for example, the early death in 1889 of William Frederic Tillotson – whom one employee described as "both poker and bellows to the establishment" – deprived the Tillotson Newspaper Fiction Bureau of the energy and enthusiasm so necessary for success in this business. Shortly after his death the company wrote in a circular letter that "The lines of business, which have been so successful in the past will be followed in the future, and no effort will be spared to maintain and extend the reputation of the Firm," and indeed the syndicate remained in operation until 1935. Unfortunately, however, it does not appear that its managers were ever again as aggressive about soliciting authors' works and selling them as its founder had been. In the cases of S. S. McClure and Irving Bacheller, the extensive travelling they did on behalf of the syndicate became quite tiresome. In November 1893 McClure wrote to his wife Hattie, "Am getting to [sic] old to travel. I can't bear being away from you." McClure recalled that "From 1890 on I was overcome more and more often by periods of complete nervous exhaustion," and he reported that in 1893, "physically, I was a worn-out man." In part, McClure established *McClure's Magazine* in the spring of 1893 because he was tired of travelling and mistakenly believed that his new role would allow him to spend more time at home. Although the McClure Syndicate would remain under family control until 1912, after 1894 S. S. McClure concerned himself less and less with it, and according to some accounts the people he left in charge of the syndicate – including his brother Tom – lacked drive and organizational skills. Bacheller, too, remembered that he disliked being away so much on business, stating, "I was not quite happy, for I was fond of my wife and home." Sometime between 1891 and November 1894 he wrote of his syndicate, "I am getting tired of it and ... am looking forward to a time when I can retire at least from any active part in newspaper work." Bacheller was also increasingly distracted by his own literary aspirations. In 1889 he had begun asking for and receiving advice from literary critic and poet Edmund Clarence Stedman about his own poetry and fiction. Bacheller remembered that when he had his first short story published in *Cosmopolitan* magazine in January 1897, "I longed then to be released from the cares of business."[5] In 1898 Bacheller left the syndicate business and subsequently served in an editorial position at Joseph Pulitzer's New York *World* in 1899. The fantastic popular success of Bacheller's novel *Eben Holden* (1900), though, guaranteed that he would never return to the newspaper world.

Another personal reason for the demise of Bacheller's and McClure's syndicates was that neither Bacheller nor McClure was a trained businessman. In 1891 McClure wrote of money matters, "I have not time to think of these things," and he later recalled, "I never kept books; a few notes jotted down from time to time kept me informed as to my accounts." John Phillips brought a great deal of financial organization and accounting to the business after he joined the syndicate staff in 1886. McClure later recalled that Phillips "'made me agree to abide by the orderly methods of keeping track of contracts with authors and sales to editors,'" but McClure continued to frequently disregard his advice. Bacheller, more a novelist than a businessman, probably operated in much the same way McClure did; he frankly acknowledged that he had "no special talent for business."[6]

If the McClure and Bacheller syndicates began to decline for purely personal reasons, though, one would have expected others to enter the field and succeed when they left it. Certainly others did try, but most failed. Only a few galley-proof syndicates, like Tillotson's – which was run by well-trained, expert businessmen who kept detailed account books – made the syndicate venture moderately successful. The lack of great success enjoyed by most syndicates, then, cannot be completely ascribed to idiosyncrasies of their managers. Instead, certain developments in newspaper and literary publishing and the very nature of the syndicate business itself militated against their success.

Despite contemporary belief to the contrary, syndicating original fiction – as opposed to syndicating advice for women, features for children, interviews of famous personages, and so forth – never proved to be very profitable. McClure should have seen the writing on the wall when he lost money on his first story in 1884, but he believed his plan would work if he only put more energy into it. By the beginning of 1885, McClure was already losing money, $600 in March 1885 alone; the only thing that kept McClure afloat was a story that Harriet Prescott Spofford gave him free that spring. By 1890 McClure reported that he was making some profits, and he told Robert Louis Stevenson fairly truthfully, "I am comparatively rich now." Yet when Stevenson provided him with South Seas letters in 1891 that were not nearly as financially lucrative as McClure had expected, McClure's prospects were substantially dimmed. Ever the financially conservative partner, John S. Phillips took a hard look at their syndicate business in 1891 and advised McClure, "Things cannot go on in this way forever – the profits do not furnish enough to materially increase the capital in proportion to the growth of the business. It is top-heavy, and it seems to me may fall of its own weight." Phillips's solution was to invite a number of newspapers to become investors in the business; however, McClure, who could brook no diminishment of his personal control, never took this step. By 1892, Phillips was again warning that the syndicate was on the verge of collapse. McClure later remembered that by 1893, after "years of the hardest kind of labor, of mental torture and nervous strain, I was exactly $2,700 ahead." In search of a larger and more regular income, McClure launched his magazine in the spring of 1893, telling his wife it would "at the worst [be] simply a temporary reduction in my profits, at the best a great & valuable property & an income inconceivably large." McClure had hoped to finance the magazine with syndicate profits, but as he noted, "As soon as the newspapers felt the pinch of the panic, they began to cut down expenses, and our syndicate service was one of the first things they could dispense with ... Every discontinuance meant a net loss to us of from twenty to seventy dollars a week." During the Depression of the mid-1890s McClure's constant difficulty – collecting the money that newspaper editors owed him for fictions they had already printed and McClure had already paid for or contracted for with authors – was exacerbated. After 1893 the syndicate produced fairly small profits for the rest of its years, and in 1904 even lost money under Tom McClure's direction.[7]

Unlike McClure, Bacheller did allow outside investors to supply needed capital and claimed to have made his syndicate profitable. He recalled that in the mid-1890s, "I was prospering. I had a comfortable cash balance. The hard times of 1893 did not bother me." However, in 1897 Bacheller wrote that because the other investors in his syndicate had cut expenses so close to the bone, the syndicate was slow to pay authors and thus lost them. Bacheller later posited that the syndicate had remained on solid financial footing even in the late 1890s but that "Side issues were the things that got me into difficulty." Possibly this is true. Bacheller was never completely satisfied with his role as manager of a fiction syndicate, as one can gather from his many other failed ventures during the late 1880s and 1890s. From October 1887 until June 1888, he published a weekly newspaper entitled the *New Yorker* (unfortunately there are no extant copies of this paper). In the early 1890s Bacheller was a partner in the New York Pictorial League, which sold advertising illustrations to newspapers. In another attempt to become an editor/publisher, Bacheller founded the *Pocket Magazine* in November 1895. Printed by the Frederick A. Stokes Company, this monthly magazine lasted until December 1901 and reportedly had an average circulation of 12,000 copies in 1895. Finally, Bacheller also invested in a number of other projects, ranging from a weekly advertising journal titled *Youth and Home* to horse breeding, both of which he says lost money. For whatever reason, by the time Bacheller sold the syndicate business to John Brisben Walker in 1898, he was personally in debt for thousands of dollars. As Bacheller candidly concluded many years later, "My greatest problem [was not] in the making of money but in keeping it after its arrival."[8]

Of the three major galley-proof syndicates, Tillotson's Newspaper Fiction Bureau was probably the most profitable. This is undoubtedly due to its being managed by experienced, prudent businessmen who kept detailed records of expenditures and revenues. Yet compared to the other businesses eventually run by Tillotson's, including the *Bolton Evening News*, a chain of Lancashire newspapers, the Premier Box Company of Liverpool, and a sizeable printing concern, the syndicate was a relatively unprofitable sideline. For the entire year of 1901 the firm spent £173.2.0 on serial fiction, and even if profits had been 100 per cent, this would have been a negligible figure. In the mid-1920s the Bureau's annual profits ranged between £1,639 and £2,156, which was respectable but not enough to justify much attention or investment. One can readily understand the sentiment of William Frederic Tillotson's son, Fred Lever Tillotson, who wrote in 1935 that he was "sorry to part with the business which has been an absorbing interest to all of us and which has been carried on so long; but our hands are full with the newspaper [the *Bolton Evening News*] and its associated businesses, and we require the accommodation which will now be free with the disappearance of the Fiction Department and its many tons of proof sheets & c."[9]

Some might argue that the way both McClure and Bacheller spent outlandish sums to procure works by famous authors exemplifies their inexperience as businessmen and helped contribute to their downfall. From the beginning, editors recognized McClure's propensity to be overly generous with these authors; in 1885 one wrote in amazement, "What enormous prices you pay your famous people!" Authors, too, noticed this. Robert Louis Stevenson, who called McClure "so little of a businessman and so much of a splasher," wrote in regard to his serial *St. Ives*, "The price [McClure offers] seems to me exorbitant. But who am I to complain?" Bacheller also was extravagant with money. Years later, ironically in an address to the Stevenson Society, he told the audience, "I remember when I was just about as poverty stricken as he [McClure], I flung large sums about with the same recklessness."[10]

Yet one cannot blame these two men for being idiosyncratic spendthrifts; they felt compelled to pay extraordinarily high prices to get what Bacheller called "sky-rockets" (works by popular authors) that they needed to sell the service to newspaper editors. By 1888, as Tillotson told Victor Lawson, authors had learned "to ask more for the manuscript from newspaper publishers [syndicates] than they have heretofore received from magazine publishers. They argue that there are more publications using the matter, and that therefore the assessment can be raised, as compared with what a single magazine publisher could afford to pay." The problem for syndicators was that although newspaper editors chiefly wanted works by these famous authors, the profit margin on these works was quite small, and in fact such works often had to serve as loss-leaders. Tillotson's responded to this situation in the 1890s by largely dropping out from the competition for such authors and relying increasingly on sales from its backlist. Because the firm had often bought "absolute" serial rights from authors, it was able to sell these works to newspapers decades after their first publication.[11] Bacheller and McClure, on the other hand, had not bought many copyrights outright and thus needed to continue procuring new works by famous authors; however, they lost money on these and could not reap enough profit from works by lesser-known authors to cover their losses.

In addition, syndicates were forced to pay high prices to the more desirable authors in the 1890s because only higher wages could convince authors to publish through the syndicates and the newspapers, both of whose reputations were declining among these authors and among literary critics. McClure's biographer notes that even after eight years of operation, his "syndicate business was still the butt of sneers by some of the more genteel authors." In hindsight, it is clear that syndicates succeeded for only a short time in persuading authors to overlook the general disdain among the Anglo-American literati for having their work appear in newspapers, a print form associated with trade, politics, ephemerality, and common people. John Phillips had told McClure in 1884 that he believed authors "would prefer (not speaking of price) to publish once in a choice journal like Century to a broader circulation through the medium of 2nd and 3rd rate papers" because although writers would receive larger remuneration for stories from the syndicate, "this is not all they look at"; later experience proved him to be prescient in this matter.[12]

Throughout the history of the syndicates, many authors had looked down their noses at them because they represented publication in a newspaper. In the 1870s, for example, a number of British authors were very reluctant to sell their works to Tillotson's. One contemporary noted that "the big writers were not at first willing cooperators. They did not like the idea of treating with a provincial publisher for the production of their stories in cheap newspapers week by week." Ouida (Louise de la Ramée) flatly refused Tillotson's offer in 1879, stating, "I do not write for newspapers." In the 1880s, however, the number of British authors who shied away from newspaper publication appears to have declined. Ouida herself published seven works through Tillotson's before her 1891 tirade against syndicates in the London *Times*. Joseph Hatton wrote in 1892 that a few years earlier, Harrison Ainsworth had damaged his reputation by publishing a novel in *The Sunday Times* but that the stigma of newspaper publication had now disappeared. Around 1889, though, authorial prejudice against newspapers appears to have begun reemerging. The *Writer* magazine reported in this year that "The sensible author of fiction laughs nowadays at any objection to this mode of coming before the public, just as he laughed in former days when it was suggested to him that he would come to look on the penny and half-penny papers as his best publishers." Yet George Gissing wrote in this same year that he would "'never dream of writing a *story* for a newspaper syndicate; the kind of stuff they publish, and the way they advertise it, is too ignoble," and Ada Ellen Boyly declined Tillotson's invitation to contribute a story, writing, "I have a dislike to publishing stories in newspapers." In another example of authorial prejudice, Arthur Conan Doyle wrote to *Blackwood's* in 1890, "'I would take 300 [pounds] for the serial rights [to *The White Company*] in a good magazine rather than 500 [pounds] which has already been offered me by a syndicate [probably McClure's].'"[13]

Some American authors shared this prejudice against newspaper publication and the syndicates. Bacheller was well aware of how difficult it would be, as he said later, "to get the gods of old New England [Holmes and Whittier] to write for the *vulgar* newspapers" (emphasis added). In 1884 Henry James wrote to a friend regarding his syndication by Charles Dana that some of his stories would soon appear "in (horresco referens!) the New York Sunday Sun!" As in Britain, the relatively high prices these syndicates paid for fiction seem to have mitigated such prejudice in the late 1880s and early 1890s. By the late 1890s, however, the situation had reversed, and there was increased authorial prejudice against syndication. Jack London probably spoke for many authors when he wrote in 1899 that although he had previously been published through the Tillotson's syndicate, "I don't like that kind of work myself," and later in the same year hinted why: "I am always afraid to send *McClures* [sic] anything that I consider good, for fear they will publish it through the syndicate."[14]

The exorbitant sums paid to authors by the syndicates, then, represent a necessary attempt to overcome the inferior status associated with newspaper publication, not a mistake of inexperienced businessmen. Where did authors get the idea that newspapers were not respectable places to publish their works? Many authors would have received this message from the growing number of articles critical of newspapers that were being published in the pages of the *North American Review*, the *Atlantic*, the *Dial*, and other magazines influential among middle and upper class readers. These journals, which to a great extent controlled literary reputation, increasingly deemed newspapers – and by association their readers – as vulgar and transient, exhibiting little taste or intelligence. In many ways such diatribes must be understood as a counterattack against what these writers believed was a threat to a unified genteel culture: the newspaper. Anthropologist Victor Turner argues that when "a person or subgroup breaks a rule" (as authors did in contributing to syndicates), clashes erupt that "mount toward a crisis of the group's unity and continuity unless rapidly sealed off by redressive public action, consensually undertaken by the group's leaders, elders, or guardians," and this is precisely how influential social and literary critics reacted to the newspapers. E. L. Godkin wrote in the *North American Review* of a growing "segregation of the newspaper-reader from the book-reader," and noted that among cultivated men, "you will have the mental food which the newspapers supply to the bulk of the population treated with ridicule and contempt." One report in 1895 implied that "the habit of a certain class of people to speak disparagingly and with a supercilious accent of the newspapers and to point out their alleged inferiority to the magazines as sources of information and entertainment" was widespread. Critics excoriated newspapers for many reasons, but one in particular must have hit close to home for authors: their ephemerality as a print form. In 1882 another writer in the *North American Review* argued that the newspaper's "ephemeral flutter, its perpetual coming and going, its very iridescence or transiency and unresting flux, constitute its *raison d'être*." Finally, in 1893 one writer concluded that the newspaper "is in its essence transient, and that to speak of a permanent expression in transient form is plainly a contradiction in terms."[15]

In the 1890s, influential magazine commentators also began to more distinctly distinguish between the act of contributing to the magazines, which William Dean Howells told the readers of *Scribner's* in 1893 "are ephemeral in form, but in substance they are not ephemeral, and what is best in them awaits its resurrection in the book" and contributing to the newspapers. The author Amelia Barr, writing in the *North American Review*, contrasted those writers who wrote various materials for the newspapers – she called them "ephemeral literary workers" – with those who produced "works demanding learning, patience, steady application," and another writer in 1891 argued in the *Atlantic* that "Men are divided broadly into journalists and eternalists, ephemera and immortals, and we can only match the multitude of the first with the permanence of the second." William Morton Payne of the *Dial* magazine rued the day that the poet Eugene Field began writing for the newspapers, arguing that "His talent deserved a better fate than that of lifelong service to journalism, the taskmaster that impelled him to many a hasty and unconsidered utterance," concluding, "Time will sift the meritorious things in his work from the heap of unsightly scoria in which they are embedded."[16]

This view of newspapers as ephemeral and undignified could not help but contribute to authorial prejudice against the syndicates that distributed works for publication in them. Julian Hawthorne indicated in 1888 that authors did "not like the idea of appearing in newspapers at all," citing as one of the chief reasons their view that "A copy of a newspaper is a thing of an hour; it costs almost nothing, and is valued accordingly by the purchaser." This is ironic, however, because the newspaper's ephemerality and its ability to reach the non-book buying public was what initially attracted many authors to the syndicates. Authors knew very well that newspaper publications were ephemeral and unlikely to enhance their reputations among leading middle-class cultural arbiters. At one time, Edward Bok noted, the ephemerality of the newspaper was precisely what attracted authors; because of it, he said, the author could make a great deal of money from a secondary work and not cause long-term damage to his or her literary reputation. He wrote that the author "likes to feel that the story which he gives to the newspaper is but casually or hastily read, and that it is soon forgotten, and he takes the chance of publishing material over his name which he is often ashamed to have mentioned to him in conversation." William Dean Howells also reported "that some short-story writers made the syndicate pay more for their wares than they got from the magazines for them, considering that the magazine publication could enhance their reputation, but the Sunday edition [of newspapers, where most syndicated fiction appeared,] could do nothing for it."[17] For authors concerned with their more permanent literary posterity, however, such ephemerality – even when it was financially remunerative – undoubtedly became less appealing.

Better-known authors also were supposedly horrified to learn that their names and fictions were being printed alongside "sensational, vulgar, and not infrequently prurient stuff which appeals to the lowest taste," and turned away from syndicates for this reason. Such reactions, however, ring of disingenuity and came only later. Initially, authors had clearly understood that their names would be used by syndicates and newspaper editors for advertising purposes; in fact, many of them had hoped that this publicity among readers with whom they usually would not have come in contact would prove financially beneficial to them. As previously mentioned, for example, Henry James contributed to Charles Dana's New York *Sun* syndicate to gain the publicity and popularity he felt he needed to procure higher prices from other publishers. James tried to have it both ways; he wanted to benefit from yet also distance himself from the newspapers and what they represented to people of his social class. After his short stories appeared in the *Sun* syndicate in 1884, for instance, James ironically castigated newspapers in *The Bostonians* (1886) for encouraging a mad drive among individuals for publicity, the very thing – besides a great deal of money – he had wanted to gain from them.[18]

In the 1880s and early 1890s the relatively high prices the syndicates offered, along with the market they represented for hundreds of stories and serials, were enough to outweigh the low reputation of newspapers among fiction authors of all levels, and to allow the syndicates to procure their works. Yet new marketplace conditions of the late 1880s and 1890s made it possible for a number of more prominent and genteel authors to avoid newspaper publication. Although Bacheller continued in the late 1890s to procure works by the likes of Jewett, Garland, and Kipling, the American Chace Act of 1891 and the establishment of numerous mass-market magazines helped lessen the syndicates' attractiveness as fiction outlets. British authors were now receiving more equitable sums for American publication, the national monthly magazines were now able to pay higher prices than the syndicates (because they could sell national advertising, they had much more money at their disposal), and these magazines had a better reputation among important members of the literary community.

The increased number and prestige of magazines among the literary community and the rising amounts they could pay were not the only reasons galley-proof syndicates had to pay higher prices to authors and accept lower profit margins. In the late 1880s and 1890s numerous new syndicates appeared, and the competition for authors grew concomitantly. Bacheller recalled that "McClure's success and my own had convinced many clever newspaper men that a fortune could be made in the business. They were flooding the market with new ideas. Our way was becoming more and more difficult." McClure, whose success was only superficial and certainly not financial, wrote that by 1892, "We had important rivals by this time, and they cut down our profits." Tillotson's business was affected by the establishment of syndicates throughout the world. W. H. Lever, who accompanied William Frederic Tillotson on his visit to the United States and Canada in 1888, wrote that since Tillotson's first trip there in 1884, "fiction bureaus had sprung up in the United States and had been a success. In addition to this, fiction bureaus had sprung up in Germany and France and other parts of the world." At various times McClure, realizing that competition was ruinous, attempted to monopolize the market, but he was never successful in his endeavors. He wrote to William Dean Howells in October 1891 that "There are continually other people coming in to take the authors whose work I have brought before this new [newspaper] public." In response to this situation, the frustrated McClure proposed to Howells a "monopoly of the great names," whereby he would arrange "with the half dozen really great novelists to agree with me for a period of time, say three to four years, to let me handle all the matter they are willing to sell to the newspapers." Surely McClure's proposals were rebuffed by these authors, just as Tillotson's efforts in the 1880s to include similar restrictive clauses in authors' contracts had been rejected. Such attempts at containing competition were doomed to failure. Whether or not he was referring to McClure's plan, a writer in the *Journalist* in December 1891 commented on the "mysterious rumor ... of an effort to combine all the 'syndicates,' so called, into one organization, a sort of syndicate trust," but noted that "So far the efforts ... have been futile, and were it possible to form the combination it would not last six months." The reason given was that syndicates – especially galley-proof ones – required so little start-up capital that any monopoly would always be threatened by newcomers. This same author concluded – ominously for the syndicates – that "The rivalry between them [McClure, Bacheller, and the United Press] is healthful for both the papers and the writers, and existing conditions are unlikely to be at present disturbed by any trust." Significantly, when listing whom the competition benefited, the writer left out the syndicates.[19]

Competition among galley-proof syndicates not only forced syndicates to pay authors higher prices and thus accept reduced profits, it also allowed newspaper editors to ask for lower prices and to remain for the most part free of long term contracts. One report stated in 1896, "Within the past few months the competition between the syndicates has degenerated into a reckless fight for the patronage of newspapers, and the rates for which they have offered their service has fallen to a ridiculously low figure." Furthermore, because of this competition editors could pick and choose among the offerings of the various galley-proof syndicates rather than commit themselves to regular payments to one syndicate with a restricted choice of materials. After signing a contract for one year with a Buffalo newspaper, McClure in November 1884 reported, "Twenty such contracts would set me up," but these never materialized. In August 1898, shortly after he had left the syndicate business for good, Bacheller indicated to one newspaper editor what he believed to be the chief reason he had failed: "Give me [guaranteed contracts with] fifty big newspapers each paying a respectable space rate and I'll agree to outbid every magazine in the world for that [sic] I want and get it too."[20]

The result of the lack of long-term contracts was an extremely uncertain cash flow which made financial success even more difficult to achieve. Functioning as classic middlemen, Bacheller, McClure, and Tillotson's had to pay authors some percentage of their selling price for a manuscript up front and promise to pay the rest at a certain future date. They tried to postpone this future date until after they would have received payments from subscribing newspapers, but often editors delayed payment and left the syndicates in debt to authors. Victor Lawson of the *Chicago Daily News*, for example, refused to help Bacheller by paying in full for a Frank Stockton story before he received the second half. Without contracts with newspapers, Julian Hawthorne prophesied in 1888, the syndicates "are liable to come to grief; [they] will be behind-hand in [their] payments to authors, and then [their] authors will distrust [them] and refuse to write when called upon." In 1886 McClure's wife described the situation that would become the norm for his syndicate: "the newspapers are in arrears to him $2000, so that he is terribly pressed for money to use in his business." Bacheller, too, recounted that in the early days of his syndicate, "I was having a hard time to make my payments [to authors] on time," and in 1897, "We were slow in paying our foreign contributors and we lost them. Kipling and Doyle had been of inestimable value to us." Even Tillotson's occasionally frustrated authors with late payments. John Maxwell, husband of novelist Mary Elizabeth Braddon, told W. F. Tillotson, "she does not like the position involved in having to wait while you gather in your harvest [payments from newspapers.]" Ever the perceptive businessman, John Phillips told McClure, "The trouble is not so much the amount we have to pay out [to authors] but a good deal of it we have to pay at definite times." McClure's financial system that was the result of few long-term contracts was, as Robert Louis Stevenson noticed, full of "shambling hand-to-mouth expedients [that] might any day tip him over the margin into the penitentiary." To make the situation even more difficult, because there were few guaranteed contracts, the possibility existed with each fiction that the syndicate – if it could not sell the work to enough editors – would still owe the author the balance without having recouped its investment. Once again, Bacheller, McClure, and Tillotson's at first appear as incompetent at business and responsible for precipitating their own failure, this time by creating an uncertain cash flow situation. Upon closer examination, however, one can see that competition – something they could not control – was responsible for discouraging the long term contracts that would have insured greater stability.[21]

One could hypothesize that these syndicates might have survived the continued uncertain cash flow if only they had had more capital at their disposal. Higher capital reserves not only would have allowed syndicates to pay authors without having to wait until payments came in from newspapers, but might also have enabled them to weather difficult times such as the 1893 depression, McClure's financial bath with the Stevenson letters, or Bacheller's loss in January 1897 of $700 in gold (this supposedly went to the bottom of the Atlantic Ocean when Stephen Crane – on assignment for and financed by Bacheller – jettisoned it to save himself from drowning). Both Bacheller and McClure operated severely undercapitalized businesses. Bacheller, however, seemed more willing to solicit loans and attract outside investors. Throughout the history of his syndicate, he regularly obtained fresh infusions of capital, usually by taking on partners. The end result, though, was that by 1896, even though the company was still known as the Bacheller Syndicate, Bacheller himself was actually just a paid employee, with a salary of $100 per week. McClure, too, started with very little capital. He remembered that in the fall of 1884, "I was utterly without resources. I had not $25 in the bank, and I had no relatives who could help me"; he added, "It wasn't as if I had had money enough to live on for six months while I gave the thing a trial." By 1893 the situation had not greatly improved, with McClure having only $2,700 in the bank, not much for such an extensive business.[22]

Yet even if these syndicates had possessed more capital, one must question if this would have been enough to have kept them afloat and made them successful. Tillotson's Newspapers, Ltd. had a great deal of capital at its disposal; in 1895 the company as a whole had declared assets of approximately £33,000, or $165,000. Yet as noted previously, the Fiction Bureau appears to have been only a very minor part of the Tillotson's operations and earned relatively small profits; company managers probably knew that further investment would not likely yield a desirable level of profit. It is evident, too, that the frequent infusions of money to Bacheller's syndicates were necessary not only to pay for losses on "side issues" but also to help make up the syndicate's operating deficit. The Tillotson's company could afford to continue operating the Fiction Bureau because it had other more profitable ventures to pay overhead costs. In the cases of

Bacheller, McClure, and other independent American syndicators, however, there is some truth to the judgment of one contemporary, that these syndicates were "bureaus of relief for necessitous and uncapitalized persons, whose energies are misspent in a hopeless business."[23]

As if these obstacles were not enough, galley-proof syndicates became less successful in the United States because their American market actually shrank. The number of Sunday editions of daily newspapers rose sharply in the 1890s, as did their circulations. Yet as the circulation area of each individual metropolitan newspaper grew with the introduction of faster trains, the number of newspapers to which the syndicates could sell a single fiction without having their circulation areas overlap actually decreased. The effects of this development might have been negated if newspaper editors had been willing to pay more for each fiction, but instead they often demanded a larger exclusive circulation area for less money. Thus, just as the purchasing power of the mass-market national magazines was increasing, the revenues the syndicates could collect and pay for each fiction were decreasing, and consequently they could afford fictions only by lesser-known authors.

Finally, the role of syndicates as middlemen was largely superseded in the 1890s by literary agents. Galley-proof syndicates had served an important function for authors at a time when the magazine and book markets were severely limited. By performing the difficult task of making arrangements with multiple newspapers, syndicates helped authors tap into a market that was previously unrecognized by and inaccessible to most of them. They thus acted as literary agents but with no guaranteed fee. In 1891 the British author Ouida lumped the syndicate and literary agent together and argued that "He does nothing which cannot just as well be done by yourself, or by your secretary, if you have one." A great number of authors, however, disagreed and appreciated how syndicates and agents freed them from the tedious, time-consuming, and distasteful task of marketing their wares to editors. Yet in the late 1880s and 1890s, more authors began engaging literary agents rather than syndicates to do such work. The syndicate, "a necessity of the time," in Bacheller's words, had in many ways become superfluous.[24]

Although the period during which syndicates purchased and distributed fiction for first publication and thus played major roles in the Anglo-American literary marketplace was relatively short, their impact on American literary culture was quite enduring. Most literary scholars, however, have overlooked their influence. Instead, the mass-market magazines established in the late 1880s and 1890s have been given almost all the credit for increasing the market and remuneration for authors' works and for reaching "a vast middle-to-lowbrow American readership that hitherto had not been addressed successfully." Richard Brodhead has recently implied that these magazines were the first "agents of a different version of culture: the establishers of literary writing in the lives of another audience, grouped around other – consumer-culture, not gentry-culture – values." Yet the syndicates were pioneers in doing this before the mass-market magazines. What has also received little attention is that these mass-market monthly magazines – filled with timely features, high quality fiction, and advertisements arranged in a visually exciting way – modelled themselves after the Sunday newspapers that the syndicates helped make possible. H. L. Mencken recognized the influence of syndicates, writing, "the truth is that its [the mass-market magazine's] real father was the unknown originator of the Sunday supplement. What McClure – a shrewd literary bagman – did was to apply the sensational methods of the cheap newspaper to a new and cheap magazine." One might argue that were it not for the syndicates, these magazines might never have evolved as they did and taken center stage in the literary marketplace.[25]

Readyprint, plate service, and galley-proof syndicates also had a substantial effect on the profession of literary authorship in the United States. The latter two especially provided authors access to a hitherto untapped inland newspaper audience and represented immense and relatively lucrative markets for short stories and serials. Through syndicated publication, too, authors gained extensive publicity among audiences that had previously not been reached. Most important, by paying high prices and by disregarding the long-standing customs of trade courtesy, galley-proof syndicates helped usher in a new era for authors in which they were free to auction their work to the highest bidder in a truly competitive marketplace.

Possibly what is most remarkable about the syndicates is that the majority of them were able to bring quality fiction to a large national audience without centralizing or exercising undue hegemonic power over authors, editors, or readers. In 1887 one report noted the "complaint loud and deep among newspaper men against the centralizing process, which finds expression in the patent insides and outsides, news bureaus, plate matter, illustrated-article bureaus and syndicates," and stated, "At first sight, it would seem as if their opposition were well founded." Yet this writer looked more closely, saw the numerous advantages such businesses afforded, and concluded that "the impartial student of history ... should rejoice in the success of such concerns."[26] Historians today should also carefully distinguish among the various types of syndicates and discern their advantages as well as their disadvantages. The word "syndicate" evokes visions of a vast, vertically-integrated corporation made up of many subsidiaries and exerting ironfisted control over production, distribution, and consumption of its product. Some newspaper syndicates were indeed large organizations, but their size did not automatically translate into marketplace control. Unlike the centrally organized and commanded businesses of the mass-market magazines, story papers, or book publishing houses, syndicates occupied a unique position in the publishing world: neither publishers nor literary agents, they responded to the commands of a loose, decentralized, and heterogeneous network of fiction authors, newspaper editors, and readers. Most of the actual control in the syndicate system remained decentralized and at the local level; newspaper editors told syndicates what to purchase from authors, decided which fictions they would purchase from syndicates, and laid out the pages of the newspapers for readers. Yet, in general, because of the organizational structures of most syndicates no one party – authors, syndicators, editors, or readers – had the power to impose its vision of what should be produced or consumed within this system and how. Rather, the cultural product offered by these syndicates, more than any other of the period, was the result of extensive negotiation and compromise on all sides. Moreover, syndicates and, I believe, editors, did not force standardized reading strategies or interpretations of the fiction texts on passive readers.

Unfortunately, the decentralized control inherent in the syndicate system at the time contributed to the decline of the syndicates, especially of galley-proof syndicates. McClure, Bacheller, Tillotson's, and others like them simply could not make this type of business succeed, because they had little control either over supply or over demand. In this system, which benefited authors, editors, and readers, the only ones left without any real benefit were the syndicates themselves, the classic cultural negotiators.

In 1934 Richard H. Waldo, who had recently bought the McClure Syndicate, wrote that the story of this syndicate was "surely worthy of preservation in our American archives for the generation to come"; I believe the same can be said for the story of all syndicates in general. Most of the fictions published through the agency of the syndicates were probably read fairly quickly before the newspaper was put to some other purpose or thrown in a trash can. "In every large [American] city," one 1895 report stated, "thousands of such little afternoon sheets are left on street cars, thrown into waste baskets or dropped in the gutters, after they have been played with a few minutes." The ephemerality of the form in which syndicated fiction was printed, however, must not be confused with its value or impact. As one commentator remarked about a syndicated work by Mary E. Wilkins, "This story appearing in a daily newspaper is not less literature than as if it had made its debut between the pasteboard covers of the bound book or had its announcements flaunted to the public on the highly colored posters of the publishers of *Harper's* or *Scribner's*."[27] There is simply no evidence that the influence on readers of fictions printed in newspapers whose ink came off on readers' hands, whose newsprint began decaying almost immediately, which was usually discarded minutes or hours after it was printed, and which was read hurriedly on a trolley car, was any less than that of a text printed on longer-lasting cotton rag paper, bound between leather or board covers, preserved on library shelves, and read slowly in the solitude and serenity of a parlor.

To appreciate the significance of the syndicates, literary scholars must overcome some long-held prejudices against and misunderstandings of the newspaper. Today, as was the case in the nineteenth century, many of those involved in literary studies and publishing view newspaper publication as less significant and prestigious because the material product is less enduring. Yet buried in the microfilm of newspapers from the late nineteenth century, in periodical discussions of the syndicates and newspapers, and in the archives of various syndicates, there are important lessons to be learned.

Foremost among these lessons is that the syndicates were pioneers and innovators in a number of areas. Equally important, though, is that the rise and fall of the syndicates can help us more fully understand how and why the schism between high and low culture widened in the late nineteenth century. "The newspaper," historian Sidney Kobre writes, "throughout this era served the function of obtaining vicariously for the middle and working class the things [of] which the upper-class boasted," and syndicates played a major role in this project of cultural democratization by procuring what was viewed as "quality" fiction for newspaper readers. One obituary of William Frederic Tillotson noted that "Through his agency fiction from the best writers has been given direct to the [British] masses, who are indebted to [him] ... for many an intellectual treat formerly enjoyed only by the well-to-do." The same, it is evident, can be said for the activities of all syndicates that distributed fiction to American newspapers. Numerous contemporary commentators noted that daily papers especially were circulated to people from all socioeconomic classes, and the noted literary critic Edmund Gosse concluded in 1891 that in the Anglo-American world, "The newspapers are the most democratic vehicles of thought." In 1887 one observer noted that the newspaper "furnishes millions of people daily with their chief subjects of conversation," and one can imagine that syndicates helped make fiction the material for daily, communal interaction with others.[28] When the syndicates declined, Americans of all socioeconomic classes throughout the country thus lost one of the most accessible ways to interact on a daily basis with fiction by many of the period's most prominent and respected authors.

Unfortunately for these readers, many of the more prominent authors turned away from the syndicates for their own financial reasons and because they were urged to do so by influential critics who scorned the newspapers and the audiences they represented. Distinct cultural boundaries were thus erected between literature for the "masses" and for the "classes." Ironically, soon afterwards these newspaper readers were increasingly criticized for not reading enough literature regarded by the literary establishment as serious and possessing artistic merit. In general, one can conclude that the decline of literary syndicates constitutes one more reason why, as Lawrence W. Levine has recently written, at the turn of the century "less and less could one find audiences that cut across the social and economic spectrum enjoying an expressive culture which blended together mixed elements of what we would today call high, low, and folk culture."[29]

Syndicates, which Irving Bacheller argued filled the need for an "adequate medium between the author and the great majority which does not read expensive books and magazines," played a major role in the American literary marketplace of the late nineteenth century.[30] The impact they had on authors, editors, and readers of the period was both significant and extensive. For these reasons, the time has clearly come for their stories to be more fully represented in the history of American literature.

Notes

INTRODUCTION

1 Edward W. Bok, "The Modern Literary King," *Forum* 20 (1895): 340; Worthington C. Ford, "Report of the Council," *Proceedings of the American Antiquarian Society* 28 (1918): 10.
2 William A. Dill, *Growth of Newspapers in the United States* (Lawrence, KS: University of Kansas Press, 1928) 28. Reliable data about newspaper production during this period, as well as about the production and circulation of other print forms, is very difficult to obtain. Because there is no central source for such data, in many places in this book I was forced to use data from many different sources; in all cases I have tried to present only the most accurate figures.
3 I obviously do not wish to imply that I agree with the distinction made in the late nineteenth century between "quality" and "popular" fiction. Indeed, one of the purposes of this book is to indicate how texts that have never been taken seriously by cultural arbiters can have meaning for readers. For traditional views of the reading audience during this period see Christopher P. Wilson, "The Rhetoric of Consumption: Mass-Market Magazines and the Demise of the Gentle Reader, 1888–1920," *The Culture of Consumption: Critical Essays in American History 1880–1980*, ed. Richard Wightman Fox and T. J. Jackson Lears (New York: Pantheon Books, 1983) 44; James L. W. West III, *American Authors and the Literary Marketplace Since 1900* (Philadelphia: University of Pennsylvania Press, 1988) 38–39; Frank Luther Mott, *A History of American Magazines: 1885–1905*, vol. 4 (Cambridge, MA: Harvard University Press, 1957) 8; and Richard Brodhead, "Literature and Culture," *Columbia Literary History of the United States* (*CLHUS*), ed. Emory Elliott et al. (New York: Columbia University Press, 1988) 475.
4 See Michael Lund, *America's Continuing Story: An Introduction to Serial Fiction, 1850–1900* (Detroit: Wayne State University Press, 1993).
5 Susan Coultrap-McQuin, *Doing Literary Business: American Women Writers in the Nineteenth Century* (Chapel Hill: University of North Carolina Press, 1990). See also Brodhead, *CLHUS* 475 and Nelson Lichtenstein,

"Authorial Professionalism and the Literary Marketplace, 1885–1920," *American Studies* 9 (1978): 35–53.
6 Editorial, *Journalist*, 15 September 1888: 8; [William H. Hills], *Writer* (New York) 2 (1888): 5.
7 Bok, "The Modern Literary King" (1895): 340, 339, 341.
8 For an account of the contest for Twain's novel, see *Mark Twain–Howells Letters. The Correspondence of Samuel L. Clemens and William D. Howells 1872–1910*, ed. Henry Nash Smith and William M. Gibson, vol. 2 (Cambridge, MA: Harvard University Press, 1960) 644n; Robert Donald, "Sunday Newspapers in the United States," *The Universal Review* 8 (September–December 1890): 79; Leon Mead, "The Practical Side of Literature," *Gunton's* 21 (1901): 443 and 444.
9 For the failure of Howells's attempts at forming a syndicate, see W. D. Howells, *Selected Letters 1892–1901*, ed. and annotated by Thomas Wortham, Christoph K. Lohmann, and David J. Nordloh (Boston: Twayne, 1981) 232–233, 237, and 244–245; Hamlin Garland's comment is found in James Lane Allen et al., "Will the Novel Disappear?" *North American Review* 175 (1902): 295.
10 Fox-Genovese, "Literary Criticism and the Politics of the New Historicism," *The New Historicism*, ed. H. Aram Veeser (New York and London: Routledge, 1989) 117.
11 Natalie Zeamon Davis, "Anthropology and History in the 1980s: The Possibilities of the Past," *Journal of Interdisciplinary History* 12 (1981): 274.

1 PREPARING THE WAY FOR THE SYNDICATES

1 Halsey, *Our Literary Deluge* (New York: Doubleday, Page and Co., 1902) 3; Norris, "Salt and Sincerity," *The Responsibilities of the Novelist and Other Essays*, 1903, vol. 7 of *The Complete Edition of Frank Norris*, 10 vols. (Garden City, NY: Doubleday, Doran & Co., 1928) 199.
2 Beard, *American Nervousness. Its Causes and Consequences* (New York: G. P. Putnam's Sons, 1881) 96, 99, 117, 134, 135.
3 For these very unreliable publication figures, quoted from contemporary reports in *American Publishers' Circular*, see Susan Geary, "The Domestic Novel as a Commercial Commodity: Making a Best-Seller in the 1850s," *Papers of the Bibliographical Society of America* 70 (1976): 366, 369, 370, 371; for overall figures after 1880 and an explanation of their limited reliability, see John Tebbel, *A History of Book Publishing in the United States* 4 vols. (New York: R. R. Bowker Co., 1972–1981) 2: 675–693.
4 Frank L. Schick (*The Paperbound Book in America: The History of Paperbacks and Their European Background* [New York: R. R. Bowker Co., 1958] 51) places the circulation range at 35–80,000, while Raymond Howard Shove (*Cheap Book Production in the United States, 1870 to 1891* [Urbana, IL:

University of Illinois Library, 1937] 7) states that the average was 50–60,000.

5   See Schick, *The Paperbound Book* 55 and Tebbel, *History of Book Publishing* 2: 486.
6   Shove, *Cheap Book Production* x and 36.
7   Story paper characterization from Michael Denning, *Mechanic Accents: Dime Novels and Working Class Culture* (New York: Verso Press, 1987) 10; *New York Weekly* figures from Quentin Reynolds, *The Fiction Factory or, From Pulp Row to Quality Street* (New York: Random House, 1955) 26 and 32, plus Mary Noel, *Villains Galore: The Heyday of the Popular Story Weekly* (New York: Macmillan, 1954) 114; *Ledger* figure from Mott, *American Magazines* 2: 359n.
8   Periodical numbers from John W. Tebbel, *The American Magazine: A Compact History* (New York: Hawthorn Books, 1969) 119; population figures from *Historical Statistics of the United States, Colonial Times to 1970*, 2 parts (Washington, DC: United States Dept. of Commerce, 1975) 2: 8; the calculation of 686 per cent is from Tebbel's figures; quotation from Richard D. Altick, *Writers, Readers, and Occasions: Selected Essays on Victorian Literature and Life* (Columbus, OH: Ohio State University Press, 1989) 227.
9   The 1860 figures are from Mott, *American Magazines* 2: 10; *Atlantic* figures from Tebbel, *Magazine* 11, and Ballou, *The Building of the House: Houghton-Mifflin's Formative Years* (Boston: Houghton-Mifflin, 1970) 453; for figures on *Harper's Monthly* and *Bazar* see Eugene Exman, *The House of Harper: One Hundred and Fifty Years of Publishing* (New York: Harper and Row, 1967) 79 and 122; for *Century* figures see Brodhead, "Literature and Culture" 472; 1900 figures from Frank Luther Mott, *American Journalism: A History, 1690–1960*, 3rd edn. (New York: Macmillan, 1962) 590.
10 Brodhead, "Literature and Culture" 476; George Britt, *Forty Years – Forty Millions: The Career of Frank Munsey* (New York: Farrar and Rinehart, 1935) 82.
11 Godkin, "Newspapers Here and Abroad," *North American Review* 150 (1890): 203.
12 The figure of 363 per cent is derived from a table in William A. Dill, *Growth of Newspapers* 11–12; see Dill 28 for 1860, 1880, 1890, and 1899 figures. For figures on newspapers in major cities see S[imon] N[ewton] D[exter] North, *History and Present Condition of the Newspaper and Periodical Press of the United States* (Washington, DC: Government Printing Office, 1884) 77, and Franklin William Scott, *Newspapers and Periodicals of Illinois, 1814–1879* (Chicago: R. R. Donnelly and Sons, n.d.) cii; the 1880 figures are from North, *History and Present Condition* 72 and 73.
13 Figures from Dill, *Growth of Newspapers* 28 and 30 (weekly circulations include a small number of non-newspaper periodicals).
14 New York *World* and New York *Journal* figures in Meyer Berger, *The*

Story of the New York Times, 1851–1951 (New York: Simon and Schuster, 1951) 112 and 569; *Boston Globe* 6 November 1884: 4, 1 November 1891: 1, and 2 January 1899: 6; *Detroit Free Press* 12 July 1885: 4; *Evening Item* figures from Mott, *American Journalism* 450; *Indianapolis News* 1 October 1891: 2; *Los Angeles Times* 7 November 1896: 24; St. Paul *Pioneer Press* figure from Sidney Kobre, *The Yellow Press and Gilded Age Journalism* (Tallahassee: Florida State University Press, 1964) 218. It should be noted that the term "daily" usually applied to all weekday editions plus Saturday.

15 The figure for Sunday papers in 1880 is from North, *History and Present Condition* 171; 1890 and 1900 figures from Alfred McClung Lee, *The Daily Newspaper in America: The Evolution of a Social Instrument* (New York: Macmillan, 1937) 719; *Boston Globe* 25 July 1891: 10.

16 *Boston Globe* figures from 2 August 1891: 20, 1 June 1891: 1, and 1 November 1899: 1.

17 Railroad statistics from *Historical Statistics* 2: 731; for an excellent discussion of antebellum transportation difficulties see Ronald J. Zboray, "The Transportation System and Antebellum Book Distribution Reconsidered," *American Quarterly* 38 (1986): 53–71.

18 Walter Sutton, *The Western Book Trade: Cincinnati as a Nineteenth-Century Publishing and Book-Trade Center* (Columbus, OH: Ohio State University Press, 1961) 285; 1880 figure from Mott, *American Magazines* 3: 26.

19 Britt, *Forty Years* 83; the International News Company is described in "In Able Hands," *Newspaper Maker* 29 October 1896: 3.

20 *Historical Statistics* 2: 805.

21 Arthur Reed Kimball, "The Invasion of Journalism," *Atlantic Monthly* 86 (1900): 122. For an overview of this issue see Richard B. Kielbowicz, "Mere Merchandise or Vessels of Culture?: Books in the Mail, 1792–1942," *Papers of the Bibliographical Society of America* 82 (1988): 169–200.

22 Figures in Wayne E. Fuller, *RFD, The Changing Face of Rural America* (Bloomington: Indiana University Press, [1964]) 14.

23 1868 and 1871 figures in Frederic Hudson, *Journalism in the United States from 1690 to 1872*, 3 vols. (New York: Harper and Brothers, 1873) 3: 775; 1880 figures from North, *History and Present Condition* 158.

24 For Curtis's beliefs see Salme Harju Steinberg, *Reformer in the Marketplace: Edward W. Bok and the "Ladies' Home Journal"* (Baton Rouge: Louisiana State Press, 1979) 4; *Atlantic* circulation in Bliss Perry, letter to Henry James, 31 October 1899, quoted in Ballou, *The Building of the House*) 465.

25 "Special Newspaper Trains," *Journalist* 22 August 1885: 4; Donald, "Sunday Newspapers in the United States" 80–81.

26 *Atlanta Constitution* 23 November 1884: 6; *Detroit Free Press* 14 June 1885: 10; Frank Angelo, *On Guard. A History of the Detroit Free Press* (Detroit: Detroit Free Press, 1981) 97; *Boston Globe* 7 February 1891: 5; Edgar Watson Howe, "Country Newspapers," *Century* 42 (1891): 782; for

Colorado Weekly Sun figures see advertisement, *Printers' Ink* 2 May 1894: 555.

27 Illiteracy figures from *Historical Statistics* 1: 382; schools in *Historical Statistics* 1: 369; population figures from *Historical Statistics* 1: 8; Harvey Graff, *The Literacy Myth: Literacy and Social Structure in the Nineteenth-Century City* (New York: Academic Press, 1979) 276 and ix; Altick, *Writers, Readers, and Occasions* 213.
28 "Columbus," "Chicago's Daily Newspapers," *Printers' Ink* 16 August 1893: 193.
29 Donald Sheehan, *This Was Publishing: A Chronicle of the Book Trade in the Gilded Age* (Bloomington: Indiana University Press, 1952) 5.
30 Scudder depiction in Ballou, *The Building of the House* 444; "Confessions of a Literary Hack," *Forum* 19 (1895): 633; Sheehan, *This Was Publishing* 124 and 127.
31 Borus, *Writing Realism: Howells, James, and Norris in the Mass Market* (Chapel Hill: University of North Carolina Press, 1989) 46; Frank Norris, "Salt and Sincerity," *The Responsibilities of the Novelist and Other Essays* 198.
32 Charvat, *The Profession of Authorship in America, 1800–1870*, ed. Matthew J. Bruccoli (Columbus: Ohio State University Press, 1968) 309.
33 Ballou, *The Building of the House* 289; Coultrap-McQuin, *Doing Literary Business* 198; Anesko, *"Friction with Market": Henry James and the Profession of Authorship* (New York: Oxford University Press, 1986) 34; N. N. Feltes, *Modes of Production of Victorian Novels* (Chicago: University of Chicago Press, 1986) 63.
34 Wilson, "The Rhetoric of Consumption" 44.
35 Henry James, letter to William James, 20 February 1888, quoted in Anesko, *"Friction with Market"* 130; Harte, letter to A. P. Watt, 21 May 1885, *The Letters of Bret Harte*, ed. Geoffrey Bret Harte (Boston and New York: Houghton Mifflin Co., 1926) 275–276. For the most complete history of the literary agent see James Hepburn, *The Author's Empty Purse and the Rise of the Literary Agent* (London: Oxford University Press, 1968).
36 "Confessions of a Literary Hack" 631–632; for pay per book see Shove, *Cheap Book Production* 36.
37 Radway, *Reading the Romance: Women, Patriarchy, and Popular Literature* (Chapel Hill and London: University of North Carolina Press, 1984).
38 S. S. McClure, letter to Seth Low, Rare Book and Manuscript Library, Columbia University.

2 THE PIONEERS

1 Clementine Cole, letter to American Press Association, 29 February 1892, APA-LC.
2 Editorial, New York *Sun* 8 November 1884: 2; Circular, 4 October 1884, MP-Lilly; S. S. McClure, letter, *Critic* 8 (1887): 42.

3 For "Journal of Occurrences" information see Frank Luther Mott, *American Journalism* 99 and 397n; for Aikens and *Staten Islander*, see *American Newspaper Directory*, part 1 (New York: George P. Rowell, 1870) 109–111; the success of British partly printed sheets is noted in Michael Turner, "The Syndication of Fiction in Provincial Newspapers, 1870–1939: The Example of the Tillotson 'Fiction Bureau,'" B. Litt. thesis, Oxford University, 1968, 13–15.

4 For the early history of readyprints see Elmo Scott Watson, *A History of Newspaper Syndicates in the United States, 1865–1935* (Chicago: n. p., 1936) 5–12; for Atwood and Rublee figures, see "Death of A. N. Kellogg," *Journalist* 3 April 1886: 8.

5 For early customers see *KAHB* 10; for 1865 figures see Ellen M. Mrja, "Ansel Nash Kellogg," *American Newspaper Journalists, 1873–1900*, Dictionary of Literary Biography 23, ed. Perry J. Ashley (Detroit: Gale Research Co., 1983) 182; 1871 figures in [M. M. Quaife], "How A. N. Kellogg Revolutionized America's Country Press," *The National Printer-Journalist* February 1922: 21; 1877 figures in advertisement, *American Newspaper Directory* (New York: [George P. Rowell and Co.], 1877) n. p.; the figure of 1,588 papers is reported in *N. W. Ayer and Son's Newspaper Annual and Directory* (Philadelphia: N. W. Ayer and Son, 1887) 947; 1900 figures (which might include many newspapers that took plate service from Kellogg) in Watson, *History of Newspaper Syndicates* 41; 1.7 million figure from *Biographical Sketches of the Leading Men of Chicago* (Chicago: Wilson, Peirce, and Co., 1876) 84.

6 The 1878 figures from *KAHB* 16; 1880 figures from Scott, *Newspapers and Periodicals of Illinois* lxxxi; 1886 figures from *N. W. Ayer and Son's American Newspaper Annual and Directory* (1887) 947.

7 Figure of 117 newspapers in *American Newspaper Directory* (1869) 323; figures for the American Newspaper Union are from an advertisement in *American Newspaper Directory* (1877) n. p.; Beals's activities are described in Watson, *History of Newspaper Syndicates* 28–29.

8 For Western Newspaper Union founding and expansion see Watson, *History of Newspaper Syndicates* 30–31; *N. W. Ayer and Son's American Newspaper Annual* (1891) 1232, 1241, 1283, 1357; Lyman Morse, *Advertisers' Handy Guide. 1895* (New York: Lyman D. Morse, 1895) 578–579.

9 Endorsement quoted in *KAHB* 65; for paper costs, see Howe, "Country Newspapers" (1891): 781, and *KAHB* 10; for numerous editorial commendations of Kellogg's presswork, see *KAHB* 62–67.

10 One writer in 1870 indicates that Kellogg had recently begun printing serial fiction (*American Newspaper Directory* [1870] 207); all statements about readyprint newspapers in 1876 are based on observations made of the Kellogg Collection of 'Patent Inside' Newspapers, Chicago Historical Society, Chicago, Illinois; 1878 quotation in *KAHB* 40; G. W. Wappiert, "Newspaper Factories," *Writer* 4 (1890): 8.

11 "The A. N. Kellogg Newspaper Co.," *Journalist* 28 May 1887: 3;

Kellogg–Bacheller combination advertisement, Watson, *History of Newspaper Syndicates* between pages 44 and 45. Wright Patterson asserted that Kellogg supplied *The Red Badge of Courage* to 200 small city daily newspapers and 250 weekly papers in plate form, plus more in the form of patent insides (letter to George Max, 31 May 1947, quoted in [Joseph Katz], "An Editor's Recollection of 'The Red Badge of Courage,'" *Stephen Crane Newsletter* 2.3 [Spring 1968]: 4–5). While some of what Patterson remembered has proven to be incorrect, this is no reason to distrust everything he says.

12 For evidence of matrixes being sent see Wappiert, "Newspaper Factories" 7; advance payment is indicated in Howe, "Country Newspapers" 781.

13 For Rowell's start, see Watson, *History of Newspaper Syndicates* 35; Joseph Katz says that Kellogg began plate service in 1871, but this is doubtful ("Bibliography and the Rise of American Literary Realism," *Studies in American Fiction* 2 [1974]: 81); for information about British plate service, see William Hunt, *Then and Now; or, Fifty Years of Newspaper Work* (Hull and London: Hamilton, Adams, and Co., 1887) 71–76; technical developments in Lee, *The Daily Newspaper in America* 141, *KAHB* 20, and Watson, *History of Newspaper Syndicates* 34–35.

14 For origins of boilerplate term see Watson, *History of Newspaper Syndicates* 36n; W. E. S. Fales notes that the Association began a "slip-service" with the title of the American Press Syndicate in 1884 (letter, *Journalist* 15 September 1888: 9); for the number of American Press Association customers in 1886 see "The American Press Association," *Journalist* 27 March 1886: 10; figures for 1890 in advertisement, *Journalist* 5 July 1890: 21; for 1892 report, see "The Story of a Great Success," *Journalist* 17 December 1892: 2.

15 How these plates were handled is indicated in *A Hand Book of Useful Information Concerning the Plate Service of the American Press Association* (New York: [American Press Association], 1891) 8–9 and 23–26, John C. Sim, *The Grass-Roots Press: America's Community Newspapers* (Ames, Iowa: The Iowa State University Press, 1969) 43, Watson, *History of Newspaper Syndicates* 36, and W. G. Benlin, letter to A. A. Hill, 11 December 1893, APA-LC; first quotation from "Bye-the-Bye," *Journalist* 29 January 1887: 9; last quotation in Howe, "Country Newspapers" 782.

16 For indications of this strategy see "The A. N. Kellogg Newspaper Co." 3.

17 "The American Press Association" (1886): 10; *A Hand Book of Useful Information* 20; Howard Fielding, "Plate Matter for Newspapers," *Book News* 7 (1889): 238.

18 Stephen Crane, letter to "My dear Sir," American Press Association, 25 August 1892, letter 12 of *The Correspondence of Stephen Crane*, ed. Stanley Wertheim and Paul Sorrentino, vol. 1 (New York: Columbia University Press, 1988) 45; Crane, letter to Editor, American Press

Association, 23 November [1895], letter 142 of vol. 1, *The Correspondence of Stephen Crane* 147; London's connection to the Association is mentioned in Lee, *The Daily Newspaper in America* 584; Charlotte Perkins Stetson, letter to Mr. I. D. Marshall, 18 July 1890, APA-LC.

19 Stetson, 18 July 1890, APA-LC; "Bye-the-Bye," *Journalist* 5 February 1887: 8.

20 W. D. Howells, letter to [Benjamin] Ticknor, 1 December 1887, *Selected Letters of W. D. Howells 1882–1891*, ed. and annotated by Robert C. Leitz III with Richard H. Zallinger and Christoph Lohmann, vol. 3 (Boston: Twayne, 1980) 210–211; see Kate Chopin, letters to A. A. Hill, 26 December 1894, 1 January 1895, 11 January 1895, and 16 January 1895, APA-LC (for other information on Chopin's dealings with the Association, see Emily Toth, *Kate Chopin* [New York: William Morrow and Co., Inc., 1990] 200, 247, and 275); Opie Read, letter to [I. D. Marshall], 17 February 1893, Opie Read Collection (#9279), CWB-Alderman; purchases of Tillotson's fiction are indicated in April 1887–March 1892 Trade Ledger, ZBEN 1/3; for evidence of McClure sales to the Association, see Robert McClure, letters to T. C. McClure, 12 April 1898, 28 March 1899, and 5 April 1899, all MP-Lilly.

21 One advertisement is seen in *Journalist* 5 July 1890: 21; the use of circulars is indicated in "Bye-the-Bye," *Journalist* 4 April 1891: 8; Rogers, "Circulation Ideas," *Newspaper Maker* 11 February 1897: 3. There is one report that the Association established a London office to market its materials in Britain, but whether this succeeded is unknown ("Bye-the-Bye," *Journalist* 23 April 1887: 9).

22 For an example of editorial suggestions made to authors see Alfred R. Calhoun, letter to [I. D.] Marshall, 25 March 1892, APA-LC; quotation from "The American Press Association" (1886) 10; 1892 list of illustrators and storage quotation in "The Story of a Great Success" 3; for indications of copyright registration see John Russell Young, letter to "Gentlemen," 25 August 1897, APA-LC.

23 For a good overview of the history of feuilletons see Lise Queffélec, *Le Roman-Feuilleton Français au XIXe Siècle* (Paris: Presses Universitaires de France, 1989).

24 "Taken at the Flood," *Bolton Weekly Journal* 30 August 1873–18 April 1874; "Notes and News," *Academy* 9 July 1881: 28; information on Leng's activities can be found in Graham Pollard, *Serial Fiction* (London: Constable, [1938]) 270, numerous letters in ZBEN 4/3, and in Victor Lawson, letters to C. D. [son of W. C.] Leng, 22 May 1888, and 8 March [1889], VLP-Newberry.

25 "Fighting the Air," *Bolton Weekly Journal* 7 November 1874–29 May 1875; Michael Turner notes the status of Marryat's work ("The Syndication of Fiction in Provincial Newspapers 1870–1939" 47); "Taken at the Flood," *Harper's Weekly* 1 November 1873–23 May 1874; for evidence of American sales in the 1880s see ZBEN 1/3 and ZBEN

4/3; the number of people in the Fiction department is in Wage Book, December 1887–September 1891, ZBEN 2/6.

26 Circular enclosed with S. S. McClure, letter to William W. Clapp, 24 May 1886 (bms Am 1518), the Houghton Library, Harvard University, Cambridge, MA; the terms of a McClure–Tillotson agreement of March 1887 are outlined in S. S. McClure, letter to John S. Phillips, 9 March 1887, MP-Lilly.

27 For the establishment of an American branch office in late 1888 see "Journalistic Enterprise," *Journalist* 12 January 1889: 11, and "Trade and Literary Gossip," *Bookseller* 9 January 1889: 5; Michael L. Turner, "Tillotson's Fiction Bureau," *Studies in the Book Trade in Honour of Graham Pollard* (Oxford: The Oxford Bibliographical Society, 1975) 363; the number of fictions circulated in America and the predominance of British authors is reported in "Bye-the-Bye," *Journalist* 3 September 1892: 9; for a good idea of such a mixture see the *Utica [NY] Daily Observer* (1899); Mr. Frank Graves's employment and the continued existence of a New York office are indicated in William Brimelow, letter to Provident Life Assurance Society, 7 August 1900, ZBEN 14/4.

28 For Sheppard description, see loose clippings in ZBEN 9/4; for account of Bennett meeting, see Frank Singleton, typescript notes, ZBEN 14/10.

29 Numerous letters from authors in ZBEN 4/1 refer inquiries to A. P. Watt; such an arrangement between Tillotson's and Watt is mentioned in S. S. McClure, letter to Hattie [McClure], 7 March 1887, MP-Lilly; see James B. Pinker, letter to Stephen Crane, 21 September 1899, letter 557 of vol. 2, *The Correspondence of Stephen Crane* 517–518; Tillotson's solicitation is evident in Cora Crane, letter to James B. Pinker, [mid-March 1900], letter 659 of vol. 2, *The Correspondence of Stephen Crane* 606.

30 Turner, "Tillotson's Fiction Bureau" 359; Leng's sales to Tillotson's are indicated in Tillotson Ledger A, pages 42 and 202, BL-Turner.

31 Nigel Cross, *The Common Writer: Life in Nineteenth-Century Grub Street* (Cambridge: Cambridge University Press, 1985) 208; for a more detailed description of the decline of the three-decker novel, see Guinevere L. Griest, *Mudie's Circulating Library and the Victorian Novel* (Bloomington: Indiana University Press, 1970) 156–175. Tillotson and Son's desire for stories is noted in "Literary Syndicates," *The Editor* 2.2 (February 1896): 51; "Notes," *Critic* 5 (1886): 37–38; William J. Bok, "Literary Leaves," *Indianapolis News* 9 October 1886: 3; Jack London, letters to Cloudesley Johns, 12 June 1899 and 26 September 1899, *The Letters of Jack London: Volume One: 1896–1905*, ed. Earle Labor, Robert C. Leitz III, and I. Milo Shepard (Stanford, CA: Stanford University Press, 1988) 83–87 and 114–115.

32 Maxwell, letter to W. F. Tillotson, 29 December 1882, ZBEN 4/3.

33 The use of Programmes in Britain is indicated in Turner, "Reading for the Masses: Aspects of the Syndication of Fiction in Great Britain," in

Book Selling and Book Buying: Aspects of the Nineteenth-Century British and North American Book Trade, ed. Richard G. Landon (Chicago: American Library Association, 1978) 66; the 1894 Programme is quoted in Turner, "The Syndication of Fiction in Provincial Newspapers" 89; see 1885 Programme attached to Tillotson and Son, letter to Henry Holt and Co., 14 October 1885, Box 127, File #3, Henry Holt Archives, Department of Rare Books and Special Collections, Princeton University Libraries; for numerous examples of both novel and short story marketing in the United States see the Victor Lawson Papers; 1882 quotation in Circular, 30 December 1882, ZBEN 4/3; Maxwell, letter to W. F. Tillotson, 28 January 1883, ZBEN 4/3; cabling is advised in Circular, 2 January 1884, ZBEN 4/3.

34 Advertisements in *Journalist* 14 November 1891: 16, *Journalist* 5 October 1892: 15, and *Journalist* 17 December 1892: 72.

35 For Braddon serials see Tillotson circulars, ZBEN 4/3; price of *The Evil Genius* is quoted in Victor Lawson, letter to S. S. McClure, 5 December [1888], VLP-Newberry; for short story offer see "Literary Syndicates" (1896): 50; Circular, 30 December 1882, ZBEN 4/3; the variables are clearly indicated in Tillotson, Notebook, circa 1885, ZBEN 4/5.

36 For information about Brimelow, Nayler, Edwards, Sheppard, and James Lever Tillotson, see Fred Evans and John Nayler, written reminiscences, ZBEN 14/10, and various clippings in ZBEN 9/4; Gibbs's position is indicated in Turner, "The Syndication of Fiction" 52–53. For samples of handwritten manuscripts, see Wilkie Collins, "The Devil's Spectacles," and Richard Marsh, "Mr. Whiting and Mary Ann," ZBEN 4/7; quotation from Nayler written reminiscence, January 1946, ZBEN 14/10.

37 See how three illustrations accompanied the first installment of The Duchess (Mrs. Hungerford), "Lady Werner's Flight," *Syracuse Herald* 21 October 1892: 9, but many others in this paper during 1894 were non-illustrated; for 1899 practice see the *Utica Daily Observer*.

38 For a description of Tillotson's plate service see Tillotson, Notebook, circa 1885, ZBEN 4/5; for availability of "copy in reprint" in 1875 see Turner, "The Syndication of Fiction in Provincial Newspapers" 43; "Reprint only" quotation in Notebook, ZBEN 4/5; American printing for Tillotson material is implied in W. Philip Robinson, letter to I. D. Marshall, 26 February 1892, APA-LC.

39 Circular, 30 December 1882, ZBEN 4/3; Maxwell, letter to W. F. Tillotson, 31 December 1883, ZBEN 4/3.

40 John S. Phillips notes that Taylor syndicated this work ("Newspaper Syndicates," *Book News* 6 [1888]: 487–488); "The King's Men," *Boston Globe*, Sundays, 8 June 1884–10 August 1884; "Royal Love" advertisement, *Boston Globe* 16 November 1884: 16; for Taylor's sale of one fiction to a Chicago newspaper, see Victor Lawson, letter to Taylor, 13 March [1888], VLP-Newberry.

41 The claim about Dana is made in Edward P. Mitchell, *Memoirs of an Editor* (New York: Charles Scribner's Sons, 1924) 280; program advertisement at head of Bret Harte, "A Blue Grass Penelope," *Syracuse Standard* 6 July 1884: 6.
42 *New York Sun* 1 January 1885: 2; Phillips, "Newspaper Syndicates" (1888): 488; manager quoted in "Continued Stories," *Journalist* 30 August 1884: 1 (it is uncertain which story Mr. Scott of the *Chicago Herald* purchased from Dana in 1884, since the Henry James and Bret Harte stories previously mentioned were published in the *Chicago Tribune*).

3 THE HEYDAY OF AMERICAN FICTION SYNDICATION

1 McClure, letter to E. D. Cope, 26 August 1891, MP-Lilly; Bacheller, *From Stores of Memory* (New York: Farrar and Rinehart, 1938) 43.
2 For a description of some of the various literary bureaus see Hepburn, *The Author's Empty Purse* (1968) 73; the advantages of literary bureaus and manuscript brokers are described in W[illiam] H. H[ills], editorial, *Writer* (New York) 5 (1891): 122–124; "An Author's Exchange," *Journalist* 8 September 1888: 8; and "Manuscript Brokers," *Journalist* 24 September 1887: 9.
3 Ouida, letter, London *Times* 22 May 1891: 3; McClure, letter to Stevenson, 12 September 1890, MP-Lilly.
4 McClure, *My Autobiography* (1913; New York: Frederick A. Stokes Co., 1914) 168.
5 Garland, *Companions on the Trail: A Literary Chronicle* (New York: Macmillan, 1931) 108; Waugh, *One Man's Road: Being a Picture of Life in a Passing Generation* (London: Chapman and Hall, 1931) 230.
6 Tarbell, *All in a Day's Work. An Autobiography* (New York: Macmillan, 1939) 119, 154; Osbourne, *An Intimate Portrait of RLS* (New York: Charles Scribner's Sons, 1924) 80–81; Baker (David Grayson), *American Chronicle: The Autobiography of Ray Stannard Baker* (New York: Charles Scribner's Sons, 1945) 96; Conrad, letter to Edward Garnett, [24 November 1899], vol. 2, *The Collected Letters of Joseph Conrad, 1898–1902*, ed. Frederick R. Karl and Laurence Davies (Cambridge: Cambridge University Press, 1986) 221–222; Howells later wrote that a friend of his youth from Ohio, Ralph Keeler, was the chief inspiration for Fulkerson (see "The Author to the Reader," W. D. Howells, *A Hazard of New Fortunes*, intro. by Everett Carter [1889; Bloomington and London: Indiana University Press, 1976] 505–506).
7 First two quotations from marginal notes made by Bacheller in Cyril Clemens, letter to Bacheller, [August 1939], B-StL; for colleague's statement, see W. E. S. Fales, letter, *Journalist* 15 September 1888: 9.
8 Fales states that Bacheller established the American Bureau of Fiction

Notes to pages 72–75 239

in December 1883 (9); a contemporary article on Bacheller also says he began in 1883 (O. W. R., "The Newspaper Syndicate King," *Journalist* 31 July 1886: 3); Alfred McClung Lee cites this article in *The Daily Newspaper in America* 584–585, and others since have cited Lee. The year 1884 is proposed by Peter Lyon (*Success Story: The Life and Times of S. S. McClure* [New York: Charles Scribner's Sons, 1963] 54); V. V. McNitt states that Bacheller began in 1887 ("Sam McClure Started Something," *Editor and Publisher* 67 [21 July 1934]: 80); R. W. Stallman and Lillian Gilkes write, "Bacheller's syndicate was not founded until late in 1894, though most likely it was in the planning stage much earlier" (Stallman and Gilkes, ed., *Stephen Crane: Letters*, with intro. by Stallman [New York: New York University Press, 1960] 41n); Frank Luther Mott describes Bacheller as an "Indiana author" (*American Journalism* 482). Elmo Scott Watson claims that Bacheller's syndicate was originally named the New York *Press* Syndicate (*History of Newspaper Syndicates* 43), but the New York *Press* did not begin publication until 1887.

9 Bacheller later wrote that he met Hatton in the autumn of 1884 (see marginal notes, Cyril Clemens, letter to Irving Bacheller, [August 1939], B-StL), but newspaper accounts of Irving's tour and the publication of Hatton's novel in early 1884 prove this is incorrect; Bacheller describes this first attempt at syndicating in *Coming Up the Road: Memories of a North Country Boyhood* (Indianapolis: Bobbs-Merrill, 1928) 260.

10 Bacheller's memories of his first sales trips are in *Coming Up the Road* 261, and *From Stores of Memory* 44; see London Letters in *Boston Herald* 25 May 1884: 16, and *Washington Post* 8 February 1885: 2; payment is indicated in C. Shackleford, letter to A. I. Bacheller, VLP-Newberry; Bacheller claimed that he quit his newspaper job right after his first sales trip in spring 1884 (*From Stores of Memory* 44).

11 Opie Read, "Old Amazin' Grace," *Utica Daily Observer* 29 November 1884: 3; Samuel D. Lee, letter to McClure, 23 May 1885, MP-Lilly. The first fiction positively identified as a Bacheller piece by virtue of an attached copyright notice of "Bacheller and Gunnison" is Julian Hawthorne, "Carlo Carrambo," *Boston Globe* 1 February 1885: 16 (Herbert F. Gunnison was a friend of Bacheller's from St. Lawrence).

12 *My Autobiography* 170; S. S. McClure, letter, *Critic* 11 (1887): 43; McClure also confesses his indebtedness to Dana in *My Autobiography* 164; Circular, 4 October 1884, MP-Lilly.

13 The best source for information on the early days of McClure's syndicate is Lyon, *Success Story* 53–109; for his duties as editorial assistant, see Autobiography notes 15, MP-Lilly; quotation from *My Autobiography* 164; for 1870 story see McClure, "And McClure Tells How He Did It," *Editor and Publisher* 21 July 1934: 82; McClure repeated this story of his *St. Nicholas* idea numerous times, including in *My Autobiography* 164–5; quotation from *My Autobiography* 165.

14 The contents of McClure's letter to Phillips can be inferred from

Phillips, letter to McClure, 10 August 1884, MP-Lilly; "S. S. McClure's 16 Words of Advice Key to Success," *Boston Globe* 9 September 1939, morning edition: 2.
15 Lyon, *Success Story* 57; *My Autobiography* 167 and 175.
16 McClure, letter to John Phillips, 9 March 1887, MP-Lilly; S. S. McClure, letter to Hattie McClure, 26 December 1889, MP-Lilly; S. S. McClure, letter to Seth Low, 29 August 1891, Rare Book and Manuscript Library, Columbia University; Rudyard Kipling, letter to S. S. McClure, [January 1890], *The Letters of Rudyard Kipling*, ed. Thomas Pinney, vol. 2 (Iowa City: University of Iowa Press, 1990) 6; Twain publication noted in Elizabeth Morrison, "Newspapers and Novelists in Late Colonial Australia: Serial Fiction in the Melbourne *Age*, 1872–1899," diss., Monash University, Clayton, Victoria, Australia, 1983, 51.
17 Robert McClure wrote to Tom McClure on 26 September 1900 that he was offering Anthony Hope's *Tristram of Blent* to newspapers in India, South Africa, and Australia (MP-Lilly).
18 For six-day service in 1885, see Robert H. Campe, letter to S. S. McClure, 30 July 1885, MP-Lilly.
19 For word count and number of foreign works see McClure, letter, *Critic* 43; Holiday Program for December 1885, Scrapbook, MP-Lilly; Circular, 27 March 1885, Unbound Publicity, MP-Lilly; and McClure, letter to Talcott Williams, 27 July 1885, in Talcott Williams Papers (Box 1, Folder 13), Special Collections, Amherst College Archives, Amherst, MA. For projected 300 stories see Circular, 10 September 1885, Publicity, MP-Lilly; for desire to increase American stories to five, see McClure to Talcott Williams, 27 July 1885, Talcott Williams Papers.
20 Quotations from *Coming Up the Road* 264 and 266; for Arthur Stedman's contact with Mary E. Wilkins, see Mary E. Wilkins, letters to Arthur Stedman, 12 February 1894 and 22 December 1895, letters 145 and 190 of *The Infant Sphinx: Collected Letters of Mary E. Wilkins Freeman*, ed. Brent L. Kendrick (Metuchen, NJ: The Scarecrow Press, 1985) 161–162 and 183–184; E. C. Stedman's duties are seen in Bacheller, letter to [Edmund Clarence] Stedman, 16 August 1895, ECSP-Columbia; Matthews returned the check with a letter to Bacheller, 30 October 1894, Henry E. Huntington Library.
21 Phelps, *Chapters from a Life* (Boston and New York: Houghton, Mifflin and Co., 1897) 245; Circular, 27 October 1884, MP-Lilly; for McClure's written solicitations see McClure, letters to "Charles Egbert Craddock" (Mary Noailles Murfree), 20 September 1884 and 25 October 1884, The Robert W. Woodruff Library, plus Frank Stockton, letter to S. S. McClure, 25 November 1884, Frank Stockton Collection (#5866), CWB-Alderman. For details of Stevenson's promise of what would eventually be known as *David Balfour*, see Roger G. Swearingen, *The Prose Writings of Robert Louis Stevenson* (Hamden, CT: Archon Books,

1980) 117 and 168; for an example of such formal agreements, see Memorandum of Agreement, attached to S. S. McClure, letter to Mr. Stevenson, 25 October 1892, Robert Louis Stevenson Papers, Beinecke Rare Book and Manuscript Library, Yale University.

22 Harriet McClure, letter to Mother, 10 September 1885, MP-Lilly; for *Le Petit Journal* subscription see Brentano Brothers, letter to S. S. McClure, 23 November 1885, MP-Lilly; McClure, letter to Bierce, 9 July 1892, Beinecke Rare Book and Manuscript Library. Norris's route to McClure is not completely clear, for while Jeannette Gilder wrote that McClure read the *Wave* and invited Norris to New York (noted in Franklin Walker, *Frank Norris: A Biography* [Garden City, New York: Doubleday, Doran and Co., Inc. 1932] 166), Norris himself said that he initiated contact with McClure by submitting *Moran of the Lady Letty* for publication in *McClure's Magazine* (see Frank Norris, letter to Isaac Frederick Marcosson, [1 December 1898?], letter 19 of *Frank Norris: Collected Letters*, compiled and annotated by Jesse S. Crisler [San Francisco: The Book Club of California, 1986] 56–58). Franklin Walker has concluded that Phillips first contacted Norris (see "Four Additional Frank Norris Letters," *Book Club of California Quarterly Newsletter* 40 [Winter 1974]: 4–5).

23 For information on the 1886 contest see "Bye-the-Bye," *Journalist* 12 June 1886: 9; for information on 1888 and 1893 prize contests, see 7 October 1888, Scrapbook, MP-Lilly, and 20 February 1893, Copybook, MP-Lilly; this instruction sheet dated 1886 is located in Scrapbook for 1899, MP-Lilly; figure of twenty stories a day (most of them probably for the prize contest) is from Harriet McClure, letter to Mother, 5 November 1885, MP-Lilly; figure of about one thousand entries in Notice, [1894], Scrapbook, MP-Lilly; Advertisement, *Boston Globe* 21 August 1885: Supplement, p. 2; Advertisement, *Journalist* 11 January 1890: 14.

24 Announcements regarding the contest won by Burton can be found in "Bye-the-Bye," *Journalist* 10 July 1886: 8; and "News and Notes," *Writer* (New York) 1.5 (August 1887): 100; Burton's status as a Bacheller employee is seen in F. R. Burton, letter, *Journalist* 6 August 1887: 9 (Burton was probably an employee during the prize contest, previous to the date of this letter); details of Bacheller's 1894 contest were reported in "Miss Wilkins a Prize-Winner in Bacheller Syndicate's Competition," *Critic* 26 (1895): 483; Brent L. Kendrick describes Wilkins's involvement in this contest in *The Infant Sphinx* 120–121.

25 Bacheller later wrote that "often my errands called me to France and England" (*From Stores of Memory* 95); Waugh, *One Man's Road* 230; *Coming Up the Road* 265.

26 Autobiography notes, MP-Lilly; for pseudonym see Lyon, *Success Story* 74; for details of Frederic's relationship with McClure, see *The Correspondence of Harold Frederic*, ed. George E. Fortenberry, Stanton Garner,

and Robert H. Woodward (Fort Worth: Texas Christian University Press, 1977) 263n; S. S. McClure, letter to John S. Phillips, 9 March 1887, MP-Lilly; S. S. McClure to Hattie McClure, 9 March 1887, MP-Lilly; McClure's attempt to market Robert Louis Stevenson's "The Outlaws of Tunstall Forest" in Britain is indicated in correspondence from editors of the *Nottingham Daily Guardian* and *Cardiff Times*, 27 June and 29 June 1888, MP-Lilly, respectively; for Conrad's comments see letter to Edward Garnett, [24 November 1899], vol. 2, *The Collected Letters of Joseph Conrad* 121; *My Autobiography* 201; "Bye-the-Bye," *Journalist* 18 October 1890: 8.

27 For details of Bacheller's visit to Doyle, see *Coming Up the Road* 271–272, and Irving Bacheller, Address to the Stevenson Society, 26 August 1922, B-StL; for details of the sale of these *South Seas Letters*, see George L. McKay, *Some Notes on Robert Louis Stevenson: His Finances and His Agents and Publishers* (New Haven: Yale University Library, 1958) 30–31; for information on the Howells arrangement see S. S. McClure, letters to W. D. Howells, 18 April 1890, 21 April 1890, and 24 December 1890 (BMS Am 1784), the Houghton Library, Harvard University; the primacy of the *Sun* in this matter is detailed in James P. Elliott, introduction and notes to W. D. Howells, *The Quality of Mercy*, (1891; Bloomington: Indiana University Press, 1979) 365n–367n; Twain wrote, "Laffan sent Mc[Clure] up here a day or two ago to offer me $300 per Century page for a few European letters for the syndicate papers" (letter to Fred J. Hall, 20 May 1891, letter 226 of *Mark Twain's Letters to His Publishers*, ed. Hamlin Hill [Berkeley: University of California Press, 1967] 276).

28 Report in "Bye-the-Bye," *Journalist* 18 January 1890: 9; *Coming Up the Road* 266.

29 Sidney Kobre, *Development of American Journalism* (Dubuque, Iowa: Wm. C. Brown Co., 1969) 514–515; Editor of New Orleans *Daily Picayune* [unreadable name], letter to McClure, 20 January 1885; Editor of Omaha *Herald* [N. J. Jackson?], letter to McClure, 20 January 1885; Mr. Keating, letter to McClure, 19 May 1885, all in MP-Lilly; Autobiography notes, MP-Lilly; McRae, *Forty Years in Newspaperdom. The Autobiography of a Newspaper Man* (New York: Brentano's, 1924) 87.

30 William H. Rideing, "Boston Letter," *Critic* 8 (1887): 6; *From Stores of Memory* 44.

31 William P. Harrison, letter to McClure, 17 October 1885, MP-Lilly; for details of the Vanderpoole scandal and his arrest in September 1887, see "Literary Forgery," *Syracuse Herald* 25 September 1887: 4, and "Disclosure and Disgrace," *Journalist* 24 September 1887: 12.

32 For an example of Bacheller's double-sided stationery see Bacheller, letter to Colonel Cockerill, 19 January 1886, New York *World* Collection, Special Collections, Columbia University; later Bacheller circular in Joseph Katz, introduction to Stephen Crane, *The Red Badge of Courage*

(1894; Gainesville, Florida: Scholars' Facsimiles and Reprints, 1967) 22–23; "Bye-the-Bye," *Journalist* 24 October 1891: 8.

33 For frequency of travel, see *Coming Up the Road* 265; quotation from Irving Bacheller, "The Rungs in My Little Ladder," *American Magazine* 85 (1918): 19; Bacheller, letter to John Brisben Walker, 14 March 1898, Special Collections and Manuscripts, Harold B. Lee Library, Brigham Young University; Johnson's travels are implied in "James W. Johnson," *Journalist* 13 September 1890: 2; "my travelling agents" are noted in Irving Bacheller, letter to [Edmund Clarence] Stedman, 10 April 1893, ECSP-Columbia.

34 Borus, *Writing Realism* 44.

35 Bacheller 1885 price in Robert H. Campe, letter to McClure, 30 July 1885, MP-Lilly; 1890 price in Victor Lawson, letter to Bacheller, 8 March 1890, VLP-Newberry; for 1894 Bacheller price see circular in Katz, introduction, *The Red Badge of Courage* 22–23.

36 Contract, 13 November 1884, MP-Lilly; for McClure prices of $8–15, see Circular, 8 November 1884, MP-Lilly; 1892 prices in Copybook, 17 May 1892, 18 January 1892, and 1 July 1892, MP-Lilly; Twain figures are in Circular, [1 July 1892?], Copybook, MP-Lilly; Bacheller's promises of possible payment at end of each month in Katz, introduction, *The Red Badge of Courage* 22–23.

37 Probable sale of second serial rights to the American Press Association is indicated in Robert McClure, letter to T[om] C. McClure, 5 April 1899, MP-Lilly; S. S. McClure, letter to the Editor of *Christian at Work*, 27 May 1891, MP-Lilly; see Joseph Katz, "Theodore Dreiser's 'Ev'ry Month,'" *Library Chronicle* 38 (Winter 1972): 59–60; for the number of syndicate pieces in *McClure's Magazine*, see undated memorandum, "McClure's Magazine" folder, MP-Lilly.

38 Vallentine's association with Bacheller is indicated in advertisement, *Journalist* 26 March 1887: 15, and Irving Bacheller, letter to O. O. Howard, 21 December 1891, Oliver Otis Howard Papers; Patterson's recollections are found in a letter dated 31 May 1947 that is reprinted in full in [Joseph Katz], "An Editor's Recollection of 'The Red Badge of Courage'" (Spring 1968): 3–5; for Bacheller's attempt to hire Stedman, see Bacheller, letter to [Edmund Clarence] Stedman, 4 September 1890, ECSP-Columbia; Bacheller, letter to [Edmund Clarence] Stedman, undated, ECSP-Columbia (its approximate date is indicated by its appearance on Bacheller and Johnson Newspaper Syndicate letterhead); Gaines's employment in *Coming Up the Road* 304.

39 "Good corp [sic] of clerks" and McClure's attempt to hire Anderson in McClure, letter to Professor Anderson, 16 December 1885, MP-Lilly; Baker, *American Chronicle* 98.

40 Burnett's editorship announced in Circular, 1 February 1889, Scrapbook, MP-Lilly, although Burnett apparently did not join the staff until October 1889; Pratt's appointment in Circular, 22 August 1891, Copy-

book, MP-Lilly; Norris's indefinite position is indicated in Franklin Walker, "Four Additional Frank Norris Letters," *Book Club of California Quarterly Newsletter* 40 (Winter 1974): 5; Marshall's involvement is indicated in Robert McClure, letter to Edward Marshall, McClure's Syndicate, 11 November 1899, MP-Lilly; Adams's editorship in Lyon 188.

41 Bacheller, letter to Mr. Stedman, undated, ECSP-Columbia; for Howells, see *The Quality of Mercy*, textual commentary, 366; for Crane, see *The Third Violet and Active Service*, vol. 3 of *The University of Virginia Edition of the Works of Stephen Crane*, ed. Fredson Bowers, introduction by J. C. Levenson (Charlottesville: University Press of Virginia, 1976) 333; for Kipling see McClure Autobiography notes, MP-Lilly.

42 McClure recalled this longhand copying in an undated radio interview, MP-Lilly; an example of longhand copying in non-aniline ink is "The Princess and the Bengaly," adapted by Harriet Hurd McClure, 1885, Scrapbook, MP-Lilly; stenographer's employment noted in an interview, "Colonel McClure, at 'Newspaper Week,' Tells of Early Struggles Syndicating," *Philadelphia Public Ledger* 27 April 1923: n.p., MP-Lilly; "One Thing and Another," *Detroit Free Press* 13 December 1885: 12; the hectograph process was capable of producing up to 100 copies (JoAnne Yates, *Control Through Communication: The Rise of System in American Management* [Baltimore and London: Johns Hopkins University Press, 1989] 50).

43 Bacheller's practice of allowing authors to revise proofs is evident in Mary E. Wilkins, letter to Arthur Stedman, 16 June [18]95, letter 170 of *The Infant Sphinx* 173–174; the usual flow of manuscript and copy to editors and illustrators in the McClure syndicate is indicated in John S. Phillips, letter to McClure, 22 October 1890, MP-Lilly.

44 Joseph Katz calls the New York *Press* "the [Bacheller] syndicate's home newspaper" at one time (introduction, *The Red Badge of Courage* 24); *Coming Up the Road* 266; Bacheller's employment of printers is evident in Irving Bacheller, letter to [Edmund Clarence] Stedman, 23 April 1895, ECSP-Columbia. One textual editor has asserted that the western sketches of Stephen Crane, syndicated by Bacheller in 1895, were typeset at the office of the *Nebraska State Journal* in Lincoln, and that these proofs were sent directly to subscribing newspapers without Bacheller having the chance to review or correct them (Bowers, ed., *Works of Stephen Crane*, vol. 8: Tales, Sketches, and Reports [Charlottesville: University Press of Virginia, 1973] 795, 884, and 887).

45 McClure describes this type of arrangement in *My Autobiography* 176; printing of proofs by various newspapers is indicated in numerous letters to McClure, 1884 and 1885, MP-Lilly; *My Autobiography* 176–177; for the arrangement with the *Boston Globe*, see Robert McClure, letter to Tom McClure, 24 August 1898, MP-Lilly, and Shurmer Sibthorp, letter to Mr. [Tom] McClure, 10 May 1900, MP-Lilly.

46 Both Hawthorne's and Cooke's stories appeared in the *Syracuse Journal*

24 December 1885: page 2 of special holiday supplement; John Young Taylor Diary, Courtesy, the Winterthur Library: Joseph Downs Collection of Manuscripts and Printed Ephemera; for Bacheller's galley-proof copy see Sarah Orne Jewett, "A Village Patriot," Houghton Library, AB85 J554 896v, Harvard University; Kauffman's position is indicated in G. Y. Kauffman, letter to B. M. Kip, 10 September 1896, B-StL; Bacheller, Johnson, and Bacheller circular, reprinted in Katz, introduction, *The Red Badge of Courage* 22–23.

47 McClure's statement regarding "Outlaws" can be found in *My Autobiography* 204 and in "Address of S. S. McClure to The Stevenson Society," 26 August 1922, MP-Lilly; McClure's first offer of illustrations is indicated in Talcott Williams, letter to McClure, 15 December 1884, MP-Lilly; Pratt appointment in Circular, Copybook, 10 October 1891, MP-Lilly; Bodfish and Newman are named in Circular, 11 November 1891, MP-Lilly.

48 The small number of papers receiving text in stereotype plate form is suggested in Bacheller, letter to [Edmund Clarence] Stedman, 23 April 1895, ECSP-Columbia; one week is the period cited in Circular, 27 March 1885, Publicity file, MP-Lilly; ten days noted in *My Autobiography* 176.

49 The only traces I have found of the Authors' Alliance are the copyright notices printed with numerous fictions and a number of post-1900 letters (lacking letterheads) in the *Archives of Grant Richards, 1897–1948* (Cambridge: Chadwyck-Healey, 1979); for information on the Literary Department of the United Press, see "Mr. Edward S. Van Zile," *Journalist* 26 April 1890: 2, and "Bye-the-Bye," *Journalist* 19 April 1890: 9, 26 April 1890: 9, and 1 November 1890: 9.

50 For information on Colles, see Robert A. Colby, "'What Fools Authors Be!' The Authors' Syndicate, 1890–1920," *Library Chronicle of the University of Texas* 35 (1986): 61 and 80; the activities and address of Chartres are evident in John Chartres, letter to Dear Sir, 22 October 1896, APA-LC; Colby says that authors had to pay only 5 per cent (63), but Colles wrote in 1890 that authors were charged 25 per cent ([William Morris Colles], "On Syndicating," *The Author* 1 [1890]: 10); James Hepburn, ed., *Letters of Arnold Bennett*, vol. 1 (London: Oxford University Press, 1966) 22; advertisement reprinted in Colby, "'What Fools'" 60; all authors except Crane are listed in Colby "'What Fools'" 82; Crane's agent, Paul Revere Reynolds, sold "The Lone Charge of William Perkins" to the Authors' Syndicate (see Crane, letter to Reynolds, 14 September [1898], letter 397 of vol. 2, *The Correspondence of Stephen Crane* 369); Colby "'What Fools'" 82.

51 *From Stores of Memory* 43; John Phillips, letter to McClure, 10 August 1884, MP-Lilly; McClure, letter to John S. Phillips, 30 June 1933, MP-Lilly.

4 WHAT LITERARY SYNDICATES REPRESENTED TO AUTHORS

1. Hills, "The Stranger in New York," *Writer* (New York) 2 (1888): 5; John P. Young, *Journalism in California* (San Francisco: Chronicle Publishing Co., 1915) 154.
2. For a good description of the light moralizing tone of much of this fiction, see David Roy Cassady, "The Content of the Rural Weekly Press in Illinois in 1882," diss., University of Iowa, 1980, 198–204.
3. Edgar Nye, letter to S. S. McClure, 28 August 1885, Edgar Nye Collection (#7949), CWB-Alderman.
4. *A Handbook of Useful Information Concerning the Plate Service of the American Press Association* (1891) 3; J. B. Naylor, letter to Dear Sirs, 21 July 1899, APA-LC; "A Word About Plate Matter," *Journalist* 9 May 1891: 8; L. E. Buckley, letter, 19 May 1896, APA-LC.
5. Emma M. Wise, letter to Gentlemen, 9 August 1895, APA-LC; "Literary Syndicates," *Editor* 2.2 (1896): 51.
6. The 1887 price is indicated in "Bye-the-Bye," *Journalist* 5 February 1887: 8; the rates paid in the early 1890s are seen in "The Local Paper," *Journalist* 21 June 1890: 8, and in Clara Brown, letter, 11 February 1893, APA-LC; Opie Read, letter to I. D. Marshall, 17 February 1893, Opie Read Colection (#9279), CWB-Alderman.
7. Edwards, *The Fiction Factory* (Ridgewood, NJ: The Editor Co., 1912) 127; quotation and price of $5 per thousand words from Kate Chopin, letter to A. A. Hill, 16 January 1895, APA-LC; the length of these works (5,000 words and 3,400 words) is given in Kate Chopin, letter to A. A. Hill, 1 January 1895, APA-LC; for sale of "A Family Affair" see Toth, *Kate Chopin* 275.
8. An agreement for a series of stories is indicated in Alfred R. Calhoun, letter to I. D. Marshall, 25 March 1892, APA-LC, and another is implied in Opie Read, letters to I. D. Marshall, 21 December 1891 and 17 February 1893, Opie Read Collection (#9279), CWB-Alderman. Charles L. Hildreth, letter, 6 November 1891, APA-LC; "no suggestion" quotation in Mrs. Julia K. Hildreth, letter to Mr. Marshall, 22 February 1892, APA-LC; Will Lisenbee, letter to Mr. Marshall, 12 December 1891, APA-LC; William Perry Brown, letter, 29 January 1892, APA-LC.
9. The storiette limit of 1,200 words is indicated in Alice Ives, letter, 21 May 1895, APA-LC; 1887 lengths are found in "Bye-the-Bye," *Journalist* 5 February 1887: 8; the minimum of 5,000 words is in W. Hibbs, letter to Mr. Hunt, 6 February 1893, APA-LC; the maximum of 6,000 words is in Charles L. Hildreth, letter to Mr. Marshall, 22 June 1891, APA-LC.
10. J. Connelly, letter to Mr. Hill, 1 April 1896, APA-LC; Alice Ives, letter to Mr. Hill, 21 May 1895, APA-LC; Will Lisenbee, letter to Mr. Marshall, 12 December 1891, APA-LC.

11 Annie I. Willis, letter, 1 February 1892, APA-LC; A. S. Cody, letter to Mr. Hill, 20 March 1896, APA-LC; Bart Kennedy, letter to Mr. Hill, [December 1894], APA-LC.
12 Jack London, *Martin Eden* (1908; New York: Macmillan, 1973) 225–226; Ouida, letter, London *Times* 22 May 1891: 3.
13 Interview with S. S. McClure, typescript notes, 1907, MP-Lilly; Bok, "The Modern Literary King" (1895): 340, 341.
14 Feltes, *Modes of Production of Victorian Novels* 64; Circular, Scrapbook, September 1890, MP-Lilly; remarks in McClure, *My Autobiography* 196 and 182, plus McClure, Autobiography notes, MP-Lilly. For McClure's boast, see Circular, 2 December 1891, Copybook, MP-Lilly; Lyon, *Success Story* 97; for charges that McClure commissioned fiction, see Lyon, *Success Story* 96 and Lichtenstein, "Authorial Professionalism" 42; J. C. Levenson, introduction, Crane, *The Third Violet and Active Service* xxxvii.
15 For a disparaging view of the syndicated version of *The Red Badge of Courage*, see Katz, introduction, *The Red Badge of Courage* 31–32; for Bacheller's largesse with Crane see J. C. Levenson, introduction, Crane, *Tales of Adventure*, vol. 5 of *Works of Stephen Crane*, ed. Bowers (Charlottesville: University Press of Virginia, 1970) lxxi.
16 For comments about "Georgina's Reasons," see Michael Anesko, *"Friction with Market"* 225n, Leon Edel, *Henry James: A Life* (New York: Harper and Row, 1985) 305, and Robert L. Gale, ed., *A Henry James Encyclopedia* (New York: Greenwood Press, 1989) 254.
17 Earl L. Bradsher, "Book Publishers and Publishing," *Cambridge History of American Literature*, ed. William Peterfield Trent et al. (1917; New York: Macmillan, 1943) 549.
18 Matthews, *Cheap Books and Good Books* (New York: American Copyright League, 1888): 11; O'Reilly, *What American Authors Think About International Copyright* (New York: American Copyright League, 1888) 8.
19 Sheehan, *This Was Publishing* 57; Coultrap-McQuin, *Doing Literary Business* 39.
20 *Harper's* figures in William J. Bok, "Literary Leaves" (12 March 1887): 3; *Ladies' Home Journal* figures in Hills, *Writer* (New York) 5 (1891): 122; Henry James, letter to William Dean Howells, 9 January 1874 and 10 March 1874, quoted in Anesko 41; *Century* quotation in Lichtenstein 38; "Confessions of a Literary Hack" (1895): 633.
21 Tillotson and Son, letters to Henry Holt and Co., 14 October 1885 and March 1889, Box 127, File #3, Henry Holt Archives, Princeton University Libraries; Maxwell to Tillotson, 28 February 1885, ZBEN 4/3.
22 Hawthorne, "Syndicate Matter," *Journalist* 14 July 1888: 4.
23 "Novels in Daily Newspapers," *Syracuse Daily Standard* 30 June 1884: 2; "Newspaper Novels," *Journalist* 14 September 1889: 10; Scribner, letter to L. W. Bangs, 13 July 1893, quoted in Sheehan, *This Was Publishing* 77; Alfred R. Calhoun, letter to Major Smith, 9 November 1896, APA-LC.

24 1884 report from "Magazine Literature and Illustrations," *Journalist* 9 August 1884: 6; 1880s figure from George McMichael, *Journey to Obscurity: The Life of Octave Thanet* (Lincoln, NE: University of Nebraska Press, 1965) 115; 1890s figure from Borus, *Writing Realism* 43; in 1895 Edward Bok also wrote that magazines paid on average $5 per thousand words, but further noted that some authors could make as much as $14 per thousand (Bok, "The Modern Literary King" [1895]: 338).

25 For Harte's rates see various account ledgers, BL-Turner; Hamlin Garland, "Irving Bacheller, Interpreter of the Old America to the New," *Red Cross Magazine* March 1920: 12; Bacheller, "The Syndicate Matter," *Journalist* 17 April 1886: 3; Circular, [December 1884], MP-Lilly; McClure wrote that he paid $250 for "A Daring Fiction" (*My Autobiography* 168), a story approximately 5,500 words long, which equals $45.45 per thousand words; W[illiam] H. H[ills] in 1888 reported that with the McClure syndicate "a 'bright story of two thousand words by a beginner' should be worth ten dollars [thus approximately $5 per thousand]. It might be worth a good deal more" ("Letters to the Editor," *Writer* (New York) 2 [1888]: 90); Phillips, "Newspaper Syndicates" (1888): 489; McClure, letter to Bellamy, 11 July 1889 (BMS Am 1181), Houghton Library, Harvard University; for prices McClure paid to Harte, see Robert McClure, letters to Tom McClure, 20 May 1898 and 19 October 1899, MP-Lilly; for Crockett prices, see Robert McClure, letter to Tom McClure, 1 November 1899, MP-Lilly; Advertisement in S. S. McClure, letter to E. D. Cope, 26 August 1891, Copybook, MP-Lilly.

26 Adelaide Cilley Waldron, "Business Relations Between Publishers and Writers," *Writer* (New York) 1 (1887): 57; Circular quoted in Turner, "The Syndication of Fiction" 104; "Bye-the-Bye," *Journalist* 4 September 1886: 9; William Dean Howells, "The Man of Letters as a Man of Business," *Scribner's* 14 (1893): 441; "Death of Mr. W. F. Tillotson, J. P.," *Journalist* 9 March 1889: 3.

27 London, *Martin Eden* 172; Ellen Moers, introduction, Lyon, *Success Story: The Life and Times of S. S. McClure* (1963; DeLand, Florida: Everett/Edwards, Inc., 1967) ix; Frank Norris, letter to John Phillips, 9 January 1900, letter 50 of *Frank Norris: Collected Letters* 102; "Scotch ass" quotation from Crane, letter to Paul Revere Reynolds, 14 January [1898], letter 355 of vol. 1, *The Correspondence of Stephen Crane* 327; Crane, letter to S. S. McClure, 27 January 1896, letter 192 of vol. 1, *The Correspondence of Stephen Crane* 192.

28 Figure of $100–$150 from Anesko, *"Friction with Market"* 52; the price of $1,200 for "Georgina's Reasons" is reported in Phillips, "Newspaper Syndicates" 448; Ellen Ballou writes that Dana paid James between $1,100 and $1,200 for "Pandora," and for "Georgina's Reasons" "probably a like amount" (*The Building of the House* 376); Henry James,

letter to T. B. Aldrich, 13 February [1884], in *The Selected Letters of Henry James*, ed. with introduction by Leon Edel (New York: Farrar, Straus and Cudahy, 1955) 79; for James's income figures, see Anesko, *"Friction with Market"* 176-177.

29 For Stevenson's income in the early years, see Hepburn, *The Author's Empty Purse* 88; for Stevenson's income in 1886 and 1887 see George J. McKay, *Some Notes on Robert Louis Stevenson, His Finances, and His Agents and Publishers* (New Haven: Yale University Library, 1958) 21; also see Jenni Calder, *Robert Louis Stevenson: A Life Study* (New York: Oxford University Press, 1980) 233; details of McClure's offer regarding "The Black Arrow" (marketed by McClure under the title, "The Outlaws of Tunstall Forest") are found in Swearingen, *Prose Writings* 84; Stevenson, letter to Baxter, 1 December 1892, *RLS: Stevenson's Letters to Charles Baxter*, ed. DeLancey Ferguson and Marshall Waingrow (New Haven: Yale University Press, 1956) 313.

30 Kenneth Robinson, *Wilkie Collins. A Biography* (London: The Bodley Head, 1951) 311. For details of the competition for *The American Claimant* see *Mark Twain–Howells Letters*, ed. Smith and Gibson 644n, and *Mark Twain's Letters to His Publishers*, ed. Hill 276n, 277n. In his address to the Stevenson Society in 1922, McClure recalled that he offered Kipling $20,000, probably for "The Light That Failed" (MP-Lilly), but in 1936 McClure recounted a somewhat different story that included how he topped Scribner's offer of $16,000 with his own of $25,000 (letter to Catherine Douglass, 7 February 1936, MP-Lilly). Bacheller, Address to the Stevenson Society, B-StL.

31 Bok, "The Modern Literary King" (1895): 341; Mary E. Wilkins, letter to Harper and Brothers, 12 August [18]93, letter 139 of *The Infant Sphinx* 158; the amounts paid to Crane are listed in a Tillotson's ledger in BL-Turner.

32 For "higher payments" quotation see Kendrick 119; for $50 figures, see Mary E. Wilkins, letter to Arthur Stedman, 12 February 1894, letter 145 of *The Infant Sphinx* 161 and Sarah Orne Jewett, letter to Messrs. Bacheller, Johnson, and Bacheller, 10 October 1894, Sarah Orne Jewett Miscellaneous Papers, Rare Books and Manuscripts Division, the New York Public Library, Astor, Lenox and Tilden Foundations. For the figure of $375, see McClure, Autobiography notes 11, MP-Lilly; for the negative reaction of editors to *The White Company* see McClure, *My Autobiography* 205; "Physician's Waiting Room" prices in John Phillips, letter to S. S. McClure, 9 November 1892, MP-Lilly; Stevenson, letter to Baxter, 14 October 1890, *RLS: Stevenson's Letters to Charles Baxter* 273.

33 For information about Braddon and Harte's fees see various Tillotson's ledgers, BL-Turner. Harte actually sold 15 works to Tillotson's, but the amount paid is available for only 14 of these.

34 Howells, "Man of Letters as Man of Business" (1893): 441.

35 S. S. McClure, letter to Charles Egbert Craddock, pseud. (Mary Noailles Murfree), 25 October 1884, the Robert W. Woodruff Library, Emory University; for Bacheller paying upon acceptance see George J. Clarke, letter, *Journalist* 12 May 1888: 9; Conan Doyle quotation in *Coming Up the Road* 271; for Bacheller falling behind in payments see *Coming Up the Road* 292; McClure, *My Autobiography* 169; Jewett, letter to S. S. McClure, 24 August [1885], Sarah Orne Jewett Collection (#6218), CWB-Alderman; Maxwell, letter to Tillotson, 5 January 1883, ZBEN 4/3.

36 Mead, "The Practical Side of Literature," 443; Donald, "Sunday Newspapers in the United States" (Sept.–December 1890): 79; *Saturday Review* article quoted in *Bolton Weekly Journal* 27 February 1885: 2; Alex. Paul, letter, *Providence Sunday Journal* 10 March 1889, typescript copy in ZBEN 14/10; Circular, 10 September 1885, Publicity file, MP-Lilly; Alice French, letter to McClure, 20 February 1893, Alice French Collection (#7194), CWB-Alderman; "Literature in Newspapers," *Newspaper Maker* 29 August 1895: 7.

37 "Mr. M'Clure [sic] and His Magazine," *American Review of Reviews* 8 (1893): 99; Franklin Walker, "Four Additional Frank Norris Letters" (Winter 1974): 4; "Live Topics of Today," *Chicago Tribune* 28 January 1897: 6.

38 Bacheller, *From Stores of Memory* 59; for Bacheller's account of Crane's sudden propulsion to fame and his reception at the Philadelphia *Press*, see Bacheller, letter to Cora Crane, 13 July 1900, Appendix 4, R. W. Stallman and Lillian Gilkes, eds., *Stephen Crane: Letters*, (New York: New York University Press, 1960) 298–299; Crane's surprise is indicated in Crane, letter to an unknown recipient, [December 15, 1894], *Stephen Crane: Letters* 43.

39 "The Fiction Bureau," *Writer* (London) 1.6 (1889): 137; Alex. Paul, letter, *Providence Sunday Journal* 10 March 1889, typescript copy in ZBEN 14/10; for an account of Crane using his clippings in this way see Katz, introduction, *The Red Badge of Courage* 38.

40 Robert Louis Stevenson, letter to Charles Baxter, 1 December 1892, *RLS: Stevenson's Letters to Charles Baxter* 313: the Burnett drama is recounted in Ann Thwaite, *Waiting for the Party: The Life of Frances Hodgson Burnett 1849–1924* (London: Secker and Warburg, 1974) 144 (in the end, McClure succeeded in obtaining "Giovanni and the Other" for syndication); James, letter to T. B. Aldrich, 13 February [1884], *Selected Letters of Henry James* 79 (James did not receive the amount he asked for: see Ellery Sedgwick, "Henry James and the *Atlantic Monthly*: Editorial Perspectives on James' 'Friction With the Market,'" *Studies in Bibliography* 45 [1992]: 318).

41 Bok, "Literary Leaves," *Indianapolis News* 9 October 1886: 3; S. C. Williams, letter to S. S. McClure, 23 November 1885, MP-Lilly; "The Fiction Bureau" (1889): 137; "Recent Publications," review of *Plantation*

Pageants by Joel Chandler Harris, New Orleans *Daily Picayune* 15 October 1899: sec. 2: 7; Twain, letter to Fred J. Hall, 20 October 1891, *Mark Twain's Letters to His Publishers*, ed. Hill 286.
42 Colby, "'What Fools!'" 66.

5 WHAT PRICE MUST AUTHORS PAY?

1 Kipling, letter to McClure, [30 January 1890], *The Letters of Rudyard Kipling* 2: 6; "Literary Syndicates" (1895): 50.
2 Nye, letter to McClure, 28 August 1885, Edgar Nye Collection (#7949), CWB-Alderman; Kipling, *Something of Myself. For My Friends Known and Unknown* (Garden City, NY: Doubleday, Doran and Co., 1937) 134–135; for examples of such contracts see Bodleian Eng.MS.Misc.f.395/1; for an example of resistance to such contracts see William Black, letter to Tillotson's, 6 January 1897, ZBEN 4/1; Tillotson's Ledger, ZBEN 4/4.
3 Circular, 10 October 1891, Copybook, MP-Lilly.
4 Richard Little Purdy, *Thomas Hardy: A Bibliographical Study* (Oxford: Clarendon Press, 1954) 72; for details of the rejection and new work, see ibid. 94; Thomas Hardy, précis, ZBEN 4/1; 1911 Programme, BL-Turner.
5 Bacheller, "The Syndicate Matter" 3; McClure, Circular letter, 10 February 1886, MP-Lilly; S. S. McClure, letter to Hattie McClure, 30 July 1890, MP-Lilly; "Instructions …," 1886, Scrapbook, MP-Lilly; Circular, 17 June 1888, Scrapbook, MP-Lilly.
6 McCarthy, letter to Tillotson, 17 July 1884, ZBEN 4/1; "Instructions…" (1886), MP-Lilly; Circular, October 1886, Scrapbook, MP-Lilly; description of *The Cosmic Bean* in Circular, [March 1891], Scrapbook, MP-Lilly; Circular, [May 1891], Scrapbook, MP-Lilly.
7 Jewett, letter to Mr. [Arthur] Stedman, 25 February 1895, quoted in David Bonnell Green, "Sarah Orne Jewett's 'A Dark Night,'" *Papers of the Bibliographical Society of America* 53 (1959): 331; for suggestion of a "New England juvenile" story to Wilkins, see Wilkins, letter to Arthur Stedman, 12 February 1894, letter 145 of *The Infant Sphinx* 161.
8 Thomas Hardy, letter to Mr. [Clement King] Shorter, 29 January 1892, Bolton Evening News, Bolton, England; John Nayler, typed reminiscence, ZBEN 14/10.
9 Wilkins, letter to Arthur Stedman, 22 December 1895, letter 190 of *The Infant Sphinx* 184; Richard Cary, introduction, *The Uncollected Stories of Sarah Orne Jewett*, ed. Richard Cary (Waterville, ME: Colby College Press, 1971) xvi; Green, "Jewett's 'A Dark Night'" 333.
10 Frank Stockton, letter to McClure, 25 October 1890, Frank Stockton Collection (#5866), CWB-Alderman; Stockton, letter to McClure, 5 October 1891, MP-Lilly.
11 McClure's requests are implied in Stockton, letter to McClure, 25 November 1884, Frank Stockton Collection (#5866) CWB-Alderman;

Twain, letter to Fred J. Hall, 16 October 1891, *Mark Twain's Letters to His Publishers* 285; McClure, letter to Joel Chandler Harris, 9 September 1885, MP-Lilly.

12 Clarke, letter, *Journalist* 12 May 1888: 9; Crane, letter to McClure, 27 January [1896], letter 192 of vol. 1, *The Correspondence of Stephen Crane* 192; Phelps, *Chapters from a Life* 246.

13 London, "The Unmasking of the Cad," *Utica Daily Observer* 13 September 1899: 3; London, "The Grilling of Loren Ellery," *Utica Daily Observer* 2 October 1899: 3; the bishop's libel suit is mentioned in A. T. Quiller-Couch, letter to Dear Sirs, 23 November 1893, ZBEN 4/1.

14 Advertisements, *Bolton Weekly Journal* 12 February 1881: 2, 14 June 1885: 5, and 27 May 1882: 2.

15 Nym Crinkle, "The Scab's Fate," *Syracuse Evening Herald* 14 November 1886: 3; Jeannette H. Walworth, "Old Sandy," *Syracuse Evening Herald* 21 November 1886: 3; Ruth McEnery Stuart, "A Christmas Gift That Went A-Begging," *Syracuse Daily Journal* 18 December 1897: 3.

16 *My Autobiography* 231; Moore description in Circular, 13 June 1892, Copybook, MP-Lilly; McClure, letter to Howells, 9 October 1891, quoted in *W. D. Howells. Selected Letters, 1882–1891* 317n; Boyesen, "A Case of Heart-Break," *Detroit Free Press* 15 February 1885: 17.

17 Bates, "Literary Affairs in Boston," *The Book Buyer* 6 (1889): 95.

18 Katz, "Bibliography and the Rise of American Literary Realism" 78; Howells, "Man of Letters as a Man of Business" (1893): 441.

19 For numerous examples of Tillotson's contracts see Bodleian.MS.Eng.-Misc.f.395/1; the requisite length for prize stories is stated in "Miss Wilkins a Prize-Winner" (1895): 483; Sarah Orne Jewett, letter to Arthur Stedman, 25 February 1895, quoted in Green, "Jewett's 'A Dark Night'" 331; Bacheller, letter to [Edmund Clarence] Stedman, 16 August 1895, ECSP-Columbia; late 1894 guidelines in Bacheller circular, reprinted in Katz, introduction, *The Red Badge of Courage* 22–23; Bacheller, letter to [Melville] Phillips, 21 January 1897, Beinecke Rare Book and Manuscript Library. McClure's 1885 limit is noted in Isabel Hapgood, letter to McClure, 23 August 1886, MP-Lilly; for 1886 length limits, see "Instructions ...," 1886, Scrapbook, MP-Lilly; for 1887 limits, see Circular, January 1887, Publicity file, MP-Lilly; 1896 limit in Adele E. Thompson, "What the Editor Wants in Fiction," *Editor* 2 (1896): 126.

20 "List of Novels and Short Stories," ZBEN 4/5; Turner, "Tillotson's Fiction Bureau" 371–378; "Bye-the-Bye," *Journalist* 3 September 1892: 9.

21 Bacheller length figures include illustrations, but these were minimal.

22 Circular, 17 November 1884, Scrapbook, MP-Lilly; Circular, 27 March 1885, Publicity file, MP-Lilly; for lack of uniformity see Scrapbook, 30 April 1899 through 28 May 1899, MP-Lilly; one novel was announced at 6,000 words per installment for sixteen weeks (Scrapbook, 3 June

1888, MP-Lilly). In 1891 the advertised serials were scheduled to run anywhere from nine to twenty installments long, and at least three serials were scheduled to be over 100,000 words long (Circular, 1891, Scrapbook, MP-Lilly).

23 McClure, letter to O. O. Howard, 20 August 1891, Oliver Otis Howard Papers; Jewett to McClure, 26 August [1886], Special Collections, Colby College; McClure, letter to Jack London, 25 March 1902, photocopy in Jack London Collection, Utah State University Library; Bacheller, letter to [Melville] Phillips, 21 January 1897, Beinecke Library.

24 Jewett, letter to Arthur Stedman, 25 February 1895, quoted in Green, "Jewett's 'A Dark Night'" 331; Wilkins, letters to Arthur Stedman, 12 February 1894 and 5 March 1894, letters 145 and 147 of *The Infant Sphinx* 161–162; for rejection of one story see Irving Bacheller, letter to [Edmund Clarence] Stedman, 16 August 1895, ECSP-Columbia.

25 McClure, letter to Harris, 9 September 1885, MP-Lilly; McClure, letter to Stevenson, 12 September 1890, MP-Lilly; McClure, letter to Howells, 28 August 1890, Houghton Library.

26 H. H. Boyesen, letter to McClure, 17 January 1885, MP-Lilly; Jewett, letter to McClure, 26 August [1886], Colby College Library; Stockton, letter to McClure, undated, Frank Stockton Collection (#5866), CWB-Alderman; Phelps, letter to McClure, 20 March 1889, MP-Lilly.

27 Sala, letter, 10 January 1889, ZBEN 4/9; Caine, letter, 12 January 1891, ZBEN 4/1.

28 Bacheller, letter to Edmund Clarence Stedman, 23 June 1894, ECSP-Columbia.

29 Jewett, letter to McClure, 22 September [1885], Sarah Orne Jewett Collection (#6218), CWB-Alderman; Phelps, letter to McClure, 5 March 1885, MP-Lilly; Wilkins, letter to Eliza Farman Pratt, 16 August 1891, letter 82 of *The Infant Sphinx* 130.

30 Wilkins, letter to Arthur Stedman, 12 February 1894, letter 145 of *The Infant Sphinx* 161; Jewett, letter to Bacheller, Johnson and Bacheller, 10 October 1894, Jewett Miscellaneous Papers, Rare Books and Manuscripts Division, New York Public Library; Bacheller circular, Katz, introduction, *The Red Badge of Courage* 22–23.

31 Corelli, letter to Tillotson and Son, 6 March 1892, ZBEN 4/9; Caine, letter to W. F. Tillotson, 13 June 1888, Bodleian.MS.Eng.Misc.f.395/1; Jacobs, letter to James Lever Tillotson, n. d., ZBEN 4/1.

32 McClure quotation from Copybook, 29 November 1893, MP-Lilly (for frustration with Kipling, see Circular, 24 March 1893, Copybook, MP-Lilly); Harte excuse, *Bolton Weekly Journal* 24 December 1880: supplement page 1.

33 Clarke, letter, *Journalist* 12 May 1888: 9; for one example of a typesetting error see "Bye-the-Bye," 2 October 1886: 9.

34 McClure, Autobiography notes, MP-Lilly; for evidence that McClure sent proofs to Stevenson in Samoa, see Swearingen, *Prose Writings* 143;

Edward Peck, editor of *Transcript*, letter to McClure, 25 December [1885], MP-Lilly.

35 McCarthy, letter to Tillotson and Son, 23 March 1889, Bolton Evening News, Bolton, England; Collins contract, Bodleian.MS.Eng.-Misc.f.395/1; Hall Caine, letters to Tillotson and Son, 18 November and 3 December 1894, ZBEN 4/9.

36 Collins contract, Bodleian.MS.Eng.Misc.f.395/1; for the biographer's charge see Ruth Odell, *Helen Hunt Jackson (H. H.)* (New York: D. Appleton-Century Co., 1939) 215–216; years later, Bacheller weakly refuted the biographer's charges, writing, "I do not think that this is true. Helen Hunt Jackson never wrote a story for me. If she had I would not have broken faith with her" (see margin notes of Cyril Clemens, letter to Irving Bacheller, [August 1939], B-StL); for an account of the dispute between Wilkins and Bacheller, see Kendrick, ed., *The Infant Sphinx* 120–121.

37 Bacheller, letter to O. O. Howard, 13 January 1892, Oliver Otis Howard Papers.

38 Ainsworth Rand Spofford, *A Book for All Readers*, 2nd edn. (New York and London: G. P. Putnam, 1900) 166; Edgar Nye, letter to McClure, 28 August 1885, Edgar Nye Collection (#7949), CWB-Alderman.

39 See "Defiant Piracy," advertisement, *Journalist* 19 April 1890: 14; the Toronto *Globe* request is seen in A. Pardoe, letter to W. F. Tillotson, 9 June 1885, ZBEN 4/3; for Tillotson's prosecution of the Montreal paper and possible action in Australia see "Notes," *Critic* 5 (1886): 37–38; Bacheller's offer of assistance in protecting Wilkins's copyright is indicated in Kendrick, ed., *The Infant Sphinx* 474n and Wilkins, letter to Arthur Stedman, 22 December 1895, letter 190 of *The Infant Sphinx* 183–184; Robert McClure, letter to Tom McClure, 23 February 1900, MP-Lilly.

40 McClure, *My Autobiography* 167; this is corroborated by Harriet McClure, who notes in a letter of 9 October 1884, "the authors write him splendid letters" (MP-Lilly); Bacheller, *From Stores of Memory* 44; Bok, "The Modern Literary King" (1895): 341.

6 PLEASING THE CUSTOMERS

1 Kellogg quoted in Lee, *The Daily Newspaper in America* 581; McClure, *My Autobiography* 167–168; Bacheller, *From Stores of Memory* 95.

2 Rowell, *Forty Years an Advertising Agent, 1865–1905* (New York: Printers' Ink, 1905) 221; Eugene C. Harter, *Boilerplating America: The Hidden Newspaper*, ed. Dorothy Harter (Lanham, MD: University Press of America, 1991) 28.

3 Edgar Watson Howe, "Country Newspapers" (1891): 781; "Ansel Nash Kellogg," *Biographical Sketches of the Leading Men of Chicago* (1876) 85; Wappiert, "Newspaper Factories" (1890): 7.

4   For indications that Kellogg solicited suggestions, see letters from editors in *KAHB* 62–67; for the varied number of columns, see *KAHB* 20; for 1878 quotation see *KAHB* 8; for the report of 300–400 different styles see "Death of A. N. Kellogg" (1886): 8; for report of 100 different versions, see Howe, "Country Newspapers" (1891): 781. The 300–400 different versions did not have entirely different materials but rather were created by rearranging approximately fifteen different sets of materials into various combinations.

5   *American Newspaper Directory* (1870) 207; for choices see *Centennial File of Kellogg's Auxiliary Newspapers*, 1876, Chicago Historical Society, Chicago, Illinois.

6   James quoted in *KAHB* 67. Harter, *Boilerplating America* 134.

7   Wappiert, "Newspaper Factories" (1890): 8; *KAHB* 37.

8   "The Story of a Great Success," *Journalist* 17 December 1892: 3.

9   "The Story of a Great Success" (1892): 2; *A Hand Book of Useful Information* (1891) 26; "The Story of a Great Success" (1892) 3; Patterson quoted in Neil M. Clark, "Patterson Helps to Edit Twelve Thousand Newspapers," *American Magazine* 104 (October 1927): 160.

10 Cassady, "The Content of the Rural Weekly Press in 1882" (1980): 204.

11 H. C. Michener, letter to Dear Sirs, 1 March 1892, APA-LC; *Hammondsport Herald* 19 December 1894: 8.

12 "The American Press Association," *Journalist* 27 March 1886: 10; *A Hand Book of Useful Information* (1891) 9.

13 "A Syndicate Syndicate," *Journalist* 21 November 1891: 8; "The Story of a Great Success" (1892): 2.

14 William Westall, "Newspaper Fiction," *Lippincott's Monthly Magazine* 40 (1890): 78; Programme, 1912, Tillotson's Programme Ledger, BL-Turner.

15 Fales, letter, *Journalist* 15 September 1888: 9; Victor Lawson, letter to Bacheller, 19 April 1889, VLP-Newberry; Bacheller, *Coming Up the Road* 265.

16 For McClure's request for copies of newspapers see Circular, Copybook, 23 October 1891, MP-Lilly; for McClure soliciting suggestions, see Circular, 27 March 1885, Publicity file, MP-Lilly; A. H. Chadbourne, letter to Dear Sir, 9 December 1885, MP-Lilly; Publicity circular, December 1885, Scrapbook, MP-Lilly; Circular, 10 October 1891, Copybook, MP-Lilly; McClure, letter to Murfree, 9 December 1884, Robert W. Woodruff Library, Emory University; French, letter to McClure, 20 February 1893, Alice French Collection (#7194), CWB-Alderman.

17 J. Lincoln Steffens, "The Business of a Newspaper," *Scribner's Magazine* 22 (1897): 450.

18 George Smith, letter to S. S. McClure, 9 January 1885, MP-Lilly; "A Woman's Page," undated, Publicity, MP-Lilly.

19 "The Serial Story Feature," *Newspaper Maker* 23 July 1896: 4; "The

Syndicate Evil," *The Editor* 2 (April 1896): 147; Spofford, *A Book for All Readers* (1900) 166; Phillips, "Newspaper Syndicates" (1888): 489.

20 *Auburn Daily Advertiser* 7 March 1885: 2; *Detroit Free Press* 1 November 1885: 5.
21 Ellis Roberts, letter to McClure, 13 December 1885, MP-Lilly; Jerome A. Hart, letter to McClure, 9 January 1885, MP-Lilly; Tillotson quoted in Westall, "Newspaper Fiction" (1890): 78.
22 Russell Jacobs, letter to McClure, 30 November 1885, MP-Lilly; H. A. Byram, letter to McClure, 7 November 1885, MP-Lilly.
23 Circular, 10 April 1887, Scrapbook, MP-Lilly.
24 S. S. McClure, Stevenson Society Address, 1922, MP-Lilly.
25 "The Story of McClure's" (N.p.: n.p., n.d.), MP-Lilly; Bok, "The Modern Literary King" (1895): 341.
26 Lawson, letter to McClure, 10 June 1890, VLP-Newberry; the middle-class status of most metropolitan newspaper editors during this period is documented in Jack R. Hart, "Horatio Alger in the Newsroom: Social Origins of American Editors," *Journalism Quarterly* 53 (1976): 14–20; Steffens, "The Business of a Newspaper" (1897): 465.
27 Platt and Platt, letter to McClure, 18 April 1885, MP-Lilly; Williams, letter to McClure, [3 December 1885], MP-Lilly; Lawson, letter to Tillotson's, 8 May 1891, VLP-Newberry; Lawson, letter to Tillotson's, 26 March 1888, VLP-Newberry; Lawson, letter to Tillotson's, 5 January 1889, VLP-Newberry.
28 Steffens, "The Business of a Newspaper" (1897): 465.
29 Bacheller, letter to [Melville] Phillips, 21 January 1897, Beinecke Library; Zola advertisement in Circular, 8 July 1888, Scrapbook, MP-Lilly; Circular, 1896, Scrapbook, MP-Lilly.
30 Lawson, letter to McClure, 9 March 1891, VLP-Newberry; H. A. Byram, letter to McClure, 7 November 1885, MP-Lilly.
31 Lawson, letter to McClure, 24 April 1890, VLP-Newberry; Edward Phelps, letter to McClure, 2 November 1885, MP-Lilly; W. B. Merrill, letter to McClure, 24 December 1884, MP-Lilly.
32 Circular, August 1890, Scrapbook, MP-Lilly; Circular, 15 April 1902, MP-Lilly.
33 Marion Cann, letter to McClure, 9 February 1885, MP-Lilly; Lawson, letters to McClure, 30 May 1890 and 14 January 1895, VLP-Newberry; Jerome Hart, letter to McClure, 9 January 1885, MP-Lilly; McClure, letter to Murfree, 9 December 1884, Robert W. Woodruff Library, Emory University; "crowding" quotation in McClure Autobiography notes, MP-Lilly; Lawson, letter to Bacheller, 4 September 1889, VLP-Newberry; Lawson, letter to McClure, 30 May 1890, VLP-Newberry.
34 *Journalist* 17 December 1892: 72; for Lawson's rejection of these stories see letters to McClure, 11 June 1890 and 27 June 1890, VLP-Newberry; for rejection by the Buffalo *News* see John S. Phillips, letter to McClure, 22 October 1890, MP-Lilly.

35 Bok's status as an innovator in ad-stripping is noted in Steinberg, *Reformer in the Marketplace* 62.
36 McClure, *My Autobiography* 204–205; Lyon, *Success Story* 99; Circular, 5 January 1891, Scrapbook, MP-Lilly; McClure, *My Autobiography* 205.
37 Bacheller contract blank reproduced in Katz, introduction, *The Red Badge of Courage* 22–23; *Coming Up the Road* 278.
38 Lawson, letter to Tillotson's, 10 March 1886, VLP-Newberry; Lawson, letter to Tillotson's, 26 March 1888, VLP-Newberry; Lawson expresses his desire for three or four installments per week in letter to McClure, 31 October 1888, VLP-Newberry; [Edward Wyllis Scripps], letter, *Journalist* 2 June 1888: 2.
39 Circular, December 1885, Scrapbook, MP-Lilly; Circular, January 1887, Publicity, MP-Lilly.
40 Tillotson's Circular, 30 December 1882, ZBEN 4/3; for information on *The Quality of Mercy* see Elliott, ed., Howells, *The Quality of Mercy* 367n–368n; for information on *The Red Badge of Courage* see Crane, *The Red Badge of Courage*, vol. 2 of *Works of Stephen Crane*, ed. Bowers with introduction by J. C. Levenson (Charlottesville: University Press of Virginia, 1975) 249–252; also see Stephen Crane, "The Red Badge of Courage," *Syracuse Daily Journal* 4–10 December 1894, and *Rochester Herald* 3–8 December 1894.
41 For an example of such a response see Lawson, letter to McClure, 5 December [1888], VLP-Newberry.
42 Edward Phelps, letter to McClure, 2 November 1885, MP-Lilly; Katz, introduction, *The Red Badge of Courage* 39; Cather, "When I Knew Stephen Crane" (1900), in *Willa Cather. Stories, Poems, and Other Writings* (New York: Library of America, 1992) 933; compare, for example, London's story as it appears in the New Orleans *Daily Picayune* (24 March 1901: section 3, page 1) and in the *Boston Globe* (24 March 1901, magazine, page 2).
43 *Chicago Tribune* 3 August 1884: 12; *Boston Globe* 4 October 1891: 25; *Utica Weekly Herald* 9 June 1885: 9.
44 For an example of such a revised and enlarged illustration, note how the main illustration provided by Bacheller to accompany the text of Mary E. Wilkins's "How Charlotte Ellen Went Visiting" (*Utica Daily Observer* 1 November 1897: 3) was redrawn and elaborated for its appearance in the *Chicago Tribune* (7 November 1897: 48).
45 J. M. Caughlin, letter to McClure, 7 January 1885: MP-Lilly; Marion Stuart Cann, letter to McClure, 24 December 1884, MP-Lilly; Circular, 27 March 1885, Publicity file, MP-Lilly; Circular, 10 September 1885, Publicity file, MP-Lilly; contract notice in Circular, 10 October 1891, Copybook, MP-Lilly.
46 McClure, letter to O. O. Howard, 22 December 1887, Oliver Otis Howard Papers.
47 "Literary Syndicates" (1896): 50; McClure quoted in Richard H.

Waldo, "The Genius of S. S. McClure," *Editor and Publisher* 21 July 1934: 88.
48 Kobre, *The Yellow Press* 366.
49 DiMaggio, "Market Structure, the Creative Process, and Popular Culture: Toward an Organizational Reinterpretation of Mass Culture Theory," *Journal of Popular Culture* 11 (1987): 443; [William Morris Colles], "On Syndicating" (1890): 10; McClure, *My Autobiography* 235; Circular, 9 November 1893, Copybook, MP-Lilly.

7 READERS' EXPERIENCES WITH SYNDICATED FICTION

1 Waldron, "Business Relations Between Publishers and Writers" (1887): 57; Williams quoted in Lyon, *Success Story* 74; Nayler, letter to James Lever Tillotson, 31 March 1917, ZBEN 7/2.
2 Williams, letter to S. S. McClure, 23 November 1885, MP-Lilly; "Continued Stories," *Journalist* 10 August 1884: 1.
3 The request of the editor of the *Inter-Ocean* is noted in McClure, letter to Howells, 9 October 1891, quoted in *W. D. Howells, Selected Letters 1882–1891* 317n; for Taylor paraphrase see Circular, 1 December 1891, Scrapbook, MP-Lilly; "Who Killed Agatha Webb?" advertisement, *Detroit Free Press* 14 May 1899: section 5, page 2.
4 Aurora editor quoted in *KAHB* 62; Henry editor quoted in *KAHB* 62 (these comments, reprinted in a Kellogg publication, were obviously chosen for their positive tone); *A Hand Book of Useful Information* (1891) 20.
5 The promise was made by McClure's partner John S. Phillips in "Newspaper Syndicates" (1888): 489; "The Serial Story Feature" (1896): 4; "New American Stories," *San Francisco Chronicle* 13 July 1884: 4; Lawson, letter to Tillotson's, 10 March 1886, VLP-Newberry; Lawson, letter to Colonel Taylor, 24 August 1888, VLP-Newberry; Lawson, letter to Tillotson's, 14 June 1890, VLP-Newberry; Editorial, *Auburn Daily Advertiser* 24 January 1885: 2; "A Month of Daily Stories," *Auburn Daily Advertiser* 25 April 1885: 2; [Edward Wyllis Scripps], letter, *Journalist* 2 June 1888: 12.
6 Elmer Davis, *History of the "New York Times," 1851–1921* (New York: New York Times Company, 1921) 209; "Women and Newspapers," *New York Times* 6 September 1896: Magazine 14; Frederick M. Crunden, "Supplying of Current Daily Newspapers in Free Library Reading-Rooms," *Library Journal* 19.12 (December 1894): 144; Howells, "The Man of Letters as a Man of Business" (1893): 441; Howells, "What Should Girls Read?" *Harper's Bazaar* 36 (1902): 960; Geraldine Bonner, "A California Novel" (1898), *Critical Essays on Frank Norris*, ed. Don Graham (Boston: G. K. Hall, 1980) 3.
7 *Kellogg's Advertising Lists* (N.p.: n.p., 1878) 5; W. D. Hughes, quoted in

KAHB 62; John M. Stahl, *Growing With the West: The Story of a Busy, Quiet Life* (London: Longmans, Green, and Co., 1930) 101; Hamlin Garland, "Up the Coolly," *Main-Travelled Roads* (1899; New York: Harper and Brothers, n. d.) 81; Laura Ingalls Wilder, *The Long Winter* (1940; New York: Harper and Row, 1953) 169; *KAHB* 72; Wayne E. Fuller, *RFD: The Changing Face of Rural America* (Bloomington: Indiana University Press, 1964) 291, 292; the estimate of five readers per newspaper is given both in *Biographical Sketches of the Leading Men of Chicago* (1876) 84, and Howe, "Country Newspapers" (1891): 781; quotations from Harter, *Boilerplating America* 128.

8 "Newspaper Reading," *Boston Herald* 15 November 1885: 12; James Parton, "Newspapers Gone to Seed," *Forum* 1 (1886): 18.

9 "Newspaper Reading" (1885): 12; G. T. C., "Reaching the Rich," *Printers' Ink* 26 June 1895: 3; W. D. Howells, *The Rise of Silas Lapham* (1885; Bloomington and London: Indiana University Press, 1971) 78–79; "The Small Change of Literature," *Critic* 12 (1889): 155, 156.

10 Samuel Gompers, *Seventy Years of Life and Labor: An Autobiography* (New York: E. P. Dutton, 1925) 81; Johnson, *The Autobiography of an Ex-Coloured Man* (1912; Garden City, New York: Garden City Publishing, n. d.) 73; Elizabeth B. Grannis, "How a Business Woman Reads the Newspapers," *Printers' Ink* 27 February 1895: 12; "The Decline of Reading Aloud," *Independent* 15 April 1909: 825.

11 Howells, *The Rise of Silas Lapham* 89, 88; "Sunday Papers Eulogized," *Newspaper Maker* 2 April 1896: 11; "Parts of the Paper Women Read," *Printers' Ink* 3 January 1894: 24. Janice Radway found in her study of romance novel readers, conducted in the early 1980s, that women often justified their reading to doubting husbands and others by saying that it provided them with valuable or useful "information" (*Reading the Romance: Women, Patriarchy, and Popular Literature* [Chapel Hill and London: University of North Carolina Press, 1984] 106–107).

12 "The Newspaper Side of Literature," *Century* 36 (1887–1888): 151; for a description of and reaction to the "vagrant and mal-odorous class" that frequented reading rooms, see Crunden, "Supplying of Current Daily Newspapers" (1894): 46.

13 "The Point of View," *Scribner's* 14 (1893): 660; this series of articles includes Grannis, "How a Business Woman Reads the Newspapers" (1895): 12–13; Richard Hyde, "How a Variety Theatrical Manager Reads the Newspaper," *Printers' Ink* 10 April 1895: 33–35; Thomas W. Keene, "How a Tragedian Reads the Newspapers," *Printers' Ink* 5 June 1895: 3–4; and Dr. Cyrus Edson, "How a Physician Reads the Newspaper," *Printers' Ink* 12 June 1895: 3–4; "Newspaper Reading" (1885): 12.

14 Fredson Bowers is the scholar who has most assiduously examined the variations of syndicated texts, specifically those of Stephen Crane (see

the ten-volume edition of Stephen Crane's works that he edited for the University Press of Virginia, 1969–1976).

15 Louis James, "The Trouble With Betsy: Periodicals and the Common Reader in Mid-Nineteenth-Century England," *The Victorian Periodical Press: Samplings and Soundings*, ed. Joanne Shattock and Michael Wolff (Leicester, England: Leicester University Press, 1982) 350–351.

16 Donald, "Sunday Newspapers in the United States" (1890): 82.

17 Gunter Barth, *The Rise of Modern City Culture in Nineteenth-Century America* (New York: Oxford University Press, 1980) 80; Advertisement, *Boston Globe* 7 February 1891: 7; Advertisement, *Boston Globe* 1 January 1891: 6; Advertisement, *Boston Globe* 7 February 1891: 7; Anzia Yezierska, *Bread Givers* (1925; New York: Persea Books, 1975) 155.

18 "A Salvation Boom in Matabeleland," *Syracuse Herald* 10 December 1899: 30; Mrs. J. K. Hudson, "Manuel: A Cuban Insurgent," *Utica Observer* 21 March 1898: 7. In 1974 Joseph Katz proposed that the syndicates helped create "a climate . . . that was almost perfectly suited to" the work of American literary realists, yet provided no specific information as to which components of this climate were most important ("Bibliography and the Rise of American Literary Realism" 86). I believe that the emphasis editors, syndicators, and readers placed on "timeliness" and relevance to contemporary events is the most important element of this environment.

19 *Chicago Tribune* 3 August 1884: 12.

20 Donald, "Sunday Newspapers in the United States" (1890): 81; "A Pinch of Salt," *Syracuse Daily Journal* 30 October 1897: 3; "Serena Ann. Her First Christmas Keeping," *Utica Daily Observer* 15 December 1894: 7.

21 David Wechsler, "When Doctors Disagree," *Utica Daily Observer* 30 November 1894: 7.

22 Crane, "A Mystery of Heroism," *Utica Daily Observer* 1 August 1895: 7, and 2 August 1895: 7; "One Dash–Horses," *Syracuse Daily Journal* 4 January 1896: 3.

23 "Georgina's Reasons," *Chicago Tribune* 20 July 1884: 3, 27 July 1884: 12, and 3 August 1884: 12; Norris, "A Salvation Boom in Matabeleland," *Syracuse Herald* 10 December 1899: 30.

24 Lawson, letter to Tillotson's, 26 March 1888, VLP-Newberry; McClure, Autobiography notes, MP-Lilly.

25 "Many Minds," *Boston Globe* 9 February 1891: 5; Radway, "Reading Is Not Eating: Mass-Produced Literature and the Theoretical, Methodological, and Political Consequences of a Metaphor," *Book Research Quarterly* 2 (1986): 9; Grimsted, *Needs and Opportunities in the History of the Book: America, 1639–1876*, ed. David D. Hall and John B. Hench (Worcester, MA: American Antiquarian Society, 1987) 208.

26 On average, 40 to 50 newspapers purchased each short story from McClure, although only 13 to 20 took each novel (see *My Autobiography*

Notes to pages 204–208

    176 and S. S. McClure, letter, *Critic* 8 [1887]: 42). Bacheller recalled that in 1885 some 20 newspapers took fiction from him (*Coming Up the Road* 264), but in 1886 the reported number varied from 80 ("Bye-the-Bye," *Journalist* 2 October 1886: 9) to 140 ("O. W. R.," "The Newspaper Syndicate King" [1886]: 3).

27 "A Word About Plate Matter," *Journalist* 9 May 1891: 8; *Biographical Sketches of the Leading Men of Chicago* 85; Alex. Paul, letter, *Providence Sunday Journal* 10 March 1899: n. p., ZBEN 14/10; Mead, "Practical Side of Literature" (1901): 444.

28 Charvat, "Literature as a Business," *Literary History of the United States*, ed. Robert E. Spiller et al., 4th edn. (New York: Macmillan, 1974) 965; Charles A. Choate, letter, *Journalist* 15 June 1889: 11; Howells, *A Hazard of New Fortunes* 101–102.

29 Bacheller, "The Syndicate Matter" (1886): 3; McClure, letter to Professor E. D. Cope, 26 August 1891, Copybook, MP-Lilly; McClure, circular letter, 29 August 1891, Copybook, MP-Lilly; *My Autobiography* 43–44.

8 THE DECLINE OF THE LITERARY SYNDICATES

1 Garland, in Allen, et al., "Will the Novel Disappear?" (1902): 295; quoted in "Books, Magazines and Newspapers," *Journalist* 25 June 1887: 6.

2 Jason Rogers, "Circulation Ideas," *Newspaper Maker* 15 October 1896: 5; "The Newspaper Syndicate," 15 December 1900, clipping pasted in a Scrapbook of William Holland Samson, Rochester (New York) Public Library; Howells, "The Man of Letters as a Man of Business" (1893): 440–441; Howells, *Literature and Life* (1902; Port Washington, New York: Kennikat Press, 1968) 1–35; for the figure of 100 syndicates, see Willard Grosvenor Bleyer, *Main Currents in the History of American Journalism* (Boston: Houghton Mifflin, 1927) 400; Elmo Scott Watson lists 145 individual syndicates in *History of Newspaper Syndicates* 90–93; James L. W. West III, "The Second Serials of *This Side of Paradise* and *The Beautiful and the Damned*," *Publications of the Bibliographical Society of America* 73 (1979) 63–74.

3 Authors mentioned in "No More Patent Insides," 10 February 1952, clipping in Western Newspaper Union Collection, Historical Society of Douglas County, Omaha, Nebraska; for an account of the expansion of the Western Newspaper Union, see Watson, *History of Newspaper Syndicates* 50–54; the number of readyprint customers in 1952 is found in "Readyprint Victim of Times; Helped in Joslyn Fortune," 8 February 1952, clipping in Western Newspaper Union Collection; "No More Patent Insides," 10 February 1952.

4 Patterson quoted in Neil M. Clark, "Patterson Helps To Edit Twelve Thousand Newspapers" (1927): 162; these reader surveys are reported

in Millard Van Marter Atwood, *The Country Newspaper* (Chicago: A. C. McClurg and Co., 1923) 29–30; A. J. Munson, *Making a Country Newspaper* (Chicago: Dominion, 1899) 29.

5   For employee's comment see typescript notes for *Bolton Evening News* 50th Anniversary Celebration (1917), ZBEN 7/2; Tillotson and Son, letter to Henry Holt and Co., March 1889, Box 127, File #3, Henry Holt Archives, Princeton University Libraries; it is unknown when Tillotson's ceased syndicating fiction in the United States; McClure, letter to Hattie McClure, 13 November 1893, MP-Lilly; McClure, *My Autobiography* 255 and 254; Bacheller, *From Stores of Memory* 95; Bacheller, letter to [Edmund Clarence Stedman], undated, ECSP-Columbia (the 1891–1894 date is indicated by the Bacheller and Johnson Syndicate letterhead); Bacheller, *Coming Up the Road* 283.

6   McClure, letter to Professor Anderson, 15 January 1891, MP-Lilly; *My Autobiography* 172; McClure quoted in Richard H. Waldo, "The Genius of S. S. McClure," *Editor and Publisher* 21 July 1934: 88; *Coming Up the Road* 95.

7   For McClure losing money in early 1885, see Hattie McClure, letter to Mother, 29 May 1885, MP-Lilly; Spofford's gift is noted in Hattie McClure, letter to Mother, 7 June 1885, MP-Lilly; McClure, letter to Stevenson, 12 September 1890, MP-Lilly; Phillips, letter to McClure, 5 January 1891, MP-Lilly; Phillips's second warning is in letter to McClure, 3 November 1892, MP-Lilly; in *My Autobiography* McClure indicates that in 1892 the syndicate had $7,300 in capital, $4,500 of which belonged to John Phillips (208), but the quotation and figure of $2,700 used here are taken from McClure's Autobiography notes, MP-Lilly; S. S. McClure, letter to Hattie McClure, 11 December 1892, MP-Lilly; *My Autobiography* 211; for the financial situation of the syndicate in later years see Lyon, *Success Story* 159 and 268–9.

8   *From Stores of Memory* 45; the tightfistedness of Bacheller's partners is noted in *Coming Up the Road* 292; Bacheller, "The Rungs in My Little Ladder" (1918): 79; for information about the *New Yorker* see Phillips, "Newspaper Syndicates" (1888): 488–489, and "Bye-the-Bye," *Journalist* 29 October 1887: 8; for Pictorial League activities see John Young Taylor Diary, Courtesy, the Winterthur Library; for circulation figures of *Pocket Magazine* see Bacheller, Johnson, and Bacheller, letter to Joseph E. Chamberlin, 17 October 1895, quoted in a footnote of letter 183 of *The Infant Sphinx* 472; for miscellaneous projects see *Coming Up the Road* 289–290 and various undated letters from Bacheller to Albert Bigelow Paine, Henry E. Huntington Library; Bacheller's debt in *Coming Up the Road* 295; Bacheller, "One Path to Glory," *New York Herald Tribune Magazine* 16 November 1930: 27.

9   Expenditures for 1901 in ZBEN 1/7; for Tillotson's profits in the 1920s see ZBEN 4/10; [Fred Lever Tillotson], letter to Ivor Griffiths, 14 March 1935, ZBEN 4/10.

10 F. A. Carle, letter to S. S. McClure, 23 November 1885, MP-Lilly; Stevenson, letter to Charles Baxter, 14 October [1891], *RLS: Stevenson's Letters to Charles Baxter* 287; Stevenson to Baxter, 9 September 1894, *RLS* 367 (although *St. Ives* was not purchased for syndication, this quotation exemplifies McClure's practice of offering great sums to authors); Bacheller, Address to Stevenson Society, B-StL.

11 Bacheller wrote, "in the newspaper syndicate business we were in constant need of sky-rockets" (*Coming Up the Road* 292); Tillotson quoted in Victor Lawson, letter to McClure, 5 December [1888], VLP-Newberry; for the small profit margin on these works see McClure, Autobiography notes, MP-Lilly; one can see Tillotson's reliance on its backlist in various sales ledgers in BL-Turner.

12 Lyon, *Success Story* 108; Phillips, letter to McClure, 10 August 1884, MP-Lilly.

13 Alex. Paul., letter, *Providence Sunday Journal* 10 March 1889, typescript in ZBEN 14/10; Ouida, letter to Tillotson's, 11 September 1879, ZBEN 4/9; Hatton, *Journalistic London* (London: Sampson, Low, Marston, Searle, and Rivington, 1882) 201; "The Fiction Bureau," *Writer* (London) 1.6 (April 1889): 136; Gissing is quoted in Cross, *The Common Writer* 208 (Cross adds that "Many authors believed that they would lose considerable caste by publishing in newspapers rather than in magazines"); Boyly, letter to Tillotson's, 5 February 1889, ZBEN 4/1; Doyle is quoted in Richard Lancelyn Green and John Michael Gibson, *A Bibliography of A. Conan Doyle* (Oxford: Clarendon Press, 1983) 47.

14 Bacheller, *Coming Up the Road* 263; James, letter to Thomas Sergeant Perry, 6 March [1884], in Virginia Harlow, *Thomas Sergeant Perry: A Biography* (Durham, NC: Duke University Press, 1950) 316; London, letter to Cloudesley Johns, 12 June 1899, *The Letters of Jack London: Volume One, 1896–1905* 85; London, letter to Cloudesley Johns, 12 September 1899, *Letters* 110. In this letter London further indicates that he knows nothing about McClure's syndicate, but this remark was probably disingenuous.

15 Victor W. Turner, "Dewey, Dilthey, and Drama: An Essay in the Anthropology of Experience," *The Anthropology of Experience*, ed. Victor W. Turner and Edward M. Bruner (Urbana and Chicago: University of Illinois Press, 1986) 39; Godkin, "Newspapers Here and Abroad" (1890): 203; "Magazines and Newspapers," *Newspaper Maker* 18 July 1895: 2; George T. Rider, "The Pretensions of Journalism," *North American Review* 135 (1882): 471; Arlo Bates, "Literary Affairs in Boston," *Book-Buyer* 10 (1893): 405.

16 Howells, "The Man of Letters as a Man of Business" (1893): 433; Barr, "The Relations of Literature to Society," *North American Review* 153 (1891): 90; W. J. Stillman, "Journalism and Literature," *Atlantic Monthly* 68 (1891): 688; [William Morton Payne], Editorial, *Dial* 16 November 1895: 278.

17 Hawthorne, "Syndicate Matter" (1888): 4; Bok, "The Modern Literary King" (1895): 341; Howells, "The Man of Letters as a Man of Business" (1893): 441.
18 Arlo Bates, "Literary Affairs in Boston," *Book-Buyer* 6 (1889): 96; see the description of Selah Tarrant in James, *The Bostonians* (1886) in *Henry James. Novels 1881–1886* (New York: Library of America, 1985) 894–895.
19 Bacheller, *Coming Up the Road* 291; McClure, *My Autobiography* 208; W. H. Lever, *Bolton Weekly Journal* and *Bolton Evening News* Souvenir (1890), ZBEN 10/1; McClure, letter to Howells, 9 October 1891 (BMS Am 1784), Houghton Library, Harvard University; "A Syndicate Syndicate" (1891): 8.
20 "The Syndicate Evil" (1896): 148; S. S. McClure, letter to Hattie McClure, 19 November 1884, MP-Lilly; Bacheller, letter to [Edward Henry] Clement, 13 August 1898, James T. Williams Papers.
21 Lawson, letter to Bacheller, 2 November 1889, VLP-Newberry; Hawthorne, "Syndicate Matter" (1888): 4; Hattie McClure, letter to "Folks at Home," 2 September 1886, MP-Lilly; *Coming Up the Road* 264 and 292; Maxwell, letter to Tillotson, 5 January 1883, ZBEN 4/3; John Phillips, letter to McClure, 3 November 1892, MP-Lilly; Stevenson, letter to Charles Baxter, 1 December 1892, *RLS* 313.
22 The impact of Crane's loss of Bacheller's money is noted in Bacheller, letter to Mr. Osborne, 2 November 1921, B-StL. Bacheller's later claim that a $250 loan from New York Governor Flower was "the only financial help I had from anyone in those hard days of my pioneering" (*From Stores of Memory* 44) is quite misleading: James W. Johnson invested $5,000 in the syndicate in about 1886 (*Coming Up the Road* 264); Bacheller wrote in April 1895 that "our money is coming in freely now and will shortly be increased by an addition of $30,000 to our working capital" (Bacheller, letter to [Edmund] Stedman, 23 April 1895, ECSP-Columbia), but the source of this money is unknown; and in May 1896 Bacheller and a group of investors bought out Johnson's share of the business, incorporating as the Bacheller Syndicate (see incorporation agreement, 15 May 1896, B-StL). McClure, *My Autobiography* 170–171.
23 For Tillotson's capital in 1895 see Partnership Agreement, 1 April 1895, Bolton Evening News, Bolton, England (Courtesy of Mr. Marcus Tillotson); Rideing, "Boston Letter" (1887): 6.
24 Ouida [Louise de la Ramée], letter, London *Times* 22 May 1891: 3; Bacheller, "The Syndicate Matter" (1886): 3.
25 West, *American Authors* 103; Brodhead, "Literature and Culture" 476; H. L. Mencken, *Prejudices: First Series* (1919; New York: Alfred A. Knopf, 1929) 175.
26 "Journalistic Centralization," *Journalist* 17 September 1887: 8.
27 Waldo, "The Genius of S. S. McClure" (1934) 80; "Quantity and Quality," *Newspaper Maker* 16 May 1895: 7; "Literature in Newspapers" (1895): 7.

28 Kobre, *The Yellow Press and Gilded Age Journalism* 70; W. F. Tillotson, Obituary, *Newcastle [England] Weekly Chronicle*, 23 February 1889, clipping in ZBEN 14/7; Gosse, "The Influence of Democracy on Literature," *Contemporary Review* 59 (1891): 532; "The Daily Press," *Critic* 7 (1887): 49.
29 Levine, *Highbrow/Lowbrow: The Emergence of Cultural Hierarchy in America* (Cambridge, MA: Harvard University Press, 1988) 208.
30 Bacheller, "The Syndicate Matter," *Journalist* 17 April 1886: 3.

Bibliography

PRIMARY SOURCES

American Press Association Papers, Library of Congress, Washington, DC.
Beinecke Rare Book and Manuscript Library, Yale University, New Haven, CT.
Bodleian MS.Eng.Misc f.395/1 and 395/2, The Bodleian Library, Oxford, England.
The Bolton Evening News Archive, Bolton Metro Library, Bolton, England.
Bolton Evening News, Private Collection, Bolton, England.
Centennial File of A. N. Kellogg's Auxiliary Newspapers, Exhibited by A. N. Kellogg at the Centennial Exhibition in Philadelphia, Pennsylvania, 1876. Chicago Historical Society Library, Chicago, IL.
The Chicago Daily News Archive, The Newberry Library, Chicago, IL.
Clifton Waller Barrett Collection, Manuscripts Division, Special Collections Department, Alderman Library, University of Virginia, Charlottesville, VA.
The Henry Holt Archives, Manuscripts Division, Department of Rare Books and Special Collections, Princeton University Libraries, Princeton, NJ.
The Houghton Library, Harvard University, Cambridge, MA.
The Huntington Library, San Marino, CA.
Irving Bacheller Papers, Special Collections, Owen D. Young Library, St. Lawrence University, Canton, NY.
Jack London Collection, Special Collections and Archives, Utah State University, Logan, UT.
James T. Williams Papers, Special Collections Library, Duke University, Durham, NC.
Knox College Archives, Seymour Library, Knox College, Galesburg, IL.
Mary Noailles Murfree Papers, Special Collections Department, Robert W. Woodruff Library, Emory University, Atlanta, GA.
Oliver Otis Howard Papers, Special Collections, Bowdoin College Library, Brunswick, ME.
Sarah Orne Jewett Miscellaneous Papers, Rare Books and Manuscripts

Division, The New York Public Library, Astor, Lenox and Tilden Foundations, New York, NY.
S. S. McClure Papers, The Lilly Library, Indiana University, Bloomington, IN.
Special Collections, Miller Library, Colby College, Waterville, ME.
Special Collections, Rare Books and Manuscripts, Butler Library, Columbia University, New York, NY.
Special Collections and Manuscripts, Harold B. Lee Library, Brigham Young University, Provo, UT.
Talcott Williams Papers (Box I, Folder 13), Amherst College Archives, Amherst College, Amherst, MA.
Tillotson and Son's materials in the possession of Mr. Michael Turner, The Bodleian Library, Oxford, England. Available through application to Mr. Turner.
Victor Lawson Papers, The Newberry Library, Chicago, IL.
Western Newspaper Union Collection, Historical Society of Douglas County, NB, Library/Archives Center, Omaha, NB.
The Winterthur Library: Joseph Downs Collection of Manuscripts and Printed Ephemera, Winterthur, DE.

NEWSPAPERS CONSULTED

Albany [NY] Argus
Atlanta Constitution
Auburn [NY] Daily Advertiser
Bolton [England] Weekly Journal
Boston Globe
Boston Herald
Chicago Daily News
Chicago Tribune
Detroit Free Press
Hammondsport [NY] Herald
Indianapolis News
Los Angeles Times
New Orleans *Daily Picayune*
New York *Commercial Advertiser*
New York *Press*
New York *Sun*
New York Times
New York *World*
Rochester [NY] *Daily Union and Advertiser*
Rochester *Democrat and Chronicle*
Rochester *Morning Herald*
San Francisco Chronicle
Syracuse [NY] Herald

Syracuse Daily Journal
Syracuse Daily Standard
Toronto *Globe*
Utica *[New York] Daily Observer*
Utica *Weekly Herald*
Washington Post

CONTEMPORARY SOURCES AND ACCOUNTS

"The A. N. Kellogg Newspaper Co." *Journalist* 28 May 1887: 1–3.
Allen, James Lane, et al. "Will the Novel Disappear?" *North American Review* 175 (1902): 289–298.
American Newspaper Directory. New York: George P. Rowell, 1869, 1870, 1876.
"The American Press Association." *Journalist* 27 March 1886: 10.
"American Press Association." *Journalist* 17 December 1887: 25.
"An Author's Exchange." *Journalist* 8 September 1888: 8.
Bacheller, Irving. "A Passion Study." *Cosmopolitan* 22 (January 1897): 319–320.
"The Syndicate Matter." *Journalist* 17 April 1886: 3.
Barr, Amelia E. "The Relations of Literature to Society." *North American Review* 153 (1891): 87–91.
Bates, Arlo. "Literary Affairs in Boston." *Book Buyer* 6 (1889): 95–96.
"Literary Affairs in Boston." *Book Buyer* 10 (1893): 405–406.
Beard, George. *American Nervousness. Its Causes and Consequences*. New York: G. P. Putnam's Sons, 1881.
Biographical Sketches of the Leading Men of Chicago. Chicago: Wilson, Peirce and Co., 1876.
Bok, Edward W. "The Modern Literary King." *Forum* 20 (1895): 334–343.
Bok, William J. "Literary Leaves." *Indianapolis News* 9 October 1886: 3.
"Literary Leaves." *Indianapolis News* 12 March 1887: 3.
Bolles, F. A. "The Ideal Country Paper." *Writer* (New York) 4 (1890): 73–75.
Bonner, Geraldine. "A California Novel." 1898. Reprinted in *Critical Essays on Frank Norris*. Ed. Don Graham. Boston: G. K. Hall, 1980. 3–7.
"Books, Magazines and Newspapers." *Journalist* 25 June 1887: 6.
Burton, F. R. Letter. *Journalist* 31 March 1888: 8.
"Bye-the-Bye." *Journalist* 12 June 1886: 9; 10 July 1886: 8; 4 September 1886: 8–9; 2 October 1886: 9; 29 January 1887: 9; 5 February 1887: 8; 23 April 1887: 9; 29 October 1887: 8; 18 January 1890: 9; 19 April 1890: 9; 26 April 1890: 9; 18 October 1890: 8; 1 November 1890:9; 4 April 1891: 8; 24 October 1891: 8; 3 September 1892: 8–9.
Cather, Willa. "When I Knew Stephen Crane." 1900. *Novels, Poems, and Other Writings*. New York: Library of America, 1992. 932–938.
Choate, Charles A. Letter, *Journalist* 15 June 1889: 11.
Clarke, George J. Letter. *Journalist* 12 May 1888: 9.
[Colles, William Morris]. "On Syndicating." *Author* 1 (1890): 10–11.

"Columbus." "Chicago's Daily Newspapers." *Printers' Ink* 16 August 1893: 193.
"Compensation of Authors." *Writer* (New York) 1 (1887): 53.
"Confessions of a Literary Hack." *Forum* 19 (1895): 629–40.
"Continued Stories." *Journalist* 30 August 1884: 1.
Crunden, Frederick M. "Supplying of Current Daily Newspapers in Free Library Reading Rooms." *Library Journal* 19.12 (December 1894): 46–49, 143–146.
"The Daily Press." *Critic* 7 (1887): 49–50.
"Death of A. N. Kellogg." *Journalist* 3 April 1886: 8.
"Death of Mr. W. F. Tillotson. J. P." *Journalist* 9 March 1884: 3–4.
"The Decline of Reading Aloud." *Independent* 15 April 1909: 824–826.
"Defiant Piracy." Advertisement. *Journalist* 19 April 1890: 14.
Didier, Eugene L. "Does Literature Pay?" *Writer* (New York) 2 (1888): 218–19.
"Disclosure and Disgrace. Vanderpoole, the Literary Impostor." *Journalist* 24 September 1887: 12.
Donald, Robert. "Sunday Newspapers in the United States." *The Universal Review* 8 (September–December 1890): 78–89.
Editorial. New York *Sun* 8 November 1884: 2.
Editorial. *Journalist* 15 September 1888: 8.
Edson, Dr. Cyrus. "How a Physician Reads the Newspaper." *Printers' Ink* 12 June 1895: 3–4.
Fales, W. E. S. Letter. *Journalist* 15 September 1888: 8–9.
"The Fiction Bureau." *Writer* (London) 1.6 (April 1889): 136–7.
Fielding, Howard. "Plate Matter for Newspapers." *Book News* 7 (1889): 237–238.
Garland, Hamlin. *Main-Travelled Roads.* 1899. New York: Harper and Brothers, n. d.
Godkin, E. L. "Newspapers Here and Abroad." *North American Review* 150 (1890): 197–204.
Gosse, Edmund. "The Influence of Democracy on Literature." *Contemporary Review* 59 (1891): 523–536.
Grannis, Elizabeth. "How a Business Woman Reads the Newspapers." *Printers' Ink* 27 February 1895: 12–13.
"G. T. C." "Reaching the Rich." *Printers' Ink* 26 June 1895: 3.
Halsey, Francis Whiting. *Our Literary Deluge.* New York: Doubleday, Page and Co., 1902.
A Hand Book of Useful Information Concerning the Plate Service of the American Press Association as Furnished to Over Six Thousand Newspapers in the United States. New York: [American Press Association], 1891.
Hatton, Joseph. *Journalistic London.* London: Sampson Low, Marston, Searle, and Rivington, 1884.
Hawthorne, Julian. "Syndicate Matter." *Journalist* 14 July 1888: 4–5.
H[ills], W[illiam] H. Editorial. *Writer* (New York) 5 (1891): 122–124.

"Letters to the Editor." *Writer* (New York) 2 (1888): 90.
"Letters to the Editor." *Writer* (New York) 3 (1889): 278.
"The Stranger in New York." *Writer* (New York) 2 (1888): 1–6.
Howe, Edgar Watson. "Country Newspapers." *Century* 42 (1891): 776–83.
Howells, W[illiam] D[ean]. *A Hazard of New Fortunes.* 1889. Intro. by Everett Carter. Notes to the Text and Text Established by David J. Nordloh, et al. Bloomington and London: Indiana University Press, 1976.
  Literature and Life. 1902. Port Washington, New York: Kennikat Press, 1968.
  "The Man of Letters as a Man of Business." *Scribner's Magazine* 14 (1893): 429–45.
  The Rise of Silas Lapham. 1885. Intro. and notes by Walter Meserve. Bloomington and London: Indiana University Press, 1971.
  Selected Letters 1882–1891. Ed. and annotated by Robert C. Leitz III with Richard H. Ballinger and Christoph Lohmann. Vol. 3. Boston: Twayne, 1980.
  "What Should Girls Read?" *Harper's Bazaar* 36 (1902): 956–960.
  See also Elliott, ed.
Hudson, Frederic. *Journalism in the United States from 1690 to 1872.* 3 vols. New York: Harper and Brothers, 1873.
Hunt, William. *Then and Now; or, Fifty Years of Newspaper Work.* Hull and London: Hamilton, Adams, and Co., 1887.
Hyde, Richard. "How a Variety Theatrical Manager Reads the Newspaper." *Printers' Ink* 10 April 1895: 33–35.
"In Able Hands." *Newspaper Maker* 29 October 1896: 3.
James, Henry. *Novels 1881–1886.* New York: Library of America, 1985.
"James W. Johnson. A Well-Known Newspaper Man." *Journalist* 13 September 1890: 2.
"Journalistic Centralization." *Journalist* 17 September 1887: 8.
"Journalistic Enterprise." *Journalist* 12 January 1889: 11.
Keene, Thomas W. "How a Tragedian Reads the Newspaper." *Printers' Ink* 5 June 1895: 3–4.
Kellogg's Auxiliary Hand-Book: Containing a History of the Origin of Auxiliary Printing; With Opinions of Publishers; and Day-Book and Journal Combined; Being a Model System of Keeping Advertising Accounts; Together with Various Useful Articles, Tables, and Calendars. Chicago: A. N. Kellogg, 1878.
Kimball, Arthur Reed. "The Invasion of Journalism." *Atlantic Monthly* 86 (1900): 119–124.
"Literary Forgery." *Syracuse [NY] Herald* 25 September 1887: 4.
"Literary Syndicates." *The Editor* 2.2 (February 1896): 49–51.
"Literature in Newspapers." *Newspaper Maker* 29 August 1895: 7.
"Live Topics of Today." *Chicago Tribune* 28 January 1897: 6.
"The Local Paper." *Journalist* 21 June 1890: 8.
London, Jack. *Martin Eden.* 1908. New York: Macmillan, 1973.
McClure, S. S. Letter. *Critic* 11 (1887): 42–43.

"Magazine Literature and Illustrations." *Journalist* 9 August 1884: 9.
"Magazines and Newspapers." *Newspaper Maker* 18 July 1895: 2.
"Manuscript Brokers." *Journalist* 24 September 1887: 9.
Matthews, Brander. *Cheap Books and Good Books*. New York: American Copyright League, 1888.
Mead, Leon. "The Practical Side of Literature." *Gunton's* 21 (1901): 436–445.
"Miss Wilkins a Prize-Winner in Bacheller Syndicate's Competition." *Critic* 26 (1895): 483.
"Mr. Edward S. Van Zile." *Journalist* 26 April 1890: 1–2.
"Mr. M'Clure [sic] and His Magazine." *American Review of Reviews* 8 (1893): 98–99.
Morse, Lyman. *Advertisers' Handy Guide. 1895*. New York: Lyman D. Morse, 1895.
Munson, A. J. *Making a Country Newspaper*. Chicago: The Dominion Co., 1899.
N. W. Ayer and Sons American Newspaper Annual and Directory. Philadelphia: N. W. Ayer and Sons, 1887, 1889, 1890, 1891.
"News and Notes." *Writer* (New York) 1 (1887): 100.
"Newspaper Novels." *Journalist* 14 September 1889: 10.
"Newspaper Reading." *Boston Herald* 15 November 1885: 12.
"The Newspaper Side of Literature." *Century* 36 (1887–1888): 150–151.
"The Newspaper Syndicate." N. p., 15 October 1896: 5. Clipping pasted in a Scrapbook of William Holland Samson, Rochester, NY, Public Library.
Norris, Frank. *The Responsibilities of the Novelist and Other Essays*. Intro. by Charles Caldwell Dobie, foreword by Grant Overton. 1903. Vol. 7 of *The Complete Edition of Frank Norris*. 10 vols. Garden City, NY: Doubleday, Doran and Co., 1928.
North, S[imon] N[ewton] D[exter]. *History and Present Condition of the Newspaper and Periodical Press of the United States with a Catalogue of the Publications of the Census Year*. Washington, DC: Government Printing Office, 1884.
"Notes." *Critic* 5 (1886): 37–38.
"Notes and News." *Academy* 9 July 1881: 28.
"Novels in Daily Newspapers." *Syracuse Daily Standard* 30 June 1884: 2.
"One Thing and Another." *Detroit Free Press* 13 December 1885: 12.
O'Reilly, John Boyle, *What American Authors Think About International Copyright*. New York: American Copyright League, 1888.
Ouida [Louise de la Ramée]. Letter. London *Times* 22 May 1891: 3.
O. W. R. "The Newspaper Syndicate King." *Journalist* 31 July 1886: 3.
Parton, James. "Newspapers Gone to Seed." *Forum* 1 (1886): 15–24.
"Parts of the Paper Women Read." *Printers' Ink* 3 January 1894: 24.
Paul, Alex. Letter. *Providence Sunday Journal* 10 March 1889: n. p.
[Payne, William Morton]. Editorial. *Dial* 16 November 1895: 278.

Peters, Alfred H. "The Compensation of Writers." *Writer* (New York) 1 (1887): 53–56.
Phelps, Elizabeth Stuart. *Chapters from a Life.* Boston and New York: Houghton, Mifflin and Co., 1897.
Phillips, John S. "Newspaper Syndicates." *Book News* 6 (1888): 487–489.
Pocket Magazine. Vols. 1–9. New York: Frederick A. Stokes Co., 1895–1901.
"The Point of View." *Scribner's* 14 (1893): 657–660.
"Quantity and Quality." *Newspaper Maker* 16 May 1895: 7.
"Queries." *Writer* (New York) 1 (1887): 170–171.
Rideing, William H. "Boston Letter." *Critic* 8 (1887): 5–6.
Rider, George T. "The Pretensions of Journalism." *North American Review* 135 (1882): 471–83.
Robinson, W. Phillip. Letter. *Journalist* 3 October 1891: 13.
Rogers, Jason. "Circulation Ideas." *Newspaper Maker* 15 October 1896: 5.
———. "Circulation Ideas." *Newspaper Maker* 11 February 1897: 3.
[Scripps, Edward Wyllis]. Letter. *Journalist* 2 June 1888: 12.
"The Serial Story Feature." *Newspaper Maker* 23 July 1896: 4.
"The Small Change of Literature." *Critic* 12 (1889): 155–56.
"Special Newspaper Trains." *Journalist* 22 August 1885: 4.
Spofford, Ainsworth Rand. *A Book for All Readers.* 2nd edn. New York and London: G. P. Putnam, 1900.
Steffens, J. Lincoln. "The Business of a Newspaper." *Scribner's Magazine* 22 (1897): 447–467.
Stillman, W. J. "Journalism and Literature." *Atlantic Monthly* 68 (1891): 687–95.
"The Story of a Great Success." *Journalist* 17 December 1892: 2.
"Sunday Papers Eulogized." *Newspaper Maker* 2 April 1886: 11.
"The Sunday Press." *Journalist* 13 June 1885: 6.
"The Sunday Standard." *Syracuse Daily Standard* 14 June 1884: 4.
"The Syndicate Evil." *Editor* 2 (April 1896): 147–148.
"A Syndicate Syndicate." *Journalist* 21 November 1891: 8.
Thompson, Adele E. "What the Editor Wants in Fiction." *Editor* 2 (1896): 123–126.
"Trade and Literary Gossip." *Bookseller* 9 January 1889: 5.
Waldron, Adelaide Cilley. "Business Relations Between Publishers and Writers." *Writer* (New York) 1 (1887): 56–57.
Wappiert, G. W. "Newspaper Factories." *Writer* (New York) 4 (1890): 6–9.
Westall, William. "Newspaper Fiction." *Lippincott's Monthly Magazine* 40 (1890): 77–82.
"William Frederick [sic] Tillotson." Obituary. *The Publishers' Circular* 1 March 1889: 224.
"Women and Newspapers." *New York Times* 6 September 1896: Magazine 14.
"A Word About Plate Matter." *Journalist* 9 May 1891: 8.

LATER SOURCES, POPULAR AND SCHOLARLY

Altick, Richard D. *Writers, Readers, and Occasions: Selected Essays on Victorian Literature and Life.* Columbus: Ohio State University Press, 1989.
American Imprints Inventory No. 11: A Check List of the Kellogg Collection of "Patent Inside" Newspapers of 1876. Chicago: The WPA Historical Records Survey Project, 1939.
Anesko, Michael. *"Friction with Market": Henry James and the Profession of Authorship.* New York: Oxford University Press, 1986.
Angelo, Frank. *On Guard. A History of the Detroit Free Press.* Detroit: Detroit Free Press, 1981.
Archives of Grant Richards. Cambridge, MA: Chadwyck-Healey, 1979.
Atwood, Millard Van Marter. *The Country Newspaper.* Chicago: A. C. McClurg and Co., 1923.
Bacheller, Irving. *Coming Up the Road: Memories of a North Country Boyhood.* Indianapolis: The Bobbs-Merrill Co., 1928.
 From Stores of Memory. New York: Farrar and Rinehart, 1938.
 "One Path to Glory." *New York Herald Tribune Magazine* 16 November 1930: 8, 9, 27.
 "The Rungs in My Little Ladder." *American Magazine* 85 (1918): 19, 79–84.
Baker, Ray Stannard (David Grayson). *American Chronicle: The Autobiography of Ray Stannard Baker.* New York: Charles Scribner's Sons, 1945.
Ballou, Ellen B. *The Building of the House: Houghton-Mifflin's Formative Years.* Boston: Houghton-Mifflin, 1970.
Barth, Gunter. *The Rise of Modern City Culture in Nineteenth-Century America.* New York: Oxford University Press, 1980.
Berger, Meyer. *The Story of the New York Times, 1851–1951.* New York: Simon and Schuster, 1951.
Binghamton and Broome County, New York. A History. 3 vols. New York and Chicago: Lewis Historical Publishing Co., 1924.
Bleyer, Willard Grosvenor. *Main Currents in the History of American Journalism.* Boston: Houghton Mifflin, 1927.
Borus, Daniel H. *Writing Realism: Howells, James, and Norris in the Mass Market.* Chapel Hill: University of North Carolina Press, 1989.
Bowers, Fredson, ed. *The University of Virginia Edition of The Works of Stephen Crane.* 10 vols. Charlottesville: University Press of Virginia, 1969–1976.
Bradsher, Earl L. "Book Publishers and Publishing." *The Cambridge History of American Literature.* Ed. William Peterfield Trent et al. 1917. New York: Macmillan, 1961. 533–553.
Britt, George. *Forty Years – Forty Millions: The Career of Frank A. Munsey.* New York: Farrar and Rinehart, 1935.
Brodhead, Richard. "Literature and Culture." *Columbia Literary History of the United States.* Ed. Emory Elliott et al. New York: Columbia University Press, 1988. 467–481.

Calder, Jenni. *Robert Louis Stevenson: A Life Study*. New York: Oxford University Press, 1980.
Cary, Richard, ed. *The Uncollected Short Stories of Sarah Orne Jewett*. Waterville, ME: Colby College Press, 1971.
Cassady, David Roy. "The Content of the Rural Weekly Press in 1882." Diss. The University of Iowa, 1980.
Charvat, William. "Literature as a Business." *Literary History of the United States*. Ed. Robert E. Spiller et al. 4th edn. New York: Macmillan, 1974. 953–968.
   The Profession of Authorship in America, 1800–1870. Ed. Matthew J. Bruccoli. Columbus: Ohio State University Press, 1968.
Clark, Neil. "Patterson Helps To Edit Twelve Thousand Newspapers." *American Magazine* 104 (October 1927): 36, 37, 158, 160–164.
[Clemens, Samuel L.]. *Mark Twain's Letters to His Publishers*. Ed. Hamlin Hill. Berkeley: University of California Press, 1967.
[Clemens, Samuel L. and W. D. Howells]. *Mark Twain–Howells Letters. The Correspondence of Samuel L. Clemens and William D. Howells*. Ed. Henry Nash Smith and William M. Gibson. 2 vols. Cambridge, MA: Harvard University Press, 1960.
Colby, Robert A. "'What Fools Authors Be!' The Authors' Syndicate, 1890–1920," *Library Chronicle of the University of Texas* 35 (1986): 60–87.
"Colonel McClure, at 'Newspaper Week,' Tells of Early Struggles Syndicating." *Philadelphia Public Ledger* 27 April 1923: n. p.
[Conrad, Joseph]. *The Collected Letters of Joseph Conrad, 1898– 1902*. Ed. Frederick R. Karl and Laurence Davies. Vol. 2. Cambridge: Cambridge University Press, 1986.
Coultrap-McQuin, Susan. *Doing Literary Business: American Women Writers in the Nineteenth Century*. Chapel Hill: University of North Carolina Press, 1990.
[Crane, Stephen]. *The Correspondence of Stephen Crane*. Ed. Stanley Wertheim and Paul Sorrentino. 2 vols. New York: Columbia University Press, 1988. See also Bowers, ed., Katz, ed., Stallman and Gilkes, eds.
Cross, Nigel. *The Common Writer: Life in Nineteenth-Century Grub Street*. Cambridge: Cambridge University Press, 1985.
Davis, Elmer. *History of the "New York Times," 1851–1921*. New York: New York Times Company, 1921.
Davis, Natalie Z. "Anthropology and History in the 1980s: The Possibilities of the Past." *Journal of Interdisciplinary History* 12 (1981): 267–75.
Denning, Michael. *Mechanic Accents: Dime Novels and Working Class Culture*. New York: Verso Press, 1987.
Dill, William A. *Growth of Newspapers in the United States*. Lawrence, KS: University of Kansas Press, 1928.
DiMaggio, Paul. "Market Structure, the Creative Process, and Popular Culture: Toward an Organizational Reinterpretation of Mass Culture Theory." *Journal of Popular Culture* 11 (1987): 436–52.

Edel, Leon. *Henry James: A Life.* New York: Harper and Row, 1985.
Edwards, John Milton (pseud. William Wallace Cook). *The Fiction Factory.* Ridgewood, NJ: The Editor Company, 1912.
Elliott, James P. Introduction and notes, W. D. Howells, *The Quality of Mercy.* Bloomington: Indiana University Press, 1979.
Exman, Eugene. *The House of Harper: One Hundred and Fifty Years of Publishing.* New York: Harper and Row, 1967.
Feltes, N. N. *Modes of Production of Victorian Novels.* Chicago: University of Chicago Press, 1986.
Ford, Worthington C. "Report of the Council." *Proceedings of the American Antiquarian Society* 28 (1918): 7–12.
Fox-Genovese, Elizabeth. "Literary Criticism and the Politics of the New Historicism." *The New Historicism.* Ed. H. Aram Veeser. New York and London: Routledge, 1989.
[Frederic, Harold]. *The Correspondence of Harold Frederic.* Ed. George E. Fortenberry, Stanton Garner, Robert H. Woodward. Fort Worth, TX: Texas Christian University Press, 1977.
[Freeman, Mary E. Wilkins]. *The Infant Sphinx: Collected Letters of Mary E. Wilkins Freeman.* Ed. Brent L. Kendrick. Metuchen, NJ: The Scarecrow Press, 1985.
Fuller, Wayne E. *RFD, The Changing Face of Rural America.* Bloomington: Indiana University Press, 1964.
Gale, Robert L., ed. *A Henry James Encyclopedia.* New York: Greenwood Press, 1989.
Garland, Hamlin. *Companions on the Trail: A Literary Chronicle.* New York: Macmillan, 1931.
——— "Irving Bacheller: Interpreter of the Old America to the New." *Red Cross Magazine* March 1920: 11–12.
[Garland, Hamlin]. *Hamlin Garland's Diaries.* Ed. Donald Pizer. San Marino, CA: The Huntington Library, 1968.
Geary, Susan. "The Domestic Novel as a Commercial Commodity: Making a Best-Seller in the 1850s." *Papers of the Bibliographical Society of America* 70 (1976): 365–93.
Geertz, Clifford. *The Interpretation of Cultures.* New York: Basic Books, 1973.
Gompers, Samuel. *Seventy Years of Life and Labor: An Autobiography.* New York: E. P. Dutton, 1925.
Graff, Harvey J. *The Literacy Myth: Literacy and Social Structure in the Nineteenth-Century City.* New York: Academic Press, 1979.
Green, David Bonnell. "Sarah Orne Jewett's 'A Dark Night.'" *Papers of the Bibliographical Society of America* 53 (1959): 331–334.
Green, Richard Lancelyn and John Michael Gibson. *A Bibliography of A. Conan Doyle.* Oxford: Clarendon Press, 1983.
Griest, Guinevere L. *Mudie's Circulating Library and the Victorian Novel.* Bloomington: Indiana University Press, 1970.
Grimsted, David. "Books and Culture: Canned, Canonized, and

Neglected." *Needs and Opportunities in the History of the Book: America, 1639–1876.* Ed. David D. Hall and John B. Hench. Worcester, MA: American Antiquarian Society, 1987. 187–232.

Harlow, Virginia. *Thomas Sergeant Perry: A Biography.* Durham, NC: Duke University Press, 1950.

Hart, Jack R. "Horatio Alger in the Newsroom: Social Origins of American Editors." *Journalism Quarterly* 53 (1976): 14–20.

[Harte, Bret]. *The Letters of Bret Harte.* Ed. Geoffrey Bret Harte. Boston and New York: Houghton Mifflin Co., 1926.

Harter, Eugene C. *Boilerplating America: The Hidden Newspaper.* Ed. Dorothy Harter. Lanham, MD: University Press of America, 1991.

Hepburn, James. *The Author's Empty Purse and the Rise of the Literary Agent.* London: Oxford University Press, 1968.

Hepburn, James, ed. *Letters of Arnold Bennett.* Vol. 1. London: Oxford University Press, 1966.

Historical Statistics of the United States, Colonial Times to 1970. 2 parts. Washington, DC: U.S. Department of Commerce, 1975.

[James, Henry]. *Henry James Letters.* Ed. Leon Edel. Vol. 1. Cambridge, MA: Harvard University Press, 1974.

The Selected Letters of Henry James. Ed. Leon Edel. New York: Farrar, Straus, and Cudahy, 1955.

James, Louis. "The Trouble With Betsy: Periodicals and the Common Reader in Mid-Nineteenth Century England." *The Victorian Periodical Press: Samplings and Soundings.* Ed. Joanne Shattock and Michael Wolff. Leicester, England: Leicester University Press, 1982.

Johnson, James Weldon. *The Autobiography of an Ex-Coloured Man.* 1912. Garden City, New York: Garden City Publishing, n. d.

Katz, Joseph. "Bibliography and the Rise of American Literary Realism." *Studies in American Fiction* 2 (1974): 75–88.

[Katz, Joseph]. "An Editor's Recollection of 'The Red Badge of Courage.'" *Stephen Crane Newsletter* 2.3 (Spring 1968): 3–6.

Introduction. Stephen Crane. *The Red Badge of Courage.* 1894. Gainesville, FL: Scholars' Facsimiles and Reprints, 1967. 9–42.

"Theodore Dreiser's 'Ev'ry Month.'" *Library Chronicle* 38 (1972): 46–66.

Kielbowicz, Richard B. "Mere Merchandise or Vessels of Culture?: Books in the Mail, 1792–1942." *Papers of the Bibliographical Society of America* 82 (1988): 169–200.

[Kipling, Rudyard]. *The Letters of Rudyard Kipling.* Ed. Thomas Pinney. Vol. 2. Iowa City: University of Iowa Press, 1990.

Kipling, Rudyard. *Something of Myself. For My Friends Known and Unknown.* Garden City, NY: Doubleday, Doran and Co., 1937.

Kobre, Sidney. *Development of American Journalism.* Dubuque, IA: Wm. C. Brown Co., 1969.

The Yellow Press and Gilded Age Journalism. Tallahassee: Florida State University Press, 1964.

Lee, Alfred McClung. *The Daily Newspaper in America: The Evolution of a Social Instrument*. New York: Macmillan, 1937.
Levine, Lawrence. *Highbrow/Lowbrow: The Emergence of Cultural Hierarchy in America*. Cambridge, MA: Harvard University Press, 1988.
Lichtenstein, Nelson. "Authorial Professionalism and the Literary Marketplace, 1885–1920." *American Studies* 9.1 (1978): 35–53.
[London, Jack]. *The Letters of Jack London*. Ed. Earle Labor, Robert C. Leitz III, and I. Milo Shepard. 3 vols. Stanford: Stanford University Press, 1988.
Lund, Michael. *America's Continuing Story: An Introduction to Serial Fiction, 1850–1900*. Detroit: Wayne State University Press, 1993.
Lyon, Peter. *Success Story: The Life and Times of S. S. McClure*. New York: Charles Scribner's Sons, 1963.
McClure, S. S. "And McClure Tells How He Did It." *Editor and Publisher* 21 July 1934: 82, 90.
My Autobiography. 1913. New York: Frederick A. Stokes Co., 1914.
McKay, George L. *Some Notes on Robert Louis Stevenson: His Finances and His Agents and Publishers*. New Haven: Yale University Library, 1958.
McMichael, George. *Journey to Obscurity: The Life of Octave Thanet*. Lincoln, NE: University of Nebraska Press, 1965.
McNitt, V. V. "Sam McClure Started Something." *Editor and Publisher* 67 (21 July 1934): 80, 84, 86, 90.
McRae, Milton A. *Forty Years in Newspaperdom. The Autobiography of a Newspaper Man*. New York: Brentano's, 1924.
Mencken, H. L. *Prejudices: First Series*. 1919. New York: Alfred A. Knopf, 1929.
Mitchell, Edward P. *Memoirs of an Editor*. New York: Charles Scribner's Sons, 1924.
Moers, Ellen. Introduction. Peter Lyon. *Success Story: The Life and Times of S. S. McClure*. Deland, FL: Everett/Edwards, Inc., 1967. vii-xv.
Morrison, Elizabeth. "Newspapers and Novelists in Late Colonial Australia: Serial Fiction in the Melbourne *Age*, 1872–1899." Diss. Monash University, Clayton, Victoria, Australia, 1983.
Mott, Frank Luther. *American Journalism: A History: 1690–1960*. 3rd edn. New York: Macmillan, 1962.
A History of American Magazines. 5 vols. Cambridge, MA: Harvard University Press, 1930–1968.
Mrja, Ellen M. "Ansel Nash Kellogg." *American Newspaper Journalists, 1873–1900*. Vol. 23 of Dictionary of Literary Biography. Ed. Perry J. Ashley. Detroit: Gale Research Company, 1983. 180–183.
Noel, Mary. *Villains Galore: The Heyday of the Popular Story Weekly*. New York: Macmillan, 1954.
[Norris, Frank]. *Frank Norris: Collected Letters*. Compiled and annotated by Jesse Crisler. San Francisco: The Book Club of California, 1986.
Odell, Ruth. *Helen Hunt Jackson (H.H.)*. New York: D. Appleton-Century, 1939.

Osbourne, Lloyd. *An Intimate Portrait of RLS*. New York: Charles Scribner's Sons, 1924.

Pollard, Graham. *Serial Fiction*. London: Constable, [1938].

Purdy, Richard Little. *Thomas Hardy: A Bibliographical Study*. Oxford: Clarendon Press, 1954.

[Quaife, M. M.] "How A. N. Kellogg Revolutionized America's Country Press." *National Printer-Journalist* February 1922: 21.

Quéffelec, Lise. *Le Roman-Feuilleton Français au XIXe siècle*. Paris: Presses Universitaires de France, 1989.

Radway, Janice A. "Reading Is Not Eating: Mass-Produced Literature and the Theoretical, Methodological, and Political Consequences of a Metaphor" *Book Research Quarterly* 2 (1986): 7–29.

Reading the Romance: Women, Patriarchy, and Popular Literature. Chapel Hill and London: University of North Carolina Press, 1984.

Reynolds, Quentin. *The Fiction Factory or, From Pulp Row to Quality Street*. New York: Random House, 1955.

Robinson, Kenneth. *Wilkie Collins. A Biography*. London: The Bodley Head, 1951.

Ross, Andrew. *No Respect: Intellectuals and Popular Culture*. New York: Routledge, 1989.

Rowell, George Presbury. *Forty Years an Advertising Agent, 1865–1905*. New York: Printers' Ink, 1905.

"S. S. McClure's 16 Words of Advice Key to Success." *Boston Globe* 9 September 1939: morning edition, 2.

Schick, Frank L. *The Paperbound Book in America: The History of Paperbacks and Their European Background*. New York: R. R. Bowker Co., 1958.

Scott, Franklin William. *Newspapers and Periodicals of Illinois, 1814–1879*. Chicago: R. R. Donnelly and Sons, n.d.

Sedgwick, Ellery. "Henry James and the *Atlantic Monthly*: Editorial Perspectives on James' 'Friction With Market'" *Studies in Bibliography* 45 (1992): 311–332.

Sheehan, Donald. *This Was Publishing: A Chronicle of the Book Trade in the Gilded Age*. Bloomington: Indiana University Press, 1952.

Shove, Raymond Howard. *Cheap Book Production in the United States, 1870 to 1891*. Urbana: University of Illinois Library, 1937.

Sim, John C. *The Grass-Roots Press: America's Community Newspapers*. Ames, Iowa: The Iowa State University Press, 1969.

Stahl, John M. *Growing With the West: The Story of a Busy, Quiet Life*. London: Longmans, Green and Co., 1930.

Stallman, R. W. and Lillian Gilkes, eds. *Stephen Crane: Letters*. New York: New York University Press, 1960.

Steinberg, Salme Harju. *Reformer in the Marketplace: Edward W. Bok and the "Ladies' Home Journal"*. Baton Rouge: Louisiana State University Press, 1979.

[Stevenson, Robert Louis]. *RLS: Stevenson's Letters to Charles Baxter*. Ed.

DeLancey Ferguson and Marshall Waingrow. New Haven: Yale University Press, 1956.
Sutton, Walter. *The Western Book Trade: Cincinnati as a Nineteenth-Century Publishing and Book-Trade Center*. Columbus: Ohio State University Press, 1961.
Swearingen, Roger G. *The Prose Writings of Robert Louis Stevenson. A Guide*. Hamden, CT: Archon Books, 1980.
Tarbell, Ida. *All in a Day's Work. An Autobiography*. New York: Macmillan, 1939.
Tebbel, John W. *The American Magazine: A Compact History*. New York: Hawthorn Books, 1969.
  A History of Book Publishing in the United States. 4 vols. New York and London: R. R. Bowker Co., 1972–1981.
Thwaite, Ann. *Waiting for the Party: The Life of Frances Hodgson Burnett 1849–1924*. London: Secker and Warburg, 1974.
Toth, Emily. *Kate Chopin*. New York: William Morrow and Co., 1990.
Turner, Michael. "Reading for the Masses: Aspects of the Syndication of Fiction in Great Britain." *Book Selling and Book Buying: Aspects of the Nineteenth-Century British and North American Book Trade*. Ed. Richard G. Landon. Chicago: American Library Association, 1978. 52–72.
  "The Syndication of Fiction in Provincial Newspapers, 1870–1939: The Example of the Tillotson 'Fiction Bureau.'" B. Litt. thesis, Oxford University, 1968.
  "Tillotson's Fiction Bureau." *Studies in the Book Trade in Honour of Graham Pollard*. Oxford: The Oxford Bibliographical Society, 1975. 351–378.
Turner, Victor W., "Dewey, Dilthey, and Drama: An Essay in the Anthropology of Experience." *The Anthropology of Experience*. Ed. Victor W. Turner and Edward M. Bruner. Urbana and Chicago: University of Illinois Press, 1986.
Waldo, Richard H. "The Genius of S. S. McClure." *Editor and Publisher* 21 July 1934: 80, 88.
Walker, Franklin. "Four Additional Frank Norris Letters." *Book Club of California Quarterly Newsletter* 40 (1974): 3–12.
  Frank Norris: A Biography. Garden City, New York: Doubleday, Doran and Co., 1932.
Watson, Elmo Scott. *A History of Newspaper Syndicates in the United States, 1865–1935*. Chicago: N.p., 1936.
Waugh, Arthur. *One Man's Road: Being a Picture of Life in a Passing Generation*. London: Chapman and Hall, 1931.
West, James L. W. III. *American Authors and the Literary Marketplace Since 1900*. Philadelphia: University of Pennsylvania Press, 1988.
  "The Second Serials of *This Side of Paradise* and *The Beautiful and the Damned*." *Publications of the Bibliographical Society of America* 73 (1979): 63–74.
Wilder, Laura Ingalls. *The Long Winter*. 1940. New York: Harper and Row, 1953.

Wilson, Christopher. *The Labor of Words: Literary Professionalism in the Progressive Era*. Athens: University of Georgia Press, 1985.

"The Rhetoric of Consumption: Mass-Market Magazines and the Demise of the Gentle Reader, 1880–1920." *The Culture of Consumption: Critical Essays in American History 1880–1980*. Ed. Richard Wightman Fox and T. J. Jackson Lears. New York: Pantheon Books, 1983. 39–64.

Yates, JoAnne. *Control Through Communication: The Rise of System in American Management*. Baltimore and London: Johns Hopkins University Press, 1989.

Yezierska, Anzia. *Bread Givers*. 1925. New York: Persea Books, 1975.

Young, John F. *Journalism in California*. San Francisco: Chronicle Publishing Co., 1915.

Zboray, Ronald J. "The Transportation Revolution and Antebellum Book Distribution Reconsidered." *American Quarterly* 38 (1986): 53–71.

Index

agents, literary 30, 66, 79, 81, 97, 222
  see also Chartres, John; Pinker, James; Reynolds, Paul Revere; and Watt, A. P.
Aikens, Andrew Jackson 36, 38
Ainsworth, Harrison 214
American News Company 20
American Press Association, general references 32, 35, 44, 207
  authors and 102–7, 150, 180
  early history of 43
  fiction, editing of 47
  fiction, illustration of 47–8
  fiction, marketing of 46–7
  fiction, procurement of 45–6
  newspaper editors and 157–9
  readers and 186
Atlantic Monthly 15, 16, 22, 26–7, 113, 195
Authors, Society of 30, 96
  see also Colles, William Morris
Authors' Alliance 96
Authors' Syndicate 36, 46, 96–7, 125
  see also Colles, William Morris, and Authors, Society of

Bacheller, Irving 64, 67, 70, 109–10, 128
  see also Bacheller syndicates and *Pocket Magazine*
Bacheller syndicates, general references 32, 35, 36, 64, 73, 134–5, 138–9, 166, 172, 175–6, 178, 205, 209, 226
  authors and 115–16, 119, 120, 121, 123, 130, 131, 132, 137, 140, 142, 143, 145, 147, 149, 169, 177
  decline, reasons for 208–22
  fiction, editing of 90–1, 92, 144–5
  fiction, illustration of 94
  fiction, marketing of 83–90, 160
  fiction, procurement of 77–83
  history of 64–7, 71–3
  Kellogg Co. and 40–1, 89, 90
  newspaper editors and 84–9, 151, 160, 171, 173

Bennett, Arnold 54, 97
Bok, Edward W. 5–6, 119, 150, 166, 172, 216–17
  see also *Ladies' Home Journal*
Bolton Weekly Journal 50, 55, 59, 109, 130, 146
  see also Tillotson, William Frederic
Boston Globe 18–19, 24, 25, 61, 62, 72, 94, 177, 185, 195, 196–7, 202
  see also Taylor, Charles
Boyesen, Hjalmar H. 116, 136, 141, 186
Braddon, Mary Elizabeth 50, 53, 58, 114, 120, 121, 165, 220
  see also Maxwell, John
Brimelow, William 58, 128
Brodhead, Richard 16, 223
Burnett, Frances Hodgson 91, 124

Caine, Hall 141–2, 143–4, 146
Century magazine 16, 25, 74, 113, 192, 195
Chace Act (1891) 13, 14, 29, 30, 40, 53, 60, 113, 148, 174, 218
  see also copyright
Chartres, John 81, 97
Chesnutt, Charles 4, 199
Chicago Daily News 58, 162, 168, 186, 220
  see also Lawson, Victor
Chicago Tribune 175, 198, 201
Chopin, Kate 46, 104
Colles, William Morris 30, 81, 96–7, 125
  see also Authors, Society of, *and* Authors' Syndicate
Collins, Wilkie 54, 58, 61, 119, 146, 165, 202
Conan Doyle, Sir Arthur, general references 4, 54
  Bacheller syndicates and 82, 119, 121, 166, 220
  McClure syndicate and 88, 120, 123, 135, 169, 172–3, 214
Conrad, Joseph 71, 82
copyright 13, 60, 107, 111, 148, 149, 174
  see also Chace Act
Corelli, Marie 143

281

Cosmopolitan magazine 16, 25, 73, 86, 104, 209
Coultrap-McQuin, Susan 5, 28, 112
courtesy, trade 77, 111–12, 223
Cramer, Aikens, and Cramer 38
Crane, Stephen general references, 4, 32, 97
   American Press Association and 45
   Bacheller syndicates and 41, 109, 117, 123, 131, 140, 145, 166, 173, 200, 221
   Kellogg, Ansel Nash, Co. and 41
   Red Badge of Courage 41, 109, 117, 123–4, 140, 145, 173, 176, 177
   McClure syndicate and 92, 109, 117–18, 133, 169
   Tillotson's Newspaper Fiction Bureau and 54–5, 119
Dana, Charles A. 35, 64, 67, 74, 82, 83
   James, Henry, and 110, 114, 118, 124, 130, 185, 186, 214–15, 217
   New York Sun syndicate history 61–2
   see also New York Sun

Detroit Free Press 18, 23–4, 92, 139, 164, 185
Dunbar, Paul Laurence 199

Edwards, John Milton 45, 104
exchange, newspaper 39, 40, 48, 84, 85, 152, 155, 160, 203

feuilletons 48–9, 50, 79, 185
(Freeman), Mary E. Wilkins, general references 4, 119, 199, 225
   Bacheller syndicates and 41, 81, 92, 120, 122, 130, 131, 140, 143, 147, 148–9
   McClure syndicate and 75, 92, 143
French, Alice (Octave Thanet) 122, 161

Garland, Hamlin 7, 32, 67, 115–16, 131, 189
(Gilman) Charlotte Perkins Stetson 45
Gosse, Edmund 91, 226

Haggard, H. Rider 54, 198
Hardy, Thomas 54, 128, 130–1, 134
Harper's Bazar 16
Harper's Monthly Magazine 15, 16, 53, 113, 195
Harper's Weekly 16, 53
Harris, Joel Chandler 41, 75, 125, 132, 140–1, 199
Harte, Bret, general references 30, 96
   Charles A. Dana and 35, 61, 62, 186
   McClure syndicate and 88, 116
   Tillotson's Newspaper Fiction Bureau and 115, 120, 144
Hatton, Joseph 72, 73, 214
Hawthorne, Julian 86, 92, 94, 114, 145, 165, 168, 170, 202, 216, 220

Hope, Anthony 81
Howells, William Dean, general references 4, 7, 46, 61, 113, 117, 141, 187, 216, 218, 242n
   Hazard of New Fortunes, A 71, 204
   Quality of Mercy, The 82, 92, 135, 170, 176, 185
   Rise of Silas Lapham, The 71, 113, 190, 191
   syndicates, comments on 117, 121, 137, 206–7, 217

Jackson, Helen Hunt 79, 147, 178
Jacobs, W. W. 144
James, Henry, general references 4, 28, 30, 113, 201, 214, 217
   Charles A. Dana and 61, 110, 114, 118, 124, 130, 177, 185, 186, 198, 201, 214–15, 217
   "Georgina's Reasons" 61, 110, 177, 198, 201
   McClure syndicate and 79, 170
   "Pandora" 61
   "Real Thing, The" 170
Jewett, Sarah Orne
   Bacheller syndicates and 120, 130, 131, 134, 137, 140, 143, 199, 218
   McClure syndicates and 75, 79, 121, 135, 139–40, 141, 143, 170
Johnson, James W. 78, 87, 160
Johnson, James Weldon 191

Kellogg, Ansel Nash 151, 207
Kellogg, Ansel Nash, Co., general references 7, 32
   authors and 101–2
   Bacheller syndicates and 40–1, 89, 90
   early history of 32, 36–7
   fiction, distribution of 41, 189
   fiction, plate service 42, 44
   fiction, procurement of 39–41
   newspaper editors and 152–6, 186
Kipling, Rudyard, general references 4, 96, 198
   Bacheller syndicates and 41, 218, 220
   McClure syndicate and 32, 76, 88, 92, 119, 123, 126, 127, 144, 166, 172
   Tillotson's Newspaper Fiction Bureau and 54

Ladies' Home Journal 5, 6, 16, 22, 113, 119, 172
   see also Bok, Edward W.
Lawson, Victor 58, 162–7, 168, 169, 170, 171, 172, 175, 186, 202, 213, 220
   see also Chicago Daily News
Leng, W. C. 50, 55

Index

London, Jack, general references 4, 45, 108, 117, 177, 207
   McClure syndicate and 117, 140, 177, 215
   Tillotson's Newspaper Fiction Bureau and 55, 108, 133, 215
Luska, Sidney (Henry Harland) 78, 124

McCarthy, Justin 129, 146, 148
McClure, Harriet (Hattie) 75, 79, 92, 209
McClure, Robert 76, 82, 91, 92, 149
McClure, Samuel Sidney 64, 67, 68, 69, 71, 109, 128–9, 205
McClure's Associated Literary Press syndicate, general references 7, 225
   authors and 79, 80, 116–25, 127, 129, 131–3, 135–50, 151, 171, 210, 212, 214, 215
   decline, reasons for 98, 209–22
   fiction, editing of 91–2, 109, 129, 145, 202
   fiction, illustration of 95
   fiction, marketing of 83–9, 160–1
   fiction, procurement of 77–83
   history of 64, 73–6
   newspaper editors and 84–9, 151, 160–76, 178–9, 181
   readers and 185, 186, 202, 203
   Tillotson's Newspaper Fiction Bureau and 53, 55, 75–6, 81–2
   Woman's page materials 95, 187
   Youth's page materials 75, 76, 91, 95, 116, 141
McClure's Magazine 16, 71, 76, 90, 91, 94, 97, 117, 181, 209, 223
McClure, Tom 76, 149, 211
Maxwell, John 56, 57, 61, 114, 121, 220
   see also Braddon, Mary Elizabeth
Meredith, George 97, 135
Murfree, Mary Noailles (Charles Egbert Craddock, pseud.) 79, 161, 171

Nayler, John 58, 59, 131, 183
New York *Sun* 35, 36, 61–2, 72, 82–3, 93, 187–8, 214–15, 217
   see also Dana, Charles A.
newspapers
   Sunday 3, 18–19, 23, 57, 61, 84, 96, 99, 117, 118, 137–8, 139, 162–3, 167, 170, 175, 185, 187, 190, 191, 192, 193, 197, 208, 214, 215, 217, 222, 223
   Women's/Woman's pages and 25–6, 32, 43, 95, 163, 187
   Youth's pages and 75, 76, 91, 95, 116, 141
   see also exchange, newspaper, *and titles of individual newspapers*
Norris, Frank 11, 27, 80, 92, 117, 123, 187–8, 241n

"Salvation Boom in Matabeleland, A" 197, 201
novels, dime 13, 31, 112, 126, 144, 149, 152, 181
Nye, Bill (Edgar) 102, 127, 148

Ouida (Louise de la Ramée) 66, 108, 134, 168, 214, 222

papers, story, 8, 14–15
Phelps, Elizabeth Stuart 79, 133, 141, 143, 170
Phillips, John S. 69, 75, 76, 79–80, 81, 82, 91, 98, 116, 117, 128, 164, 209–11, 213, 220
Pinker, James 30, 54–5, 81, 144
plate service, stereotype
   history of 42, 207–8
   newspaper editors and 47, 156–9
   readers and 157, 208
   technical operations of 42–4
   see also American Press Association, Kellogg, Ansel Nash, Co., *and* Western Newspaper Union
Pocket Magazine 90, 147, 211–12
   see also Bacheller, Irving, *and* Bacheller syndicates
postal system, United States 20–3, 40, 189
Pratt, Eliza Anna Farman 91, 92, 143

Radway, Janice 31, 202
railroads 3, 20, 21, 22
Read, Opie 46, 73, 104
readers 183–205, 226
   autonomy of 28, 31
   gender and 25–6, 187–8, 191–2
   literacy of 24–5
   rural 188–9, 208
   urban 189–90, 225
readyprint (patent insides/outsides)
   authors and 101–2
   fiction, procurement of 39–41
   history of 36–9
   newspaper editors and 39, 153–6
   readers and 186, 188, 189, 208
   technical operations of 41–2
   see also Kellogg, Ansel Nash, Co., *and* Western Newspaper Union
Reynolds, Paul Revere 30, 81

St. Paul Pioneer-Press 18, 189
Sala, George Augusta 141
Scripps, Edward 175, 186
Sheppard, Robert 54, 59, 160
Spofford, Harriet Prescott 79, 165, 210
Stedman, Arthur 78, 81, 130, 131, 140, 143

Stedman, Edmund Clarence 78, 90, 92, 142, 209
Stevenson, Robert Louis, general references 4, 66, 71, 79, 123, 124, 141, 145, 198, 212, 220
  "Outlaws of Tunstall Forest, The" (*The Black Arrow*) 82, 95, 118, 145
  South Seas Letters 76, 82, 120, 210
Stockton, Frank 75, 79, 96, 129, 132, 141, 177, 220

Taylor, Charles 61, 64, 185
  see also Boston Globe
Tillotson, Fred Lever 212
Tillotson, James Lever 59
Tillotson, William Frederic *49*, 53, 54, 128, 146, 149–50, 165, 205, 208, 226
Tillotson's Newspaper Fiction Bureau, general references 7, 8, 32, 35, 46, *51*, *52*, 107, 160, 166, 173, 183, 212, 218, 221
  authors and 50, 54, 55, 108, 109, 113–14, 115, 116, 119, 120–3, 127–31, 133–4, 141–2, 143–4, 146, 148, 149–50, 165, 214
  decline, reasons for 208–9, 212, 221, 224
  fiction, editing of 58–9, 146
  fiction, illustration of 59
  fiction, marketing of 56–8, 173–4
  fiction, procurement of 54–5, 160, 165
  history of 49–54, 58–9

McClure, S. S. and 53, 55, 75–6, 81–2
  New York office of 53, 54, 55, 57, 59
  newspaper editors and 56–8, 60–1, 129, 138, 168, 169, 171–2, 175
  stereotype plates and 50, 59–60
Turner, Michael 53, 138
Twain, Mark 4, 78, 82–3, 132
  American Claimant, The 6, 76, 88–9, 119, 125

unions, newspaper
  American Newspaper Union 35, 38
  Chicago Newspaper Union 35, 38, 207
  New York Newspaper Union 35, 38
  see also readyprint *and* Western Newspaper Union
United Press 46, 96, 178, 219
Utica Daily Observer 177–8, 199–200

Watt, A. P. 30, 54, 66, 81
Waugh, Arthur 81
Wells, H. G. 4, 54, 97
Western Newspaper Union 35, 38, 42, 44, 157, 179–80, 207, 208
Weyman, Stanley 81, 123
Wilder, Laura Ingalls 189

Yezierska, Anzia 197

Zola, Emile 129, 134, 169